Transformations of Musical Modernism

Profound transformations in the composition, performance and reception of modernist music have taken place in recent decades. This collection brings fresh perspectives to bear upon key questions surrounding the forms that musical modernism takes today, how modern music is performed and heard and its relationship to earlier music. In sixteen chapters, leading figures in the field and emerging scholars examine modernist music from the inside, in terms of changing practices of composition, musical materials and overarching aesthetic principles, and from the outside, in terms of the changing contextual frameworks in which musical modernism has taken place and been understood. Shaped by a 'rehearing' of modernist music, the picture that emerges redraws the map of musical modernism as a whole and presents a full-scale re-evaluation of what the modernist movement has been all about.

ERLING E. GULDBRANDSEN is a professor at the Department of Musicology, University of Oslo, where he leads the research group, '20/21 – Musical Trajectories Today'. He has carried out research at IRCAM (Paris) and at the Paul Sacher Foundation (Basel) and received the King's Gold Medal for his work on Boulez. His 2006 article on Mahler and Boulez was awarded the Norwegian prize 'Scientific Article of the Year'. He has published widely on Wagner and musical drama, musical modernism, music history, analysis, performance practice and aesthetic experience.

JULIAN JOHNSON is Regius Professor of Music at Royal Holloway, University of London. He has written five books, including *Webern and the Transformation of Nature* (Cambridge, 1999) and *Mahler's Voices* (2009). His most recent, *Out of Time: Music and the Making of Modernity* (2015), considers music's constitutive relation to modernity from the sixteenth century to the present. In 2005 he was awarded the Dent Medal of the RMA for 'outstanding contributions to musicology' and, in 2013, became the first holder of the Diamond Jubilee Regius Chair of Music.

Music Since 1900

GENERAL EDITOR Arnold Whittall

This series – formerly Music in the Twentieth Century – offers a wide perspective on music and musical life since the end of the nineteenth century. Books included range from historical and biographical studies concentrating particularly on the context and circumstances in which composers were writing, to analytical and critical studies concerned with the nature of musical language and questions of compositional process. The importance given to context will also be reflected in studies dealing with, for example, the patronage, publishing and promotion of new music, and in accounts of the musical life of particular countries.

Titles in the series

Jonathan Cross
The Stravinsky Legacy

Michael Nyman
Experimental Music: Cage and Beyond

Jennifer Doctor
The BBC and Ultra-Modern Music, 1922–1936

Robert Adlington
The Music of Harrison Birtwistle

Keith Potter
Four Musical Minimalists: La Monte Young, Terry Riley, Steve Reich, Philip Glass

Carlo Caballero
Fauré and French Musical Aesthetics

Peter Burt
The Music of Toru Takemitsu

David Clarke
The Music and Thought of Michael Tippett: Modern Times and Metaphysics

M. J. Grant
Serial Music, Serial Aesthetics: Compositional Theory in Post-War Europe

Philip Rupprecht
Britten's Musical Language

Mark Carroll
Music and Ideology in Cold War Europe

Adrian Thomas
Polish Music since Szymanowski

J. P. E. Harper-Scott
Edward Elgar, Modernist

Yayoi Uno Everett
The Music of Louis Andriessen

Ethan Haimo
Schoenberg's Transformation of Musical Language

Rachel Beckles Willson
Ligeti, Kurtág, and Hungarian Music during the Cold War

Michael Cherlin
Schoenberg's Musical Imagination

Joseph N. Straus
Twelve-Tone Music in America

David Metzer
Musical Modernism at the Turn of the Twenty-First Century

Edward Campbell
Boulez, Music and Philosophy

Jonathan Goldman
The Musical Language of Pierre Boulez: Writings and Compositions

Pieter C. van den Toorn and John McGinness
Stravinsky and the Russian Period: Sound and Legacy of a Musical Idiom

David Beard
Harrison Birtwistle's Operas and Music Theatre

Heather Wiebe
Britten's Unquiet Pasts: Sound and Memory in Postwar Reconstruction

Beate Kutschke and Barley Norton
Music and Protest in 1968

Graham Griffiths
Stravinsky's Piano: Genesis of a Musical Language

Martin Iddon
John Cage and David Tudor: Correspondence on Interpretation and Performance

Martin Iddon
New Music at Darmstadt: Nono, Stockhausen, Cage, and Boulez

Alastair Williams
Music in Germany Since 1968

Ben Earle
Luigi Dallapiccola and Musical Modernism in Fascist Italy

Thomas Schuttenhelm
The Orchestral Music of Michael Tippett: Creative Development and the Compositional Process

Marilyn Nonken
The Spectral Piano: From Liszt, Scriabin, and Debussy to the Digital Age

Jack Boss
Schoenberg's Twelve-Tone Music: Symmetry and the Musical Idea

Deborah Mawer
French Music and Jazz in Conversation: From Debussy to Brubeck

Philip Rupprecht
British Musical Modernism: The Manchester Group and their Contemporaries

Amy Lynn Wlodarski
Musical Witness and Holocaust Representation

Carola Nielinger-Vakil
Luigi Nono: A Composer in Context

Erling E. Guldbrandsen and Julian Johnson
Transformations of Musical Modernism

Transformations of Musical Modernism

Edited by

Erling E. Guldbrandsen and Julian Johnson

University of Oslo
Royal Holloway, University of London

CAMBRIDGE
UNIVERSITY PRESS

University Printing House, Cambridge CB2 8BS, United Kingdom

Cambridge University Press is part of the University of Cambridge.

It furthers the University's mission by disseminating knowledge in the pursuit of education, learning and research at the highest international levels of excellence.

www.cambridge.org
Information on this title: www.cambridge.org/9781107127210

© Cambridge University Press 2015

This publication is in copyright. Subject to statutory exception and to the provisions of relevant collective licensing agreements, no reproduction of any part may take place without the written permission of Cambridge University Press.

First published 2015

A catalogue record for this publication is available from the British Library

Library of Congress Cataloguing in Publication data
Transformations of musical modernism / edited by Erling E. Guldbrandsen and Julian Johnson.
    pages cm
Includes bibliographical references and index.
ISBN 978-1-107-12721-0
1. Modernism (Music)   2. Music – 20th century – History and criticism.
3. Music – 21st century – History and criticism.   I. Guldbrandsen, Erling E., 1960–
II. Johnson, Julian.
ML197.T73   2015
780.9′04–dc23

2015021263

ISBN 978-1-107-12721-0 Hardback

Cambridge University Press has no responsibility for the persistence or accuracy of URLs for external or third-party internet websites referred to in this publication, and does not guarantee that any content on such websites is, or will remain, accurate or appropriate.

Contents

List of music examples   page ix
Notes on contributors   xii
Acknowledgements   xvi

Introduction   1
Erling E. Guldbrandsen and Julian Johnson

Part I Rethinking modernism   19

  1   The lure of the Sublime: revisiting the modernist project   21
     Susan McClary

  2   Return of the repressed: particularity in early and late modernism   36
     Julian Johnson

  3   Expressionism revisited: modernism beyond the twentieth century   53
     Arnold Whittall

  4   Erik Bergman, cosmopolitanism and the transformation of musical geography   74
     Björn Heile

  5   Sharing a stage: the growing proximity between modernism and popular music   97
     David Metzer

Part II Rewriting modernism   117

  6   Ritual and Eros in James Dillon's *Come live with me*   119
     Michael Cherlin

  7   Montage in modernity: scattered fragments, dynamic fragments   145
     Jean-Paul Olive

  8   Transformations of appearance: suddenness and the modernist fragment   155
     Marion Hestholm

  9   Rethinking Boulez: schemes, logics and paradigms of musical modernity   172
     Edward Campbell

10 Remembrance and prognosis in the music of György Ligeti   190
   Peter Edwards

11 Valentin Silvestrov and the symphonic monument in ruins   201
   Samuel Wilson

Part III Replaying modernism   221

12 Playing with transformations: Boulez's *Improvisation III sur Mallarmé*   223
   Erling E. Guldbrandsen

13 Performance as critique   245
   Arnulf Christian Mattes

14 'Unwrapping' the voice: Cathy Berberian and John Cage's *Aria*   264
   Francesca Placanica

15 Radically idiomatic instrumental practice in works by Brian Ferneyhough   279
   Anders Førisdal

16 The ethics of performance practice in complex music after 1945   299
   Tanja Orning

Bibliography   319
Index of names   336
Index of subjects   347

Music examples

3.1 Richard Emsley, *for piano 15*, bars 1–25. © Copyright Richard Emsley 2005. 58
3.2 Richard Emsley, *for piano 15*, bars 717–730. © Copyright Richard Emsley 2005. 58
3.3a Rebecca Saunders, *Crimson*, bars 1–6. Edition Peters No. 11004. © Copyright 2005 by Henry Litolff's Verlag. Reproduced by permission of Hinrichsen Edition, Peters Edition Ltd., London. 61
3.3b Rebecca Saunders, *Crimson*, bars 136–145. Edition Peters No. 11004. © Copyright 2005 by Henry Litolff's Verlag. Reproduced by permission of Hinrichsen Edition, Peters Edition Ltd., London. 62
3.3c Rebecca Saunders, *Crimson*, bars 270–279. Edition Peters No. 11004. © Copyright 2005 by Henry Litolff's Verlag. Reproduced by permission of Hinrichsen Edition, Peters Edition Ltd., London. 62
3.4 James MacMillan, *St John Passion*, 'The Reproaches', bars 3–11 (vocal line only). © Copyright by Boosey & Hawkes Music Publishers Ltd. Reproduced by permission of Boosey & Hawkes Music Publishers Limited. 65
3.5 James MacMillan, *St John Passion*, 'Sanctus Immortalis, miserere nobis', bars 1–6, 23–28. © Copyright by Boosey & Hawkes Music Publishers Ltd. Reproduced by permission of Boosey & Hawkes Music Publishers Ltd. 67
3.6 Simon Holt, *Black Lanterns*, ending. © Copyright 1984 Chester Music Limited. All rights reserved. International copyright secured. Used by permission of Chester Music Limited. 68
3.7 Simon Holt, *Boots of Lead*, bars 1–16: offstage clarinet in A only. © Copyright 2002 Chester Music Limited. All rights reserved. International copyright secured. Used by permission of Chester Music Limited. 69
4.1 Serial structure of Erik Bergman's *Aubade* for Orchestra, Op. 48 85
4.2 Erik Bergman, *Colori ed Improvvisazioni* Op. 72, bars 50ff. Reproduced by permission of Boosey & Hawkes Music Publishers Ltd 88
4.3 Erik Bergman, *Bardo Thödol* Op. 74, 1st movt., bars 10ff. Reproduced by permission of Boosey & Hawkes Music Publishers Ltd 92
4.4 Erik Bergman, *Lament and Incantation* Op. 106, Incantation, beginning. Reproduced by permission of Boosey & Hawkes Music Publishers Ltd 94

List of music examples

6.1 James Dillon: *Come live with me*, opening 12 bars: setting of 2.1, without vocalization (score pages 1–2). Edition Peters No.7248. © Copyright 1982 by Hinrichsen Edition, Peters Edition Ltd., London. Reproduced by kind permission of the publisher. 127

6.2 James Dillon: *Come live with me*, bars 31–43: setting of 2.3 (score pages 4–5). Edition Peters No.7248. © Copyright 1982 by Hinrichsen Edition, Peters Edition Ltd., London. Reproduced by kind permission of the publisher. 130

6.3 James Dillon: *Come live with me*, bars 98–166: setting of 2.7 (score pages 17–20 (third and full iteration)). Edition Peters No.7248. © Copyright 1982 by Hinrichsen Edition, Peters Edition Ltd., London. Reproduced by kind permission of the publisher. 134

6.4 James Dillon: *Come live with me*, bars 176–191: setting of 2.9 (score page 22). Edition Peters No.7248. © Copyright 1982 by Hinrichsen Edition, Peters Edition Ltd., London. Reproduced by kind permission of the publisher. 139

6.5 James Dillon: *Come live with me*, bars 213-250: setting of 2.12 (score pages 25–9). Edition Peters No.7248. © Copyright 1982 by Hinrichsen Edition, Peters Edition Ltd., London. Reproduced by kind permission of the publisher. 140

8.1 Beethoven, *Pastoral* Symphony, 2nd movement (Szene am Bach), clarinet motive (bars 69-70). 164

11.1 Valentin Silvestrov, Symphony No. 5, figs. 10–12 (upbeat to bar 73–88), reduction. 204

11.2 Valentin Silvestrov, Symphony No. 5: first harp, bar 300. © 2001 by M. P. Belaieff, Frankfurt. 212

11.3 Valentin Silvestrov, Symphony No. 5, figs. 90–92 (upbeat to bar 758–777), reduction. 213

11.4 Valentin Silvestrov, Symphony No. 5, bar 772 to end, reduction. 213

11.5 Valentin Silvestrov, Symphony No. 5, returning melody, first violins, from bar 727 (fig. 87). © 2001 by M. P. Belaieff, Frankfurt. 216

11.6 Valentin Silvestrov, Symphony No. 5, first clarinet's solo line, bars 611–615. © 2001 by M. P. Belaieff, Frankfurt. 216

11.7 Valentin Silvestrov, Symphony No. 5, bars 479–483, beginning of the piano's solo material. © 2001 by M. P. Belaieff, Frankfurt. 217

12.1a '"Improvisation III", harps, page 1, first version'. 229

12.1b '"Improvisation III", harps, page 1, revised version'. 229

12.2 'Basic figures'. 232

12.3 'Permutations and multiplications'. 232

12.4 'Superposition and displacement'. 233

12.5 'Reduction of polyphony'. 233

12.6 'Alpha series'. 234

12.7 'Beta series'. 234

List of music examples

12.8 'Gamma series'.   234

15.1 Brian Ferneyhough, *Unity Capsule*, opening. Copyright © 1975 by Hinrichsen Ed. Used by permission of C. F. Peters Corporation. All rights reserved.   284

15.2 Brian Ferneyhough, *Unity Capsule*, page 5, end of middle stave and opening of bottom stave. Copyright © 1975 by Hinrichsen Ed. Used by permission of C. F. Peters Corporation. All rights reserved.   285

15.3 *Kurze Schatten II*, mvt. 1, bars 1–6. Copyright © 1989 by Hinrichsen Ed. Used by permission of C. F. Peters Corporation. All rights reserved.   289

15.4 *Kurze Schatten II*, mvt. 2, bars 1–4 (example 15.4a) and 31–32 (example 15.4b). Copyright © 1989 by Hinrichsen Ed. Used by permission of C. F. Peters Corporation. All rights reserved.   292

15.5 *Kurze Schatten II*, mvt. 2, bar 7. Copyright © 1989 by Hinrichsen Ed. Used by permission of C. F. Peters Corporation. All rights reserved.   293

15.6 *Kurze Schatten II*, mvt. 4, bars 6–8. Copyright © 1989 by Hinrichsen Ed. Used by permission of C. F. Peters Corporation. All rights reserved.   295

15.7 *Kurze Schatten II*, mvt. 4, bars 26–27. Copyright © 1989 by Hinrichsen Ed. Used by permission of C. F. Peters Corporation. All rights reserved.   295

15.8 *Kurze Schatten II*, mvt. 4, bars 34–35. Copyright © 1989 by Hinrichsen Ed. Used by permission of C. F. Peters Corporation. All rights reserved.   296

16.1 Klaus K. Hübler, *Opus breve*, page 1. © 1988 by Breitkopf & Härtel, Wiesbaden. Reproduced by permission.   301

16.2 *Time and Motion Study II* by Brian Ferneyhough. Copyright © (1978) Used by permission of C. F. Peters Corporation. All rights reserved.   312

Notes on contributors

Edward Campbell is Senior Lecturer in Music at the University of Aberdeen and a member of the university's Centre for Modern Thought. He specializes in contemporary European art music and aesthetics including historical, analytical and aesthetic approaches to European modernism, the music and writings of Pierre Boulez, contemporary European opera and the interrelation of musical thought and critical theory. He is the author of the books *Boulez, Music and Philosophy* (Cambridge, 2010) and *Music after Deleuze* (2013), and co-editor of *Pierre Boulez Studies*, to be published by Cambridge in 2016.

Michael Cherlin is the author of *Schoenberg's Musical Imagination* (Cambridge, 2007) and *Some Varieties of Musical Irony* (Cambridge, forthcoming), and the editor of *Music Theory Spectrum* (2013–15). He is Professor of Music Theory at the University of Minnesota.

Peter Edwards is a postdoctoral fellow and lectures in musicology at the University of Oslo. His current project 'Style and Modernity', funded by the Research Council of Norway, studies the implications of modernist aesthetics on theories of style across a range of musical genres and traditions. He is also a guitarist and composer and has received commissions from leading ensembles and performers.

Anders Førisdal is a Norwegian guitarist and musicologist. As a soloist and artistic director of the group asamisimasa, he has collaborated with many of the major composers of our time, including Brian Ferneyhough, Helmut Lachenmann and Mathias Spahlinger, and given numerous world premieres. He wrote his master's thesis on Aldo Clementi, and his first solo CD, a double disc devoted to the experimental guitar music of Bjørn Fongaard, was released in February 2015. At the time of writing, Førisdal has recently finished a doctoral thesis on radically idiomatic instrumental practice in the works of Ferneyhough, Richard Barrett and Klaus K. Hübler.

Erling E. Guldbrandsen is Professor at the Department of Musicology, University of Oslo, where he leads the research group '20/21 – Musical Trajectories Today'. He followed the doctoral programme 'Musique et musicologie du XXème siècle' at IRCAM (Paris) and studied Pierre Boulez's music at IRCAM and at the Paul Sacher Foundation (Basel), resulting in his dissertation on Boulez which was awarded His Majesty the King's Gold Medal in 1996. A 2006 article on Mahler and Boulez was awarded the Norwegian prize 'Scientific Article of the Year'. Guldbrandsen has published widely on contemporary music, Boulez, Mahler, Bruckner, Wagner, J. S. Bach, Norwegian music and opera, often combining music analysis, performance studies, literary criticism, music history and aesthetics.

Björn Heile is Reader in Music Since 1900 and Head of Music at the University of Glasgow. He is the author of *The Music of Mauricio Kagel* (2006), the editor of *The Modernist Legacy: Essays on New Music* (2009), co-editor (with Martin Iddon) of *Mauricio Kagel bei den Darmstädter Ferienkursen für Neue Musik: Eine Dokumentation* (2009) and co-editor (with Peter Elsdon and Jenny Doctor) of *Watching Jazz: Encountering Jazz Performance on Screen* (forthcoming). He is currently preparing a large collaborative research project on the performance practice of Mauricio Kagel's experimental music and co-editing (with Charles Wilson) *The Ashgate Research Companion to Modernism in Music*.

Marion Hestholm earned her doctoral degree in June 2011. Her dissertation 'Fragments, Flights, and Forms: Montage as a Constructive Principle of Twentieth-Century Music' investigates the mechanisms of montage as it takes shape in music by Ives, Berio and Kagel. She is particularly interested in the reciprocity between twentieth-century music and philosophy, and of how that century's musical innovation actualizes concepts such as organicism, narrativity and poetic logic. Hestholm is also a trained pianist from the Norwegian Music Academy. At present, she works as a radio host and reporter in the Norwegian Broadcasting Corporation.

Julian Johnson is Regius Professor of Music at Royal Holloway, University of London. His writing on music history has focused particularly on musical modernism but he has published widely on music from Beethoven through to contemporary music, and in relation to philosophy, literature, visual art and landscape. He has written five books, including *Webern and the Transformation of Nature* (Cambridge, 1999) and *Mahler's Voices* (2009). His most recent, *Out of Time: Music and the Making of Modernity* (2015), considers music's constitutive relation to modernity from the sixteenth century to the present.

Arnulf Christian Mattes is Associate Professor at the University of Bergen Centre for Grieg Research. He studied the cello at the Staatliche Musikhochschule Trossingen and gained a PhD at the University of Oslo with a dissertation on Schoenberg's late chamber works. In 2009 he received a three-year research grant from the Norwegian Research Council for the postdoctoral project 'Musical Expression in Transforming Cultures: A Comparative Study of Rudolf Kolisch's Performance Practice'. Mattes has previously published articles on Schoenberg and Kolisch in the *Journal of the Arnold Schoenberg Center* and *Twentieth-Century Music*.

Susan McClary is Professor of Music at Case Western Reserve University and Distinguished Professor Emerita, UCLA. She focuses her research on the cultural criticism of music. Her books include *Feminine Endings: Music, Gender, and Sexuality*; *Georges Bizet: Carmen*; *Conventional Wisdom: The Content of Musical Form*; *Modal Subjectivities: Renaissance Self-Fashioning in the Italian Madrigal*; *Reading Music, Desire and Pleasure in 17th-Century Music*; and *Structures of Feeling in 17th-Century Expressive Culture*. Her work has been translated into at least twenty languages. McClary received a MacArthur Foundation 'Genius' Fellowship in 1995.

David Metzer is Professor of Music at the University of British Columbia. He is the author of *Quotation and Cultural Meaning in Twentieth-Century Music* and *Musical Modernism at the Turn of the Twenty-First Century*. His articles have appeared in *Modernism/modernity*, *Journal of Musicology* and *Popular Music*, among other journals. He is currently working on a history of the ballad in American popular music from the 1950s to the present day.

Jean-Paul Olive is a professor in the Department of Music at Paris 8 University, where he teaches musical analysis and aesthetics. After being director of the department 'Arts, Philosophy and Aesthetics', he directed the Doctoral School's programme in 'Aesthetics, Science and Technology of the Arts'. He also founded the 'Arts 8' series and is co-director of the musicology journal *Filigrane*. His major publications include a book on the work of Alban Berg (*Alban Berg: Le tissage et le sens*, 1997), an essay about montage in music (*Musique et montage: Essai sur le matériau musical au début du XXème siècle*, 1999) and a book on the musical texts of the philosopher Theodor W. Adorno (*Un son désenchanté*, 2008). He also directed numerous edited collections including: *Expression et geste musical*, 2013 (with Suzanne Kogler); *Réfléchir les forms: Autour d'une analyse dialectique de la musique*, 2013; and *Gestes, fragments, timbres: la musique de György Kurtág*, 2009.

Tanja Orning is a cellist and musicologist active in the fields of contemporary and experimental music. She performs with groups such as asamisimasa, BOA trio and DR.OX, as well as in her solo-project Cellotronics. She studied in Oslo, London, and at Indiana University with Janos Starker as a Fulbright Research Fellow. Since earning her PhD at the Norwegian

Academy of Music in contemporary performance practice (2014), Orning has worked as an associate professor at the Department of Musicology, University of Oslo, and teaches contemporary music at the Academy of Music, besides being an active performer.

Francesca Placanica is the co-editor of *Cathy Berberian: Pioneer of Contemporary Vocality* (2014) and has worked extensively on primary sources from Cathy Berberian's private archives while completing her master's thesis 'Cathy Berberian: Performance as Composition' at Southern Methodist University, Dallas, Texas, in 2007. She holds a PhD in Music from the University of Southampton (2013) and has lectured in Performance and Musicology at Maynooth University in 2014. An active professional singer, she is now an associate researcher at Orpheus Institute (Ghent), where she is leading her artistic research project on twentieth-century monodrama and vocality.

Arnold Whittall is Professor Emeritus of Music Theory and Analysis at King's College London. His latest books are *The Wagner Style: Close Readings and Critical Perspectives* (2015) and *Introduction to Serialism* (Cambridge, 2008). A contributor to *Maxwell Davies Studies* (Cambridge, 2009), *Elliott Carter Studies* (Cambridge, 2012), *Rethinking Britten* (2013) and *Harrison Birtwistle Studies* (Cambridge, 2015), he has recently completed an extended series of articles on 'British Music after Britten', published principally in *Tempo* and *The Musical Times* between 2001 and 2015.

Samuel Wilson is Lecturer in Contextual Studies at London Contemporary Dance School and Tutor in Music Philosophy and Aesthetics at Guildhall School of Music and Drama. His research focuses principally on subjectivity and music in the context of recent modernity. He completed his PhD in 2013 at Royal Holloway, University of London (supervised by Julian Johnson), and has since published in *Contemporary Music Review* and *International Review of the Aesthetics and Sociology of Music*. He is a member of the central organizing committee for the annual *London Conference in Critical Thought* (londoncritical.org).

Acknowledgements

This collection of essays originates from an international symposium held in Paris in October 2011, organized by Erling Guldbrandsen and the Musical Modernism Research Group based at Oslo University. It brought together a number of established figures in the field with emerging scholars in order to examine the transformation of musical modernism that has taken place in recent decades. It became clear during the three-day meeting that not only did the papers present a particularly rich set of perspectives on this central question but together they formed a powerful and coherent analysis which was considerably more than the sum of its parts. To help realize this as a full-length book publication, Julian Johnson was invited to act as the co-editor. The resulting volume includes the work of many of those who participated in that meeting as well as contributions by other invited scholars. In bringing this wonderfully rich set of approaches to publication, the editors are necessarily grateful to a number of key people.

The seminar series promoted by the Musical Modernism Research Group of the Department of Musicology at Oslo University was invaluable in creating the context for both the Paris meeting in 2011 and the subsequent development of ideas. The group continues to flourish, under the leadership of Erling Guldbrandsen, under its new name '20/21 – Musical Trajectories Today'. The Paris meeting was generously supported by the Centre Franco-Norvégien in Paris, directed by Bjarne Rogan. The editors are very grateful to Victoria Cooper, Senior Commissioning Editor at Cambridge University Press, for her enduring support and encouragement; to Arnold Whittall, who welcomed the volume into the 'Music in the Twentieth Century' series, of which he is the editor; to Fleur Jones at Cambridge University Press, who piloted the book manuscript through to publication; and to Sam Wilson, for his invaluable administrative help. Finally, our thanks go to the other fourteen authors whose work has created this volume. The process of sharing ideas from which this book emerges, always conducted in a spirit of enthusiastic openness and generosity, has been a great pleasure for us both.

Introduction

Erling E. Guldbrandsen and Julian Johnson

The transformation of what?

What is musical modernism? Is it a musical *style*, inescapably marked by rebarbative traits such as dissonance, atonality and a fragmented musical surface, confronting listeners with insurmountable difficulties in its resistance to traditional ideas of musical beauty, its avoidance of melody or familiar harmony, its lack of regular pulse, rhythm or groove, its rejection of recognizable musical forms and ideas of expression? Or, is modernism rather a musical *epoch*, starting with the outburst of atonal expressionism of the Schoenberg school before 1910 and finally coming to an end with the advent of minimalism, neo-tonality, new simplicity, neo-romanticism and postmodernism around 1970? Is modernist music still, as Stockhausen and Boulez once saw it, the prophetic art of the future, a project of progress, enlightenment, critique and liberation, invoking new aesthetic forms and 'nie erhörte Klänge', or has it ultimately imploded into the hermeticism of its own ivory tower? Is it a morally superior attack on easy listening, musical laziness and the instant gratification of a ubiquitous consumerism, or is it, regardless of whether one sees it as a style or an epoch, something that has long since lost any power of attraction it may have once held for audiences, musicians or scholars? Was post-war modernism, as Richard Taruskin proclaimed, nothing more than an epiphenomenon of the Cold War,[1] a playing out of politics in the cultural sphere? And today, in the second decade of a new century and sixty years or more after some of its defining works, is modernist music, as Arved Ashby has noted, despite his otherwise sympathetic attitude,[2] close to becoming irrelevant?

According to the authors of this book, modernism is neither a style nor an epoch; it has neither imploded nor come to a historical end. Rather, musical modernism is an attitude of musical practice – in composition, performance and listening – that involves an increased awareness of its

---

[1] Richard Taruskin, *Music in the Late Twentieth Century: The Oxford History of Western Music*, 5 vols. (Oxford University Press, 2010), vol. V, pp. 18–22.
[2] Arved Ashby, *The Pleasure of Modernist Music: Listening, Meaning, Intention, Ideology* (University of Rochester Press, 2004), p. 36.

own historical situation and remains alive and kicking as a vibrant musical force among musicians, festivals and audiences on all continents of the contemporary world. As soon as music starts reflecting upon its own language – its means of expression – it takes on a historical self-awareness that amounts to modernist, critical reflection. From this view, musical modernism simply involves a heightened consciousness of the relations between present and past, between present and future and between continuity and discontinuity in the history of music; in brief, it provokes an acute awareness of the condition of historicity that has always been embedded in the present moment of musical experience.

Such a historical awareness was already a characteristic of Beethoven's world and of the modernity that erupts with the French Revolution and the philosophy of Hegel. What is the late style of Beethoven if not a compositional wrestling and musical meditation on this condition of temporal and historical fragility? To be sure, Rimbaud's imperative that 'il faut être absolument moderne' and Nietzsche's call to 'forget about history to be able to live' are both countered by a sense that one must incorporate and reflect upon history in order to be able to transcend it. From this longer historical gaze, musical modernism – in the midst of its enduring search for new soundscapes and new modes of expression – is inextricably tied to an earlier age, because modernism is a product of the historical self-consciousness that what is now has not always been and will not always be the case. It is subject to constant change, or – as we prefer to call it in the title of this book – it is subject to perennial transformation. On closer study, there is no violent break, no simple rupture with the past but rather processes of gradual transformations taking place from within, taking place and taking time.

For that reason, this book takes the long view of musical modernism, a perspective that has perhaps become possible only after the changes within modernist practices that have happened over the last six decades. It begins from the sense that modernism denotes a musical attitude that not only stretches back further than we might previously have imagined but is still ongoing. The idea of transformation thus displaces the familiar periodizations of music history which miss the bigger picture because of a narrow idea of music history as the history of musical 'style'. Therefore, not only do the contributors to this volume refer back to classical and romantic musical culture, but equally they show little interest in the idea of 'postmodernism', a term which appears relatively rarely in the pages that follow. Compared to other cultural forms, musical practice and musical criticism were late to adopt the term, which, after a brief but provocative currency in the early 1980s, seems now to have been largely abandoned. What proponents of postmodernism suggested as contrary or even anti-modernist elements of cultural practice now seem, from the longer view of a transformed modernism, simply part of its inherently contradictory nature. Lyotard's insistence that the postmodern denotes not a coming after but a moment of self-reflection within modernism thus becomes self-evident from this longer view.[3] Modernism, from this perspective, shows no sign of having reached its end, either as a historical era or as a cultural and aesthetic force. Instead, one might talk of a 'Second Modernism' (Claus-Steffen Mahnkopf)[4] emerging after 1980, a transformation of the trajectory of the modernisms both of the early part of the twentieth century and of the post-1945 period.

Modernism and tradition

On the one hand, then, musical modernism itself has changed: it is no longer what it was, either in the post-1945 decades or in the years around 1910. On the other hand, the idea of a transformed modernism presumes a certain coherence and belonging together of the diverse musical practices of well over a hundred years. This is the contradictory nature of transformation, one played out most obviously in musical modernism in its complex relation to tradition – a relation that retroactively contributes towards changing what we conceive of as the basic traits of that tradition. A single example illustrates the point: Schoenberg's 'break' with tonality around 1909 has generally been regarded as a clear rupture with the past, yet Schoenberg himself insisted that his work continued rather than rejected musical tradition. An essential formative trait of music from Bach to Brahms – the interrelation and integration of motifs and themes to create a play of similarities and differences – was taken up by Schoenberg and magnified, both in the free atonal works and in dodecaphony. It was only through his 'break' with tradition that this previously unreflected and latent aspect of music was taken up and articulated, that is, the recognition that structural integration, and not tonality in itself, was the decisive tool in giving musical form to a work. Schoenberg's contribution to the history of music is thus not restricted to the creation of new works of music; he also retrospectively changed our view of what, in fact, are the essential traits of that tradition. To put it

---

[3] Jean-François Lyotard, *The Postmodern Condition: A Report on Knowledge*, trans. Geoff Bennington and Brian Massumi (Manchester University Press, 1984).

[4] Claus-Steffen Mahnkopf, Frank Cox and Wolfram Schurig, *Facets of the Second Modernity: New Music and Aesthetics in the 21st Century* (Hofheim: Volke Verlag, 2008).

more strongly, new music not only retroactively alters our view of tradition but may in fact change the tradition itself.

Musical tradition is thus not a given, but rather a kind of chameleon, the colours and appearance of which change according to posterity's shifting basis of understanding. Modernism and tradition are entities interwoven in complex and even paradoxical ways, one dependent upon the other, one defined by its other. At least four typical attitudes towards tradition emerge within modernism. There is the desire to forget about tradition, discard it and break with it (as with Russolo, Varèse, Scelsi, Cage, Xenakis, the historical avant-garde or the early advocates of integral serialism in the 1950s like Stockhausen, Nono, Boulez); the desire to recall tradition, become conscious of it and perpetuate it (as with Schoenberg, Berg, Britten, Henze, Rihm, Gubaidulina, Pärt or Silvestrov); the attempt to create tradition anew, (re-)construct it and change it retroactively (as in Stravinsky, Bartók, Webern, Messiaen, Lachenmann, Ferneyhough, Dillon, Saariaho or the late Boulez); and the aim even to put the temporal and structural paradoxes of modernism and tradition into play in the music itself (as in Ives, Zimmermann, Ligeti, Berio, Kagel, Kurtág, Reich, Adams or Schnittke).[5] That many of these composers might easily be placed in more than one category underlines the complexity at hand: breaking with tradition, carrying on tradition and 'creating' tradition anew become inseparably interwoven enterprises. Such paradoxes lie at the heart of the concepts of both 'modernism' and 'tradition', making the historical idea of a rupture with the past and determining a new start in history too simplistic to be tenable. The literary historian Paul de Man sees, in his reading of Nietzsche, how the spontaneous move to forget the past which characterizes all of modernity immediately falls back into remembering it: 'One is soon forced to resort to paradoxical formulations, such as defining the modernity of a literary period as the manner in which it discovers the impossibility of being modern.'[6]

What becomes clear is that the nature of the transformations witnessed in the past five or six decades forces us to rethink a narrow conception of modernism itself, in part because it forces a reappraisal of its relation to tradition. Later modernism, far from being some final phase or

---

[5] Erling E. Guldbrandsen, *Tradisjon og tradisjonsbrudd. En studie i Pierre Boulez: Pli selon pli—portrait de Mallarmé* (Oslo: Scandinavian University Press, 1997). Chapter 1, 'Modernisme og tradisjon', pp. 13–126.

[6] Paul de Man, 'Literary History and Literary Modernity' in *Blindness and Insight: Essays in the Rhetoric of Contemporary Criticism*, 2nd edn (Minneapolis, MN: Methuen, 1983), pp. 142–65, p. 144.

Introduction

progression from earlier modernism, thus shows itself to be a reworking and recouping of many of its earlier concerns. Understanding this as a process of transformation, contained within a relatively 'steady state',[7] suggests ways not only of understanding recent musical practice but also of rethinking the historiography of modernism more broadly. Put simply, the transformations taking place in recent decades – in composition and performance practice, and in the theoretical frameworks of musicology – imply a redrawing of the map of musical modernism as a whole. One might go further, and suggest that it is precisely the changes in musical practices of recent decades that have allowed us not only to see *modernism* in a different perspective but to do so because we now see the history of musical *modernity* as a whole in a different perspective. The reconfiguring of our understanding of the history of the modern has its roots in the 1960s – witness Michel Foucault's analysis of the historical epistemes of Western culture – but it was not until relatively recently that the writing of music history began to rethink its idiosyncratic set of periodizations. The latter still tends to reinforce a narrowly stylistic definition of modernism, cut off from previous eras by a rhetoric of rejection. A number of publications of the last decade propose a wider view, suggesting that the idea of modernity might be a more useful model for understanding music history; one consequence of this – but perhaps also one point of departure – has been a much richer and more contradictory conception of modernism.[8]

Musicology and modernism

Modernism remained a central preoccupation of musicological study throughout the twentieth century, unsurprisingly since it was in this century that the discipline of musicology came of age. Not only the teleological conception of music history but also ideas of formalist musicology, structural music analysis, a certain objectivism in the view of the artwork

---

[7] Arnold Whittall, *Musical Composition in the Twentieth Century*, revised edn (Oxford University Press, 1999).
[8] Karol Berger and Anthony Newcomb (eds.), *Music and the Aesthetics of Modernity: Essays* (Cambridge, MA: Harvard University Press, 2005); John Butt, *Bach's Dialogue with Modernity: Perspectives on the Passions* (Cambridge University Press, 2007); Andrew Bowie, *Music, Philosophy, and Modernity* (Cambridge University Press, 2007); Jonathan Goldman, Jean-Jacques Nattiez, and François Nicolas, *La Pensée de Pierre Boulez à Travers ses Écrits* (Paris: Delatour, 2010); Jeremy Begbie, *Music, Modernity, and God: Essays in Listening* (Oxford University Press, 2014); Julian Johnson, *Out of Time: Music and the Making of Modernity* (Oxford University Press, 2015).

and the idea of music theory conceived as hard-core science, all went neatly together with modernist ideas of high art, objectivism and elitist aesthetics. Thus, when formalist musicology was profoundly challenged during the 1990s, so too was the general idea of modernist music as a historical 'telos' and aesthetic centre of the musical world. The subsequent changes can be summarized as a long series of dichotomies following the simple model of a 'turn' from *this* to *that*: a turn from musicological formalism to cultural studies, from absolute music to socio-historical context, from elitist art to popular music, from Western biases to globalized perspectives, from a presumedly masculine worldview to feminist and gender theory, from authors' intention to listeners' experience, from score to performance, from construction to perception, from closed work to open text, from structure to gesture, from *ratio* to pleasure, from brain to body, from intellectual distance to social participation, from unity to plurality of meaning, from 'meaning' to 'use' and from closed institutions of autonomous art to multimedia events, crossover genres and festivals, new technologies and interactive social media. Such a list is not devoid of paradoxes, not least because almost all of these 'turns' had already occurred within the realm of modernist music itself and have been successively propelled and disseminated from there. The very model of conceiving historical development through simple dichotomous 'turns' is in itself nothing more than a historiographical trope, a narrative of progress, a model of thought that modernism had long since problematized within its own compositional and performative self-reflection. The evidence of this is massive, spanning from modernism's early embrace of open form, aleatoricism and new technologies to its inclusion of the sounds and instruments of world music, of radical idiomatics and new blends of global and historical styles. While critical dismissals of modernism are perennial outside of modernism – most recently from cultural studies on the one hand and cognitive sciences on the other – modernism's own attitudes of constant self-criticism and self-transformation remain undiminished and belie the many proclamations of its historical death.

The starting point for the diverse set of investigations collected in the present book is thus neither the theorization of cultural epochs and ideas of history nor the over-hasty announcement of the end of modernism. The starting point is, instead, the material practice of musical composition, performance and reception – not simply in and for themselves but also in terms of the way they take up, question, remember and reformulate music of an earlier modernism. If what emerges is a rethinking of the idea of musical modernism as a whole, from the 1890s through to the present (a long twentieth century), it is one that is derived from a study of recent music's engagement with its own past. The book makes no attempt to give any account of canonic composers, trends and directions of modernist music and does not aim in any way to be historically representative, let alone exhaustive. There are plenty of key figures not covered here (Messiaen, Stockhausen, Xenakis, Feldman, Kagel and several others), and there is little discussion of the American avant-garde, minimalism, spectralism or neo-romanticism. The exploration of musical modernism here is, instead, largely a consideration of European practice and one rooted mainly in considerations of acoustic musical works and their performances (as opposed to electronic music and questions of new technologies and media).

In place of any survey or overview of modernism, the topic of this volume is instead the idea of its *transformation*, explored here from three different but clearly interrelated perspectives:

Part I, 'Rethinking modernism', discusses the changing relation between modernist music and its wider contexts of cultural reception and historical reinterpretation – the way this music plays with historical elements inside constantly shifting and new frameworks.

Part II, 'Rewriting modernism', discusses transformations in the poetics and aesthetics of compositional writing, in musical analysis and in listening experience – the way this music plays in the tensions between strictness and freedom, necessity and chance.

Part III, 'Replaying modernism', discusses the way in which the role of the performer takes on a far more significant status in relation to the concept of the modernist work, not only in so-called theatrical pieces but also in works where the composer's authority appears to govern the most meticulous details – in the presentation of the music in fluid and transient performative acts of interpretation, playing and listening.

Rethinking modernism

Part I of this book considers the changing contextual frameworks in which musical modernism has taken place and by means of which it has been understood – history and historiography, culture and listening, politics and geography – and a changing relationship of modernism to its audience, including signs of a growing rapprochement with aspects of popular music. The map of musicological and critical conceptualizations has changed over recent decades – from formalist structural analysis towards criticism and cultural contextualization, from issues of composition (the musical text, compositional techniques, aesthetic theory) to issues of performance (the performing body, radical idiomatics) and listening (aesthetic experience, subject position, sound studies), from concerns of universality and abstraction towards the historically and geographically particular, from spatial hierarchies (centre and periphery, high and low) to a decentred and paratactic field of musical genres and cultures.

Key to rethinking the discourse of musical modernism is rehearing the music, and all the chapters in Part I proceed by bringing musical works into productive and critical tension with the categories through which we understand them. The rethinking of musical modernism from a historical viewpoint is certainly one part of the recent transformations in how we think and write about it. But it is surely in the material practices of musical composition and performance – as sound – that the greatest transformations have taken place.

In that respect, Susan McClary's 'The lure of the Sublime: revisiting the modernist project' is itself a highly significant sign of a transformation in the reception of this repertoire. Her highly polemical and influential essay 'Terminal Prestige' of 1989,[9] itself instrumental in helping to create that change – as an articulation of what began to emerge as a postmodern position in music – expressed a sense of frustration with the institutional insularity of high modernism, especially what she calls the 'institutionalized prohibition against addressing meaning'. Her remarkable revisiting of the topic twenty-five years later, in the chapter presented here, not only discovers quite the opposite in more recent modernist repertoires but finds through them a way of rehearing the music of an earlier modernist tradition. With reference to three recent operas (by Kaija Saariaho, George Benjamin and Salvatore Sciarrino), she explores the idea of a transformed modernism in terms of music that foregrounds the sensuality of desire, embraces lush and opulent soundworlds and is not afraid to be directly communicative. How should we understand the return of models of human emotion in music that an earlier modernism had apparently expunged? McClary does not only find a new emphasis on the expressive and rhetorical power of music and its intelligibility to audiences; she also offers a more sympathetic historical reading of 'why' earlier modernist music was as it was, acknowledging the situation in which post-war composers found themselves. In a new interpretive effort, taking up the long historical gaze, she traces back the problem to the opposition of the beautiful and the sublime in the late eighteenth century, suggesting that

---

[9] Susan McClary, 'Terminal Prestige: The Case of Avant-Garde Music Composition', *Cultural Critique*, 12 (1989), 57–81.

the presumedly masculine, rational ideal of the sublime eventually came to overrule the feminine, sensual qualities of musical beauty in the normative poetics of high modernism. Although presenting a political recontextualization of modernism as seen through the lenses of aesthetics, history, gender study and cultural institutionalization, McClary does not contest the historical problem of 'beauty' falling into ideology in the mid-twentieth century (from Schoenberg to Stockhausen and from Adorno to Boulez). Her search for a recovery of the category of the beautiful thus represents a vivid challenge to the idea of what a critical music might be in the middle of the second decade of the twenty-first century.

In 'Return of the repressed: particularity in early and late modernism', Julian Johnson traces a transformed musical compositional aesthetic in two relatively late works by two key composers of the post-war avant-garde that recoup a sense of memory and particularity of voice and place: Ligeti's sonata for solo viola (1994) and Berio's *Voci* (1984) for solo viola and ensemble. This shift in compositional focus offers a perspective from which the whole of musical modernism might be rethought. Ligeti's sonata for solo viola resonates with Bartók's sonata for solo violin of fifty years earlier. Bartok's concern for particularity of musical voice is linked to his own ethnomusicological work beginning as early as 1906, with its insistence on the particularity of musical sound that escaped the 'rationalization' of musical notation. Johnson concludes that, 'the relays between the later and earlier parts of the twentieth century suggest a continuity of concern rather than a narrative of rejection and overstepping, a transformation of recurrent tensions rather than any trajectory of development'. The problem, he suggests, lies with the conceptualization of twentieth-century music history, a 'telling' of the story of musical modernism that later practice forces us to rethink.

Arnold Whittall, in 'Expressionism revisited: modernism beyond the twentieth century', offers a specific illustration of this long view of musical modernism by taking the category of 'expressionism', so often confined to a thinking of modernism pre-1920, and rediscovering it in the music of five British composers working at the start of the twenty-first century – Richard Elmsley, Rebecca Saunders, Simon Holt, James MacMillan and Jonathan Harvey – in accordance with what Whittall has explored elsewhere in terms of a 'modern classicism'. Through close readings of musical texts he shows how this music, very much of the early twenty-first century, nevertheless relates back to earlier modernist concerns (as far as Wagner), providing a sense of modernism that 'is not just persistent but multifarious', multiple and transformational. Moreover, not least in the introductory pages of his chapter, Whittall offers a compressed survey and a vigilant rethinking of how musicology has been constantly wrestling with the conceptualization of modernism throughout the twentieth century and beyond. Maybe modernism has survived for so long, Whittall suggests, precisely because its evolving identity reflects its capacity to interact with a succession of different aesthetic and compositional tendencies, spanning from expressionism to the avant-garde, neoclassicism, experimentalism, spectralism, new complexity and even minimalism, none of which tendencies have precluded the others' existence, but have rather endured and supplemented each others' presence.

In 'Erik Bergman, cosmopolitanism and the transformation of musical geography', Björn Heile considers the rethinking of musical modernism not just historically and temporarily but in spatial and geographic terms – so often neglected in accounts of music history that prioritize technical issues. Its focus on the Finnish composer Erik Bergman, a composer who himself embodied so many of the stylistic twists and turns of musical modernism, through dodecaphony, serialism and aleatoricism, then proceeds to examine Bergman's pioneering attitudes to world music which later modernism may be seen to have taken up (a topic that Heile has previously discussed in regard to Stockhausen and others). In the face of a narrow idea of abstract internationalism and alleged 'universalism' espoused by the post-war avant-garde, Heile explores a theory of 'critical cosmopolitanism' in relation to Bergman's music, by narrating the composer's long career as a voyage in three stages: at first exploring outwards from his native Finnish origins, exploring the realm of the Other and then returning back to his own, transformed musical self.

The idea that musical modernism was somehow opposed to popular culture is both true and false – Satie and French neoclassicism, to say nothing of Eisler and Weill, chart a course that arcs out in a quite different trajectory from that of Schoenberg and Webern. Once again, more recent transformations of modernist practice force us to rethink the binary oppositions implied by the aesthetics of Adorno and the Darmstadt generation. David Metzer's 'Sharing a stage' charts the growing proximity between modernist music and popular idioms – a convergence that provokes some serious questions about our understanding of what modernism is and has been. This is not a debate about 'high' and 'low' culture, but rather a cross-genre inquiry into a new ease of coexistence between presentations of modernism and popular music. Metzer finds shared interest in musical ideas of sonic flux, fragmentation, purity, density and simultaneity that produce common ground between the music of Sonic Youth, Public Enemy and Aphex Twin and that of modernist 'concert' composers. His conclusion is that modernism is a continuing and vital force capable of ever new formulations, as evidenced in the coexistence of quite different genres in the new creative spaces and 'changing landscape of musical practices, festivals, club spaces and journalism'.

Rewriting modernism

As Paul de Man underlines, in his words quoted earlier, the relationship between modernism and tradition is complex to the point of being paradoxical. If the objective is to break with tradition and start all over, one does nothing but continue a long tradition of revolt. Conversely, if one wants to perpetuate tradition by repeating it, it is robbed of its motion and grinds to a halt. So, if tradition is to be carried on, it needs to be transformed into something different – in other words, it must be created anew. Not until tradition is left behind is it even perceivable *as* tradition; it is first and foremost the rupture that confirms it, retroactively. In this way, tradition follows from modernism just as much as modernism follows from tradition; it derives from a modernism that discards tradition, presumes it, takes nourishment from it and folds it back into itself – that is, into its own manners of writing. Paradoxes like these are historiographical in character and pertain to the way music history is written, but they are also compositional, pertaining to the way modernism reflects upon tradition by musical means. Each aspect can be understood only in light of the other.

Our response to this inevitable paradox, according to de Man, has to be a renewed close reading of the texts – in other words, to explore how such historical paradoxes are actually handled and played out in modernism's own manners of writing. In short, we need to re-enter and rethink the practices of modernist composition. Accordingly, Part II proceeds by exploring modernist music from the inside, in terms of musical materials and their organization, as well as overarching aesthetic principles and listening experiences. It includes discussion of the relations between fragments and totality, between systems and singular ideas, as well as changes in compositional writing (*écriture*) from the 1950s to the 1990s and beyond, revisions of works and their scores and the sometimes radically changing conceptions of musical form, genre and modes of expression. Each of the five chapters in this part focuses on the work of one or more composers, namely Dillon, Zimmermann, Kurtág, Nono, Berio, Boulez, Ligeti and Silvestrov.

Michael Cherlin's 'Ritual and Eros in James Dillon's *Come live with me*' finds in the music of a composer associated with a kind of aggressively secular new complexity a focus on more ancient senses of ritual and 'a spiritual sense of the strangeness of being'. The piece he explores here, a setting of part of *The Song of Songs*, offers a case study of a transformed modernism. On the one hand, Cherlin finds strong overlaps between Dillon's music and earlier modernist practices – with the role of erotic love in Schoenberg's early music, for example, and with the play between diegetic and mimetic modes in Stravinsky's more ritualized music (*Les Noces, Abraham and Isaac, Oedipus Rex*). On the other, these ideas are reworked in Dillon's quite specifically twenty-first-century voice. As an introduction to his delving into the opulent soundscapes and the modernist sensuality of Dillon's piece, Cherlin opens up a wider perspective on the question of how a tradition – any tradition – may be transformed in a general sense, taking Walter Benjamin and Harold Bloom as antithetical ways of thinking: the one envisioning an intergenerational interdependence of fulfilment, the other seeing a quasi-Oedipal reaction of necessarily 'misreading' the heritage from the stronger precursors of tradition.

As part of a rethinking of a modernist orthodoxy of compositional unity and structural coherence, the idea of montage and the modernist fragment is explored in two chapters. In 'Montage in modernity: scattered fragments, dynamic fragments', Jean-Paul Olive explores montage as an importing into the artwork of aspects of material reality. Drawing on Adorno and Benjamin, Olive explores the idea of modern art as necessarily fragmented and heterogeneous. This is already evident in Mahler's work – as Adorno showed – in that it embodies a modernism at the level of formal and structural process rather than 'musical material' in a more restrictedly technical sense. Olive draws out that Mahler's material resists its neutralization and, in its fragments, is a music 'of ruin' (an idea developed further in Samuel Wilson's later chapter on Silvestrov). While Mahler has no direct heirs, Olive finds 'the problematics of the fragment' in the work of a number of post-war composers, such as Zimmermann (simultaneity and spherical time), Kurtág (the problematics of memory) and Nono (relating *Fragmente-Stille* to late Beethoven quartets). All three use the fragment as a resistance to all-encompassing and closed systems of thought.

Marion Hestholm discusses some of the same works but takes a slightly different angle on the topic. In 'Transformations of appearance: suddenness and the modernist fragment', she draws on the perspective of a phenomenology of listening and the experience of 'appearance' which the fragment induces in the temporality of the 'moment' (after Karl-Heinz Bohrer). Modernism foregrounds the latter at the apparent expense of the coherently structural whole. Key to the fragment is the mix of allusions to past music, as in Berio's *Sinfonia*, but the idea of the fragment itself connects modernist practices with earlier ones – certainly to literary romanticism around 1800, and in music including late Beethoven and

Schumann, not least through the function of irony and wit. In other words, this is a reading that pulls back the idea of modernism more than 200 years, joining modernist practice to that of early romanticism.

In 'Rethinking Boulez: schemes, logics and paradigms of musical modernity', Edward Campbell begins by presenting a picture of Boulez as emblematic of certain ideas of high musical modernism, standing as he is, midway through the second decade of the twenty-first century, as the sole surviving member of the 'serialist' generation of composers that came to prominence after 1945. Tracing the composer's position through his writings, Campbell asks whether instead one might talk about a period of 'modern classicism' (Whittall) in Boulez's music from the 1980s onwards or at least of 'a more circumscribed modernism'. He considers how we might conceptualize Boulez's trajectory differently by reference to the writings of Gilles Deleuze and Félix Guattari, Alain Badiou and Jacques Rancière, investigating Boulez's singular handling of the continuous, yet transformed, nature of present-day modernist composition, placed as he is in a complex position of 'in-betweens': between modernist musicianship and post-modernist philosophers' thinking, between his own musical practices and his own verbal writings, between compositional creation of new works and interpretive recreation as a conductor of canonical music, and between acoustical 'musicking' and live-electronic expansion of the field of listening.

In 'Remembrance and prognosis in the music of György Ligeti', Peter Edwards explores 'the transitions or transformations that his compositional development might be said to perform'. Key to this is the manner in which Ligeti's music engages with its past as a 'sedimentation of tradition' and an 'overloaded memory', with the 'past concealed in overabundance'. A survey of his music suggests three relations to the past: 'as saturated present, as associative stream, and as vivid, yet contorted reminiscence'. The transformation of modernism that Edwards traces in Ligeti's music is thus a transformation of a modernist relation to the past, a dialogue of 'absence and concealment', 'remembering and forgetting'. This chapter thus offers a useful and powerful lens through which to view the whole of musical modernism, exploring an aporetical dynamics of forgetfulness and remembrance that both runs through and across modernism but also allows us to see its transformations.

A similarly self-conscious engagement with the musical past is explored by Samuel Wilson in 'Valentin Silvestrov and the symphonic monument in ruins'. Just as Hestholm's exploration of the fragment led back to the self-critical play of musical language in the eighteenth century, so the idea of the ruin is characteristic and immanent to modernity as a whole from the eighteenth century onwards (Huyssen). Wilson considers Silvestrov's Symphony No. 5 as a symphonic ruin, a 'post-symphony', thus exploring a way in which modernism transforms its own past – specifically through its engagement with Mahler. His focus is what happens to subjectivity when the musical vehicle of its monumental expression is literally ruined during the symphony's formal process. Wilson explores a process of ruination in Silvestrov's symphony by means of three categories – musical time (and stasis), musical space (traces of past subjectivities appear as distant and written over) and a semiotics of musical nature. His point is not about merely looking back, but a kind of compositional writing that foregrounds its own historical transience. His chapter, focused on Silvestrov's 'off-modernist' position outside of the presumed musical centres of European music, thus continues some of the themes of the earlier chapters on Ligeti, Kurtág, Berio and Nono – opening up dimensions of memory, history and pastness, and also of ruins and of self-reflection in contemporary music.

Replaying modernism

Part III proceeds by taking up the so-called performative turn in musicology and reassessing the music of high modernism from the angle of musical performance, instrumental idiomatics and playing, an area almost entirely neglected by other volumes on musical modernism. Inherent in the latter perspective lies the idea of a performative transformation of the musical object – from a closed concept of the musical 'work' to notions of the work as an emergent phenomenon in a continual process of musical and cultural reinterpretation. The five chapters here consider the relation between composition and performance from the perspectives of the guitar, cello, violin, voice and the conductor. They do so across a historical span that reaches back to an idea of performance that emerges from the aesthetics of the Schoenberg School (in the performance practice of Kolisch as theorized by Adorno) to the 'radical idiomatics' of recent complex music in which the performing body and its relation to the musical instrument becomes itself the material of composition. There is still a need to overcome the tendency that theoretical reflection about music is lagging behind the other arts. This book contends that knowing is always interpretive (in terms of conceptual articulation), just as much as music is always interpretive (in terms of performance and listening). Nowhere is that articulated more powerfully and in more concrete detail than in these concrete relays between compositional thought and performance practice.

Such interrelations between performance practice, compositional aesthetics and our conceptualization of musical modernism are drawn out in Erling E. Guldbrandsen's 'Playing with transformations: Boulez's *Improvisation III sur Mallarmé*'. The familiar picture of Boulez's notion of modernism as a progressive rationalization of musical material is challenged by the changes in Boulez's approach to composition. Guldbrandsen questions the discourses surrounding this music and suggests that the model of 'unity and control' falls short of the listening experience and of Boulez's changing approach. Instead, he suggests that 'non-rational' elements have been seriously misrepresented in approaches to this repertoire. He pursues this idea with a study of the third Mallarmé improvisation from *Pli selon pli* to examine how five kinds of transformation can be traced in the life of this work: performative, structural, transformations of Mallarmé's poetics and Mallarmé's actual text, and of the historiographical models in which we understand this music. Examining Boulez's career as a conductor (of earlier modernist repertoire but increasingly of romantic repertoire too), Guldbrandsen considers how this might relate to parallel shifts in his compositional aesthetic (such as the 'open form' of the 1959 version giving way to the 'fixed' version in 1983, and how episodic form and pointillist articulation give way to more continuous formal processes and an enriched texture). Considering how Boulez generates his material in relation to serial structures, the chapter concludes that the degree of free choice may be far more than usually acknowledged, pointing back to the idea of aesthetic judgement in the Third Critique by Kant at the onset of modernity. This reading of Boulez evokes a complex and paradoxical relation of tradition and innovation, system and free aesthetic choice in his modernist project.

Boulez's changing experience as a conductor of earlier modernist music, and then romantic repertoire, including Wagner and Mahler, finds fascinating parallels elsewhere in the changing aesthetics of new music. Arnulf Mattes, in 'Performance as critique', explores the way that the post-Darmstadt aesthetic of performance constricted the role of the performer to an objective reproduction of minutely defined scores. Paradoxically, for all of his association with that movement, it was Adorno's lesser-known aesthetics of performance, looking back to a pre-war Viennese tradition and his work with Kolisch, that offered a timely critique to the serial performance aesthetics. Mattes suggests that Kolisch/Adorno offer 'a corrective to the narratives of musical modernism that promote composer-oriented perspectives' and make the different roles of composer, performer and critic 'more transparent'. In this way, both Kolisch's performances and Adorno's writings offered 'a critique of contemporary performance culture' – in its place, a performance 'created instead by the cognitive comprehension of musical relationships, and most of all, the knowledge of all the structural and spiritual moments beneath the surface'.

While in the case of Boulez the close relays between performance practice and compositional poetics are located in his own career as a performer, the career of Cathy Berberian offers a striking example of how a single performer has exerted a profound effect on the transformation of others' work. In '"Unwrapping" the voice: Cathy Berberian and John Cage's *Aria*', Francesca Placanica examines the mutually defining influence of Cage and Berberian through a work that 'transformed both Berberian's and Cage's aesthetics of the performative' and was key to Berberian's self-fashioning as a performer and the development of the new vocality. In this, Berberian herself underlined that the 'new vocality' had its roots not just in modernism but in a larger idea of modernity going back to Monteverdi and was thus part of a restoration of something lost to classical (textual) practices of performance.

At the heart of the new vocality was of course an insistence on the centrality of the body in new music. This is key to developments in relation to instrumental performance practice explored in the final two chapters of the book. In 'Radically idiomatic instrumental practice in works by Brian Ferneyhough', Anders Førisdal considers two works of Ferneyhough to explore the idea of 'an approach to composition that incorporates various idiomatic resources as musical material on a structural level in a composition'. His close readings of *Unity Capsule* for flute (1975) and *Kurze Schatten II* for guitar (1988) are informed by his own experience as a performer of this repertoire and the new position which such scores define for the performer. Drawing on Michel Foucault's notion of discursive practices and the writing of Jacques Derrida, he finds here a kind of 'double writing' of the music and of the body, one inscribing the other but also resisting the other, a deconstruction of the work and body that he sees both as a transformation of earlier modernist writing and as a critique of the expressive apparatus and the conditions of new music.

Tanja Orning addresses the ethical dilemma that such a condition poses for the performer of this repertoire in 'The ethics of performance practice in complex music after 1945'. Her study of Klaus K. Hübler's *Opus breve* (1987) for solo cello, again informed by her own experience as a performer, examines a 'shift of focus from the score as musical text to the action embodied in performance, a shift that calls for a complementary shift in performance practice'. As with the earlier chapters on Berberian and Ferneyhough, Orning's concept of a radically idiomatic instrumentalism brings the body of the performer centre stage, in musical composition that takes the physicality of playing as its material, a development of Lachenmann's *musique concrète instrumentale*, and the focus on how sound is produced rather than how it should be heard. The new situation for the performer thus represents another kind of transformation of an earlier ideal of performance practice in high modernism and a new situation characterized by three key aspects: a new emphasis on the role of the body, a move from the ideal of *Werktreue* to one of the ambiguity of the work and a heightened critical and self-reflective role for the performer.

At the heart of every one of the sixteen chapters that make up this book is an encounter with music. While all the authors approach their topics alert to the theoretical frameworks in which we might 'rethink' musical modernism (theories of musicology, analysis, history, philosophy, cultural studies), it is the 'rehearing' of musical modernism that most powerfully shapes this volume. What emerges on almost every page is a sense of the vibrancy and vitality of a music whose multiple and contradictory character demands critical thought while at the same time confounding it. By turns urgently sensuous and physical; pressing on the performing and listening body; and then self-reflective, ironic and playful, a transformed musical modernism refuses the attempts of music history to define it by some narrow set of stylistic traits. Way before musicology woke up to the fact, the *practice* of musical modernism – in performance, listening and composition – has been transforming itself for more than five decades.

It has done so in relation to literature, theatre, film, visual art, architecture, installations and new technologies, in relation to its own historical tradition and to musical traditions from outside the practices of Western classical music. The medium of this relation to the world, in every case, is irreducibly material, located in the sonic 'stuff' of which music is made. In that material, and in the experiential moment of aesthetic experience, this music quite literally takes place in the contemporary world. The aesthetic 'moment' of musical modernism remains a critical one – it opens up distance and difference inside the singularity of the musical moment. A part of social reality, and at the same time apart, the stubborn insistence of modernism on the realm of the aesthetic remains a condition of its critical force. Constantly self-critical of its own past, musical modernism is also an unfinished 'pro-ject', in Lyotard's sense, as something thrown out towards the future.

Historical understanding and the analysis of works and events are thus intertwined in this book – by no means towards any final synthesis or reconciliation but, like the work of musical modernism itself, in the always faltering, always revitalizing grip of self-interpretation. For that reason, our task is to encounter and think about musical modernism in the materiality of its present practice as compositional writing, performance, listening, conceptual interpretation and its changing cultural contexts. This is where the following chapters begin.

PART I

Rethinking modernism

1 The lure of the Sublime

Revisiting the modernist project

Susan McClary

In 1988 I delivered a paper titled 'Terminal Prestige: The Case of Avant-Garde Music Composition' at the conference 'The Economy of Prestige'. This interdisciplinary conference, held at the University of Minnesota, sought to explore the ways in which prestige operates as a system of reward and recognition. At the time, this topic seemed particularly relevant to music studies, which still vaunted 'non-commercial' but institutionally supported artists and held popular success and even communication with contempt. My paper appeared in print for the first time the following year in a special issue of *Cultural Critique* dedicated to that conference, and it has been reprinted in English and other languages several times since then.[1]

An early salvo against the stringent version of post-war modernism still dominating many North American music departments, the article stirred up considerable controversy. It also contributed to the emergence of a self-aware Postmodernism among composers, many of whom had been exploring eclecticism and neo-tonal sonorities in their music without using this label. A careful reading of that article will reveal that I was not attacking modernist music per se but only some of the ideologies that had upheld its hegemony: in particular, an institutionalized prohibition against addressing meaning (imposed not only on new musics but even on repertories from previous eras) and an insistence that serialist procedures comprised the necessary future for genuine music.[2]

Now, nearly thirty years later, many things have changed. First, what had appeared then in North America as the nearly unbreakable stranglehold of academic serialism suddenly weakened and vanished, leaving scarcely a

---

[1] 'Terminal Prestige: The Case of Avant-Garde Music Composition', *Cultural Critique*, 12 (Spring 1989), 57–81. For reprints see David Schwarz, Anahid Kassabian and Lawrence Siegel (eds.), *Keeping Score: Music, Disciplinarity, Culture* (Charlottesville, VA: University Press of Virginia, 1997), pp. 54–74; and my *Reading Music: Selected Essays* (Aldershot: Ashgate, 2007), pp. 85–109.

[2] Joseph Straus, among others, has claimed that no such imperative existed. See his 'The Myth of Serial "Tyranny" in the 1950s and 1960s', in *The Musical Quarterly*, 83/3 (Fall 1999), 301–43. He must not have been there at the time. I know dozens of composers who left the field as a result. See, for instance, the testimonies of Philip Glass concerning Princeton and John Adams concerning Harvard.

trace. Former metal guitarist Steve Mackey replaced Milton Babbitt on the Princeton composition faculty; John Zorn received major prizes for his fusions; and the *Norton History of Western Music* (if not so much the *Oxford*) includes blues, jazz and rock in its account of music since 1900. A flood of serious scholarly research on popular idioms has made genres such as hip hop respectable topics for intellectual inquiry. If 'Terminal Prestige' now seems antiquated, it is largely because the battles in which it engaged have long since been won.

Yet something else has occurred in the intervening years, namely the rise of a new, twenty-first-century version of modernism. For the avant-garde of the 1950s now has – in addition to its Oedipal rebels – some highly productive and successful progeny. Composers such as Kaija Saariaho, Salvatore Sciarrino and George Benjamin, unwilling to throw out the baby with the bathwater, have returned to techniques and sonorities pioneered by Messiaen, Boulez and others. In contrast to some of their predecessors, however, these artists openly acknowledge the expressive and rhetorical power of their strategies. Because staged works necessarily include actors, voices and lyrics, such music humanizes its post-tonal idiom, making its power intelligible to audiences.

The recent resurgence of modernism now appears less like the terminal stage of a fatal disease than a repository of resources for innovation. It invites us to think again about post-war modernism – not as the way European music was predestined to develop organically from within itself or as a reaction formation against popular idioms but rather as an array of relationships between artistic expression and cultural contexts. At this point in time, in other words, it has become possible to treat these repertories as yet another chapter in history.

But a strange chapter it is. We have grown so accustomed in the academy to recognizing Boulez's *Marteau sans maître* and Stockhausen's *Gesang der Jünglinge* as mid-century masterworks that we may no longer perceive how radical they were when they emerged. The requisite perspective is easily restored, however, as soon as one tries to introduce them to a class of canon-devoted conservatory students. So strong is their sense of indignation that one sometimes fears suffering the fate of all messengers bringing bad news when reaching this point in the syllabus.

For, in fact, such music *does* communicate to the uninitiated, though perhaps in ways that differ from its modes of self-justification. The soundtrack compiled by Robby Robertson for Martin Scorsese's 2010 film *Shutter Island*, for instance, featured music by Ligeti, Morton Feldman, John Adams and John Cage, among others, all of which were meant to sound like manifestations of the insane asylum in which the film was set. To today's filmgoer, this soundtrack registered quite simply as nuthouse music. And this would have made sense to Expressionists such as Schoenberg (*Erwartung*) and Berg (*Wozzeck*), both of whom developed their musical languages in part to convey psychological disorder. If we do not simply try to cudgel our students into obedient acceptance (the pedagogical strategy of decades past), their indignation when confronted with this repertory might lead us to consider fundamental questions concerning the purposes of music.

What would have motivated sensitive artists to take up the positions they maintained so fiercely in the 1950s and beyond? Audience appeal certainly does not spring to mind as an explanation. Although the alienation between composers and listeners intensified after World War II, the problem dates back at least forty years before that. For a while people in the academy and isolated sites such as IRCAM (Institut de Recherche et de Coordination Acoustique-Musique) and Darmstadt tried to ensure the continuation of modernist music even if – especially if – no one else much cared. If we discount the argument of historical necessity, how do we explain this moment to our students or even to audiences, who might give the music another chance under the right circumstances?

Several important factors come to mind. First, the world was still reeling from the shock of what had transpired during the war itself. Both the Nazis and the Soviets had harnessed the arts to their political programmes, censoring whatever seemed not to accord with their purposes and appropriating anything that suited them as propaganda. One need only watch the film footage of Wilhelm Furtwängler conducting Beethoven's Ninth in front of Goebbels and other Nazi brass to witness how musical energies can be channelled to support and animate insidious agendas. To be sure, societies have sought to control music and the other arts from Plato's Republic to Louis XIV's absolutist monarchy. But the new media of sound recording, amplification, radio and film raised the stakes immeasurably during World War II.

It is no great wonder then that serious artists reacted by writing music that refused the heated rhetoric that made so much of the traditional canon vulnerable to totalitarian abuses. They preferred to withdraw their work to a place where music would address the cool intellect rather than the emotions, which had proven all too easily swayed by propaganda machines. The nationalist fervour that had fuelled so much art in the previous hundred years had also led to unspeakably inhumane atrocities. In the face of this unprecedented level of catastrophe, the very notion of conveying meanings seemed tantamount to manipulation. Better then to operate within the cerebral sphere of electronic experimentation or high degrees of abstraction or even chance. In retrospect, this ethical position appears not only understandable under the circumstances but also laudable.

Second, the traditional centres for musical production – Vienna, Berlin, Paris, Moscow, Rome, London and New York – found themselves on fiercely opposing sides during the war, and modes of communication across that abyss had disintegrated. But there arose the hope that if music were cleansed of ideological trappings, then it could serve as a conduit for healing. One of the first international communities to emerge from the ashes of the war comprised composers who shared with each other the excitement of developing new musical procedures. For this reason many government agencies, including the US State Department, actively encouraged institutes for experimental music. And surely this climate of international cooperation, with sites such as Darmstadt and IRCAM, represented genuine progress.[3]

Third, the unparalleled advances in technology during the war, capped by the dropping of atomic bombs on civilian populations, created an emphasis on the hard sciences. Institutions of higher learning – even sleepy liberal arts colleges previously dedicated to the life of the mind – suddenly changed their priorities to focus on physics, mathematics and engineering. Because faculties devoted to philosophy and poetry had no claim to economic productivity or technological advancement, they found themselves increasingly on the margins of the educational process. Federal funding poured into the development of computers, and the Cold War race to compete with Sputnik or to put humans on the moon transformed even elementary school curricula.

Music, of course, has always had a precarious perch within mainstream education, especially in the puritanical English-speaking world. Whereas most schools in North America boasted a band, a chorus and perhaps even an orchestra, few offered courses beyond those in music appreciation designed to add a thin veneer of culture to the hordes of first-generation college students who showed up after the war, courtesy of the GI Bill. Some universities had a music historian on their staff or someone who could teach basic musicianship, but these tended to be lightly trained amateurs; only with the wave of Jewish refugees from Central Europe did more

---

[3] See the heated debate between Richard Taruskin and Charles Rosen over the extent to which this support affected cultural production. Taruskin, 'Afterword: *Nicht Blutbefleckt?*', *The Journal of Musicology*, 26/2 (2009), 274–84; and Rosen's response, 'Music and the Cold War', *New York Review of Books* (7 April 2011).

rigorous versions of musicology and music theory take root in North America.[4]

Up against that background, we suddenly had composers such as Milton Babbitt, Vladimir Ussachevsky and Otto Luening, who were able to speak the language of laboratories, experimentation and advanced technologies. They brought unprecedented prestige and external funding to their departments, for they made their projects appear closer to the objective sciences than to the subjective humanities. Of course, the question of whether to locate music with mathematics or with the rhetorically based arts goes back as far as Pythagoras. After the war, for both pragmatic and philosophical reasons, composers opted for allegiances with the Quadrivium rather than the Trivium. A sympathetic reading of Babbitt's article, published as 'Who Cares If You Listen' (which he had titled, much less aggressively, 'The Composer as Specialist'), reveals this argument quite clearly. Music was now to be one of the sciences, comprehensible – like the advanced physics of Babbitt's colleague at Princeton, Albert Einstein – principally to other experts.[5]

My last point concerns popular music. With the rapid development of sound recording and broadcast media, popular music had taken centre stage in Western music history. The apparatus connected with (what do we call it?) classical music bears some of the responsibility for its own eclipse. Our museum-oriented enterprises, our symphony orchestras and opera houses, have continued to cater to nineteenth-century tastes. Historians have shown that this calcification of the repertory began to occur soon after Beethoven, with fewer and fewer composers added to the rosters as the decades passed.[6]

And it wasn't even that audiences learned how to listen to the content of the canon; they became familiar with the principal melodies and tuned out the rest. Performers themselves have restricted their function to executing the notes on the page as accurately as possible, inflecting them indiscriminately with what is termed 'musicality', and most conservatory students still object vehemently to any discussion of musical values or

---

[4] For an account of this transformation and its consequences, see Joseph Kerman, *Contemplating Music: Challenges to Musicology* (Cambridge, MA: Harvard University Press, 1985). See also David Josephson, 'The German Musical Exile and the Course of American Musicology', *Current Musicology*, 79 and 80 (2005), 9–53.

[5] Milton Babbitt, 'Who Cares If You Listen?', *High Fidelity* (February 1958). Something similar happened in the visual arts in the United States. See Serge Guilbaut, *How New York Stole the Idea of Modern Art: Abstract Expressionism, Freedom, and the Cold War*, trans. Arthur Goldhammer (University of Chicago Press, 1985).

[6] William Weber in particular has painstakingly traced the history of concert programming. See his *The Rise of Musical Classics: A Study in Canon, Ritual and Ideology* (Oxford University Press, 1992).

interpretation. I hope that Julian Johnson's *Who Needs Classical Music?*, Larry Kramer's *Why Classical Music Still Matters*, my own *Reading Music* and Greg Sandow's blogging campaign to salvage classical music can turn the situation around, but I fear it may be too late.[7]

Indeed, long before the war, Theodor Adorno had warned that easy listening habits and automatic-pilot performances were inviting many cultivated Germans to lower their critical guard. As he explains, the music that might have accustomed his contemporaries to thinking seriously about moral tensions came to be perceived merely as elite entertainment or to be rejected altogether for the easier demands of a debased form of dancehall jazz. This slippery slope, according to Adorno, led inexorably to the rise of the Nazis in Germany and, eventually, to the Holocaust.[8]

Adorno's jeremiads indicate that the battle for listeners had already been lost. After the war, people of my father's generation were still encouraged at least to pretend to like classical music; they learned to attend symphony concerts if they aspired to professional careers. But by the time I started my undergraduate studies in the 1960s, many intellectuals were finding greater stimulation and even greater ethical fibre in the jazz of John Coltrane or the protest rock of Bob Dylan. The old browbeating methods that had shamed educated people into acquiring a modicum of music appreciation no longer had any effect.

Given the unbridgeable gap between 'serious' music and the popular music that had long since become dominant, the valiant attempts by the post-war avant-garde to uphold and continue the development of an ever more complex and uncompromising canon appear heroic. In statement after statement, Boulez, Babbitt, Roger Sessions and many others posited as their goal nothing less than the survival of music *tout court*. The analogue is the Fall of Rome to the barbarians, when a handful of scholars like Boethius fought to hold on to a few remnants of their civilization's former glory. And who could blame them for that?

So here I am, relatively late in my own career, becoming something of an apologist for modernism – or at least attempting to see matters from their

---

[7] Julian Johnson, *Who Needs Classical Music?: Cultural Choice and Musical Value* (Oxford University Press, 2002); Lawrence Kramer, *Why Classical Music Still Matters* (Berkeley and Los Angeles, CA: University of California Press, 2007); McClary, *Reading Music*; Greg Sandow, 'Greg Sandow – Blog', www.gregsandow.com/blog.

[8] Adorno elaborated these arguments throughout his career and in many places. See the compilation of some of his major pieces in *Essays on Music*, ed. Richard Leppert, trans. Susan H. Gillespie (Berkeley and Los Angeles, CA: University of California Press, 2002). For a pointed indictment of casual listening, see Adorno, *Introduction to the Sociology of Music*, trans. E. B. Ashton (New York: Seabury Press, 1976).

point of view. I suppose this is something like the process that occurs to us all when we get old enough to view our parents not as tyrants of discipline but as vulnerable human beings who made the best choices they could, given their array of options. The post-war modernists did not create the cultural circumstances in which they found themselves as they embarked on their careers, any more than people of my generation invented the Cold War or the Vietnam War, to which we have responded throughout our conscious lives. Given the resources, conditions and aesthetic assumptions of the post-war era, what they accomplished was truly remarkable.

But many of those aesthetic assumptions and social priorities went unstated or, worse, were stated in ways that provoked more animosity – especially among musicians of my generation – than sympathy. In 'Terminal Prestige' I called not for the silencing of Milton Babbitt's *Philomel* (which I greatly admire) but rather for a discussion of its meanings. The late music theorist David Lewin more than satisfied my challenge with his beautiful humanist account elucidating the relationships between Babbitt's thorny modus operandi, its allegorical significance and the affective force of the piece performed so memorably by Bethany Beardslee.[9] In countless stimulating theory conversations that often lasted for hours, Michael Cherlin has laboured since the 1980s to help me understand the positions held by Babbitt, one of his most-loved teachers.[10] And contact with Erling E. Guldbrandsen and his seminar students over the last four years in Oslo has engaged me in stimulating discussions of Boulez and Ligeti.[11]

So allow me to ask once again: why was it so difficult for the composers of such works to speak that eloquently about what they were doing? Why did they seek to deny cultural meanings, choosing instead to assert their agendas as the next necessary stage in the evolutionary trajectory of Western music? Why did formal complexity itself and the deliberate shunning of listeners seem like badges of honour?

I want to suggest that they had succumbed – like so many of their predecessors and like not a few of their Postmodernist successors – to the lure of the Sublime. A product of the new public sphere emerging in eighteenth-century England and, later, German-speaking domains, aesthetic theory posited a binary opposition between the Beautiful and

---

[9] David Lewin on Philomel in *Studies in Music and Text* (Oxford University Press, 2006).
[10] See, for instance, Cherlin's attempt to trace Schoenberg's development from his tonal roots instead of back from serialism in his *Schoenberg's Musical Imagination* (Cambridge University Press, 2007). His arguments depart quite radically from historical narratives that interpret Schoenberg's serialism as a necessary stage between late-Romantic tonality and the total serialism of the 1950s.
[11] See Erling E. Guldbrandsen's interviews with Boulez in *Tempo*, 65/255–258 (2011) and Peter Edwards, 'Tradition and the Endless Now: A Study of György Ligeti's *Le Grand Macabre*', unpublished PhD dissertation, University of Oslo (2012).

the Sublime. The Beautiful emphasized pleasure, symmetry and order, while the Sublime reached beyond such domesticated sensations to simulate the wild untamable forces of nature. In Goethe's *Sorrows of Young Werther*, for instance, the eponymous hero leaves Charlotte's genteel garden to brave the savage storm; a river that had previously provided the backdrop for their lovely outings now rages beyond its banks, uprooting trees and dragging everything along in its wake.

As long as music operated under the patronage and tastes of aristocratic courts, most of it aspired to the status of the Beautiful. But the post-revolutionary undercurrents that soon burst through that placid surface with the gothic novel, the rantings of William Blake and the horrendous paintings of Goya all gave vent to other impulses. In their descriptions of this binarism, Edmund Burke and Emanuel Kant identified the Beautiful with feminine qualities, the Sublime with the masculine. No longer would art cater to the merely pretty and congenial. It also would break out of those bounds and, like Prometheus, defy the very gods. In music Beethoven stood as the hero who threw off the fetters of balanced formal procedures and inherited harmonic practices, thereby challenging the social contracts represented by convention. Many of his compositions feature the explicit dismissal of Beauty by the erupting Sublime: think, for example, of the move from the exquisite slow movement of the Ninth Symphony to the Finale's cruelly dissonant opening, which shatters that carefully wrought island of bliss. We celebrate him for having had the courage to do so.

Beethoven's example set the tone for the artists of subsequent generations. Thereafter any idea already in circulation would qualify as a domesticated element that had to be superseded. Over the course of the nineteenth century, composers shredded conventions as soon as they began to coalesce. They created extraordinary masterworks in doing so, but they also quickly exhausted the options available to them – at least the options that could still communicate with listeners. Any whiff of convention – in other words, the social contract that allowed listeners to follow the logic of the music they heard – had to be resisted. By the early twentieth century only unrelieved dissonance would do.[12] Not a few pieces played out their transgressions with topics that featured violence against women: Strauss's *Salome*, Stravinsky's *Rite of Spring*, Berg's *Lulu* and Hindemith's *Murder, Hope of Women* come immediately to mind.

Of course, some composers still aspired to the Beautiful. In the twentieth century, Sergei Rachmaninoff and Aaron Copland continued to write

---

[12] See McClary, *Conventional Wisdom: The Content of Musical Form* (Berkeley and Los Angeles, CA: University of California Press, 2000). Chapter 4, 'The Refuge of Counterconvention', pp. 109–38.

gorgeous melodies much loved by listeners. But they received their reward in the form of audience popularity rather than within the institutional economy of prestige; they don't get to count among the Big Boys, for the chroniclers who traced the path of music history largely ignored or belittled them.[13] It was the Sublime or nothing at all.

When I first started writing about Postmodernist music in the 1980s, I believed that we might be witnessing a break away from the modernist trajectory. Critiques of what Jean-François Lyotard called the Master Narrative and a swerve away from the ultracomplex machinations of post-war composers held out some hope for a different set of aesthetic priorities.[14] But art historian Maggie Nelson's *The Art of Cruelty* traces a lineage from Antonin Artaud that has valued ever-greater transgressions.[15] The fetishizing of violence even escalated: recall the case of Chris Burden, who once had someone shoot a bullet into his arm as part of a performance art piece.

Of course, performance art of this sort qualifies as Postmodernist; indeed, Lyotard himself wrote of a 'Postmodern Sublime'. And it is in such circumstances that aspects of modernism become indistinguishable from those of its Oedipal successors, which often felt the need to push the already distended envelope yet further in order to claim the right of ascendency. What nineteenth-century French poets such as Rimbaud celebrated with the slogan 'épater la bourgeoisie' turned into the imperative to spit on just about everyone in the interest of a progress narrative that demands a scorched-earth treatment of all previous values. Nor is popular culture immune from this pattern as escalating levels of violence and sexual transgression appear in films, music videos, internet sites and computer games. The prestige of the Sublime reigns as soon as it makes an appearance within a new genre.

So what are the alternatives? A large part of the problem I have been describing goes back to those two eighteenth-century categories, one of which was always already fatally tainted by associations with the feminine. Aesthetician Alexander Nehemas tries to revitalize that category in his book, *Only a Promise of Happiness: The Place of Beauty in a World of Art*.[16] But the Beautiful has long since been demoted to the merely pretty, and

---

[13] For a historical analysis of this phenomenon, see Peter Franklin, *Reclaiming Late-Romantic Music: Singing Devils and Distant Sounds* (Berkeley and Los Angeles, CA: University of California Press, 2014).

[14] Jean-François Lyotard, *The Postmodern Condition: A Report on Knowledge*, trans. Geoff Bennington and Brian Massumi (Minneapolis, MN: University of Minnesota Press, 1984).

[15] Maggie Nelson, *The Art of Cruelty: A Reckoning* (New York: W. W. Norton, 2012).

[16] Alexander Nehemas, *Only a Promise of Happiness: The Place of Beauty in a World of Art* (Princeton University Press, 2010).

few serious artists dare pitching their tents in that terrain for fear of ridicule.

There could and should be other categories, however. When I teach Berlioz, I always lament the fact that the Fathers of Aesthetic Theory failed to recognize the Hilarious among their types, thus condemning us to unrelieved earnestness in the arts. Occasionally a serious composer ventures over into hilarity – think of Stravinsky's *Renard*, for instance – but this option by and large got consigned to the trash heap. We may acknowledge the playfulness of Erik Satie or Virgil Thomson from time to time, but we refuse to locate those artists within our principal canons. Note that all the composers I have just mentioned operated within the orbit of French culture. Is it possible that C. P. E. Bach was the last hilarious German composer? How sad is that! And why did we all allow the Germans to set the rules?

The Spiritual also makes appearances now and then in post-war music. It is no accident that our eighteenth-century philosophers avoided listing this among their categories, for they sought to establish secular alternatives to systems based on Christian precepts. Among the religious masterworks written by twentieth-century composers ordinarily associated with the modernist Sublime are Stravinsky's *Symphony of Psalms* and Schoenberg's *Moses and Aron*.

In the post-war era, Olivier Messiaen stands out as an artist whose experiments all revolved around his deep commitment to Roman Catholicism. A father figure for Boulez and Stockhausen, as well as Saariaho and Benjamin, he fashioned a musical language grounded not on defiance but on his love of birdsong, his interest in non-Western musical procedures and his mystical contemplation of the Divine. Because of this grounding, his music has continually reached out to include listeners and to move them. Think of the extraordinary scene in his *Saint Francis of Assisi* in which the saint heals the leper by kissing him, gradually leading us back into blissful triadic harmonies for the end of the opera's first act. The so-called Holy Minimalists who emerged from the collapse of the Soviet Bloc also participate fully in the aesthetic category of the Spiritual. In the United States, Steve Reich has returned to his Jewish heritage for sustenance; in England, John Taverner and Jonathan Harvey have turned unapologetically to spiritual themes. A few musicologists, for instance Marcel Cobussen, have begun to theorize the relationships between music and spirituality.[17]

---

[17] Marcel Cobussen, *Thresholds: Rethinking Spirituality through Music* (Aldershot: Ashgate, 2010).

At a more basic level, we have the long-dismissed category of Pleasure, which eighteenth-century Germans resisted in part because of its strong associations with the absolutist French court. Pleasure never has disappeared from music, of course. Whenever artists begin to pursue the Sublime, whether in classical or popular culture, many music-lovers just turn to ballads, dance music and other forms of entertainment. Historian Andreas Huyssen has shown how such activities came to be linked in the nineteenth century not only with the feminine but also with the lower classes and despised races, with austere modernism set up as a bulwark against cultural contamination.[18] But popular taste often ignores arguments based on cultural hierarchies. Recall how poor Don José in Bizet's *Carmen* tries to carry the banner of serious music in the face of the gypsies' much catchier habañeras, seguidillas and toreador songs. Even after José resorts to Sublime violence to stifle the sounds of those Others, we leave the opera house humming Carmen's tunes.[19]

In the twentieth century, the songs of Irving Berlin, Cole Porter and George Gershwin celebrated a version of urban modernity with which ivory tower composers could scarcely compete. Cerebral bebop and cool jazz got displaced by R&B, rock and soul. When rock musicians decided to experiment with strange metres in the name of progress, many people just switched to disco, which still invited its listeners to dance.[20] An old cliché opposes the Sublime and the Ridiculous. But maybe the Sublime itself, with its self-importance, exudes more of the Ridiculous than we like to admit.

Perhaps more than anything else, we have forgotten that we are in the business of what my late friend Christopher Small termed 'musicking'.[21] Chris moved after the war from New Zealand, where he had composed scores for ballets and other full-length works, to study with Luigi Nono. But faced with the choice between serialism and teaching in a high school, Chris opted for the latter. Within that context he wrote books that have transformed musicology, music education, ethnomusicology and music criticism.[22] Although he preferred playing Mozart and listening to Sibelius,

---

[18] Andreas Huyssen, 'Mass Culture as Woman: Modernism's Other' in his *After the Great Divide: Modernism, Mass Culture, Postmodernism* (Bloomington, IN: Indiana University Press, 1987), pp. 44–63.

[19] See my *Georges Bizet: Carmen* (Cambridge University Press, 1992).

[20] Elijah Wald, *How the Beatles Destroyed Rock and Roll: An Alternative History of American Popular Music* (Oxford University Press, 2009).

[21] Christopher Small, *Musicking: The Meanings of Performing and Listening* (Middletown, CT: Wesleyan University Press, 1998).

[22] Before he wrote *Musicking*, Small had published *Music, Society, Education* (London: John Calder, 1977; 2nd edn, Middletown, CT: Wesleyan University Press, 1998) and *Music of the Common Tongue: Survival and Celebration in African-American Music* (London: John Calder, 1987; 2nd end,

he became so disgusted with the narrow perspectives of many of his professional colleagues that he set about finding a way of putting the activity of music making back in the centre of attention. Instead of fetishized works, he argued, we should be observing how and why human beings engage in producing and sharing meaningful sounds. And in a world so fraught with anxieties and dangers, we surely cannot afford to sneer at pleasure, as if 'our' music were self-evidently morally superior. We all require music in our lives, perhaps for purposes of survival itself. Otherwise why would human societies have persisted in investing their limited energies in this enterprise?

It is for such reasons that I cannot bring myself to regret the arguments in 'Terminal Prestige' concerning popular music. With the advent of sound recording, the history of Western music became a radically different story from the one still too-often presented in our textbooks and curricula. For all the undeniable brilliance of Richard Taruskin's *Oxford History of Western Music*, it stumbles when it reaches the twentieth century.[23] Not even most composers today, many of whom channel pop musics in their own work, would restrict 'Western music' to the continuation of the Schoenberg legacy.

In any case, Postmodernism supplanted post-war modernism beginning in the 1960s with Berio's *Sinfonia* and George Crumb's *Ancient Voices of Children*. Minimalists such as Philip Glass and Steve Reich moved as far away from abstract modernism as they could in explicit defiance of the prohibition against repetition. We're now in a phase some call Postminimalist, though the prefix 'post' in all these labels points more to rejection of what came before than to new directions. Indeed, the concept of 'modernity' itself announces that process of radically splitting off from the past. We seem destined to live in an infinite series of 'posts'.

So it may seem strange, after so many episodes of eradicating connections with tradition, to inquire into the long-term cultural contribution of modernism. Did the post-war generation leave a legacy besides that of reaction? Or, better, does anyone – other than the odd serialist still rattling around inside an academic department – now choose to claim that legacy? And how is that legacy understood?

I want to close by dealing briefly with three contemporary artists who draw heavily from the modernist tradition yet have attracted a relatively

---

Middletown, CT: Wesleyan University Press, 1998), both of which deal insightfully – critically yet with evident love – with the canon and twentieth-century modernism. Indeed, he even published a monograph on Schoenberg (London: John Calder, 1978).

[23] Richard Taruskin, *The Oxford History of Western Music*, 6 vols. (Oxford University Press, 2005). See my review-essay in *Music and Letters*, 87/3 (2006), 408–15.

large and enthusiastic following. Finnish composer Kaija Saariaho picks up the spectral harmony and electronic sound sources associated with IRCAM and the sonorities associated with Messiaen. I am interested in Saariaho in part because she is among the most successful women composing today but even more because I find her music ravishing. She is also by far the best-known Nordic composer on the international stage.

Saariaho often chooses female characters and points of view in her operas: think, for instance, of *L'Amour de Loin, Adriana Mater, La Passion de Simone* and (most recently) *Émilie*. But she goes far beyond simply marking her subject matter as woman oriented; she has also developed a musical vocabulary designed to simulate a very different quality of desire by means of what I call smouldering intensities: a dense fabric of low drones and spectral harmonies, extended trills and static ostinatos disrupted occasionally by violent eruptions or rushes of passion. Before she went to Darmstadt and IRCAM, Saariaho studied composition in Helsinki along with Esa-Pekka Salonen as a fellow student, and that connection has no doubt given her greater access to concert programming and recording than may have been feasible otherwise. But it is surely the lush, sensual version of modernism of her music that attracts and holds listeners.

Although Saariaho occasionally makes use of sounds familiar to traditional audiences, her music operates outside the sphere of tonal practice. The open fifths that resonate with her troubadour, Jaufré Rudel, in *L'Amour de Loin* serve to anchor his *chansons* in the Middle Ages, but his own utterances refuse the comfort of triadic convention. Yet the opera communicates powerfully with audiences through its gestures, its brilliant orchestration and its ability to produce moods. For all that she chooses her pitches through spectral devices, Saariaho explicitly refuses to write what she calls 'paper music': music designed for cerebral analysis. It is no coincidence that she came to operatic composition through the urging of Peter Sellars – the long-time collaborator with John Adams – and the model of Messiaen's *Saint François d'Assise*, which Sellars staged. He also staged the extraordinary first production of *L'Amour de loin*.[24]

My second composer, George Benjamin, similarly descends from Messiaen, with whom he studied. Benjamin's recent *Written on Skin* (premiered in 2012) has taken the opera world by storm. Simultaneously austere and opulent, this work shares with *L'Amour de loin* a story taken from the troubadour tradition, in this case the tale of the eaten heart. And

---

[24] Kaija Saariaho, *L'Amour de loin* (2000). DVD: Peter Sellars (dir.), libretto by Armin Maalouf. With performers Gerald Finley and Dawn Upshaw, and conducted by Esa-Pekka Salonen (Deutsche Grammophon, 2005); CD conducted by Kent Nagano, with Daniel Belcer and Ekaterina Lekhina (Harmonia Mundi, 2009).

like Saariaho, Benjamin makes his music immediately comprehensible through his deployment of gesture and mood. The menacing quality of The Man, the repressed sexuality of The Woman, the uncanny quality of The Boy, who doubles as an angel: all of these seize listeners and pull them inexorably towards the opera's grisly end.[25]

It bears mention that both *L'Amour de loin* and *Written on Skin* eschew the usual male/female dichotomy by featuring an important intermediate figure: Saariaho's Pilgrim, who is given no gender in the libretto, and Benjamin's The Boy, sung by a countertenor. A mere twenty years ago, countertenors still sounded repellent to many audiences. But we have witnessed a boom in recent years, thanks to the historical performance movement and the development of virtuoso singers dedicated to falsetto singing. If Benjamin Britten made use of this voice to convey the queerness of Oberon in *Midsummer Night's Dream* and Philip Glass to signal a kind of deformity in *Akhnaten*, countertenors now allow for a more complex array of gender types.[26]

Salvatore Sciarrino drew his inspiration for *Luci mie traditrici* from Carlo Gesualdo's murder of his wife and her lover, but he takes his source music from a highly chromatic chanson by Claude le Jeune rather than from Gesualdo. The chanson runs through the opera, presented first as just a tune and later – as the drama becomes more fraught – in distortions that render it all but unrecognizable. Sciarrino has his characters whisper menacingly at each other, as if reluctant to sing at all. Whenever they begin to give a word full voice, they soon distort it to a raspy hiss or else break off as if a hand had been clamped down over the mouth. In the context of the extended performance techniques movement, these sounds are right at home. But to move them onto the operatic stage is quite another matter. Yet Sciarrino's deft control of temporality and mood make this a gripping experience.[27]

In a recent piece on the resurgence of Richard Strauss in the *New York Times*, critic Anthony Tommasini quipped, 'The polemical era when brainy uptown composers battled downtown exponents of postmodernism is, thankfully, past.'[28] Indeed, no one pays much attention any longer to the preponderance or absence of triads from scores. What matters now is musical and dramatic effectiveness. Thus, although I have been tracing composers

---

[25] George Benjamin, *Written on Skin* (2012). DVD: Katie Mitchell (dir.), libretto by Martin Crimp, with performers Barbara Hannigan and Bejun Mehta, and conducted by George Benjamin (Opus Arte, 2013).

[26] For a fuller discussion of this issue, see my 'Soprano Masculinities' in Philip Purvis (ed.), *Masculinity in Opera* (London: Routledge, 2013), pp. 51–79.

[27] Salvatore Sciarrino, *Luci mie traditrici* (1998). DVD: with Nina Tarandek and Christian Miedl, cond. Marco Angius (EuroArts, 2011).

[28] Anthony Tommasini, 'Drifting Back to the Real World', *New York Times* (8 June 2014).

who would identify themselves with a kind of modernity, I might well also have considered works by Thomas Adès or John Adams, who might at one time have seemed aligned with the swerve away from modernism but who freely engage as well with devices and sonorities from the post-war era. For all these composers, the whole world of sound is their oyster.

Adolescents often feel the need to break violently with their fathers and mothers; recall not only the Postmodernists lashing out against their post-war predecessors but also Boulez's savage 'Schoenberg est mort' pronouncement. Yet close affinities sometimes emerge between grandparents and grandchildren, helping to knit ruptured families back together into some semblance of continuity. My young composition students these days are avid fans of Boulez, Ligeti and Feldman. They don't care about the old arguments concerning the survival of music and the necessity of toeing the modernist line; they simply love the compositions for their own sakes, for the ways they put sounds together. And they mine them for ideas, as composers have done forever. For the return of this particular prodigal daughter to the fold, I owe a particular debt of gratitude to my former student Ethan Braun, who has continued to correspond with me concerning these issues even after both of us moved on to other institutions.

In the public realm, composers such as Saariaho, Benjamin and Sciarrino have done a great deal to guarantee the modernist legacy by taking up elements from post-war composition and fashioning pieces that communicate powerfully with large audiences. No one studying their music can avoid reflecting upon the works of those who developed so many of the materials with which they operate. As their operas send us back to Messiaen, Ligeti or Boulez, they invite us to hear the post-war modernists again with new ears. Our post-Postmodern modernists thereby remind us of the aesthetic richness in the music of their forebears, especially the emotional qualities they tried by and large to deny but that now glow unapologetically in their new music.

2 Return of the repressed

Particularity in early and late modernism

Julian Johnson

Ligeti: Sonata for Solo Viola

In the preface to the score of his Sonata for Solo Viola of 1994, György Ligeti considers the difference between the violin and the viola. Where 'the violin leads, the viola remains in the shade', he suggests, because the viola lacks the high E-string, which 'lends the violin a powerful luminosity and metallic penetrating tone'. 'In return', he continues, 'the low C-string gives the viola a unique ascerbity, compact, somewhat hoarse, with the aftertaste of wood, earth and tannic acid'.[1] As with all things to do with Ligeti, we might be cautious about reading this too seriously; Richard Steinitz, for one, suggests that Ligeti's wine-tasting metaphor is 'tongue-in-cheek'.[2] But the preface also underlines that the tone Ligeti imagined was not simply that of the viola 'in general' but the particular sound of one player, Tabea Zimmermann, whom he had heard at a concert in Cologne in 1990, and the Sonata provides ample evidence that its starting point lies in such particularity – of tone, accent, intonation and gesture.

The first of the six movements to be composed were 'Loop' (placed second in the published order) and 'Facsar' (placed third) – embodying between them the qualities Ligeti had most admired in Zimmermann's playing – 'vigorous and pithy – yet always tender'. His prefatory note to 'Facsar' continues the intensity and specificity of his earlier sensory metaphor: 'Facsar', he tells us, is a Hungarian verb meaning 'to wrestle' or 'to distort' but 'is also associated with the bitter sensation felt in the nose when one is about to cry'.[3] Ligeti instructs the player to deliver the first twelve bars of its slow dance melody on the C-string alone, but it is the first movement, 'Hora lungă', which presents the most single-minded and sustained exploration of this elemental quality of the instrument. Played entirely on the C-string throughout its nearly six-minute duration, it turns the viola into some ancient monochord in which intonation,

---

[1] György Ligeti, Sonata for Solo Viola, Preface (Mainz: Schott Music, 2003).
[2] Richard Steinitz, *György Ligeti: Music of the Imagination* (London: Faber, 2003), p. 337.
[3] Ligeti, Sonata for Solo Viola, Preface.

unstructured by the relationship between strings and the usual architecture of learned hand positions, is more akin to that of the human voice. Ligeti makes this explicit by his detuning of the equal-tempered scale to achieve what he calls 'natural intervals'. The piece is conceived as sounding in the natural harmonic series arising from a fundamental F, which means, in practice, a very slight tuning down of the A to make a natural major third, a slightly larger tuning down of the E-flat to achieve a natural seventh and about a quarter-tone tuning down of the B-natural to approximate the eleventh harmonic (indicated in the score by three different downward-facing arrows). The result is a musical voice whose palpable particularity disorientates the listener, the very specificity of its presence making it hard to place.

If the Sonata foregrounds a preoccupation with the particularity of sound – the tone of the viola's C-string, Tabea Zimmerman's playing, and an intonation that resists the abstract ratios of equal temperament – it also implies a particularity of musical voice in terms of the resonances of time and place. 'Facsar' is dedicated to Sándor Veress, Ligeti's composition teacher some forty-five years earlier at the Franz Liszt Academy in Budapest, whose death in 1993 occurred soon after the movement's completion. One need not be aware of the dedication to hear a homage in this music to Bartók (Veress's own teacher) and to the engagement of both these composers with traditions of folk music from Hungary to the Balkans.[4] On the one hand, Ligeti was keen to emphasize the wider origins of his fascination with musical materials from outside European art music – he relates 'Hora lungă' to the music of Andalusia and Rajasthan, and the fifth movement of the Sonata, 'Lament', to the music of the Balkans, the Ivory Coast and Melanesia. The Piano Etudes famously extend such references to sub-Saharan Africa, Jazz and Gamelan.[5] But at the same time, it is hard to escape the sense of an absolute specificity of voice and also place.[6] 'Hora lungă', Ligeti writes, 'evokes the spirit of Romanian folk music, which, together with Hungarian folk music and that of the gypsies,

---

[4] Benjamin Dwyer identifies 'a more than passing tribute to Béla Bartók' in the Sonata. See 'Transformational Ostinati in Györgi Ligeti's Sonatas for Solo Cello and Solo Viola' in Louise Duchesneau and Wolfgang Marx (eds.), *György Ligeti: Of Foreign Lands and Strange Sounds* (Woodbridge: Boydell and Brewer, 2011), pp. 19–52, p. 19.
[5] Ligeti credits his debt to the ethnomusicologist Simha Arom in his use of African polyrhythms in the Etudes. The seventh Etude, 'Galamb Borong', shows a clear link to gamelan music, but elsewhere Ligeti references Ugandan xylophone playing and the Jazz pianism of Thelonius Monk and Bill Evans (as in the fifth Etude, 'Arc en ciel'). Bartók's presence is clear in No. 4, 'Fanfares', with its 3 + 2 + 3 ostinato figure.
[6] It is perhaps not irrelevant that Ligeti's beloved brother Gabor, murdered in a concentration camp at the age of seventeen by the Nazis in 1945, also played the viola. See Steinitz, *György Ligeti*, p. 17.

made a strong impression on me during my childhood'. Keen to distance himself from any kitsch use of folklore, he immediately locates this in a very particular place – the Maramures province in the far north of Romania, in the Carpathian Mountains. But as Benjamin Dwyer points out, the link is also to Bartók, who first came across the *hora lungă* in the territories of Maramures and Sata-Mare in 1912, an encounter that Bartók later described 'as the most important development of his musical career'.[7]

Such particularity of geography and voice is glaringly at odds with the cultivated anonymity and abstraction of the musical avant-garde of the mid-century. Ligeti's use of natural tuning, a kind of refusal of the progressive rationalization of pitch that takes place from the Renaissance onwards, was of course contemporary with spectralism's *recherches* in the 1980s into the natural acoustic properties of sound, but his 'rude' pleasure in premodern tuning is curiously at odds with the precision of that aesthetic. Spectralism, as a product of the hyper-modern capacity of computer-generated analysis, seems a quite opposite thing to the archaic quality of Ligeti's viola, to say nothing of the 'natural' horns and the detuned warblings of the four ocarinas in the Violin Concerto, completed in 1992, the year in which the Viola Sonata was began. One might note that the shock of the horns and ocarinas is first heard in the Concerto after the extended solo violin opening of the second movement 'Aria', played entirely on the G-string for the first seventy-four bars.

Commenting specifically on Ligeti's musical topic of lament, Amy Bauer noted that across the composer's work, and as early as his music from the 1960s and 1970s, 'the lament topic often appeared as an interruption, a rhetorical apostrophe or exclamatory passage ... as a stain that both mars and marks ... [disrupting] the ethos and formal continuity of a work, altering the movement or piece in which it was embedded'.[8] It is, to be sure, a startling effect of Ligeti's music that intensely lyrical music has the effect of creating a dissonance not only in the formal structure of an individual piece but in the larger context of the musical language in which it operates. His exploration of natural tunings has a similar effect, most obviously demonstrated by the anarchic and carnivalesque character of the quartet of horns in his *Hamburg Concerto* (1999, rev. 2003), whose title marks out its relation of non-identity to a Brandenburg Concerto.[9] The

---

[7] Dwyer, 'Transformational Ostinati', p. 26.
[8] Amy Bauer, *Ligeti's Laments: Nostalgia, Exoticism and the Absolute* (Farnham: Ashgate, 2011), p. 3.
[9] The use of a quartet of horns playing natural harmonics and the foregrounding of the tone of the solo viola are both prominent features of Gérard Grisey's *Les espaces acoustiques* (1974–85), which begins with an extended solo for viola in its Prologue, returning in the sixth movement, Epilogue, before the re-entry of the full orchestra led by the detuned whooping of the four horns.

Sonata for Solo Viola similarly draws attention to a deliberate historical disjunction, as if to use J. S. Bach as a kind of symbol for the rationalizations of modernity which Ligeti's work acknowledges while distancing at the same time. In the last movement of the Sonata, a 'Chaconne chromatique', Ligeti draws attention to the relation by denying it: 'Allusions to the famous Bach Chaconne should not be expected! My sonata is much more unassuming, does not historicize and also cannot support monumental forms. I use the word chaconne in its original meaning: as a wild exuberant dance in strongly accented three-four time with an ostinato bass-line.'[10]

Ligeti seems to reclaim the chaconne from the grand, abstract, highly rationalized cleverness of the Baroque, in order to restore its bodily nature as a dance. But the physicality of the rhythmic energy is tied up with a highly chromatic harmonic palette and an upper line that is often simply a descending chromatic scale, as if the bodily exertions of the dance were opposed to the disintegrating effect of the rationalized chromatic scale. The sense of an agonistic relation between these two opposing forces is underlined by the increasing density of triple and quadruple stopping and a 'crescendo estremo' to a dynamic of *fffff*. At this point the wedge form reaches its point of maximum intensity and, by means of a short transitional passage (bs. 74–79), it gives way to a pianissimo epilogue (Meno mosso, molto cantabile), its marking of 'da lontano' underlined by the *sul tasto* tone maintained to the end.

The sudden simplicity with which the chaconne material is treated is startling. Its increasingly diatonic language suggests echoes of some of Stravinsky's chorale endings (as in the *Symphonies of Wind Instruments*, for example). And, after all six movements of the Sonata have used the open C-string as their reference point, the ending of the last movement now reads that C as a II^b, a Neapolitan tonal relation, to end on a first inversion B major triad – on one level, a display of wit typical of the composer, on another, a utopian twist performed without a trace of irony.

Bartók: Sonata for Solo Violin

Ligeti's Chaconne has other historical resonances, of course, not least Bartók's use of the form in the first movement ('Tempo di Ciaccona') of his Sonata for Solo Violin, written fifty years earlier in 1944. Bartók's movement displays the same astringent chordal texture and the wrestling with the instrument that this embodies, referencing its baroque model even as it departs from it with exaggerated registral separations and textural

---

[10] Ligeti, Sonata for Solo Viola, Preface.

dislocations; both composers use the chaconne's repetitions as a vehicle for the progressive accumulation of intensity in writing that pushes at the boundaries of the technically possible. But what binds Ligeti's movement to Bartók's is not just this sense of a working out of formal and historical tensions but also the shared attempt to *break out of* or *break through* this historical tension in order to arrive at something else, at a simpler musical statement contained in the idea of melody. Such a trajectory is staged in a direct way in the final movement of Ligeti's Sonata, with its clear caesura dividing the 'recovered' modal melody in the final section from the violent struggle of the earlier music. Bartók's Chaconne is a first movement, not a last, and such a breakthrough is not so much delivered here as implied – particularly in the brief passages of more lyrical, modal writing (b. 49) and the intrusion of dance rhythms from a peasant musical tradition (b. 84) both distant to the baroque chaconne and, at the same time, recalling its origins in the 'wild exuberant dance' referenced by Ligeti. Taken as a whole, however, Bartók's Sonata allows a progressive recovery of material that we might hear as repressed by the strict logic of the rationality of musical modernity (enshrined here in the chaconne form). The idea is immediately reframed by the second movement, 'Fuga', in which the abstract logic of the fugue finds itself at odds with the raw and rebarbative tone of Bartók's violin. The tension between a brittle and uncompromising formal discipline and the bricolage of the violin's physical gestures eventually snaps with the sidestep into a moment of peasant dance music (bs. 88–92). The repetitive rhythm and the open fifth that frames the simple middle-voice melody suggest a contained musical space that is the opposite of the teleology of the fugue.

But it is the opening of the third movement, 'Melodia', which makes the most resonant link to Ligeti's Sonata. The extended passages to be played on a single string foreground the particular voice of each string in turn, ensuring a quality of tone quite different to that produced by a violinist making use of a more regular division between the strings. Thus, bars 1–6 are delivered entirely on the G-string, bars 7–8 on the D-string and so on. Bars 9–11 are carefully divided to produce a very particular sequence of tones: first, the upward phrase F-G-C-D is given on the G-string for the first three notes but uses a natural harmonic of the D-string for the final note; this is answered by the falling dyad F#-D on the A-string, and then an interpolated passage on artificial harmonics on the G-string (the lowest string is thus employed to produce the highest, most ethereal and extra-territorial phrase).

Two decades before the solo sonata, Bartók's two mature sonatas for violin and piano, written in 1921 and 1922, demonstrate a similar dialectic between modernism's exploration of musical technics and an attempt to break through to the naked fragility of an unadorned voice. In the first movement of the Sonata for Violin and Piano No. 1, the trajectory of the sonata discourse becomes increasingly conflicted and violent until, in an unprepared gesture, the linearity of the music is abruptly suspended by the curiously static monotone of the violin (Fig. 10, sostenuto molto), a meditation on the open D-string that produces, after all the urgent and complex activity of the preceding music, a moment of self-reflection. Where before the violin was engaged in an altercation with the piano, driving forwards at every turn, it now pauses, holding up the action by simple pivoting on the axis of its open D-string, a sense enhanced by the widely spaced spread octaves in the piano (five bars after Fig. 10).

This suspension of linear and discursive action now acts as a threshold to a quite different sound world. The piano moves in euphonious parallel thirds, a familiar triadic harmony, but as if through a distorting lens. It makes for a very extended structural hiatus, a sustained arrest of the opening energy of the movement that, in turn, becomes the threshold for a new sense of melody introduced at Figure 13 (meno lento, ma sempre molto tranquillo) – withdrawn, distant, muted but utterly intense. Although it will in turn be interrupted by the furious energy of the initial material, this tranquillo melody will later return (Fig. 20) in the furthest reaches of the violin's upper register, like a fantastical bird soaring high above the piano.

The real 'opposition' of this sonata form movement is thus the interaction between two different kinds of musical discourse, one marked in terms of the discursive techniques and technologies of modernity and the other in terms of the recovery of a more direct and embodied melodic voice, a duality immediately underlined by the start of the second movement (Adagio) which opens with the solo violin, unaccompanied, in a searching and rather fragile melodic line.

The particularity of tone, rhythm, gesture and intonation in Bartók's music is hardly separable from his exploration of the same qualities in his own pioneering ethnomusicological work. The origins of the latter appear to be located in a moment of concrete specificity worthy of Proust. While on holiday in Gerlicepuszta in Northern Hungary in the summer of 1904, the twenty-three-year-old Bartók was forcibly struck by the singing of a young serving girl, Lidi Dósa. His folk song collecting odyssey, consisting of countless trips made between 1906 and 1918, had its beginnings in this event.[11] It is important to remember that, from 1907, Bartók was a

---

[11] See Stephen Erdely, 'Bartok and Folk Music' in Amanda Bayley (ed.), *The Cambridge Companion to Bartók* (Cambridge University Press, 2001), pp. 24–44, p. 27.

full-time professor of piano at the Academy of Music in Budapest. His folk song collecting trips were thus made almost entirely in the vacations, usually Christmas and Easter. The difference between the context and aesthetic values of the piano repertoire he taught in Budapest and that of the music he recorded in the far-flung provinces must have struck Bartók on multiple levels – from the material conditions of peasant life in winter and the strangeness of accent and manner to the approach to an entirely oral musical tradition whose function and value were woven into material life.

Bartók's collecting trips were aided by phonograph recordings which he insisted were necessary for capturing those elements of particularity which resist notation. 'Folk singing is full of characteristic peculiarities deserving of precise annotation, such as, for example, the vocal *portamento*, irregular rhythm, and so forth, none of which can be recorded with the aid of conventional musical signs', to say nothing of the variants of any tune that is the essence of true folk music.[12] This latter quality, Bartók insisted, was 'one of the most characteristic, integral peculiarities of folk melodies', to the extent that 'a folk melody is like a living creature: it changes minute by minute, moment by moment'.[13] The phonograph was thus, for Bartók, a way of capturing the absolute particularity of a musical encounter, at this time and in this place, sung by this particular peasant in this unrepeatable manner. Moreover, to understand such particularity, the folklorist would ideally have an understanding of all the contexts in which it takes place – an understanding of language, customs, history, dance as well as music. As Erdeley comments, 'by the 1930s, his sophisticated notation turned his transcriptions into musical portraits of the singer or instrumentalist. No note, however slight, no vocal slide, pitch inflection, rhythmic nuance, tempo or articulative detail escaped his attention.'[14] Bartók was acutely aware of the gap between the intensely concrete particularity of his musical encounters in the field and the neat boundaries of the notated page. No matter how experienced the collector, or how precise the notation, he recognized that much of what defined the character of the music he heard simply resisted the framework of notation. It is a telling irony that, years later, having notated quarter-tone and third-tone tunings in the final movement for the Sonata for Solo Violin, he was persuaded by Yehudi Menuhin, who had commissioned the work, that he should take these out and restrict himself to the usual semitone divisions.

[12] See Bela Bartók, 'Hungarian Folk Music' (1929) in *Essays*, ed. Benjamin Suchoff (London: Faber, 1993), p. 4.
[13] Bartók, 'Why and How Do We Collect Folk Music' (1936), in *Essays*, p. 10.
[14] Erdely, 'Bartók and Folk Music', p. 32.

Berio: *Voci* (1984)

The link between Ligeti and Bartók, and between both composers and the folk musical heritage of their native regions, is of a special kind. But it would be a mistake to separate and thus marginalize the material economies of their musical languages from the rest of musical modernism. In using them as examples of a powerful current that connects early and late modernism by means of the idea of particularity and materiality, I do not want to re-inscribe the rhetoric of marginalization by which this music has often been bracketed off from some notional mainstream. To that end, my third example of a composer foregrounding the particularity of a solo string instrument, in relation to material redolent of a specific time and place, is Luciano Berio.

Berio's *Voci* was composed in 1984 for solo viola and two groups of instrumentalists. Like Ligeti's solo sonata, Berio's piece originated in relation to a particular player – the violist Aldo Bennici. Like Bartók's music, Berio's here draws on a close relationship to folk song – in this case, to songs from Bennici's native Sicily. And just as Bartók insisted on treating such songs in terms of their acoustic materiality (by means of phonograph recordings) so Berio's starting point was a set of field recordings made in the 1960s, held by the Ethnomusicological Archives of the Accademia Nazionale di Santa Cecilia in Rome.[15] The voices heard on these are raw, untutored and very distant from the quasi-scientific, hyper-precision of the world of contemporary music. In a kind of companion work, *Naturale* (1985) for solo viola and a single percussionist, Berio makes use of the recordings directly, so the interaction between instrument and voice is more explicit. *Voci* does not employ this level of literalness, but instead foregrounds the capacity of the viola to evoke the specific qualities of the vocal material it references. Because Berio's starting point was recorded sound, not notated transcriptions, those qualities are almost entirely to do with tone, texture, ornament and gesture.

Specific folk songs are named in the score as they appear, delivered by the viola in such a way as to stand out from the rest of the piece. The centrality of this source is also underlined by the work's subtitle, *Folk Songs II*, making a deliberate reference back twenty years to Berio's *Folk Songs* of 1964. But where the earlier piece comprises songs drawn from several countries and foregrounds a singer (originally, Cathy Berberian), the later piece draws its materials from a single

---

[15] Examples of the field recordings can be heard on the CD recording of *Voci* and *Naturale* recorded by ECM in 1999 and 2000: Kim Kashkashian (viola), Robyn Schulkowsky (percussion), Luciano Berio (conductor), Vienna Radio Symphony Orchestra.

place and foregrounds a violist in place of a singer.[16] The work's title, *Voci*, resonates in a variety of fascinating ways: the viola is clearly not an actual singing voice, but mediates between the instrumental and the vocal, and thus between the historical tradition of classical instrumental music and the specificity of voice and place implied by the Sicilian folk songs, upon which it draws. The forty-nine instrumentalists of the two ensembles start with very little sense of voice – merely providing various acoustic backdrops for the soloist – yet by the end, they seem to join in with the singing.

This is marked in several ways by the viola as it foregrounds the corporeal qualities of tone over any abstract compositional ideas derived from melodic motifs, made clear in a series of passages in which the soloist dwells on a single pitch, re-voicing the note by alternating strings and using harmonics and different bow positions. In the opening pages, for example, the soloist dwells on a high F#, moving across all four strings as well as harmonics to constantly vary the tone of the same pitch. This is a preamble to the introduction of the first folk melody, 'A la Sciacchitana', where the high F# becomes the first note of the viola's melody.[17]

The oscillations in pitch, the portamenti, the quarter-tone tunings, the ornaments and phrase shapes, all draw upon, without exactly imitating, aspects of the raw voices heard in the field recordings. Like those repeated F#s, what matters here is the particularity of the presence affirmed by the viola's 'voice', rather than an idea of compositional material understood in abstract categories such as interval. Put another way – the particularity of the voice *is* the compositional material here.

This foregrounding of the solo viola is typical of Berio's piece, for much of which the ensemble is given little space to expand; in fact, only twice does the ensemble play without the soloist. But as *Voci* unfolds, there is a far greater degree of engagement, interaction and dialogue between the solo voice and those of the ensembles. The final section dwells on the way in which the other instruments take up fragments of the folk melodies outlined by the viola, as if 'learned' from the soloist. The polyphonic richness of the final section is thus quite different from the relative isolation of elements at the start of the work. Combined with the vestige of a functional bass line, and echoes of quasi-tonal harmonies in a rather Ivesian heterophony, there is a sense here in which the particularity of

---

[16] *Coro* (1976), by contrast, is a multilingual patchwork of twenty-nine folk songs from around the world, a musical heteroglossia comparable to Stockhausen's *Hymnen*.

[17] The parallel with Bartók's Sonata for Violin and Piano, No. 1 (discussed above) is striking. In the first movement of Bartók's work, the elaboration of tone colour on a single pitch is similarly the prelude to a new sense of melodic directness.

the solo viola line is multiplied rather than lost when taken up by the whole, producing a cumulative meeting place of collective melodiousness.

In his liner notes for the ECM recording, Jürg Stenzl invokes Levi Strauss's opposition of 'the raw and the cooked' as a way of thinking about Berio's play with folk and art music traditions. But *Voci* replicates neither the binarism of those categories nor the one-way temporal sequence they imply (with the raw inevitably becoming cooked; never the opposite). Taken as a whole, *Voci* presents a series of constantly shifting exchanges: between the soloist and the ensemble, between signifiers of 'folk' and those of the art music tradition, between tonal reference points and atonality, between foregrounded solo instruments and backgrounded soundscapes, between the order of equal temperament and the transgressions of its detuning. But the music presents none of these as binaries; rather, it constantly moves between them, with the solo viola 'teaching' particularity to the ensemble, and ending the piece with an inconclusive oscillation between the raw and the cooked, re-voicing the single pitch 'A', the viola's highest open string, against the mechanical ticking of percussion – a kind of mirror image of Ligeti's fascination with the instrument's lowest string.

In this way, *Voci* neither imports the concrete materiality of its Sicilian folk voices into an art-music frame nor subjects the voice to the kind of radical decomposition that Berio explored in the 1960s, in works like *Visage* (1961) and *Sequenza III* for female voice (1966). Steven Connor suggests that *Visage*, in common with Stockhausen's *Gesang der Jünglinge* (1956), deploys its electronic resources to stage a breaking up of the human voice, fragmenting the singing voice into merely articulative and gestural noises which 'appears to neutralize the voice, making it a merely disposable resource to be articulated with the range of electronic sounds that Berio generated for the piece'.[18] Heard one way, this is undoubtedly true, but listen again. The microphone makes possible the aural equivalent of the photorealism that was developed in painting at exactly the same time – a means of amplifying the materiality of the sonic, exaggerating the particularity of tone and texture and highlighting every nuance of oral articulation – exactly what Connor describes elsewhere, in relation to genres of pop music performance, as the tactility of the voice in 'close, wet and "dirty" proximity' to the microphone.[19] At the heart of *Visage* is the absolute particularity of Cathy Berberian's voice and an assertion of the

---

[18] Steven Connor, 'The Decomposing Voice of Postmodern Music', *New Literary History*, 32/3 (2001), 467–83, p. 477.

[19] Steven Connor, 'Edison's Teeth: Touching Hearing' in Veit Erlmann (ed.), *Hearing Cultures: Essays on Sound, Listening and Modernity* (Oxford: Berg, 2004), pp. 153–72, p. 165.

primacy of the corporeal and sonic aspects of vocal utterance over the abstract semantics of language. This is also exactly what the viola takes up from the songs and calls of Sicilian fisherman in *Voci*.

Modernism and modernity

It would not be difficult to multiply the examples I have considered: the particularity of the Jewish-Bohemian voice in some of the scherzi of Mahler's symphonies; the inflections of tone and cadence of the Moravian language in the operas of Janáček; the unique *Klang* of orchestral sonorities in Sibelius; the specific vocabulary of bodily deportment in de Falla or Albéniz; the rude bricolage of Cage's prepared piano, displacing the anonymity of the piano's pure tone through a kind of aural graffiti; the irreducibly material and particular recorded sounds of Schaeffer's *musique concrète*; the exploration of the corporeality of the voice, grounded in the individual performer, from Berio to Saariaho. The relays between the later and earlier parts of the twentieth century suggest a continuity of concern rather than a narrative of rejection and overstepping, a transformation of recurrent tensions rather than any trajectory of development. It has become a truism that the history of twentieth-century music looks utterly different depending on where you stand to tell the story. And it has been broadly acknowledged for a while that the version that begins in Vienna with the Schoenberg school and runs, as if inevitably, to the serialism of the Darmstadt school and beyond is no longer adequate as a way of understanding the multiple strands that make up the fabric of twentieth-century music history. But we have been remarkably slow to elaborate alternative models and tell different stories. A history of the twentieth century that began with Debussy, that took sound as its starting point rather than the abstract idea of interval, would make for a quite different map – to say nothing of giving priority to questions of geography.

So how should we hear, within this historiographical voice-leading, the line that breaks the surface with Bartók and reappears in the later music of Ligeti? As a kind of inner part? One scored for the viola, perhaps? A voice that merely thickens the texture and adds colour? Of course not; and yet, even though Bartók's music is far from inaudible in the concert hall nor neglected in historical accounts of the twentieth century, it remains *conceptually* marginalized within modernism. We do not know how to think of it, how to place it in our stories of music. Let me be absolutely clear: my point is not to champion the cause of Bartók; Janáček and several others would suit my purposes just as well. I cite Bartók here merely as an example in order to elaborate the idea that the failure to hear certain aspects of twentieth-century music produces a misunderstanding of the broader movement of modernism; or, to put it the other way round, our theoretical misconceptions make us deaf to key aspects of the music.

Let's take a step back. One of the most startling moments in Theodor W. Adorno's *Philosophie der Neuen Musik* (1949) is hidden away in a footnote. It has subsequently become a well-known, if not notorious, point in the text. It occurs as Adorno sets out his theory of the 'inherent tendency of musical material', that is to the say, the necessity and inevitability of its historical progress and decay. Music that uses 'obsolete forms' of material is, by Adorno's logic, historically false, since the material itself has lost the historical meaning or 'weight' it once possessed. This historical process, he says, 'is irreversible.'[20] At which key point, Adorno betrays a moment of self-doubt by inserting a lengthy footnote. I quote it in full from the translation by Robert Hullot-Kentor:

> Where the developmental tendency of occidental music was not fully carried through, as in many agrarian regions of southern Europe, it has been possible right up to the present to use tonal material without opprobrium. Mention may be made here of the extraterritorial, yet in its rigor magisterial, art of Leoš Janáček, as well as much of Bartók's, who in spite of his folkloristic penchant at the same time counted among the most progressive composers in European art music. The legitimation of such music from the periphery in every case depends on it having developed a coherent and selective technical canon. In contrast to the productions of Nazi blood-and-soil ideology, truly extraterritorial music – whose material, while common in itself, is organized in a totally different way from occidental music – has a power of alienation that associates it with the avant-garde and not with nationalistic reaction. Ideological blood-and-soil music, by contrast, is always affirmative and allied with the tradition, whereas it is precisely the tradition of all official music that is suspended by Janáček's diction, modelled on his language, even in the midst of all the triads.[21]

Having discarded Sibelius a page or so earlier for not being sufficiently progressive, Adorno thus manages to 'save' Janáček and Bartók by means of an escape clause worthy of a legal document. In the process, however, he merely reinforces the Hegelian ideology of historical progress that runs through the *Philosophie der Neuen Musik* like a cantus firmus. As Leon Botstein has subsequently suggested, Bartók 'challenged the dominant ideological premises of music history in ways that were

---

[20] Theodor W. Adorno, *Philosophy of New Music*, trans. and ed. Robert Hullot-Kentor (Minneapolis, MN: University of Minnesota Press, 2006), p. 35.
[21] Adorno, *Philosophy of New Music*, p. 176.

prescient',[22] precisely by diverting this Hegelian trajectory of history-as-progress; in the face of a flight into increasing abstraction, Bartók's modernism insists stubbornly on the materiality of time, place and person, so forcefully experienced on his collecting trips. It is not that he literally brings into the concert hall the mud of the fields or the smoke of peasant cooking fires, but that his music is rooted in a parallel kind of tactile particularity, embodied in that of the tone, accent and the bodily gestures of musical sound.

One shocking aspect of the direction that modernist music took in the 1980s and 1990s (for some, an embarrassing *volte face*) was its renewed focus on such particularity in the face of a dominant aesthetic of abstraction that had dominated new music for nearly three decades. Ligeti's reference to a slow peasant dance from a northern province of Romania is less the issue here than the quality of rude presence that the viola player creates, circling around the same set of notes on a single string, the accent of its voice defined by its refusal of standard intonation (the musical equivalent, perhaps, of what the English call 'received pronunciation' in speech). In the same way, Berio's use of Sicilian folk song is, and is not, rooted in Sicily. *Naturale* (the version with a recorded folk singer) arguably is tied to the specific location; but *Voci*, in which the viola mediates between human voice and instrument, has to do with particularity itself, whether or not its Sicilian origin is identified. In such pieces, late twentieth-century modernism revisits and recovers a key concern of early modernism. It is not the specific materials (the chaconne or *hora lungă*) that join Bartók to Ligeti, but a shared concern with the particularity of voice, just as the tendency of heterogeneous character to overspill structure connects Berio's music to that of Gustav Mahler.

So what happens if we take Adorno's *Philosophie der Neuen Musik*, itself a key statement of the historical assumptions that underpin the mid-century avant-garde, and invert it around this point? What happens if we take hold of it by this footnote and turn the entire thing inside out (like pulling out the lining of a pocket and turning the whole jacket inside out around it)? A strange thing begins to happen if we do. What looked like a mere thread or an insignificant patch on the fabric of the larger argument begins to give. As you start to pull at it, the structure to which it is appended begins to unravel; you hardly need to pull at all, for more and

---

[22] Leon Botstein, 'Out of Hungary: Bartók, Modernism, and the Cultural Politics of Twentieth-Century Music' in Peter Laki (ed.), *Bartók and His World* (Princeton University Press, 1995), pp. 3–63.

more material to emerge (like the magician who starts to pull a handkerchief from his sleeve only for it to go on and on, in all the colours of the rainbow). In the end, you have the same whole but turned inside out. But this is no symmetrical inversion, no precise geometrical retrograde; the same material takes on a quite different aspect. My serious point here is that listening for different things is enabled by conceiving of music in different ways and – crucially – vice versa. If the discursive musicological frameworks (of history, analysis, aesthetics, politics, geography) can make us deaf to certain aspects of music, reconfiguring them can equally allow new sounds to emerge from the same music. That is exactly what I think is suggested by the kind of music we have been discussing.

It is not coincidental that Bartók pursued his ethnographical research into folk music, returning with sound recordings of individual musicians made in specific places at specific times, just as Schoenberg, separating intervallic relations from sound as such, moved irreversibly towards the logic of abstraction. Nor is it coincidental that the intellectual purity of Webern's serial masterpieces of the 1920s are contemporary with Janáček's radically concrete and empirical operas and instrumental music. Nor, that while Ligeti embarked on fieldwork on Romanian folk music in 1948, Boulez was composing the Second Piano Sonata. There are two divergent aspects of modernism at stake here – one radically abstract, the other radically particular. In the middle of the century, as these two facets of modernism bifurcated apparently beyond return, and in the same year that Adorno published his *Philosophie der Neuen Musik*, Harry Partch summed it all up in the simple opposition between a 'Corporeal' and an 'Abstract' music, the opposition that defines his book *Genesis of a Music*. Though this was published in 1949, it is a neat historical coincidence that he had been working on it since 1923, the very year in which Schoenberg first formulated the serial method.

The examples I have given here are no more than threads, unaccompanied lines on a solo viola. But tugging gently on them might result in a similar unravelling of the frameworks which have regulated our thinking about musical modernism. One might have pulled at many others – the viola d'amore in Janáček's *Kát'a Kabanová* and in his second string quartet, '*Intimate Letters*'; or the fragile but enduring presence of the viola in Morton Feldman's *The Viola in My Life* (1970), stubbornly persistent like a character from Samuel Beckett, and echoing across the space of *Rothko Chapel* (1971), a piece the viola ends with a passage of melody unique in Feldman's work, described by Alex Ross as 'a keening, minor-key, modal song, redolent of the synagogue'.[23] Or, from a quite different tradition, we might hear the solo viola in Gérard Grisey's *Espaces Acoustiques* (1974–85) as a single thread that gradually leads the ear to the elaborated spectral richness of the larger work, massively expanded as the piece progresses, but already opened up by the astonishing Prologue in which the viola moves from short melodic fragments to huge waves of sound. Like the echoing arpeggiations that conclude Boulez's *Répons* (1984), Grisey's music makes resonant the entire *corps sonore* of his musical material – both that of the instruments themselves and the 'bodies' that set them in motion. But in this, both Boulez and Grisey elaborate what can already be heard in the piano music of Debussy and Ravel – witness the manner in which, for example, Ravel sets in resonant motion the entire body of the piano in a work like 'Une barque sur l'océan' (*Miroirs*, 1905).

Such exchanges between early and late musical modernism suggest that we might reconsider the frameworks in which we have understood the idea. Theory has failed to keep step with musical practice, in part because music's recovery of its own particularity, always present though strangely repressed in the mid-century, has often been achieved only by ignoring dominant theoretical frameworks. Put another way, the radical particularity of early modernism, so vital to its oppositional and critical force, returns to later modernism having often been largely lost amid the dominance of radical abstraction in the mid-century. What had looked, by the 1970s, like a kind of historical end point, a fizzling out of the force of the modernist avant-garde in a cul-de-sac of abstraction, now looks, from the standpoint of the twenty-first century, more like a kind of righting of the balance, a reassertion of those elements that post-1945 had been all but repressed.

We are only just beginning to redraw this historical map and to realize that modernism, in all its forms, looks and sounds quite different when approached from the wider perspective of modernity as a whole. From that longer view, it is remarkable to what extent our conceptual frameworks for thinking about modernism have been shaped by the thinking of the nineteenth century, especially the ideology of progressive rationalization articulated most powerfully by Beethoven's contemporary Hegel. It is telling, therefore, to discover a thread, running through the work of twentieth-century composers, in the form of a fascination with another contemporary of Hegel and Beethoven, the poet Friedrich Hölderlin.

---

[23] Ross points out that Feldman had written this melody decades earlier, as a student, during World War II. We might therefore see this as a backward glance of memory that parallels Ligeti's evocation of Bartók. See Alex Ross, 'American Sublime', *The New Yorker* (19 June 2006).

Settings of his poetry appear in the works of composers as diverse as Richard Strauss, Max Reger, Paul Hindemith, Viktor Ullmann, Hanns Eisler, René Leibowitz, Benjamin Britten, Wilhelm Killmayer, Stefan Wolpe, Dmitri Smirnov, Friedrich Cerha, Wolfgang Rihm, György Kurtág and Kaija Saariaho. Ligeti made a setting of Hölderlin's late poem 'Der Sommer' in 1989, a setting whose calm melodic lines and triadic reminiscences perfectly match the distancing effect of the poem's own deliberate linguistic simplicity. Hölderlin's poem, and Ligeti's song setting, emphasize a quiet refusal of the historicity of Hegel and Beethoven. Time pauses here and is allowed to expand without purpose. As the last line has it, 'the year appears majestically to linger'.

Friedrich Hölderlin, 'Der Sommer'

Noch ist die Zeit des Jahrs zu sehn, und die Gefilde
Des Sommers stehn in ihrem Glanz, in ihrer Milde;
Die Feldes Grün ist prächtig ausgebreitet
Allwo der Bach hinab mit Wellen gleitet.

So zieht der Tag hinaus durch Berg und Tale,
Mit seiner Unaufhaltsamkeit und seinem Strahle,
Und Wolken ziehn in Ruh, in hohen Räumen,
Es scheint das Jahr mit Herrlichkeit zu säumen.

[There is yet time in the year, and the fields/ Of summer stand in their glory, in their softness;/ The green of the plain is sumptuously spread out,/ The tranquil stream ripples through./ And so the day stretches out through hill and valley,/ In its radiance, unceasingly,/ And clouds move in peace through lofty skies,/ The year appears majestically to linger.]

The recovery, in the music of the later twentieth century, of the repressed particularity of an earlier modernism was often condemned at the time as a kind of caving in or selling out of high modernist principles, a retrogressive and regressive return to the comfort of older styles. Such things may sometimes have happened. But Ligeti's setting of 'Der Sommer', or the Sonata for Solo Viola, might be better understood in the way that we understand a composer's 'late style' – here, not just Ligeti's, but the 'late style' of late modernism. In conversation with the English viola player Paul Silverthorne, about Ligeti's Solo Sonata, he remarked to me that, aside from posing all the technical difficulties of Bach's solo string music ('but times-ten!'), the experience of playing the Sonata was akin to that of performing late Beethoven.[24] It is a resonant remark and makes an insightful link between the sense of recovered melodic simplicity in Ligeti and that

---

[24] Private conversation with the author, October 2011.

in the late quartets and piano sonatas of Beethoven where, as Joseph Kerman has explored at length, instrumental music tries to recover an earlier immediacy of vocal expression.[25] It is from just such a longer view that we might begin to perceive the reconfiguring of musical modernism. The transformation of modernism in recent decades is also, retrospectively, a transformation of early modernism. The constitutive tension between the material particularity of music and the abstract schemes of its organization does not disappear, but it has metamorphosed significantly over the last century in ways that we may only now be beginning to understand.

---

[25] Joseph Kerman, *The Beethoven Quartets* (New York: W. W. Norton, 1979).

3 Expressionism revisited

Modernism beyond the twentieth century

Arnold Whittall

Terminologies

If it moves between the general and the particular, writing about music involves a struggle between trying to do justice to the specifics of an individual composition and trying to say something useful about that composition's context within musical history. The various 'isms' that serve to frame such narratives are necessarily open-ended and imprecise, introducing possibilities rather than certainties: so it is unsurprising that combining these concepts into notions like 'expressionistic modernism' risks achieving even greater distance from clarity and coherence than is the case when using either term on its own. Nevertheless, it might not be too challenging to consensus to suggest that expressionism is better understood as a specific subcategory of modernism: expressionism is a particular manifestation of the modernist aesthetic, not the other way round.

The most useful dictionary definitions of musical expressionism, while emphasizing its early twentieth-century associations with trends in painting and literature, soon open out with reference to 'an extravagant and apparently chaotic surface' which 'conveys turbulence in the composer's psyche',[1] or to 'the ruthless expression of disturbing or distasteful emotions, often with a stylistic violence that may involve pushing ideas to their extremes or treating the subject matter with incisive parody'.[2] Modernism is usually defined more broadly – less directly linked to particular places during the years around 1908–14, but suggesting basic affinities with expressionism stemming from 'the fundamental conviction among successive generations of composers since 1900 that the means of musical expression in the twentieth century must be adequate to the unique and radical character of the age'.[3] Modernism has survived for so

---

[1] David Fanning, 'Expressionism' in Stanley Sadie and John Tyrrell (eds.), *The New Grove*, 2nd edn, 29 vols. (London: Macmillan, 2001), vol. IIX, p. 472.

[2] Paul Griffiths, 'Expressionism' in Alison Latham (ed.), *Oxford Companion to Music* (Oxford University Press, 2002), p. 437.

[3] Leon Botstein, 'Modernism' in Stanley Sadie and John Tyrrell (eds.), *The New Grove*, 2nd edn, 29 vols. (London: Macmillan, 2001) vol. XVI, p. 868.

long because its evolving identity reflects its capacity to interact with a succession of different aesthetic tendencies: not only expressionism (which might have been thought rather avant-garde when it first exploded onto the musical scene) but – for example – neoclassicism, experimentalism, new complexity and spectralism. Nor does the presence of one of these tendencies preclude that of others: modernism is not just persistent but multifarious, and it even endures alongside features – minimalism for example – which are commonly regarded as post- or anti-modernist.

1900–2000

The aim of this chapter's narrative is to explore how technical features usually associated with expressionism have adapted to a range of aesthetic and formal contexts, not all of which are explicitly or entirely expressionistic in character; the narrative will involve some initial consideration of generalities, followed by short studies of five British composers active since 2000.

Music historians tend to agree that something unprecedentedly as well as incontrovertibly modernistic came about around the year 1909, when composers under the age of forty, like Schoenberg and Webern in Vienna and Charles Ives in New England, fractured the harmonic and formal moulds that had thus far offered ultimate stability. As the bonds of classical unity were loosened, it became possible to see early signs of modernism in many compositions written between 1820 and 1900. Yet around 1909 the leap beyond what Wagner, Liszt and Mahler were seen, technically, as standing for, brought with it the possibility of something fundamentally different: consistently dissonant rather than ultimately consonant, more atonal than tonal, more centrifugal than centripetal in design. So intensively and so darkly expressive did this new music appear – so disruptive, so expressionistic – that 'modernist' as a response to rather than rejection of classicism could seem (if only in retrospect) an inadequate label for it. Perhaps 'avant-garde' better suited its determinedly radical and anti-traditional manner?

These issues, these terminologies, have been debated at great length by a multitude of scholars. Developments in musical composition between 1900 and 1945 suggested that retaining aspects of classical thinking, especially in respect of formal design and thematic process, was relevant well beyond the relatively explicit echoes and pastiches associated with neoclassicism – itself often characterized by modernist destabilizations: for instance, Schoenberg's initiative in introducing the twelve-tone method in the 1920s brought with it a new kind of tension between expressionism and neoclassicism, and between atonality and tonality, an expressionistic quality persisting within a manner of compositional thinking that was pluralistically modernist rather than singularly avant-garde.

Even in his final years Schoenberg was capable of moving towards a fully realized modernism in one work (the Piano Concerto of 1942, with its suggestions of suspended tonality), and then back towards something potentially avant-garde and atonal a few years later (the String Trio of 1946); and the input from expressionism in each is correspondingly differentiated. The new initiatives in composition promoted in the aftermath of World War II added further levels of complication. While the likes of Dmitri Shostakovich and Benjamin Britten flourished between 1945 and 1975 despite degrees of anti-modernism (and also despite their occasional use of melodic twelve-tone constructions within tonal designs), the signal divergence from mutual regard of Pierre Boulez and John Cage (when seen in retrospect) offered an exemplary instance of the renewed opposition between the modernist and the avant-garde. Cage's radicalism was eventually reconfigured terminologically as 'experimental' and was notable for accepting the possibility of Satie-esque simplicity while also often displaying an extreme remoteness from traditional concepts of the musical work.[4] After 1970, the experimental freed itself from many (if not all) aspects of mainstream modernism, while at the same time a new phase of the hyper-expressionistic avant-garde emerged in the so-called 'new complexity'. The old post-tonal complexity might have been best exemplified in the concentrated density of Schoenberg's pre-twelve-tone compositions but – ironically, perhaps – new complexity seemed most palpable when musical genres with long histories (the string quartet, opera) became repositories for music of unprecedented difficulty and elaboration. Only in an age when absolutely precise realization of the most intricate shadings of pitch and rhythm might be achieved electronically could the full challenge of 'acoustic' complexity be realized.[5]

After 2000: five British case studies

Since 2000, the complex music of composers like Brian Ferneyhough (b. 1943) and Michael Finnissy (b. 1946) has shown some features that move in the direction of a more mainstream ethos, thereby coming closer

---

[4] See Michael Nyman, *Experimental Music: Cage and Beyond*, 2nd edn (Cambridge University Press, 1999). James Saunders (ed.), *The Ashgate Research Companion to Experimental Music* (Farnham: Ashgate, 2009).

[5] See Richard Toop, 'Against a Theory of Musical (New) Complexity' in Max Paddison and Irène Deliège (eds.), *Contemporary Music: Theoretical and Philosophical Perspectives* (Farnham: Ashgate, 2010), pp. 89–97.

to the kind of modernism found in Boulez for much of his long career, and in embodying a more insistent degree of expressionism than either Boulez or Carter, such compositions reinforce the continuing vitality and adaptability of roots in music – by Bartók and Webern as well as Schoenberg – written more than a century ago.

The importance of modernism to the music of composers who emerged before 2000 and have remained prominent since is clear, as seen in the other chapters of this book. If a steady-state of 'anything goes' has become the defining characteristic of serious composition since the emergence of minimalism and of attempts to speak of 'post-modernism' after 1970, the persistence of 'high' or 'late' modernism within that musical *bouillabaisse* is no less evident. The popular success of minimalism pure or applied – of Reich, Glass, Pärt and Tavener – is easily associated with a rejection of expressionism as something mimetic of the twentieth century's darkest and most disruptive ethos. The anti-expressionist ideal seems to be that even serious art should aspire to forms of instant gratification similar to those provided by pop music and the new technologies; but when the music of less-than-wholehearted minimalists like John Adams indicates elements of affinity with modernism, the possibility emerges of a mainstream that explores new kinds of interaction between tonal and post-tonal materials.[6] In such an aesthetic environment it might be thought that expressionism is more likely to survive or be revived from a perspective more avant-garde than modernist. The reality, however, is less clear-cut – even when approached, as in what follows, through the relatively narrow frame of a quintet of British-born composers, all of whom have made important contributions to music since the year 2000.

Still moving: Richard Emsley

Between about 1990 and 1996 Richard Emsley (b. 1951) experienced a state of 'creative paralysis' brought about, he concluded, by an 'over-complexity of design' of the kind that had characterized his earlier music. Returning to composition in 1996, Emsley decided that 'automated processes of generation' should be involved, 'pre-programmed to maximize the accidental arising of certain kinds of result (those affording a depth of structure)'. The outcome was an extended cycle for solo piano, consisting so far of fifteen movements written between 1997 and 2005: *for piano 1, for piano 2* etc. Using 'massive amounts of material ... generated and auditioned quickly

---

[6] See Keith Potter, Kyle Gann and Pwyll ap Siôn (eds.), *The Ashgate Research Companion to Minimalist and Postminimalist Music* (Farnham: Ashgate, 2013).

with a computer, passages which "caught the ear" were isolated and used as a movement, or possibly distorted to create further movements'. An element of the didactic emerges here in Emsley's liking for material distanced to a degree – by automation – from the composer. He has also written of his desire to reactivate 'sensual channels atrophied by familiarity and complacency by means of the shock of the strange. Strangeness as a retort to positivist accounts of experience. Strangeness, perhaps, as nostalgia in the face of the dis-Enchantment of the world', and with the aim of 'jolting the listener into momentary glimpses of the possible contingency of the human mode of experiencing the world'.[7]

'Strangeness' and 'contingency' are modernist rather than classical qualities, and their presence can be traced in *for piano 15* (2005). Lasting some forty minutes and written throughout on a single treble stave, the piece's 773 bars at crotchet 60 in 4/4 time and an unvaried *mezzo piano* compromise twenty-four versions of a 69-note gamut. The twenty-four units are separated by pauses (the pedal is depressed throughout) varying from seven to nineteen crotchet beats – and all begin with the same high E, with only the final statement presenting the first four notes of the gamut simultaneously. Given that the twenty-four statements are not identical in every respect and also that the variants resist reductive systematizations, a feeling of circling that is enigmatically free yet focused is one predominant result. An organizing response might quite soon sense that the first statement (Example 3.1), its durational values limited to quavers, crotchets, dotted crotchets, minims and combinations summing to a maximum of nine quavers, is preliminary – a launch-pad for the much more diverse rhythmic patterns that ensue. No pattern of intervals and rhythms emerges that might be understood as 'thematic', and no phrasing – a single slur extends across all eighteen bars of the initial unit. It is therefore counterproductive to attempt an interpretation in which certain units or groups of units favour certain aspects of musical identity, leaving others to be dealt with elsewhere, and the increase in the number of smaller-size grace notes in units 21 to 23 (Example 3.2 shows the beginning of unit 23) is more a visual than an audible distinction.

It seems that the sense of similarity without identity is what matters here rather than a process of evolutionary change and complementation. The listener has to receive rather than control, and the experience of form (sound in time) is much more to do with spirit than with shape. The challenge is therefore to discover sufficient depth to compensate for the absence of those linear factors that music conventionally relies on to

---

[7] Richard Emsley, programme notes (2008) and private correspondence. All subsequent citations relate to these sources.

Example 3.1 Richard Emsley, *for piano 15*, bars 1–25.

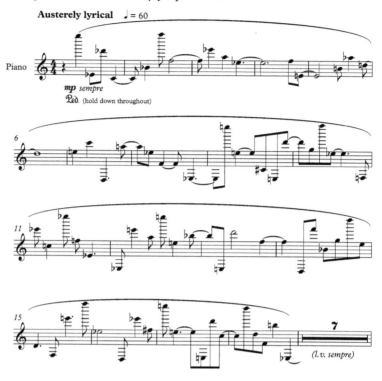

Example 3.2 Richard Emsley, *for piano 15*, bars 717–730.

involve a listener in following its passage through time. As Emsley has suggested, 'it is typically those moments in music when a seemingly paradoxical combination of temporal "opposites" occurs – persistence and change, movement and stillness – that a cancellation of single linear time is achieved'. Such an objective is bound to remain controversial in a culture whose values are predominantly secular and commercial. Most people – even 'cultured' ones – prefer to enjoy time while it lasts, rather than cultivate an unreal timelessness. As a result, what Emsley advocates as 'quiet focussing on minutiae of detail' might be easier to achieve once the listener has understood the timescale of *for piano 15* and the ethos of music balanced between the presence of gestural similarity and the absence of 'thematic' identity – what Ian Pace neatly defines as 'a unity of purpose rather than a clear direction'.[8] To cultivate the ability to alter one's mode of consciousness purely through contact with a work of art, and to experience 'non-everyday' modes of perception, as Emsley claims to be able to do when contemplating a painting by Rothko, and arguably seeks to encourage listeners to his music to emulate, is to advance into a very different world that few can currently expect to access. As with plenty of other composers who might loosely be grouped under the 'experimental' label, if you approach an Emsley composition in the same spirit as more mainstream modernist works, you may find its otherness a barrier.

Emsley's primary principle is to focus on 'depth of structure, thus suggesting that Time is manifold by nature, not merely one-dimensional and linear. This manifold nature often involves Time passing simultaneously at different rates, or "scales" of movement, the gap between these scales conceived as being possible infinitely large, the slowest "rates" thus having for us the appearance of stasis'. Bringing 'movement' and 'stasis' into conjunction comes naturally to many post-tonal or atonal composers who have moved beyond the dynamic structural hierarchies provided by the templates of the major–minor tonal system. Sometimes they will link their aesthetic preoccupations with those of practitioners of other arts to whom they feel affinity: in notes associated with another cycle of compositions called *Still/s*, begun in 2002, Emsley has referred to the cycle's connection with Jean Kay's *Six white paintings for composition* alongside his description of Samuel Beckett's work as moving towards 'whiteness, absence, stillness and silence'. Of this project, which will comprise twenty-four pieces for all the solo, duo and trio combinations of a five-instrument 'Pierrot' ensemble (flute, clarinet, violin, cello, piano), Emsley says that 'the

---

[8] Ian Pace, 'Music, Time and Timelessness', liner notes with *Richard Emsley: Flowforms*, Metier Sound and Vision CD, MSV CD92044 (2002).

materials ... have something of the bare, almost "white cell" feel of much Modernist architecture. They are extremely pared down, in an attempt to draw the listener into a quiet focussing on minutiae of detail, to "still" in the contemplative sense. This material is often presented between extended silence, as if in quotation marks – it is not there to participate in some ongoing rhetoric, but in the spirit of non-action, a concept found in many Eastern philosophical traditions'. Emsley also instances Daoism, 'one of whose many aphorisms refers to the ability of the enlightened individual to sense the innate life-span of every living thing. This is relevant to what is perhaps the cycle's most distinctive concern, to endow each sound with its own innate span ... There is also an attempt to arrive at a kind of naturalness, or "rightness", for the pulsations, which frequently coalesce in twos, oscillating with delicate randomness'. As with the *for piano* cycle, one notes the presence of modernist tropes – time as 'manifold by nature' and the 'quiet focussing on minutiae of detail', and there is even a sense of expressionism suppressed or suspended in music of such contemplative intensity, its fragile sound objects adrift in space and time.

The colour of crisis: Rebecca Saunders

The reappearance of an expressionistic modernism with roots in Webern and Schoenberg of the years around 1910 as well as in its post-1960 revival by Heinz Holliger, Helmut Lachenmann and Brian Ferneyhough is unusually strong in the music of Rebecca Saunders (b. 1967). Saunders might also be compared with James Dillon (b. 1950) or James Clarke (b. 1957), who since the 1980s have both retreated more decisively from extreme elaboration than have Ferneyhough or Finnissy. Back in 1999 Robert Adlington wrote of Saunders: 'the overriding impression is of an immediacy and directness of sound' celebrating 'the grit and noise that remind us of the presence of a fallible physical body behind the sound'; and the elemental, if not quite minimalist, quality of the 1999 work called *Cinnabar* is captured in Adlington's description of it as 'almost Rothkoesque: two distinct, grainy patinas [are] boldly juxtaposed'.[9]

Another commentator on Saunders's music – the unrelated James Saunders – has proposed a contrast between what he calls the 'confrontational collages' of her earlier works and the presence of 'more of a through-composed continuity' in the piano piece *Crimson* (2004–5).[10] This

---

[9] Robert Adlington, 'Into the Sensuous World: The Music of Rebecca Saunders', *The Musical Times*, 140/1868 (1999), 48–56.
[10] James Saunders, Liner notes with Rebecca Saunders, *Crimson*, Kairos CD 0012762KAI (2008).

Expressionism revisited

apparent seeking out of continuity nevertheless remains impeccably modernist in the way it enhances rather than eliminates the tensions between connection and disconnection, reflectiveness and rage. Rather like Dillon in his twenty-first-century music, Saunders allows for some elemental generic associations: in the chorale-like chordal homophony of *Crimson*'s final section, for example – though the chorale genre (traditionally an emblem of collective stability) is strikingly estranged when the constituent harmonies are aggressively asserted clusters (Example 3.3 shows the beginnings of each part).

Saunders also uses small-scale repetition to point out the contrast with minimalism's sustained and generally euphoric reiterations. Indeed, repetitive insistence is her music's most immediate and disturbingly expressionistic aspect. The close-position clusters which predominate in *Crimson*'s first part are subject to intensifying assaults from decorative flourishes and sudden silences. The faster second part then reinforces the role of obsessive rhythmic reiterations with a sound spectrum involving noise as much as pitch: brutal glissandi, inside the piano as well as on the keyboard, knocking on the wood of the frame, stamping on the pedals: all this displays a primitivism that seems more experimental than avant-garde and counters any tendency to move into the motivic sculpting of mainstream modernism. Part three then provides *Crimson*'s most conventionally textured and expressively restrained music. This

Example 3.3a Rebecca Saunders, *Crimson*, bars 1–6.

Example 3.3b Rebecca Saunders, *Crimson*, bars 136–145.

Example 3.3c Rebecca Saunders, *Crimson*, bars 270–279.

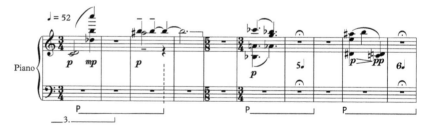

third part is much less dense, promising to be more conventionally chorale-like or sarabande-like, though the kind of textural connectedness and rhythmic regularity necessary to ground such genres proves elusive. But in comparison with what precedes it, the music of part three is wistful, even gentle in character, circling around recurrent sonorities in a spirit of Feldmanesque quiescence to set against the earlier violence.

Any associations you might expect with crimson as a warm, even comforting colour are resolutely resisted by Saunders. Rather, her notes at the front of the score offer citations from the *Oxford English Dictionary* and Joyce's *Ulysses*, which emphasize crimson's dark, potentially dangerous associations: the Joyce quotation refers to 'that awful, deep-down torrent' and 'the sea crimson sometimes like fire', and comparable states, with their textural and stylistic implications, are central to later works. In Saunders's Violin Concerto (2011) the mix of febrile agitation and anguished lamenting is given a very personal refit in what she describes as an exploration of 'two starkly contrasting states, in a fragile state of equilibrium'. One state is that of the first main section, originally called 'Rage', while the music of the second section has more of that sense of stasis fitting the title subsequently given to the concerto as a whole – *Still*. The concerto is one of several works to acknowledge Samuel Beckett's last piece of prose, *Stirrings Still*. As with *Crimson*, there is little trace of those hints of more traditional harmonic formations that lurk in some of her earlier works; she is less disposed to continue the intensely intricate kind of elaboration, relative to both pitch inflections and rhythmic values, that Ferneyhough placed at the heart of his version of the new complexity. Clusters rather than chords are also a particularly persistent feature of Saunders's *Shadow (2013). Study for piano*. With 'an acoustic shadow is to sound as a mirage is to light' as an epigraph, the composer's notes with the score include a quotation from C. G. Jung: 'everyone carries a shadow, and the less it is embodied in the individual's conscious life, the blacker and denser it is. In spite of its function as a reservoir for human darkness – or perhaps because of this – the shadow is the seat of creativity.' Another recent piece – *Solitude* for solo cello – inhabits a similarly shadowy world, its unremittingly febrile and fragmented textures further intensified by special tunings that can sound like electro-acoustic modification.

Dark corners: Simon Holt and James MacMillan

In a rare instance of a teacher commenting objectively and positively on a pupil, Anthony Gilbert has praised Simon Holt (b. 1958) for 'the *duende* quality, the dark fire, the quasi-demonic impishness that all his music has', and went on to relish its 'brilliance with dark corners'.[11] Yet Mike Seabrook avoids labelling Holt as an expressionist, perhaps in order not to risk

---

[11] Mike Seabrook, '"Dark Fire": Simon Holt and His Music', *Tempo*, 201 (1997), 21–7, p. 21. Subsequent page references in text. See also Antony Bye, 'Darkness at Noon: Anthony Bye Explores the Music of Simon Holt', *The Musical Times*, 134/1804 (1993), 313–16.

marginalizing his position on the British scene. Instead, Seabrook writes of 'the profound romanticism of his musical nature ... he is a sensualist. For all the lack of obvious melodic strains in his music, there is a distinctly sumptuous, almost sybaritic feel about his work' (23). As Seabrook does not quite say, Holt's music might be dark, but it is neither cold nor dry; Holt is described as disliking 'Lachenmann and Co., whom he finds far too arid to listen to with any pleasure' (27).

If mainstream modernism is, by definition, modernism not pushed to extremes, and even including a sense of 'profound romanticism', then it might also embrace what Ivan Hewett, with reference to *The Confessions of Isobel Gowdie* (1990), James MacMillan's early orchestral tribute to a seventeenth-century Scottish victim of cruel persecution, describes as 'modernist discoveries ... co-opted to anti-modern purposes'. As Hewett attempts to explain the apparent paradox in MacMillan's attitude to modernism, 'the idea that music need not be a unity, that it could be made of parts that proceed in ignorance of each other, was one of the great discoveries of the post-war modernists. It was anti-subjective, anti-expressive in its intention. But in MacMillan's piece the effect [of superimposing two radically different kinds of music] is full of pathos; the injustice of the verdict on Gowdie, and her piteous death, are simply '"expressed" in a new way. The means may be different, but the relation between idea and musical material is basically a nineteenth-century one'.[12]

Hewett's claim that unrelated elements in a structure that emphasizes diversity rather than unity 'proceed in ignorance of each other' in modernism after 1945 is questionable – at least as a generalization. However, his conclusion that MacMillan's 'seizing of modernist devices like clusters, discontinuity, dissonance for romantically expressive purposes is becoming a widespread, if not dominant trend in new music' (196) points to connections with mainstream late modernism along with elements of both early and high modernism. Hewett's sweepingly negative verdict on MacMillan (b. 1959) – that his music is 'pure gesture', from which all 'discourse' – that 'objective substratum which makes the music genuinely musical' is missing – might be unduly harsh. But it is still worth interrogating the claim that MacMillan's 'relation to modernism is an odd mixture of embarrassment and desire. He's embarrassed by the ideological and intellectual convictions of modernist music, but he wants the expressive *frisson* of its gestures' (197, 198).

---

[12] Ivan Hewett, *Music: Healing the Rift* (New York and London: Continuum, 2003), p. 196. Subsequent page references in text.

Example 3.4 James MacMillan, *St John Passion*, 'The Reproaches', bars 3–11 (vocal line only).

In his writings and interviews, MacMillan reveals absolutely no 'embarrassment' in the consideration of modernism's 'ideological and intellectual convictions'. This is because the convictions that matter to him are not so much aesthetic or technical as religious, and the explicit and for some distastefully primitive expressionism of *Gowdie* is fuelled by MacMillan's commitment to a view of 'the Christian narrative' as embodying 'a continual poetic tension between peace and violence'.[13] While this tension can indeed generate the kind of extreme textural and expressive contrasts that Hewett describes, those contrasts are poetic, not merely 'gestural'. MacMillan's immense creative energy is directly related to his Roman Catholic faith and to the exploration of how this fuels his involvement in the progress of present-day Scottish politics and Scottish institutions, as well as to the effort needed to ensure that Roman Catholicism, in Scotland and the wider world, resists marginalization. In consequence, MacMillan distances himself from the 'conscious decisions to avoid violence and turbulence' (25) of other composers with strong religious beliefs, like Arvo Pärt and John Tavener, in whose music there is little sense of the need for a 'Church Militant' in a rampantly secular age. In MacMillan's large-scale *St John Passion* (2007) the contemplative aspects of the drama are offset by much that is angry and aggressive, especially in the anguished solo lines of 'The Reproaches' (Example 3.4). This Jesus is not gentle, but consistently strident, even hectoring.

MacMillan has commented that music from his opera *The Sacrifice* (2005–6) 'has drifted quite naturally into the new sphere. I was also aware of the paradoxical tensions created between the two highly

---

[13] Mandy Hallam, 'Conversation with James MacMillan', *Tempo*, 62/245 (2008), pp. 17–29, p. 25. Subsequent page references in text.

contrasted musical contexts – liturgical chant and music drama. Balancing, creating opposition sometimes, and at other times elision and cross-fertilisations'.[14] With his tendency to resolve the most complex harmonies onto plain triads, MacMillan might even be thought of as an intensifier of early modernism working in the era of late modernism; yet those 'paradoxical tensions' still become especially striking when, as at the beginning of the work's purely orchestral final section, 'Sanctus immortalis, miserere nobis', he places a literal quotation from the ending of the Prelude to Wagner's *Tristan* within harmonies initially emphasizing *Tristan*'s ultimate B major triad. This leads to a citation of the Prelude's opening phrase, and chord (Example 3.5). This material is also referenced in MacMillan's *a cappella* setting of Psalm 51, *Miserere* (2009).

In the *St John Passion* such allusions (which recur) might be thought incongruous in the extreme. However, in his 2008 interview with Mandy Hallam, MacMillan praised Roger Scruton's 2004 book about *Tristan*, with its claim that '*Tristan* inspired a search for the sacred in modernism which secularists have tried to avoid talking about in the development of the arts' (22). It seems that – although Scruton has little sympathy with music that embodies aspects of post-tonal modernism – MacMillan would also agree with his claim that the voices of those 'serious artists' still concerned with the task of 'resacralizing a desacralized world', as *Tristan* did, 'have been overwhelmed by a culture of desecration'. Scruton believes that 'humanity cannot live by desecration', and that 'if we do not rediscover the sacred moment we shall lose the perspective in which our freedom resides. Our lives will become literally meaningless'.[15] The anger and intensity, as well as those moments of authentically modernist disjunction, in the *St John Passion*, suggest that MacMillan agrees. The work's wordless final message seems to be that we, who are able to mourn and to be penitent, merit compassion. But, for MacMillan the Christian, that position is meaningless without belief in an immortal power able to grant absolution. Clearly, his music is never likely to betray that conviction.

Simon Holt's concerns are quite different. As Mike Seabrook declared in 1997, and it seems to remain the case, 'one area of music is barren to him: he has no urge to write religious music at all'. If the early essence of

---

[14] James MacMillan, Liner notes with MacMillan, *St John Passion*, LSO Live CD LSO0671 (2009). For detailed commentary on MacMillan's Wagner quotations and allusions, see Dominic P. Wells, 'James MacMillan: Retrospective Modernist', unpublished PhD dissertation, University of Durham (2012); Dominic P. Wells, 'In the Footsteps of Bach: Passion Settings of David Lang and James MacMillan', *Tempo*, 67/264 (2013), 40–51.

[15] Roger Scruton, *Death-Devoted Heart: Sex and the Sacred in Wagner's Tristan und Isolde* (Oxford University Press, 2004), p. 198.

Expressionism revisited 67

Example 3.5 James MacMillan, *St John Passion*, 'Sanctus Immortalis, miserere nobis', bars 1–6, 23–28.

MacMillan is in *Gowdie*, that of Holt is in . . . *era madrugada* (1984), a work for seven instruments inspired like much of Holt's music by the poetry of Lorca, and 'eerie, rather surrealist, menacing' (23), or in *Black Lanterns*, an eight-minute piano piece originally written to mark Harrison Birtwistle's fiftieth birthday in 1984, and revised twenty years later, prior to publication and recording. Its initial, stark confrontation between ideas marked 'dolcissimo' and 'strepitoso' is mitigated by the sustained quality – with plenty of internal repetitions – of both elements, which can be thought of as

Example 3.6 Simon Holt, *Black Lanterns*, ending.

composing out background sonorities centring in different ways on the potentially stable perfect fifth, F sharp-C sharp. The eventual outcome is a conclusive move from flickering to sustained, and a final, 'distant' chorale-like phrase whose persistent F sharps are embedded in widespread counterpoints to evoke the spirit of lament (Example 3.6).

The unsettling, often surreal images – as with light having a quality of blackness – is a consistent trait of Holt's, which remains vividly functional in his 2002 setting of Emily Dickinson's 'Boots of Lead' for mezzo-soprano and a thirteen-strong instrumental ensemble. Despite its surrealistic aspects, Dickinson's poem is in essence intensely mundane, having to do with mortality and the earthiness of heavily tramping feet; it is not clear whether the speaker is reporting being buried alive or whether she is describing some strangely nightmarish out-of-body experience of falling, helplessly subject to gravity, ending up in the middle of (or buried beneath) a funeral procession, and ultimately unable to describe what, finally, she knows or understands – the poem ends with a dash, not a full stop.

There is plenty there to explain the poem's appeal to Holt, and Dickinson also provides various musical cues: a funereal tread, a beating drum, a tolling bell, the speaker reduced to being 'an Ear', as aware of

Example 3.7 Simon Holt, *Boots of Lead*, bars 1–16: offstage clarinet in A only.

silence as of sound. Holt describes his setting as 'a stately, claustrophobically slow, frozen dirge', and the implication of focusing down to an incantatory lament is clear from the beginning's stifled, Varèse-like summons from an offstage clarinet, which prolongs and decorates a simple semitonal descent before developing a much more florid profile (Example 3.7). The distinction between fundamental and ornamental elements is soon made clear, with repetitions and sustained pitches preventing the music from migrating from the mainstream into a side channel of 'complex' rhythmic, pitch-bending formulas, such as Holt's close contemporary and avant-garde connoisseur of 'dark matter', Richard Barrett, has explored.

Holt, like Rebecca Saunders, has a certain affinity with the hypnotically repetitive expressionism of James Clarke (b. 1957). He also shares Clarke's interest in American abstract painting – Clyfford Still for Clarke, Ellsworth Kelly for Holt (see the third section of the orchestral piece *Troubled Light* (2008) and *Ellsworth 2* for orchestra (2012)). Holt's gravitation towards places and things Iberian rather than Germanic means that a touch of Mediterranean warmth can be part of the stylistic mix, however subordinate or ambivalent in character. Nevertheless, an essentially wintry sensibility predominates in the violin concerto called *Witness to a Snow Miracle* (2005–6). The title refers to the gruesome martyrdom of the young Spanish Saint Eulalia, who was burned alive, only for 'a blanket of snow to fall on her ashes'. 'Ashes, ashes' is the title of a short piano piece that Holt placed with four others in a collection called *A Book of Shadows*, published in 2012 but composed between 1980 and 2005. The nature of such prevailing images – reinforced in the menace-laden sound world of the flute concerto

Morpheus Wakes (2011) – underlines Holt's willingness to remain within the dark and dangerous realm in which dreams and fantasies offer little or no hint of escape, still less of anything 'beyond'.

Sounding the spiritual: Jonathan Harvey (1939–2012)

The commitment to, and facility with, new technology in Jonathan Harvey's tape piece *Mortuous plango, vivos voco* (1980) was the result of work at IRCAM, but it marked him out as closer to Stockhausen's kind of spirituality than to Boulez's much more secular aura. By 1989, when a CD of *Bhakti* (1982) was chosen to launch the NMC record label devoted primarily to new British music, Harvey had consolidated his position within the musical establishment. Although most of his compositions in the 1980s were relatively small scale, they included the church opera *Passion and Resurrection*. Despite affinities with Benjamin Britten's concern for his music to be useful to the living, Harvey was also persuaded that elaboration – even complexity – could be potent conveyors of spiritual as well as emotional intensity. In a Foreword for a volume of writings by Brian Ferneyhough, Harvey referred to the 'spiritual crisis' that is the experience of many:

> a profound anxiety engendered by the nihilism of circularity ... Trapped in the imprisoned arguments that do not let us escape our location in history, we sense only the darkness beyond. Inevitably, anything less than a multi-faceted model is inadequate as a response. Hence complexity. Hence ambiguity, polyphony, perpetual flux. Ferneyhough's music is uniquely valuable in having the courage to hold the mirror up to that sensibility without flinching. We may not agree, as I do not, that it is the only model, but it is certainly the most widespread in the Western world today.[16]

Distancing himself in these words from the expressionistic extremism of the complex avant-garde, the alternative model which Harvey hinted at was something akin to the spectralist initiative he later defined as 'a new grammar based on nature'[17] – nature in the context of technology, that is, and his best guarantee of avoiding the risk of any 'New Age' tweeness that a concern with spirituality could so easily bring with it. Around the time of *Madonna of Winter and Spring* for orchestra and electronics (1986), Harvey wrote about 'the mirror of ambiguity' which, among many other

---

[16] Jonathan Harvey, 'Foreword' to Brian Ferneyhough, in James Boros and Richard Toop (eds.), *Collected Writings* (Amsterdam: Harwood Academic Publishers, 1995), p. xii.
[17] Julian Johnson, 'An Interview with Jonathan Harvey' in Peter O'Hagan (ed.), *Aspects of British Music of the 1990s* (Aldershot: Ashgate, 2003), pp. 119–30, p. 127.

things, sought to affirm that complexity need not be negative or intimidating but could be enriching and inspiring – especially when it became ever more likely to involve aspects of a renovated kind of post-tonal harmonic thinking from which tonal centres and even consonances were not on principle excluded.[18] During the 1990s Harvey focused even more productively on complex expressions of ritualized spirituality, with some of his most visionary instrumental works, including the Cello Concerto (1990), *Tombeau de Messiaen* and *Advaya* (both 1994). In such compositions Harvey came closest to a full realization of his personal brand of expressionistic sublimity, whose most fundamental expressive quality was forceful without menace, and (in the end) consoling without complacency.

Another decade would pass before Harvey undertook two substantial works which enshrined his radical yet unaggressive sense of his own place in a tradition of music where drama and spirituality converge, and for which Messiaen and Wagner stood as particularly important avatars – *Birdconcerto with pianosong* (2001–3) and the opera *Wagner Dream* (first performed in 2007). The opera is three times the length of *Birdconcerto*, and even more ambitious and intricate in its alignment of live, recorded and processed sounds – one reason why reproducing score extracts cannot convey the actual sound experience. Harvey's fascination with Wagner had much to do with the awesome achievement represented by the canon of romantic operas and music dramas which are probably more frequently performed and more widely studied in the twenty-first century than at any time since their creation, despite debates about the Wagner family's complicity in National Socialist ideology and the degree to which the works themselves might have anticipated, stimulated and condoned the imperialism and anti-Semitism of that ideology.

Harvey was particularly struck by Wagner's unfulfilled ambition to compose a drama on Buddhist themes, *Die Sieger*. His own aim was not to provide the *Die Sieger* that Wagner failed to produce, but to offer a dream-like presentation of a treatment of the *Die Sieger* outline in counterpoint with a spoken dramatization of the events surrounding Wagner's death that would evoke nineteenth-century stylistic conventions much more obviously than the surrounding music would. Calling *Wagner Dream* 'a fantasy based on fact',[19] Harvey imagined that, during his fatal heart attack in Venice on 13 February 1883, Wagner was particularly

---

[18] Jonathan Harvey, 'The Mirror of Ambiguity' in Simon Emmerson (ed.), *The Language of Electronic Music* (London: Macmillan, 1986), pp. 177–90.
[19] Jonathan Harvey, 'Note from the Composer' with score and libretto of *Wagner Dream*. See also Michael Downes, *Jonathan Harvey: Song Offerings and White as Jasmine* (Farnham: Ashgate, 2009), pp. 122–7.

disturbed by recalling his failure to write *Die Sieger* and might even have imagined its enactment.

It remains questionable whether opera in the opera house was a proper medium for the kind of aesthetic experience that Harvey had to offer; *Wagner Dream* has probably divided opinion more sharply than any other Harvey work, mainly because of the fissure it imposes between the operatic – the Buddhist drama – and the melodramatic: the acting out of Wagner's death in dialogue spoken by actors. The gulf between these separate worlds is meant to be bridged, and also contextualized, by the electro-acoustic music: instead of which, perhaps, the sheer strangeness of the gulf is enhanced, in an archetypal reinforcement of modernist aesthetics. For Harvey the undertaking returned him to his early operatic ambitions and his early contact with Britten. *Wagner Dream* could never be called *Death in Venice 2* except in jest. But Thomas Mann's story and Britten's opera are fundamentally about two cultures – the Germanic ethos of the repressed and bookish writer Gustav von Aschenbach, and the Grecian rites of Apollo and Dionysus that take place in Aschenbach's dreams around the idolized form of Tadziù. In turn, Harvey's dream-fantasy places the bourgeois European secular culture within which Wagner lived (Bavaria, Venice) alongside the ancient Eastern world of Prakriti, Ananda and the Buddha.

Those who believe that a Wagner who declaims in English is even more absurd than an Aschenbach who (in Britten's *Death in Venice*) sings in English are unlikely to be persuaded that the absurdity might be alleviated by having Wagner speak in German (as happened in the first British stage production of *Wagner Dream* by Welsh National Opera in 2013) or sing in any language. The opposition between reality and fantasy is simply too extreme for comfort, and possibly also for art. Harvey's own recognition of this might have emerged in the more homogeneous context for speech and singing he devised for *Weltethos* (2011), where all the texts speak of spirituality. Also, the 'Glasgow trilogy' of orchestral works – *Body Mandala, Speakings* and ... *towards a Pure Land* – undertaken between 2003 and 2008 can be conceived as a more abstract and allusive complement to the opera's explicitness, centring as it does on an instrumental and electro-acoustic representation of speaking or vocal articulation, and absorbing the purely instrumental work called *Sprechgesang* – but without any actual words. Here, especially, *Speakings* makes a final attempt to 'intermodulate' real and imagined, pure and processed. By contrast, *Messages* (2009), without electronics, and with the names of angels as text, joins *Weltethos* in making 'live' human vocality explicit, and therefore more immediately communicative.

Harvey's music is never purely, austerely other-worldly. The 'new grammar based on nature' was also intensely human, not merely a portal to the divine. There could be turbulence or tension. Yet powerful conceptions of his later years, pre-eminently *The Summer Cloud's Awakening* (2001) for choir, flute, cello and electronics and the orchestral *80 Breaths for Tokyo* (2010), show how metaphysical imaginings were always at the heart of that human, natural musical voice. This is music that gives some (earthly) sense of what it might be like when – as the Buddhist text used in *The Summer Cloud's Awakening* puts it – 'the end of craving is achieved'.

At such moments Harvey, while less raptly austere than Emsley, is at his most distant from the raging darkness of Saunders and the eerie secularism of Holt, and as close as he came to a kind of post-expressionistic modernism that is technically more radical than anything in MacMillan. At one extreme, expressionistic modernism drives music towards such states, but at the other, it seems at least tenuously compatible with a more compassionate and restrained ethos – even, as with MacMillan and Harvey, an ethos that is not just spiritual but religious. Perhaps it is this capacity within expressionistic modernism to generate visions of, and insight into, the sublime that helps to ensure its ability to renew itself regularly within the prevailing turbulence of post-2000 culture. Nevertheless, that easy revivability can provoke exasperation. Julian Anderson (b. 1967) has written about the false start he made on his opera *Thebans* (first performed in 2014) and his recomposition of the first act: 'basically I got Act 1 badly wrong the first time I did it. . . . It was a very shrieky, shouty, expressionist, splurgy thing, hopeless'.[20] For at least one important composer, expressionism is a problem, not a solution.

---

[20] Richard Morrison, 'Julian Anderson in conversation with Richard Morrison', *The Times* 2 (30 April 2014), 8–9.

4 Erik Bergman, cosmopolitanism and the transformation of musical geography[1]

Björn Heile

Erik Bergman (1911–2006) was without a doubt a modernist composer. He engaged and at times battled with many of the defining musical techniques of the twentieth century, from the post-romantic nationalism of his earliest works through a brief dabbling with neoclassicism, the adoption of dodecaphony in the early 1950s, followed soon after by integral serialism and controlled aleatoricism to the experimental exploration of sound of his often austere late works. Despite this almost suspiciously neat match between individual stylistic development and the general trajectories of canonic music history, a detailed engagement with Bergman's work troubles any whiggish textbook history of musical modernism as a linear story of innovation and progress. To be fair, such accounts no longer bear the authority once accorded to them, but what an investigation of Bergman's work brings to light is not simply the asynchronicity and diversity of twentieth-century music history or the difficulty of establishing clear criteria for what could be considered 'avant-gardist', 'progressive', 'mainstream', 'traditional' or 'conservative', 'dominant' or 'marginal' at any given historical moment. Rather, what emerges most clearly is that modernism has to be thought of as a geographically as much as historically defined phenomenon. Bergman's music engages with musical geography in at least two ways: by unambiguously embracing modernism from a position at the very periphery of modernism and European culture more widely, and by drawing on non-Western traditions. In other words, Bergman's music problematizes what the postcolonial critic Homi Bhabha has called 'The Location of Culture'.[2]

---

[1] Much of the material for this chapter was first presented in a keynote lecture at the Bergman Centenary Conference, Åbo Akademi, Turku (Finland), in September 2011. I wish to thank Juha Torvinen for inviting me and the other delegates as well as the delegates at the 'Transformations of Musical Modernism' symposium for many stimulating comments. A generous grant from the Carnegie Trust for the Universities of Scotland enabled me to study Bergman's sketches and manuscripts at the Paul Sacher Stiftung (Basel, Switzerland). Thanks are also due to the PSS and the curator of the Erik Bergman Collection at the time, Ulrich Mosch. Finally, I wish to pay tribute to Gerard Delanty, who first introduced me to Cosmopolitan Studies, at the University of Sussex, where I was based at the time.

[2] Homi Bhabha, *The Location of Culture* (London: Routledge, 1994).

In the following, after sketching relevant theoretical approaches to the cultural geography of musical modernism, I provide an account of Bergman's career as the progressive development of a cosmopolitan vision. While, in common with other recent commentators, I draw on the burgeoning field of cosmopolitan studies – or more specifically, critical cosmopolitanism – to address certain blind spots of historical musicology and present Bergman's work as a case study, I am mindful of Ryan Minor's cogent warning against a tendency for hagiography in musicological approaches to cosmopolitanism.[3] As will be seen, my general sympathy for Bergman does not occlude aspects that I find problematic or even disturbing. Yet, this too is instructive from a cosmopolitan perspective: although cosmopolitanism is driven by a normative ethics, this does not mean that there is a simple consensus on what represents a perfectly cosmopolitan act in any given situation. On the contrary, cosmopolitan ethics is procedural, and it is based on negotiation and mediation. Intercultural communication is fraught with difficulties and dangers, but the response cannot be to avoid it altogether. In a globalized world, trying and failing may be preferable to not engaging with the other at all.

The place of musical modernism

Despite a spate of publications on broadly related topics, historical musicology has typically found it difficult to conceive of cultural geography.[4] One reason for this blind spot may be found in the traditional division between historical musicology and ethnomusicology, as if a neat separation of history and geography, time and place were possible. Another may be found in the ideology of universalism, a disavowal of cultural difference, which is arguably foundational for Western classical music and which has rarely been interrogated. It is instructive, therefore, to look at accounts of Western classical music from outside musicology. The following excerpt is from a textbook in cultural geography, by Mike Crang:[5]

---

[3] Ryan Minor, 'Beyond Heroism: Music, Ethics, and Everyday Cosmopolitanism', *Journal of the American Musicological Society*, 66/2 (2013), 529–34.

[4] Examples of recent approaches to cultural geography from within historical musicology include Erik Levi and Florian Scheding, *Music and Displacement: Diasporas, Mobilities, and Dislocations in Europe and Beyond* (Lanham, MD and Plymouth, UK: Scarecrow Press, 2010); Brigid Cohen, *Stefan Wolpe and the Avant-Garde Diaspora* (Cambridge University Press, 2012); Dana Gooley, 'Cosmopolitanism in the Age of Nationalism, 1848–1914', *Journal of the American Musicological Society*, 66/2 (2013), 523–49; Brigid Cohen, 'Limits of National History: Yoko Ono, Stefan Wolpe, and Dilemmas of Cosmopolitanism', *The Musical Quarterly*, 97/2 (2014), 181–237, among others.

[5] Mike Crang, *Cultural Geography* (London: Routledge, 1998), pp. 90–1.

> The geography of music has often contrasted local and universal, rootless and rooted. It has thus been led into a search for regional folk types – the mapping of styles and influences.
>
> This treatment of music as embedded in a locale differs starkly from classical music where traces of the local have been gradually removed. Classical music has tended to treat itself as a universal, neutral standard – folk and ethnic music are measured as deviations from it. While notable developments occurred in specific places and at specific times, it is suggested the qualities of the music transcend this. Rather like the model of classical science, music became marked by its reproducibility. And just as in science this entailed the spread of particular spaces of controlled conditions and techniques – laboratories – in classical music there is the spread of the concert halls and particular practices of listening.

This quotation is hardly free from problematic generalizations, and it is easy to pick holes in it. What about, for instance, the local and national styles in the eighteenth century or nationalism in the nineteenth? Even standard histories of music allow for some national or regional variation, say when covering the specifically French tradition of *tragédie lyrique*, and 'art' music rarely lost touch with vernacular popular traditions entirely, witness the infatuation with folk and popular dance music from *Ländlers* to tangos and beyond. But, simplified as his account may be, Crang surely has got a point. Note too that the objections made above could with some justification be described as local variants of an underlying universal phenomenon or, in the case of nationalism, as an 'invented tradition'.[6]

The most influential textbook on music history, Richard Taruskin's *Oxford History of Western Music*, has next to nothing to say about what constitutes the 'West' in the title, other than to suggest that it encompasses Europe and 'America' (whether he means the continent, the USA or North America is not clear),[7] and, although Taruskin has been rightly praised for raising the profile of Russian and Eastern European music, he remains almost entirely silent about the music of Latin America and Asia, not to mention Africa. Surely, the expansion of this form of music from the heartlands of Europe to, progressively, the entire world is a remarkable phenomenon which is worth studying in its own right and which forms a central element of its history.[8] Why did the elites (for it was usually

---

[6] See Eric Hobsbawm and Terence Ranger (eds.), *The Invention of Tradition* (Cambridge University Press, 1983).

[7] Richard Taruskin, *The Oxford History of Western Music*, 6 vols. (Oxford University Press, 2005), vol. I, xxi.

[8] This argument is indebted to Nicholas Cook and Anthony Pople's *Cambridge History of Twentieth-Century Music*, which, quite uniquely, reflects deeply on the transformations of modernist musical geography; see Nicholas Cook, 'Introduction:

primarily them) in such diverse places as Russia, North and South America, Japan, Korea and China embrace this music, and why did newly independent or modernizing states feel the need to set up conservatoires and symphony orchestras as tokens of statehood almost on a par with flags, passports and currencies? And why did forms of musical modernism, in whatever guise, gain a foothold in countless countries and regions around the world? The answers to these questions have to do with geopolitics, colonialism and globalization, and, although this is not the place to go into detail, it is my contention that as the product of these forces, Western classical music bears their imprint. Indeed, the adjective 'Western' has to be called into question, given the long history of adoption and adaptation of this music outside the West (which is itself an increasingly questionable construct). Nor can we assume that these developments at the 'margins' had no effect on the 'centre'. The history of musical modernism may therefore be one not only of geographic expansion but also of diversification and hybridization.

It is noticeable, therefore, that terms such as 'globalization' and 'colonialism' or 'postcolonialism' are rarely encountered in historical musicology. By contrast, they are hotly debated in ethnomusicology: there is wide agreement that traditional and popular music are subject to these forces, but the assumption appears to be that classical and modernist music are not. An (apparent) exception to this rule is the study of musical exoticism and orientalism.[9] Although this undoubtedly represents a valuable contribution, it remains a somewhat limited engagement with musical otherness. At heart, this type of research is about the Western self; the non-Western other figures only in its represented form.[10] It cannot talk back. The wider questions about musical constructions of self and other are rarely asked, and the very concepts of Western and non-Western remain unquestioned.[11]

An interesting case in point of the difficulty in theoretical approaches to the cultural geography of musical modernism is the infamous footnote in Adorno's *Philosophy of New Music*:[12]

Trajectories of Twentieth-Century Music' in Nicholas Cook and Anthony Pople (eds.), *The Cambridge History of Twentieth-Century Music* (Cambridge University Press, 2004), pp. 7–9.

[9] See Jonathan Bellman (ed.), *The Exotic in Western Music* (Lebanon, NH: Northeastern University Press, 1998); Ralph P. Locke, *Musical Exoticism: Images and Reflections* (Cambridge University Press, 2009), among others.

[10] Cf. Sindhumathi Revuluri, 'Review: Musical Exoticism: Images and Reflections', *Journal of the American Musicological Society*, 64/1 (2011), 253–61.

[11] A corollary of musicology's obsession with exoticism is the prominence given to Edward Said's *Orientalism* (London: Penguin Books, 2003). This is not to deny the significance of the book, but it is hardly the only example of postcolonial scholarship with relevance for musicology.

[12] Theodor W. Adorno, *Philosophy of New Music*, trans. and ed. Robert Hullot-Kentor (Minneapolis, MN: University of Minnesota Press, 2006), p. 176.

> Where the developmental tendency of occidental music was not fully carried through, as in many agrarian regions of southern Europe [orig. 'south-eastern Europe'], it has been possible right up to the present [orig. 'most recent past', *jüngste Vergangenheit*] to use tonal material without opprobrium. Mention may be made here of the extraterritorial, yet in its rigor magisterial, art of Leoš Janáček, as well as much of Bartók's, who in spite of his folkloristic penchant at the same time counted among the most progressive composers in European art music. The legitimation of such music from the periphery in every case depends on its having developed a coherent and selective technical canon. In contrast to the productions of Nazi blood-and-soil ideology, truly extraterritorial music – whose material, while common in itself, is organized in a totally different way from occidental music – has a power of alienation that associates it with the avant-garde and not with nationalistic reaction. Ideological blood-and-soil music, by contrast, is always affirmative and allied with 'the tradition,' whereas it is precisely the tradition of all official music that is suspended by Janáček's diction, even in the midst of all the triads.

Clearly Adorno is troubled by music which does not fit into his universalist account, but which, to his credit, he appreciates. His response is the recourse to the traditional geography of centres and peripheries (although his usage of 'extraterritorial' overstates even that case), whereby, as in the classic account by Kenneth Clarke,[13] the technical standard in the periphery is behind that of the centres according to a spatio-temporal logic. This thinking in terms of centres and peripheries, which is key to the history of musical modernism, is not necessarily innocent, mirroring as it does the spatial order of colonialism. This would explain the centrality of the notion of 'time lag', which in one sense can be interpreted as that between the metropolis and the colony: in the thought of Bhabha, for instance.[14]

In any case, it is easy to see that Adorno's treatment of the music of Janáček and Bartók as an exception to 'the developmental tendency of occidental music' is hardly adequate; the more far-reaching response would be to interrogate the concepts of 'developmental tendency' and/or 'occidental music' so that they may accommodate them. To be fair, more recent approaches have generally had little difficulty in including Janáček and Bartók, but that does not mean that the problem of centres and peripheries and of music that 'doesn't fit' the narrative as a consequence has gone away; it has only been pushed further to 'the margins': witness the unreflected restriction to America and Europe in Taruskin.[15] Although it

---

[13] Cited in Franco Moretti, *Atlas of the European Novel, 1800–1900* (London: Verso, 1998), p. 164.
[14] Bhabha, *The Location of Culture*, pp. 338–67.
[15] Taruskin, *The Oxford History of Western Music* (see n. 7).

would be wishful thinking to confine centres and peripheries firmly to the past, there is wide agreement that this model is inadequate in dealing with the cultural dynamics of globalization.[16]

For approaches to modernism which acknowledge the formative function of place and the history of colonialism, decolonization and globalization, one has to look largely beyond musicology at literary studies.[17] As mentioned above, however, there has been a recent surge in approaches to modernist music which resemble mine in crucial aspects. Among the most far-reaching and the most relevant in the present context are Brigid Cohen's studies of Stefan Wolpe and, more recently, Wolpe and Yoko Ono.[18] Like me, Cohen also bases her account on cosmopolitan studies. Although I am in full agreement with her approach, some of my emphasis here is slightly different. Cohen focuses on the importance of migration for modernism and the contributions made by migrants, represented by Wolpe and Ono. As someone who has worked on another prominent migrant, Mauricio Kagel, and as an immigrant myself (albeit one of opportunity rather than necessity), I am more than sympathetic to this approach. Nevertheless, in my view migration is not the only, and not necessarily the most significant, aspect of the cultural geography of music overlooked by the continuing dominance of national history which Cohen deplores. Moreover, for cosmopolitanism to function as an ethics, it must not be regarded as the preserve of either the privileged or the unfortunate. After all, it was Kant, who famously never moved far from his native Königsberg, who based cosmopolitanism on the principle of 'universal hospitality'.[19] In other words, it is not only or not necessarily the refugee who is cosmopolitan but the one who gives her shelter, not the traveller but his host. As Bhabha has put it, 'cosmopolitanism must always begin at home!'.[20] Although it may come more naturally to some of us than others, we can all be cosmopolitan. As we will see, Erik Bergman travelled frequently and widely and, at least in later years, was able to do so due to his relative wealth and the privileges provided by a first-world passport. But his interest in and openness towards others preceded his journeys; he travelled *because* he was cosmopolitan by instinct if not by persuasion;

---

[16] See, for example, Arjun Appadurai, *Modernity at Large: Cultural Dimensions of Globalization* (Minneapolis, MN: University of Minnesota Press, 1996), p. 32.
[17] Laura Doyle and Laura A. Winkiel, *Geomodernisms: Race, Modernism, Modernity* (Bloomington, IN: Indiana University Press, 2005); Peter Brooker and Andrew Thacker (eds.), *Geographies of Modernism: Literatures, Cultures, Spaces* (London and New York: Routledge, 2005).
[18] Cohen, *Stefan Wolpe* and 'Limits of National History'.
[19] Immanuel Kant, *Perpetual Peace* (Minneapolis, MN: Filiquarian Publishing, LLC., 2007), p. 21.
[20] Bhabha, *The Location of Culture*, p. xv.

that is, he did not become cosmopolitan *as a result of* travel (even if that experience may have confirmed his beliefs).

Although this is not the place for a comprehensive account of cosmopolitanism or its significance for music, some brief remarks on the idea of 'cosmopolitanism' employed in this chapter are in order, notably since the scholarly concept diverges quite widely from the everyday use of the term, which can lead to confusion.[21] In the words of Anthony Appiah, cosmopolitanism 'begins with the simple idea that in the human community, as in national communities, we need to develop habits of coexistence: conversation in its older meaning, of living together, association'.[22] There are two principles to this: '[o]ne is the idea that we have obligations to others, obligations that stretch beyond those to whom we are related by the ties of kith and kind, or even the more formal ties of a shared citizenship', and 'the other is that we take seriously the value not just of human life but of particular human lives, which means taking an interest in the practices and beliefs that lend them significance'.[23] Over and above these points, the principles and values of cosmopolitanism are hotly debated and widely contested not only between its opponents and proponents but also among the latter. Nevertheless, there seems to be an almost concerted effort to disprove certain popular prejudices, namely that it is essentially Western or that it is primarily associated with privilege and multinational corporations. For instance, James Clifford has argued that 'the project of comparing and translating different travelling cultures need not be class- or ethnocentric', looking, for instance, at the experiences of Pakistani labourers in Gulf countries.[24] Critical cosmopolitanism, in particular, is intended as an ethical corrective to the unregulated process of globalization

---

[21] Despite their undoubted merits, some earlier accounts of cosmopolitanism in music, notably Martin Stokes, 'On Musical Cosmopolitanism', *The Macalester International Roundtable* (2007), http://digitalcommons.macalester.edu/intlrdtable/3 and Cristina Magaldi, 'Cosmopolitanism and World Music in Rio de Janeiro at the Turn of the Twentieth Century', *The Musical Quarterly*, 92/3–4 (2009), 329–64, suffer from the somewhat uncritical employment of everyday notions of cosmopolitanism.

[22] Anthony Appiah, *Cosmopolitanism: Ethics in a World of Strangers* (New York: W. W. Norton, 2006), p. xix.

[23] Ibid., p. xv.

[24] Quoted in Pnina Werbner, 'Anthropology and the New Ethical Cosmopolitanism' in Gerard Delanty (ed.), *Routledge Handbook of Cosmopolitan Studies* (Abingdon: Routledge, 2012), pp. 153–65, p. 156. See also Carol A. Breckenridge (ed.), *Cosmopolitanism*, Millennial Quartet (Durham, NC: Duke University Press, 2002); Fuyuki Kurasawa, 'A Cosmopolitanism from Below: Alternative Globalization and the Creation of a Solidarity without Bounds', *European Journal of Sociology / Archives Européennes de Sociologie*, 45/02 (2004), 233–55; Pnina Werbner, 'Global Pathways. Working Class Cosmopolitans and the Creation of Transnational Ethnic Worlds', *Social Anthropology*, 7/1 (1999), 17–35.

and, in common with critical theory, with which it explicitly aligns itself, is aimed at transforming the present, over and above describing it.[25]

Most significant for our purposes is cosmopolitanism's conflicted stance towards universalism and diversity or relativism. Although Chernilo, for instance, has defended certain conceptions of universalism from a cosmopolitan perspective (though his heavy qualification should be noted),[26] most cosmopolitan thinkers reject such an association, stressing on the contrary that, in the words of Hannerz, cosmopolitanism 'includes an aesthetic stance of openness towards divergent cultural experiences, a search for contrasts rather than uniformity', whereas universalism assumes sameness.[27] Likewise, Bhabha has associated cosmopolitanism with Julia Kristeva's notion of a 'right to difference in equality',[28] and Fred Dallmayer has proposed a 'hermeneutics of difference' which would negotiate between Enlightenment and modernist ideas of universalism on one hand and postmodernist and postcolonial notions of identity politics on the other.[29] In a similar way, most proponents are at pains to stress that forming allegiances with distant others does not mean repudiating local ties. Indeed, several commentators have called for 'rooted cosmopolitanism' or, like Bhabha, 'vernacular cosmopolitanism'.[30] Denigrating the local and particular in favour of the distant and universal is therefore not a cosmopolitan position. As will be seen, I believe that Bergman's practices embodied many of these precepts (if I insist on 'practices' over his professed beliefs, it is not only because 'actions speak louder than words' but also because I have to admit that I know relatively little about the latter, although my views at least do not conflict with published accounts and have met with agreement from those who knew him better).

It goes without saying that Bergman is not necessarily the only or even the best example of a cosmopolitan perspective in modernist music. Nor, as

---

[25] Gerard Delanty, 'The Idea of Critical Cosmopolitanism' in Gerard Delanty (ed.), *Routledge Handbook of Cosmopolitan Studies* (Abingdon: Routledge, 2012), pp. 38–46.
[26] Daniel Chernilo, 'Cosmopolitanism and the Question of Universalism' in Gerard Delanty (ed.), *Routledge Handbook of Cosmopolitan Studies* (Abingdon: Routledge, 2012), pp. 47–59.
[27] Ulf Hannerz, 'Cosmopolitans and Locals in World Culture', *Theory, Culture & Society*, 7/2 (1990), 237–51: p. 239. See also Ulrich Beck, *The Cosmopolitan Vision* (Cambridge: Polity Press, 2006), pp. 48–53.
[28] Bhabha, *The Location of Culture*, p. xvii.
[29] Fred R. Dallmayr, *Beyond Orientalism: Essays on Cross-Cultural Encounter* (Albany, NY: SUNY Press, 1996), p. xi.
[30] See Pnina Werbner, 'Anthropology and the New Ethical Cosmopolitanism', p. 154 for rooted and Homi Bhabha, 'Unsatisfied: Notes on Vernacular Cosmopolitanism' in Laura Garcia-Morena and Peter C. Pfeiffer (eds.), *Text and Nation: Cross-Disciplinary Essays on Cultural and National Identities* (London: Camden House, 1996), pp. 191–207 for vernacular cosmopolitanism.

I think my earlier remarks have made clear, do I think that there can be a stable or uncontroversial definition of what constitutes 'cosmopolitanism in music'. In concluding this section, I would like to point to two instances of a cosmopolitan attitude in musical life (rather than composition more narrowly) from the first half of the twentieth century. The first concerns Paul Bekker, who coined the term 'new music',[31] which Adorno later adopted, and who argued forcefully for an 'amalgamation of cultured humanity',[32] and although he seemed to be instinctively more drawn to the likes of Mahler and Schoenberg, consistently tried to be similarly generous to Debussy, Stravinsky and others, apparently reflecting on and countering his own instincts (in ways Adorno signally failed to do). Similarly, for all its flaws, the International Society for Contemporary Music attempted to break down national barriers and to promote '[a]rtistic diversity in musical creation, without prejudice on differences in musical expressions, styles, genres or media; nor regarding race, religion or politics'.[33] I would argue that it is these kinds of views to which Bergman's work seems to be committed.

Cosmopolitanism I: from nationalism to internationalism

Despite the problematic nature of the centre–periphery model implicit in standard music historiography, any account of Bergman's career and work has to reckon with the peripheral nature of musical life in Bergman's native Finland in the first half of the twentieth century, which, despite (or maybe because of) the stature of Sibelius and the efforts of earlier modernists, such as Aarre Merikanto, by most accounts was considerably more provincial than Janáček's Brno or Bartók's Budapest to which Adorno alluded.[34] Indeed, although his training and career took place in Helsinki, Bergman was actually from Nykarleby (Uusikaarlepyy) in Ostrobothnia in Western Finland and, like Sibelius, was a member of the Swedish minority. Although Finland-Swedes were traditionally part of the elite (from the time of the Swedish empire) and are well integrated, their status is slightly

---

[31] Paul Bekker, *Neue Musik* (Berlin: E. Reiss, 1920; reprinted Nendeln, Liechtenstein: Kraus Reprint, 1973).

[32] Paul Bekker, 'Kunst und Krieg: Zwei Feldpostbriefe' in *Kritische Zeitbilder (Gesammelte Schriften, vol. 1)* (Berlin: Schuster & Loeffler, 1921), pp. 177–97, p. 182.

[33] International Society for Contemporary Music, 'ISCM Statutes and Rules of Procedure for the Organization of the International Music Events (May 2010)', http://www.iscm.org/sites/default/files/rules_and_forms/Statutes%202010.pdf (accessed 15 December 2014).

[34] Cf. Tim Howell, *After Sibelius: Studies in Finnish Music* (Aldershot, UK and Burlington, VT: Ashgate, 2006); Kalevi Aho, Pekka Jalkanen, Erkki Salamenhaara and Keijo Virtamo, *Finnish Music*, trans. Timothy Binham and Philip Binham (Keuruu: Otava, 1996).

precarious. All in all, it is not surprising that Bergman started off in a style that was pretty much mandatory, not only in Finland, but, with some variation, in many other regions and countries like it: romantic nationalism, to be superseded before long by dabbling in neoclassicism. So far, so predictable.

He wanted more, however, and, at that time and in that place, this meant going abroad. According to Ulrich Mosch, it was Max Trapp, then on tour in Finland, who recommended that he study with Fritz Tiessen.[35] Bergman's studies with Tiessen between 1937 and 1939 and again 1942–43 are mentioned in every biographical sketch – with astonishing equanimity, as if there is nothing unusual about a composer being drawn to Nazi Germany of all places, and, on the second occasion, during the height of the war, of all times. Things are somewhat murky: while Trapp was pretty much an impeccable Nazi, having joined the NSDAP well before Hitler assumed power,[36] Tiessen was actually from the political left; he had been a member of the *Novembergruppe* of expressionist artists (named after the November Revolution in the Soviet Union) as well as the socialist *Arbeitersängerbund*.[37] While his career did not entirely end under the Nazis, he was not a major opportunist and undertook little to shake off the suspicion with which he was viewed. Why Trapp would have recommended a political enemy is difficult to see, although both composers shared similar stylistic tendencies (somewhere between Richard Strauss and Hindemith) – which, incidentally, says much about the political signification of musical style. The current state of knowledge about Bergman's activities in the Third Reich is thus quite confusing, and there is clearly a need for further research.

As is well known, Bergman subsequently became the first Finnish composer to employ dodecaphony, then virtually unknown in Finland, in the *Espressivo* Op. 40 for piano (in 1952). There is no evidence, however, that he learned the technique from Tiessen, and the long period between his study periods with him and Bergman's first dodecaphonic works makes this connection unlikely. Despite a lack of experience and available models, the following Three Fantasies Op. 42 for Clarinet and Piano (1953–1954) is without doubt an accomplished composition. Nevertheless, his understandable difficulties with twelve-note technique led him to study with

---

[35] '"Ihre Lieder Sind Stimmungsvoll Und Schön, Nur … ": Erik Bergmans Studien Bei Heinz Tiessen Zwischen 1937 Und 1943', *Mitteilungen Der Paul Sacher Stiftung* 24 (2011), 12–18, http://www.paul-sacher-stiftung.ch/de/forschung_publikationen/publikationen/mitteilungen/nr_24_april_2011.html, p. 12.
[36] Fred K. Prieberg, *Handbuch deutsche Musiker 1933–1945* (Fred K. Prieberg, 2004), pp. 726–31.
[37] Ibid., pp. 7192–5.

Wladimir Vogel in Ascona, another pupil of Tiessen's and veteran of the left-wing *Novembergruppe*. Again, like Tiessen, Vogel was, although respected, hardly at the centre of musical developments. However, he was a recognized specialist in dodecaphony, having organized the international twelve-tone music pre-conference in Osilina (1949), attended by Dallapiccola, Malipiero and others.[38]

Bergman's use of serial techniques can be reconstructed comparatively easily on the basis of his sketches and manuscripts, which are collected at the Paul Sacher Stiftung (Basel). Although this is not the primary focus of this chapter, it is necessary to clear up some misunderstandings in the existing research on this area and to contextualize his work more firmly in relation to the prevailing trends of the time. In many cases, Bergman wrote out row tables and even highlighted serial strands in his sketches. Although Heiniö and Oramo, in their respective entries on the composer in *Komponisten der Gegenwart* and *Musik in Geschichte und Gegenwart*, both state that Bergman used the series vertically and nonthematically,[39] the sketches and manuscripts reveal that, particularly in later years, he often preferred linear exposition of the series. The Adagio Op. 47a for Baritone, Flute, Male Choir and Vibraphone (1957), for instance, features horizontal unfolding of the series throughout, starting with a quasi-canon in the choir on different transpositions of the prime form of the series. Nor is it strictly true that Bergman's serial phase ended in 1962, as Aho claims:[40] serial elements are in evidence at least up to *Circulo* Op. 58 (1965), although it is true that, at least on the surface, serialism played a progressively less important role in Bergman's compositions from the 1960s onwards.

The design of the rows themselves is also quite sophisticated, frequently involving specific intervallic characteristics or symmetrical structures. The row for *Aubade* Op. 48 for orchestra (1958) is an interesting case in point. It is neatly divided into two hexachords (see Example 4.1), with the second one being the transposed inversion of the first. Both hexachords consist entirely of tritones and major seconds; indeed, they each make up a whole-tone set. In the course of the composition, Bergman mostly works with

---

[38] Tamara Levitz, 'Vogel, Wladimir' in Stanley Sadie and John Tyrrell (eds.), *The New Grove Dictionary of Music and Musicians*, 2nd edn. Version at *Grove Music Online*.

[39] Mikko Heiniö, 'Bergman, Erik' in Hanns-Werner Heister and Walter-Wolfgang Sparrer (eds.), *Komponisten Der Gegenwart*, 10. Lfg. (Munich: Edition Text + Kritik, 1992); Ilkka Oramo, 'Bergmann [sic], Erik (Valdemar)' in Friedrich Blume (ed.), *Die Musik in Geschichte Und Gegenwart: Allgemeine Enzyklopädie der Musik*, revised 2nd edn, ed. Ludwig Finscher (Kassel, Stuttgart, etc.: Bärenreiter, Metzler, 1999), vol. 2, pp. 1271–7.

[40] Kalevi Aho, 'Bergman, Erik', *Komponisten der Gegenwart*, 32. Lfg. (Munich: Edition Text + Kritik, 2006).

Example 4.1 Serial structure of Erik Bergman's *Aubade* for Orchestra Op. 48.

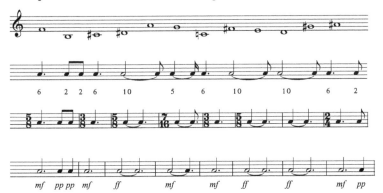

individual hexachords, rather than the twelve-note row as a whole. This is in fact a common trait of his mature serial practice, as indeed of serial composition in general, illustrating that he was by that point well informed about common trends and skilled in their application.

Indeed, he had visited the Darmstadt summer courses during the previous year, 1957,[41] attending Luigi Nono's and Karlheinz Stockhausen's lectures: 'Die Entwicklung der Reihentechnik' ('The Development of Serialism') in Nono's case and 'Music and Language' (Stockhausen), the latter including a brilliant, albeit misguided, analysis of Nono's *Il Canto sospeso*.[42] This seems to have been Bergman's only direct encounter with the international avant-garde in one of its centres, however.

Another fairly predictable result of this experience can also be found in *Aubade*: the application of integral serialism (seemingly for the first time in Bergman's work). Again the sketches reveal the process clearly. Bergman derived rhythmic and dynamic values from the intervals in the pitch series in a fairly basic way. For durations, a minor second upwards is defined as a semiquaver, with all larger intervals being multiples thereof (this obviously only works for ascending intervals, so the falling major seconds in the series are reinterpreted as rising minor sevenths, yielding a duration of ten semiquavers). The dynamic values are applied in a similar way, with two (the lowest value occurring in the series) representing pp, rising to ff (for the ascending minor seventh). Similar techniques are used in other

---

[41] John D. White and Jean Christensen, *New Music of the Nordic Countries* (Hillsdale, NY: Pendragon Press, 2002), p. 155; Martin Anderson, 'Erik Bergman [Obituary]', *The Independent* (9 May 2006).

[42] Martin Iddon, *New Music at Darmstadt: Nono, Stockhausen, Cage, and Boulez* (Cambridge University Press, 2013), p. xix.

pieces, such as *Simbolo* Op. 52 (1960), another orchestral composition. This is, however, only intermittently applied in the piece with any rigour; one such moment occurs in a passage marked *poco meno allegro* (bars 131ff.), which first presents only unpitched percussion (playing serially generated rhythms) before the other instruments enter with a linear statement of I_3 split up between the instruments; this is followed by a gradual thickening of the orchestral texture (homophonically and polyphonically).

In much of the remainder of the piece, however, the serial structures are harder to follow, and Bergman seems to have employed them less strictly. This too appears to be a common trait in his oeuvre, although more systematic analysis would be required.

Although from the standpoint of serial technique alone *Aubade* is a relatively simple work, both in its serial ordering (notably the generation of rhythm) and application, compared to otherwise similar compositions from the time, such as Stockhausen's *Gruppen* (1956) or Nono's *Il canto sospeso* (1956), it is undoubtedly a masterpiece and demonstrates that Bergman had learned the lessons from the serialist avant-garde with astonishing speed (very few composers at that, or any other, time went as far as Stockhausen or Nono in seeking to base the entirety of the musical structure from one serial kernel; nor should this be regarded as some kind of music-historical shibboleth). It must not be forgotten that he had only recently encountered dodecaphony and that he was already at an age when most other composers prefer to stick to what they know and have mastered. In addition to his rejection of nationalism and embrace of what could be considered an 'international style' in music, it is Bergman's openness towards the new and willingness to learn (from much younger composers) that demonstrates his cosmopolitan spirit.

Although integral serialism is often depicted as a dull homogenizing force, it presented exciting new ideas to many at the time, particularly in places with a hide-bound musical culture. As Paavo Heininen has pointed out, Bergman was 'the man to usher in the new wave of musical modernism in Finland [and] he was also responsible for bringing Finland into the mainstream of European avant-garde music by going further than the first generation of Finnish modernists, rejecting the expressive ideals and sound of romanticism and adopting a contextual [by which he means serial] compositional technique'.[43] This commitment to what Heininen calls (somewhat oxymoronically) 'the mainstream of European avant-garde music' has to be regarded as quite radical, and it led Bergman to become

---

[43] Paavo Heininen, 'Erik Bergman's Path to the New Music' in Jeremy Parsons (ed.), *Erik Bergman: A Seventieth Birthday Tribute* (Helsinki: Pan, 1981), pp. 113–50.

something like the adopted father of the 'Ears Open!' group of younger Finnish modernists (whose founders were Magnus Lindberg and Esa-Pekka Salonen), who, at last, also found wide recognition abroad.[44] This wider international recognition has largely remained elusive for Bergman himself: it is almost a cruel irony that self-exoticism is eminently saleable abroad, while avant-gardism tends to be less highly valued if it hails from what is perceived to be a periphery. A comparison with Bergman's younger contemporary Einojuhani Rautavaara is instructive in this regard. A parallel can be drawn with the Argentine composer Juan Carlos Paz, Bergman's senior by ten years, who was instrumental in bringing the international avant-garde to Latin America – he adopted twelve-note technique in 1934[45] – but who failed to achieve a similar recognition abroad to someone like Alberto Ginastera, who was far more willing to play up to prevailing ideas of folkloristic nationalism – not to mention the strange career of Astor Piazzolla.

In the following years, Bergman also adopted forms of controlled aleatory technique. The dissemination of this technique is itself an interesting case of the cultural geography of new music. As Howell has pointed out, Bergman's use of the technique is most closely related to that of Witold Lutosławski;[46] Lutosławski in turn got the inspiration from John Cage, although both the aesthetic intent behind the technique and his technical employment of it differ quite radically from that model.[47] The key work most frequently mentioned in this respect is the haunting *Colori ed improvvisazioni* Op. 72 (1973), which abandons bar lines about halfway through the first of its three movements (see Example 4.2), using time–space notation for the remainder of the work. What sets Bergman's work from this period apart is his varied, imaginative and practical use of notational techniques, with minutely differentiated degrees of variability and interpretive freedom with regard to pitch, duration and timbre. His vast experience as a choral director will almost certainly have played a role in this context. In relation to his employment, he also wrote numerous vocal compositions, in which he explored the possibilities of the human voice well beyond the norms of lyrical pitched singing, to include speaking, *Sprechstimme* and a host of gradations in between. These are by their nature often difficult to notate and indeterminate with respect to, for

---

[44] Aho et al., *Finnish Music*, pp. 138–41.
[45] Omar Corrado, *Vanguardias al sur: la música de Juan Carlos Paz* (Buenos Aires: Univ. Nacional de Quilmes Ed., 2012).
[46] Howell, *After Sibelius*, p. 60.
[47] Witold Lutosławski, *Lutosławski on Music*, ed. and trans. Zbigniew Skowron (Lanham, MA: Rowman & Littlefield, 2007), pp. 42 and 99.

Example 4.2 Erik Bergman, *Colori ed Improvvisazioni* Op. 72, bars 50ff.

example, pitch. Bergman's practical experience would have given him an incomparable understanding of how different types of symbols are realized by singers and what effects they create (one is reminded of Duke Ellington, who liked to experiment with his players and whose work as a composer can likewise not be separated from that of a bandleader). While the technical practicalities differ somewhat between different types of instruments and between instruments and voices, scores such as that for Bergman's opera *Det Sjungande Trädet*, Op. 110 (1988) illustrate that the composer used similar techniques for singers and instrumentalists in order to achieve comparable effects.

What this survey demonstrates, then, is how Bergman throughout his compositional career responded creatively to and took part in musical developments from abroad. What has become clear is that his guiding principle in that was a musical internationalism, arguably a form of universalism. He seemed to have no truck with musical nationalisms or with any kind of special pleading. That doesn't mean that he slavishly followed whatever trend he perceived, but that he adopted and modified those developments that suited his own artistic ends. For what follows, it is important to recognize that this form of internationalism is not fully 'cosmopolitan' in the way I am using the term, or only to a relatively limited extent (many theorists envisage degrees of cosmopolitanism). Likewise, the post-war avant-gardes like the 'Darmstadt school' are sometimes called 'cosmopolitan', but this reflects a colloquial usage of the term, which I want to distinguish from the idea of cosmopolitanism exposed above. The reason the internationalism of the post-war avant-gardes cannot be considered fully cosmopolitan is that they do not recognize cultural difference: they proclaim an unvarying absolute standard. Boulez's infamous remark that 'any musician who has not experienced ... the necessity of dodecaphonic music is USELESS' illustrates the point neatly.[48] As pointed out above, although internationalist universalism could be considered an advance over nationalism from a cosmopolitan perspective, the cosmopolitan does not simply favour the global over the local or the universal over the particular.

Cosmopolitanism II: encountering the other

Following this line of argument, it is Bergman's complementation of the international with the global that marks his cosmopolitanism. What I am referring to is his interest in traditional and non-Western musics. Such an interest is often somewhat rashly and sweepingly equated with a colonialist or neo-colonialist mindset.[49] As will become clear, although

---

[48] Pierre Boulez, *Stocktakings from an Apprenticeship*, collected and ed. Paule Thévenin, trans. Stephen Walsh (Oxford: Clarendon Press, 1991), p. 113.

[49] Cf. Georgina Born and David Hesmondhalgh (eds.), *Western Music and Its Others: Difference, Representation, and Appropriation in Music* (Berkeley, CA: University of California Press, 2000); also see Björn Heile, 'Weltmusik and the Globalization of New Music' in Björn Heile (ed.), *The Modernist Legacy: Essays on New Music* (Farnham: Ashgate, 2009), pp. 101–21.

there are problematic aspects in his thinking, Bergman can be said to have developed an increasingly cosmopolitan approach. It may be somewhat surprising if I suggest that this fascination with non-Western music is already perceptible in his study of Catholic music at the Vatican in the 1950s. This music is of course not non-Western and it is seemingly related to Bergman's employment at the Roman Catholic Church in Helsinki. Yet, for a Protestant Finland-Swede, the liturgical practices of the Vatican may seem quite foreign. In any case, from a cosmopolitan perspective, the binary division of the world into Western and non-Western and the consequent attribution of self and other along these lines is untenable; the cosmopolitan sees degrees of familiarity and looks for sameness in the other and difference in the self.

Perhaps not surprisingly, it is predominantly religious music that attracted Bergman's attention, an interest that finds most direct expression in choral works (with or without instruments). As is well known, Bergman went on extensive travels across the world, in the process amassing a sizeable collection of instruments. Hans Oesch, one of the most authoritative specialists on cross-cultural composition, accompanied him on occasion and testifies that Bergman's interest went deeper than that of a musical tourist: he learned to play various instruments and studied both primary sources and secondary literature on a range of musical traditions.[50] According to Oesch, the relatively early *Rubaiyat* Op. 41 (1953) on texts by the great Persian poet, philosopher, astronomer and mathematician Omar Khayyam emulates but does not imitate the *maqām*, the modal structures of Middle-Eastern and Islamic musical traditions.[51] This, for Oesch, differentiates the work from a superficial, merely modish reception and instead demonstrates Bergman's endeavour to respond to musical ideas and concepts at a deep level, thereby unintentionally approaching what he calls the 'character of the universal'.[52] If I cautiously agree with Oesch, it is not without noting that, in the debates on cross-cultural composition, the criteria for judgement are often back to front compared to Oesch's: one could just as well argue that only a full adoption of musical material can be regarded as 'authentic' and that any partial appropriation, as practised here by Bergman, has to be regarded as a superficial exoticism. It all depends on the wider circumstances and artistic intentions, and the

---

[50] Hans Oesch, 'Exotisches Bei Erik Bergman' in Jeremy Parsons (ed.), *Erik Bergman: A Seventieth Birthday Tribute* (Helsinki: Pan, 1981), pp. 183–206.
[51] Ibid., p. 188.   [52] Ibid., p. 188.

kind of binary division between deep and authentic on one side and superficial exoticism on the other according to simple criteria that Oesch, like so many others, wishes to undertake may not be possible or indeed desirable. There is space between the sanctimonious condemnation as 'exoticism' or 'tourist folklore' and the celebration of perfect examples of genuine intercultural composition. What Bergman is trying is to come to terms with otherness, to mediate between Western modernist composition and non-Western music. This should be regarded as an open process and not judged as a final outcome. What is noteworthy too is that the work came well before the discovery of non-Western music by both the American and European avant-gardes and the sometimes heated debates associated with them, so Bergman had very few models to work from.

It is interesting to note that the *Rubaiyat* sits between the aforementioned *Espressivo* and Three Fantasies in Bergman's oeuvre; in other words, it falls into the period of his most intensive investigation of dodecaphony, of which there are few if any traces in *Rubaiyat*. What this demonstrates is that at no stage did Bergman conceive of dodecaphony as the only legitimate musical technique, but that he always envisaged a diversity of simultaneous and, at least in principle, equally valid traditions.

The apex of this strand in Bergman's work is arguably represented by the cantata *Bardo Thödol* Op. 74 (1974), a setting of the Tibetan Book of the Dead (see Example 4.3). As Oesch states, the work is based on the actual study of rituals in Nepalese monasteries,[53] so once again, it is the product of deep immersion within the culture represented. That said, I cannot deny certain reservations against the recreation of actual religious rituals, particularly death rituals, in a secular context, essentially for aesthetic delectation. Would we be happy with the enactment of Christian funerals in comparable contexts? Having said that, his period of study in Nepalese monasteries may have given Bergman reasons to feel justified in his approach.

Like his other interests, Bergman continued with his studies of musical traditions for the rest of his life. A late flowering is the dance poem *Le voyage* Op. 142 (1999), written as a reflection of a journey around the world with his wife-to-be (his fourth), which uses musical impressions received during various parts of the journey for the individual movements, namely Aboriginal Landscape, Maori Fantasy, Polynesian Rhythms, À la

---

[53] Ibid., p. 191.

Example 4.3 Erik Bergman, *Bardo Thödol* Op. 74, 1st movt., bars 10ff.

Buenos Aires, Samba and finally South African Finale. The accusation of 'tourist folklore' is difficult to avoid, despite Bergman's lifelong and undeniably deep immersion in different musical cultures and traditions.

Cosmopolitanism III: rediscovering the self

What these examples speak to is the endeavour to make the other the self. What is equally evident in Bergman's work, however, is the attempt to make the self other, and it is arguably this which makes Bergman a true cosmopolitan. It is only in his late phase that Bergman (re)engages with the music and sounds of his native environment or at least closer to home. As Juha Torvinen has shown, works such as *Lapponia* Op. 76 (1975) and *Loleila* Op.75 (1974) take up the yoiks of the Sami, and *Arctica* Op. 90 (1979) and *Borealis* Op. 101 (1983), among many others, respond to the Nordic landscape.[54] To this can be added works such as *Lemminkäinen* Op. 103 (1984) and *Lament and Incantation* Op. 106 (1984), which, perhaps to the surprise of those who saw in Bergman only the international avant-gardist, engage with the runic chanting of the *Kalevala*, hitherto more likely to be associated with nationalist aesthetics. In contrast to what I have earlier described as the self-exoticising of musical nationalism, Bergman's exploration of the self is clearly informed by the experiences he gained with encountering the other. He is not interested in easily codifiable and superficial local colour but instead in uncovering genuinely strange but beautiful sounds. Listening to the bare sonorities and minute fluctuations around single notes in *Lament and Incantation* Op. 106 (1984) (see Example 4.4), for instance, with its exploration of phonetic materials and vocal techniques, is quite unlike any other musical experience, including that of Bergman's own *Det Sjungende Trädet*, for instance, with its fluid and lyrical vocal lines which sometimes verge on the conventional and even routine. An example of an exploration of the natural environment is *Borealis* Op. 101 for two pianos and percussion (1983), which seems to consist of nothing but elemental noise, from the minutest murmur to a deafening roar, often changing its nature almost imperceptibly over long stretches of time.

To be clear, Bergman did not hail from the Far North, and he certainly wasn't a Sami. Nykarleby lies in central Finland (on a North–South axis) and although Bergman travelled frequently to Sápmi (the area inhabited by the Sami, formerly called Lapland),[55] which played a pivotal role in his late work, he cannot be considered a local of the region. Nevertheless, there is clearly a sense in which Bergman is intently observing and listening to the world around him in one place and over long periods of time, rather than, or in addition to, travelling far and wide.

---

[54] Juha Torvinen, 'The Tone of the North', *Finnish Music Quarterly* (September 2010), http://www.fmq.fi/2010/09/the-tone-of-the-north/.

[55] Oesch, 'Exotisches Bei Erik Bergman', p. 183.

Example 4.4 Erik Bergman, *Lament and Incantation* Op. 106, Incantation, beginning.

What is most striking about these late works – as of any earlier period in his career – is that instead of adjusting the musical material to his established methods and preconceived ideas, the composer allowed himself to be changed by *it*, to start afresh. As I have shown, what distinguishes pieces such as *Rubaiyat* or *Lapponia*, to name works initiating a new phase or strand in Bergman's work, is that, beyond some technical features that point to Bergman's authorship, they sound radically unlike any of his, or anybody else's, earlier work.

In my view, this reconceptualization of the self is the true sign of the cosmopolitan. Modifying Bhabha's[56] statement, one could say thus: cosmopolitanism must always *end* at home! As pointed out above, it is a common fallacy to believe that cosmopolitanism involves a denigration of local attachments in favour of lofty notions of 'world citizenship'. All that this would amount to is a dichotomy between the local and the international, which more or less reproduces the binary division between self and other characteristic of nationalism. A cosmopolitan response is the recognition that we are all locals and that we have to learn to appreciate both what we share and what is different and unique to each of us. This process requires us both to encounter the other and to look at the self through the eyes of the other, and this is what I believe Bergman's exploration of the sounds and musics of distant places and, following this, of his more immediate environment teaches us.

As pointed out above, this is not to deny problematic aspects. Clearly, questions have to be asked about Bergman's activities in Nazi Germany, his representation of the Tibetan Book of the Dead, the somewhat shallow musical snapshots of *Le voyage* or maybe too about his representation of the Sami and the Far North. But the point cannot be a simple alternative between hagiography and sanctimony. More than anything else, cosmopolitanism involves a process of accommodation, negotiation, mediation – and learning. What characterizes Bergman's approach more than anything else is going beyond what is customary and expected: beyond romantic nationalism to embrace the international avant-garde, beyond the international avant-garde to embrace the global, beyond the global to encounter the strangeness within the self. In many respects, Bergman's personal development once again mirrors the wider transformations of modernist musical geography, from nationalism through internationalism, globalism to a reappraisal of the self. Yet,

---

[56] Bhabha, *The Location of Culture*, p. xv.

more than in the evolution of musical style, he is not so much retracing but anticipating and pushing beyond general developments. It is in this area too that his personal perspective, impacted as it is by his experiences as a member of the Swedish minority in Finland, with its specific history and marginal position vis-à-vis the centres of musical modernism, comes to the fore.

5 Sharing a stage

The growing proximity between modernism and popular music

David Metzer

New York City. Merkin Concert Hall. 21 February 2013. I have been to countless new music concerts, but none like this one. I expressly went to the concert because I knew that it would be different, yet the differences were more striking than I had anticipated. In the lobby before the show, it seemed as if this was a typical new music concert. There was a familiar cast of characters: the guy in his sixties with a forlorn ponytail who had chronicled more new music than I probably ever will and the young composition student looking around for student friends. But then I noticed the hipsters, guys with manicured beards and stovepipe jeans. That there were hipsters there was not surprising. What caught me off guard was how many were chatting away in the lobby. At one moment, I was in Merkin Concert Hall, the next it seemed as if I was in a Brooklyn club.

The concert was a little bit of both. The first half of the show was devoted to the music of the young Brazilian composer Marcos Balter, performed by the new music group Ensemble Dal Niente. This could have been the beginning of any new music concert, and an especially engaging opening with Balter's imaginative works. The second half brought to the stage the indie rock group Deerhoof – the draw for the hipsters in the lobby. Merkin Concert Hall became a club, although the acoustics were a little too alive for an amplified rock group, especially one that juxtaposes blasts of noise and heavy drumming with pop sing-songy vocals. How to finish the concert? Perhaps the only way was to bring everyone together on stage with a piece for both ensembles by Balter.

So, yes, a different type of new music concert, but, it turns out, far from a unique one. In this and other concerts, the Ecstatic Music Festival has put down bridges between the new music and indie rock worlds. So too have other festivals and new music groups. Several composers also travel back and forth between the two worlds. Then there is me, the musicologist. As much as I enjoyed the music of Balter and Deerhoof, I did not go to the concert specifically to hear either one. I instead went to experience first-hand an idea that I had been contemplating, an idea that the concert captured.

That idea is a growing proximity between modernist music and popular idioms. The two were nothing but proximate in the Ecstatic Music Festival concert – sharing the same stage. They, however, are not always so pressed up against each other. The closeness between the two takes different forms. In my book *Musical Modernism at the Turn of the Twenty-First Century*, I discussed one such form: the interest in certain musical and aesthetic ideals shared by musicians in both idioms. My references to this proximity, though, were brief, quickly closed off with a remark that this could be a topic for another book.[1] The topic is indeed large enough to warrant a book. In regard to popular styles, it covers a range of music, from 1960s groups like the Beatles and The Velvet Underground to present-day indie bands. It is also a largely unexplored topic. While connections between the two musical realms have been touched upon here and there in discussions of individual bands or composers, the increased closeness between new music and popular styles has not been identified as a larger historical development.[2] Once ascertained as such, questions quickly arise. What does that nearness say about the contemporary musical scene? How does it fit into the history of modernism?

These are pertinent questions for a collection entitled *Transformations of Musical Modernism*. The proximity between modernist and popular idioms not only reveals a modernism that has been transformed but it also transforms our conceptions of modernism. To appreciate the extent of those transformations and to answer the above questions, I will approach the topic from two contrasting perspectives. The first is a theoretical perspective that focuses on mutual interests in musical material and aesthetic ideals. To get at those affinities, I will discuss the lines of inquiry that have crossed the two idioms. The second approach looks at what is happening on the ground, that is, at concerts like the Ecstatic Music Festival show at Merkin Concert Hall. I will examine the infrastructure of festivals, clubs, record labels and magazines that has emerged to support the connections between new music and popular styles and consider the types of musical and cultural connections that those organizations are making between the two.

******

My studies of modernism build upon a conventional understanding of the concept, that of the far-reaching departures in musical language that took

---

[1] David Metzer, *Musical Modernism at the Turn of the Twenty-First Century* (Cambridge University Press, 2009), p. 245.

[2] Christopher Ballantine has recently offered an illuminating discussion of the intersections between modernist and popular idioms. Ballantine, 'Modernism and Popular Music', *Journal of the Royal Musical Association*, 139/1 (2014), 200–4.

place around the beginning of the twentieth century. I, however, depart from that standard view by focusing on what I call lines of inquiry. The inquiries are into compositional and aesthetic ideals of modernism, and the lines are formed by works that explore those ideals over the course of decades. The inquiries deal with such states as sonic flux, fragmentation, purity, density and simultaneity. Let's look at the first of these, sonic flux, which is the conception of sound as a restless realm of constant transformation in which sounds are always changing in terms of colour, density and volume. Modernist works of different types have inquired into the mutability of sound. In my book, I pursued a line of that inquiry that extends from the 1920s works of Varèse to recent pieces by Kaija Saariaho, Helmut Lachenmann and Olga Neuwirth. All three composers expand Varèse's vision of sound as existing in a state of perpetual metamorphosis by shaping sound masses that significantly change over the course of a work.[3]

The moulding of sound masses evokes what has been called musical material, the stuff not only of works but also of theories of modernism. Adorno, for example, described modernist pieces as capturing advanced material, the most challenging sounds and ideas existing at a particular historical moment.[4] In the visual arts, Clement Greenberg described the history of modernism as the gradual stripping away of the extraneous to get at the 'pure' material of painting, which consists of line, colour and texture.[5] The concept of lines of inquiry has similarities with these older theories of material but also important differences. A key difference is that of stylistic range. For both Adorno and Greenberg, 'modernism' and 'material' are synonymous. Advanced or pure materials are the stock of modernism, and modernism is the way of accessing advanced material or achieving pure forms of it. Neither type of material could ever appear in popular genres. If anything, they would be inimical to popular styles. Adorno and Greenberg would most likely find a closeness between the two absurd. More than that, the two critics used modernism as a refuge from the kitsch of mass culture.

---

[3] Metzer, *Musical Modernism*, pp. 175–237.
[4] Theodor W. Adorno, *Philosophy of New Music*, trans. and ed. Robert Hullot-Kentor (Minneapolis, MN: University of Minnesota Press, 2006), pp. 31–4. For discussions of Adorno's concept of advanced material, see Carl Dahlhaus, 'Adornos Begriff des musikalischen Materials' in *Schönberg und andere: Gesammelte Aufsätze zur Neuen Musik* (Mainz: Schott, 1978), pp. 336–9; Max Paddison, *Adorno's Aesthetics of Music* (Cambridge University Press, 1993), pp. 88–9 and p. 149; and Metzer, *Musical Modernism*, p. 5 and p. 9.
[5] Clement Greenberg, 'Modernist Painting' in John O'Brien (ed.), *Clement Greenberg: The Collected Essays and Criticism, Modernism with a Vengeance (1957–1969)*, 4 vols. (University of Chicago Press, 1993), vol. IV, pp. 83–93.

My theory of lines of inquiry, in contrast, opens up to popular genres, or I should say that the inquiries that I have followed have done so. Inquiry is a concept foreign to Adorno and Greenberg's ideas of material. Adorno, for example, describes advanced material as rarefied elements that a small number of innovative works can catch only particles of, while Greenberg presents modernism as an independent and inevitable historical process. Inquiries, on the other hand, are open, broad and unpredictable, guided by musicians' curiosity rather than a set historical path. The results can be advanced and pure as well as simplistic and dead end. With curiosity as the guide and rich ideas as the field, the inquiries that I have discussed cannot be confined to any one genre. They may have begun in modernist idioms, but they have long since been taken up by musicians working in popular genres. I would like to present three brief examples of these inquiries and compare how popular musicians have pursued them to the explorations conducted by modernist composers. In particular, I would like to show what popular musicians, far from merely copying modernist precedents, have added to those inquiries.

The first to be discussed is the inquiry into sonic flux, and the first group is Sonic Youth. The pairing is far from a surprising choice. The band is one of the seminal noise rock groups and known for the swelling, mercurial sounds they create from the standard rock setup of guitars, bass and drums.[6] In their first press release in 1981, guitarist Thurston Moore described the band's sound in this way: 'Crashing mashing intensified dense rhythms juxtaposed with filmic, mood pieces. Evoking an atmosphere that could only be described as expressive fucked-up modernism. And so forth.'[7] Of course, the word 'modernism' sticks out in that blare of rich adjectives and nouns. This would be far from last time that the word has found its way into descriptions of the group, be it those by the band members or press.

What is so 'expressive' about the group's brand of modernism can be heard in the song 'Silver Rocket' (1988). Typical of many songs in the post-punk scene of New York, it has its punk bearings. In particular, 'Silver Rocket' is similar to the amphetamine versions of older rock styles perfected by New York punk groups like the Ramones. As with that group's aphoristic blasts, it is fast, raucous and short, and keeps to a basic verse/chorus form. Sonic Youth, though, add their own touches to these punk trappings. The chord choices (A minor/F major in the verse and C major/E♭ major in the chorus) are not the staples of the 'one-chord wonders'

[6] For a discussion of the sonic qualities of the band's music, see Caroline O'Meara, 'Clarity and Order in Sonic Youth's Early Noise Rock', *Journal of Popular Music Studies*, 25 (2013), 13–30.
[7] Alec Foege, *Confusion Is Next: The Sonic Youth Story* (New York: St. Martin's Press, 1994), p. 71.

mockingly prized in punk, nor are the group's characteristic alternate tunings.[8] In addition, the poetic snarls – 'nymphoid clamor' and 'psycho helmet' – are out of place in the blunt crassness of punk lyrics.[9]

What especially separates 'Silver Rocket' from its punk forebears is Sonic Youth's 'modernism'. After only a minute and a half, the tune falls into a sonic storm created by feedback miasmas, swirling high guitar lines and drum barrages. Varèse's depiction of sound as a realm of colliding and repelling sound masses does not seem so far off here, as heard in the clash between the rumbling guitars and drums and high swirling lines; nor does the modernist line of inquiry into sound as a state of flux. The guitar sonorities constantly change in terms of colour, register and density, and the feedback forms wafting, drifting sonic clouds. This is a space where sounds exist in a state of unrelenting fluidity. It is also a state of disintegration, as, after a minute (a third of the overall length of the song), the streams of sound dwindle, which is typical of modernist works using sound masses. To take the example of two seminal sound mass compositions, the sonorities in Ligeti's *Atmospheres* and Penderecki's *Threnody for the Victims of Hiroshima* build into dense, swelling clouds, but they eventually diminish to traces. As the mass in 'Silver Rocket' crumbles, the alternating chords of the verse come in as an underpinning and lead back to the song we knew before this spell of sonic flux began.

There are several popular music precedents for 'Silver Rocket' – like the feedback-infused solos of Jimi Hendrix – but, I believe, that placing the song in the inquiry into sonic flux brings out how multidimensional and volatile the sound worlds created by the group in this and other songs can be. It also reveals what the group adds to that inquiry, what is so unique about what it has to say about sonic instability. One striking feature of 'Silver Rocket' is the compressed juxtaposition between the hard-driving, motor-like rock song and the suspended welter of the middle section. Modernist works exploring sonic flux, or Hendrix's songs, for that matter, do not contrast the two – regularity and flux – so abruptly or severely. With such a sharp juxtaposition, sound comes across as all the more unstable and changeable.[10]

Let's stick with inquiries into sound and stay in late 1980s New York, but we will move from rock to hip hop. Public Enemy's CDs *It Takes a Nation*

---

[8] The Adverts built a song around that idea, 'One Chord Wonders', which includes more than one chord.

[9] Punk, of course, had its poetic lyricists, notably Patti Smith and Richard Hell.

[10] The connections with modernism are directly made in Sonic Youth's recording *Goodbye Twentieth Century*, which includes performances of works by John Cage, Christian Wolff, Cornelius Cardew and Steve Reich, among others.

of Millions to Hold Us Back (1988) and *Fear of a Black Planet* (1990) have attained the status of classics. The accolades typically single out the sound of the albums, particularly the thick mixes of samples, beats and rap. In his review of *Fear of a Black Planet*, Simon Reynolds called the recording a 'work of unprecedented density for hip hop'.[11] Writing almost twenty years later, Alex Ross accorded the CD a broader historical significance, holding it up as 'one of most densely packed sonic assemblages in music history'.[12] As for the group, MC Chuck D referred to the album as 'probably the most elaborate smorgasbord of sound that we did' and added that it was 'completely an album of found sounds'.[13] Just how packed and elaborate the mix of found sounds is can be heard in 'Night of the Living Baseheads' (1988), which rap historian Tricia Brown, writing in the early 1990s, called 'one of the most dense and cacophonous raps to date'. She estimated that there are around forty-five sampled tracks in the recording.[14] On the mix of samples and original music tracks in the recording, rap producer Eric Sadler came up with this vivid description: 'You got stuff darting in and out absolutely everywhere. It's like somebody throwing rice at you. You have to grab every little piece and put it in the right place like in a puzzle. Very complicated.'[15]

The above comments draw attention to two inquiries: those into sonic density and the use of found sounds. Earlier modernist idioms twinned the two inquiries, particularly *musique concrète*. Pierre Schaefer's works, for example, capture the hectic clamour of modern life by using and piling on bits of real-world sounds, including voices, trains and sirens. Public Enemy stands out in the history of these inquiries, not only by pairing them but also by pushing them to extremes. At such extremes, one inquiry could diminish the other. The denser the mix, the less likely that individual found sounds can be spotted and recognized. The clearer the individual sounds, the less thick the mix is likely to be. Public Enemy, though, pulls off those extremes. In the crowded mix of 'Night of the Living Baseheads', samples emerge here and there, bits of political speeches, horn lines, wails and street noise. The samples are often fleeting, but they can be recognized. Some come across as a general type of sound – a political speech, horn line – or a general style of song, like funk or soul. Other samples can be identified as a

---

[11] Simon Reynolds, 'Review: Public Enemy, *Fear of a Black Planet*,' *Melody Maker* (April 1990).
[12] Alex Ross, *Listen to This* (New York: Farrar, Straus and Giroux, 2010), p. 60.
[13] Kembrew McLeod and Peter DiCola, *Creative License: The Law and Culture of Digital Sampling* (Durham, NC: Duke University Press, 2011), p. 25.
[14] Tricia Rose, *Black Noise: Rap Music and Black Culture in Contemporary America* (Hanover and London: Wesleyan University Press, 1994), p. 80. For a list of individual samples, see the website 'whosampled.com', which lists around twenty-four samples.
[15] Quoted in Rose, *Black Noise*, p. 80.

specific sound – a particular political speech (like the samples of speeches by Jesse Jackson and Khalid Abdul Muhammad) or horn line (the abrasive two-note riff from The J.B.'s' 'The Grunt') or a specific song, like those by James Brown and Public Enemy itself.

Rather than cancelling each other out, the inquiries combine to make incisive cultural commentary about racial injustice in American society and the potential for violence.[16] The dense mix, for example, captures the unstable, threatening qualities of noise. As if the group's name was not menacing enough, it brandished the word 'noise' in tracks like 'Bring the Noise' (sampled in 'Night of the Living Baseheads') and took pride in their music being dismissed as noise, which, for them, was a powerful and powerfully disruptive sound.[17] The noise made from found sounds could also be political. Many of the samples in 'Night of the Living Baseheads' have strong political associations. Public Enemy draws upon songs with connections to the 1960s and 1970s Civil Rights and Black Power movements, including James Brown's 'Soul Power' and 'Get Up, Get Into It, Get Involved' and Sly and the Family Stone's 'You Can Make It If You Try'.[18] The songs preached self-empowerment and reliance, beliefs upheld as necessary in overturning centuries of racial injustice. 'Night of the Living Baseheads' asserts that that message needed to be heard again in contending with the crack cocaine epidemic afflicting urban black neighbourhoods in the late 1980s. One way of hearing it again – and a way very much of that time and not the 1960s – was to place samples of those songs in a vibrant, ever-changing mix, in which their messages join and fortify a new attack on racial inequality.[19]

For my final example of modernist inquiries taken up in popular music, I will jump across genre lines to electronic dance music and into the twenty-first century. That electronic dance music would appear in this discussion should not come as a surprise. Many DJs have settled into what one critic has called the 'shadowy divide between electronic and modernist

---

[16] For a discussion of the social commentary made by the song and video, see Rose, *Black Noise*, pp. 115–23.

[17] In the video for 'Night of the Living Baseheads', the group mocks those who call their music 'noise'.

[18] Some of these samples appear in the group's 'Anti-High Blood Pressure Encounter Mix' version of the song.

[19] Public Enemy's recordings could also be placed in another modernist context, that of African American modernism. The musical lineage of that tradition would include Louis Armstrong, Duke Ellington, Charlie Parker, Miles Davis, Ornette Coleman, Sun Ra and Anthony Braxton. In particular, connections can be drawn between the sonic density in Public Enemy's recordings and those of free jazz musicians like Coleman, Sun Ra and Braxton. On the general concept of an African American modernism, see Paul Gilroy, *The Black Atlantic: Modernity and Double-Consciousness* (Cambridge, MA: Harvard University Press, 1993).

contemporary classical'.[20] Why that divide is so shadowy is that DJs have taken up the inquiry into sonic flux, as to be expected for musicians who assemble, combine and shape electronic sounds. One of those DJs is Richard David James, better known as Aphex Twin. Rather than discussing his mutable, fascinating sound worlds, I will focus on his participation in another modernist inquiry. His 'Cock/Ver10' (2001) joins the inquiry into simultaneity, that is, of superimposing highly contrasting layers. Charles Ives, Conlon Nancarrow and Elliott Carter are three modernist composers who took up this inquiry. They created dense textures by overlaying strands separated by metre, tempo or style, among other elements. Aphex Twin creates similar contrasts. 'Cock/Ver10' has two basic layers. One is the fast-tempo line made up of percussive blips that does not follow any regular, let alone discernible, metre or phrase structure. This layer unfolds throughout the whole song, but never once repeats a particular pattern. The second layer is the opposite of the first. It is a repeated slow-tempo melodic line harmonized in B minor and that follows a set metre and falls into a four-measure phrase. For electronic dance music fans, there is also a stylistic contrast. The first layer evokes the fractured, askew breakbeats of hard-driving dance styles like drum 'n' bass, while the second one suggests more relaxed, chill or ambient tracks that are often used to conjure moments of emotional reflection, like the 'melancholy' that Aphex Twin said fills the album featuring 'Cock/Ver10'.[21] The two styles had certainly been mixed before, notably in the works of Goldie and other DJs from the mid-1990s as well as in early recordings by Aphex Twin, but rarely is the juxtaposition between them so severe.

Set apart by tempo, rhythm and style, the two layers appear as if on distant planes, an impression reinforced by there being no type of interlocking between them, like shared accented notes. Nor does the slower layer return at any predictable moments within the jittery percussive stream. With 'Cock/Ver 10', listeners of Aphex Twin's music enjoy an experience that those of Ives, Nancarrow and Carter's works know well, that is, the experience of being between two or more separate planes and never being able to tie them together for any one moment.[22]

So what to make of these examples? First, I should be clear about what *not* to make of them. I am not saying that these three songs are modernist.

[20] Kafka Garden, 'Press Quotes', http://www.kafkagarden.com/quotes.html (accessed 24 March 2015).

[21] Paul Lester, 'Tank Boy', *The Guardian* (5 October 2001), http://www.guardian.co.uk/culture/2001/oct/05/artsfeatures3 (accessed 24 March 2015).

[22] For his part, Aphex Twin has not drawn a connection between his music and that of Ives, Nancarrow and Carter. He has, though, made some linkages with new music. In particular, he collaborated with Philip Glass in creating a new version of his 'Icct Hedral'.

They remain part of their own genres. Nor do I want to give the impression that these genres have been 'colonized' by modernism, that they have come under the influence of a distant modernist power. Far from being a power (distant or not), modernism has little acknowledged presence in such works for most popular musicians, and listeners of that music would not identify those elements as modernist – different and experimental perhaps, but not modernist. The unawareness of a modernist connection results in part from a lack of familiarity with modernist works. It also shows how integrated the ideas in modernist lines of inquiry have become in popular genres, so much so that they do not seem to have come from some remote stylistic land. Finally, I do not want to suggest that what I am describing is yet another case of the mixing of genres, say a bit of modernist collage in a hip hop track. Consistent with the idea of lines of inquiry, the affinities between modernist idioms and popular genres come more from the mutual interests of musicians in both categories, interests that are most often explored independently.

As to my question of what to make of these examples, it would be best to answer it from the perspectives of both a historian of modernism and one of popular music. For the former, the examples show the range of modernist inquiries. So broad has that range become that the inquiries can no longer be considered exclusively modernist. They may have originated in modernism and have become strongly linked to that music, but they are now part of the rich and vital kinds of musical creativity being carried on today across genres. Once revealed, these cross-genre inquiries can significantly transform our conceptions of modernism. Rather than being the withdrawn and dwindling, if not dead, music that it has been made out to be, modernism emerges as an enduring wellspring of ideas and a music interacting with other genres. This is a new view of modernism, and one that enhances larger arguments made by me and others that modernism was not supplanted by a postmodern movement or period in the 1960s and 1970s but rather that it continues to be a force in contemporary arts.[23]

There may be no such grand historical conclusions for popular music scholars, but nonetheless these cross-genre inquiries can offer them new perspectives. In particular, the inquiries can inspire different ways of understanding aspects of popular music idioms. For example, we can be aware of the fascination with the idea of sound as a state of constant flux

---

[23] Heinrich Klotz, *Kunst im 20. Jahrhundert: Moderne-Postmoderne-Zweite Moderne* (Munich: C. H. Beck, 1994); Marjorie Perloff, *21st-Century Modernism: The 'New' Poetics* (Oxford: Blackwell, 2002); and Claus-Steffen Mahnkopf, Frank Cox and Wolfram Schurig, *Facets of the Second Modernity. New Music and Aesthetics in the 21st Century* (Hofheim: Volke Verlag, 2008).

and examine the similar and different ways musicians in diverse genres have realized that idea.

I also believe that these cross-genre inquiries offer a way of dealing with one of the biggest critical challenges facing us today, that is, pluralism. We are frequently told that we live in a time of unprecedented stylistic plurality. That may be the case, but we need to come to terms with that diversity, to figure out what is going on in the stylistic sprawl. There has been theoretical wrestling with pluralism, notably theories of postmodernism that concentrate on the binding of stylistic and historical fragments in the arts and architecture that become prominent in the 1960s and 1970s.[24] Such theories, though, rest upon the ideas that modernism has been depleted, being, at best, another historical element in these combinations. That conclusion obviously misses how energizing modernist elements continue to be in contemporary arts.[25] One approach to dealing with pluralism is by drawing connections, to reveal the links, say, between Varèse and Sonic Youth. Only by doing such basic mapping can we detect larger patterns and groupings in that plurality. We can also perceive historical shifts occurring within it, like the growing proximity between modernism and popular genres.

So this is my grand critical call. It sounds like I have taken a page from E.M. Forster's *Howard's End*: connect – 'only connect'. My call may also come across as idealistic, if not naïve. All we have to do is to connect the pieces, to put together the seemingly distant and random, and all will be revealed. The plural realm will become a beautiful mosaic in which we can see fascinating patterns and shapes. We might not ever get that mosaic, but we can see patterns and groupings, as I have shown in this chapter and in my work on contemporary modernist music. These groupings, for example, can lead us to question some of the lines that have been firmly drawn in histories of post-1945 music, like that between modernism and postmodernism. Instead of that boundary, we can start to see new larger patterns. The best example of such a pattern is the increasing closeness between modernist idioms and popular genres. This mapping, though, needs to be aware of questions of balance and influence that arise between the connected pieces, as I was earlier in discussing how to understand the role of modernist idioms in the growing adjacency with popular styles. The drawing of lines of connection is part of the basic work that historians need to do in confronting the pluralist expanse surrounding us.

---

[24] Charles Jencks, *What Is Post-Modernism?* (New York and London: St. Martin's Press, 1986); Kenneth Gloag, *Postmodernism in Music* (Cambridge University Press, 2012).

[25] For more on my questioning of the rise of a postmodern movement or culture, see Metzer, *Musical Modernism*, pp. 101–3, 137–43 and 241–7.

Musicians, though, are busy doing that work. No better example can be found than the transcription of 'Cock/Ver10' by the new music ensemble Alarm Will Sound. The scattershot electronic blips are now played by strings and winds as well as through the heroically hyperactive efforts of the trap drum kit player. Alarm Will Sound has a repertoire that includes works by Varèse, Stockhausen and Nancarrow. Drawing upon their deep familiarity with modernist idioms, they apparently heard the modernist affinities in Aphex Twin's music; in other words, they, like me, made a connection between the two, a link that they brought out by recording a whole album of Aphex Twin transcriptions.

A new infrastructure

With Alarm Will Sound, I would like to turn my attention to the infrastructure of ensembles, festivals and magazines mentioned above, to see how it has constructed the relationship between modernism and popular genres. The infrastructure supports a new creative space that has emerged over the last decade. The space welcomes listeners and musicians of new music and popular genres and smoothes over the once imposing lines that separated the two. What is distinctively new about this space is not the mixing of the two categories, which had been going on well before the space appeared, but rather how easily new music and individual pop genres coexist. In this space, new music, hip hop, indie rock and electronic dance music are all considered to be part of the search for the new and different. A hip hop mix can be regarded as innovative and noteworthy as a string quartet or electronic dance music track. Rarely has the new sheltered a creative space as broad and inclusive as the one being shaped by these ensembles, composers, magazines and clubs. That there has been so much activity over such a short period of time in that space shows how inspiring it is and how much larger and more important it is likely to become.

To get to know this space, I will first turn to the various participants in it. They are part of what I will be calling a new scene that is largely based in New York City, although similar activities are occurring throughout North America and Europe. A good place to begin is with some of the ensembles active in this scene. Although I will be focusing on ensembles that have formed in recent years, I should mention Bang On A Can, a group founded in 1987 and that, through its links with rock styles and the festivals that it has staged, has laid the foundation for these younger ensembles. To return to a group that I have mentioned a few times so far, Alarm Will Sound claims that its album of Aphex Twin transcriptions gave them 'an important platform from which to pursue a wide-ranging artistic vision that doesn't worry too much about genre – electronic vs. acoustic, high-modernist vs. pop-influenced'.[26] As we will see, not many other participants in this scene 'worry much about genre'. They move freely between genres, and that freedom has become a mandate, if not mantra, for the scene. For example, in its mission statement, the American Contemporary Music Ensemble declares that it 'does not subscribe to one stylistic movement or genre'.[27] The string quartet ETHEL bills itself as 'a leading force in concert music's reengagement with musical vernaculars, fusing diverse traditions into a vibrant sound that resonates with audiences the world over'.[28] As with Alarm Will Sound, the wide-ranging repertoires of both groups support their claims.

Turning to composers, Judd Greenstein claims that he and like-minded colleagues do not so much cross genres but have instead moved beyond them, what he calls 'post-genre'.[29] He has even gone so far as to describe 'the absence of genre in a genuinely post-genre world', an observation that he says is so obvious as to no longer be 'interesting'.[30] Contrary to such assertions, the composers in this scene have been placed in a new genre, what has been called 'alt-classical' or 'indie-classical'.[31] Many of them, though, have shunned the terms. None other than Nico Muhly, the poster boy of indie-classical, has argued that the term is a trendy name of use only to 'PR people' and that it says little about the musicians and works that it purports to describe.[32] Other composers, however, have used the term. Both 'indie-classical' and 'post-genre', for example, appear in Greenstein's promotional materials for his New Amsterdam Records, a label devoted to the music of composers involved in this new scene.[33] So who are the composers who have willingly or unwillingly been put in these categories? Some are classically trained composers who have connections with the indie rock scene, including Muhly, Missy Mazzoli and Owen Pallett. Others are electronic dance music or indie rock musicians making their

[26] Alarm Will Sound, 'About', http://www.alarmwillsound.com/about.php (accessed 24 March 2015).
[27] American Contemporary Music Ensemble, 'About', http://www.acmemusic.org/about.html.
[28] Ethel Quartet, 'About', http://www.ethelcentral.org/about/band/ (accessed 28 June 2012).
[29] Judd Greenstein, 'Why?' http://www.juddgreenstein.com/why.html (accessed 24 March 2015).
[30] Kaufman Music Center, 'News', 22 January 2013, http://www.kaufmanmusiccenter.org/kc/article/ecstatic-music-festival-curator-judd-greenstein-introduces-the-2013-festiva (accessed 24 March 2015).
[31] Greg Sandow claims to have coined the label 'alt-classical'. 'Rebirth: The Future of Classical Music – Rebirth and Resistance', http://www.gregsandow.com/BookBlog/RevisedCh1Riffs.pdf (accessed 24 March 2015).
[32] Nico Muhly, 'Hindi Classical', http://nicomuhly.com/news/2012/hindi-classical/ (accessed 24 March 2015).
[33] New Amsterdam Records, 'Judd Greenstein', http://newamrecords.com/judd-greenstein (accessed 24 March 2015).

way into concert music, like Dan Deacon, Bryce Dessner and Sufjan Stevens. The coming-and-goings between the two worlds are getting to the point that as a *Pitchfork* article put it: 'Lately, it is hard to even tell an indie rock musician and a composer apart.'[34]

Many of these composers appear in a group of festivals that are an important part of the infrastructure of this new scene, including the Ecstatic Music Festival (curated by Greenstein), MusicNOW and Crossing Brooklyn Ferry. Then there are clubs that programme both new music and innovative stripes of popular genres. The flagship club is Le Poisson Rouge in Greenwich Village, in which during the course of a week you could hear Xenakis, indie rock and underground hip hop. According to co-founder David Handler, the club caters to the 'curious listener who wants to push their palette' and 'inhabit a different musical space than they are typically used to'.[35] Finally, I would like to mention the UK-based magazine *The Wire*, which offers readers 'adventures in sound and music'. Adventurous is perhaps the best way to describe the coverage of genres in the magazine, which can jump between modernist idioms, noise rock, micro house, drone music, early computer music and sound art.

So there is a quick tour of this new musical scene. Much of what has been written about it comes from journalists, blogs and social media. These sources largely parrot the line about being post-genre. A few writers have upheld indie-classical as saving classical music or being the future of classical music.[36] This new scene demands a more critical look than that provided by catchy slogans like 'post-genre' or 'indie-classical', although, as we will see, an examination of both concepts does offer insights into the new scene. A critical perspective can be gained by taking up two topics key to my theoretical approach, those of material and pluralism, as well as a concept central to the new scene, that is, genre. Another relevant topic is that of separation, the degree to which new music is removed from or integrated into public musical life.

Regarding 'material', musicians and writers in the new scene have little to say about it. The term itself is rarely mentioned, although there are references to elements that could be considered as material, like beats,

---

[34] Jayson Greene, 'Making Overtures: The Emergence of Indie Classical', *Pitchfork* (28 February 2012), http://pitchfork.com/features/articles/8778-indie-classical/ (accessed 24 March 2015).

[35] Joonbug, 'Joonbug Interview: David Handler, Founder of Le Poisson Rouge', 1 October 2010, http://joonbug.com/newyork/frequency/Joonbug-Interview-David-Handler-Founder-of-Le-Poisson-Rouge/nC7t9xdE94w (accessed 24 March 2015).

[36] Sandow sees alt or indie classical as a promising development for the future of classical music. Greg Sandow, 'Long overdue', 16 November 2009, http://www.artsjournal.com/sandow/2009/11/long_overdue.html (accessed 24 March 2015) and 'Rebirth: The Future of Classical Music – Rebirth and Resistance'.

mixes and types of electronic sounds. What these musicians and writers do have much to say about is genre. Adorno and Greenberg, in contrast, emphasize material over genre. For them, individual genres – opera and string quartet or painting and sculpture – were not as important as the larger modernist project in which both critics placed them. In the new scene, there are several different genres, with musicians freely travelling between them and mixing them. With all that travelling, it is no wonder that musicians and writers in the new scene have emphasized genre. Regarding material, it is the common currency that makes the exchange between genres possible, so common as to go unidentified as such.

In talking about genre, I will consult, to paraphrase Derrida, the 'law' of genre, particularly what have emerged to be the old and new laws of genre.[37] The old law is one of taxonomic purity that upholds genres as discrete categories and depicts works as comfortably fitting into those boxes. Codified into critical theory over the last fifty years, the new law presents genres as fluid, open-ended, promiscuous and hybrid, among other qualities. This view, as Hayden White has remarked, has become the 'rule' for discussing genre today.[38] The rule, though, has become so broadly accepted and unquestioningly applied that genre is in danger of becoming a genre, in the sense of the old and supposedly superseded law. In that past edict, works neatly belonged to genres and little attention was paid to what was going on outside of a genre box or how unstable genre categories actually were. Now genres neatly fit the new standard definitions of genre and those definitions give little idea of what is happening to genres in the larger, broader field surrounding a genre.

The scene in which modernist and popular idioms converge, however, gives us plenty to think about in considering not just the connection between those two idioms but also the status of genre in contemporary arts and our theoretical approaches to genre. The scene, for example, makes us aware of the pluralist space in which genres circulate. Recent theories of genre, on the other hand, do not look out at that space. Pluralism, a reality of contemporary artistic life, is rarely mentioned in genre theory. Nor does that theory account for the types of genre behaviour typical of pluralist spaces. With its emphasis on hybridity, genre theory does capture the mixing of genres that is to be expected in spaces where genres crowd up against each other. It does not, though, describe the connections established between genres that do not blend but that rather stand near to each other and share mutual interests, like those into lines of

---

[37] Jacques Derrida, 'The Law of Genre', *Critical Inquiry*, 7 (1980), 55–81.
[38] Hayden White, 'Anomalies of Genre: The Utility of Theory and History for the Study of Literary Genres', *New Literary History*, 34 (2003), 597–615, p. 602.

inquiry. Proximity and affinity have little currency in contemporary genre theory, unlike hybridity and promiscuity. Also neglected is the expanse of the pluralist realm occupied by genres. The hybrids praised by theories of genre typically involve genres that are close to each other and that can easily fit together, such as romance and comedy with the romantic comedy in film. There is little idea of distant genres, like new music and rock, coming closer together but yet standing apart and therefore no sense of the stretches traversed by those genres in the process of meeting.

So focused are theories of genre on a particular concept of genre, that they disregard what happens to those categories in their larger surroundings. In a pluralist space, genres are both weakened and reinforced. Weakened in the sense that the cluster of defining characteristics of a genre becomes less concentrated and distinct when a genre is continuously interacting with other ones, be it actual mixing or the increased proximity described in this chapter. The critical ideal of hybridity does not let on to that effacement. It instead upholds blending as the defining characteristic of genres. If anything, mixing makes genres stronger, much like cross-breeding supposedly creates healthy and resilient mutts. Yet with either thick mixtures or increased adjacency, the identities of the individual genres involved in these connections become less clear. We have less sense of what those categories mean in the blur of pluralism.

In a pluralist realm, genres may be weakened from within, but they are also strengthened from without. They are reinforced by the need for known categories, that is, to have contexts in which to group works. Genres are born from that need, and it is more fundamental than any law of genre, old or new. The need is especially pressing in a pluralist environment, where there are myriad categories and the lines between them are obscured. So although the defining features within a genre may have become less clear, the constant references to and reliance on genres give them a firm presence. They serve as landmarks around which listeners orient themselves. The larger and more diverse the terrain, the more important the landmarks. Genres play that part throughout the new scene. The club Le Poisson Rouge and the magazine *The Wire*, for example, emphasize genre in describing either the line-up for a week's concerts or categories for CD reviews. Given the different types of music that they cover, the club and magazine have to offer patrons and readers a quick and clear idea of what they will be encountering. A mere mention of rock, new music or hip hop can do just that. It does not matter how unconventional the songs in those genres may be. The genre names alone say and do so much. With this in mind, the proclamations of this new scene being 'post-genre' appear rather rash, if not self-congratulatory. There is no getting beyond genre.

Speaking of irksome phrases, there is that other one: indie-classical. Like Nico Muhly, I groan when I hear it. The phrase may very well be, as Muhly claims, a flashy publicity label, but its brief flash illuminates much about the role of genre in both the new scene and surrounding pluralist world. First, the phrase shows genres continuing to fulfil their fundamental roles, once again very much needed in a pluralist world. Just as with the creation of genres over centuries, what struck many as a new type of music appeared, so a new genre category was formed to distinguish it from other types of music. In this case, the age-old need for classification is met by a new type of classification, one befitting a pluralist environment. As a prefix 'indie' – be it for classical or rock music – does not hold much stylistic information. It instead defines genre along different lines, which is what makes it apt for a pluralist world in which the stylistic profiles of genres grow less clearly defined.

The initial line drawn by 'indie' was an industry one: the distribution between independent production and corporate labels. That line, though, has grown fainter with the increased cooperation between indie and corporate labels, and it has become even dimmer with internet distribution. Now anyone – big stars and nobodies can release their own recordings online; no recording company is needed. 'Indie', though, has drawn a deeper cultural line. As scholars have discussed, it has served as an oppositional term, setting the arts on the indie side apart from the mainstream, which is depicted as the mass production of conventional, conformist popular culture goods.[39] The two sides of the line, it should be said, are far from well defined and are malleable. Those identifying with indie, for example, often construe the mainstream to be whatever they need it to be to make their points, which is easy to do with such a large and amorphous category. Indie, on the other hand, is often defined by what it is not – not the mainstream, whatever that exactly is. Drawn along such lines, the category can be adaptable and changeable. Nonetheless, a line is drawn, and while the terms of that line might not be clear, the need behind it is. Indie responds to a desire to stand apart from the conventional and the commercial. So pervasive have mainstream popular culture goods become that people have sought refuge from them in scenes or styles that are upheld as being more serious, demanding and not swayed by commercial influences or pressures. Indie has provided such a refuge.

No matter how strong the desire to stand apart from the mainstream is, the line between indie and mainstream is far from firm. It is constantly

---

[39] Michael Z. Newman, 'Indie Culture: In Pursuit of the Authentic Autonomous Alternative', *Cinema Journal*, 48/3 (2009), 16–34, pp. 19–22.

being debated and negotiated. Such is the case whenever a group that has won over a small, devoted audience with its captivatingly new sound starts to attract a larger fan base. These familiar moments set off familiar squabbles: is the group still indie? Has it sold out? More often than not, the group maintains its indie credentials as the line between indie and mainstream holds. Michael Newman describes how that flexibility is characteristic of the indie film world. He holds up the films of Steven Soderbergh as an example.[40] Soderbergh has directed art-house fare like *The Girlfriend Experience* and *Eros* along with studio successes like *Erin Brockovich* and *Ocean's Eleven*. Even with those hits, Soderbergh is still considered to be indie, as his hit films are viewed as being stamped by his personal, artistic style. Both the successful indie band and Soderbergh films remain indie because of the need for artistic experiences considered removed from the mainstream. The need is strong enough to withstand any questioning of indie ideals.

Just how strong and adaptable that need is comes through when considering that the indie/mainstream line has been replicated in various popular genres, not just rock. The line goes by various names, all of them suggesting some other side to a popular genre, or as singer Claudia Gonson puts it in her definition of indie, 'somewhat under the radar, or difficult to define, or left of centre, or difficult to grasp'.[41] In other words, not mainstream or conventional: for example, we now have indie pop, alt-folk, alt-country, underground hip hop and intelligent dance music. Whatever it is called, the line separates more challenging – musically and culturally – forms of popular music from more accessible styles. It is not coincidental that two of the three examples that I presented – Sonic Youth and Aphex Twin – come from that side of the line. All sorts of genre labels have been applied to Sonic Youth, including noise rock, alternative rock and punk rock. Whatever the label, they convey that the group's sound breaks away from more conventional rock styles. Aphex Twin was once placed in the category of intelligent dance music, a label that he and others rejected for being elitist, although they never backed down from their challenging unconventional styles. For their part, Public Enemy, my third example, has enjoyed mainstream success while being groundbreaking and provocative in the way they handle sound.

Of all the things to call the new scene, I am not surprised that 'indie-classical' was coined. The term acknowledges the direct links between indie rock and new music created by indie musicians crossing over into the latter

---

[40] Newman, 'Indie Culture', p. 21.
[41] Quoted in 'Mark Oppenheimer, "Poetry's Cross-Dressing Kingmaker"', *New York Times*, Sunday Magazine (14 September 2012).

idiom or classical composers who either played in indie bands or have connections with them. 'Indie-classical' also emerges from the breadth and lines of distinction embedded in conceptions of indie. All sorts of styles, some not very rock-like, have been labelled indie. So it is not surprising that the junction between popular music and new music would end up attracting the indie heading. 'Indie' often serves as a catch-all for the innovative and different.

Like 'indie', 'indie-classical' also draws a line, but in this case there are two lines. The first is that between indie and mainstream, which becomes even wider with the dissonances and unconventional structures of modernist styles. New music also adds to what Pierre Bourdieu would call the cultural capital enjoyed by indie participants. As many scholars have suggested, indie scenes are fertile ground for Bourdieu's theories of distinction, as members separate themselves from the mainstream by showing that they possess specialized knowledge and tastes.[42] Knowing an obscure band can increase one's cultural capital; so too can liking new music, which surely comes across as obscure and specialized in the larger world of popular music.

The second line drawn by 'indie-classical' is that between itself and new music, or, to be specific, more established styles and settings of new music. Classical musicians in the indie-classical scene have used the term and the scene as a way of separating themselves from the more standard formats of new music as well as older generations of musicians. 'Indie', after all, is a term best suited to the young. Plus they have enjoyed the cultural capital of hipness and freshness that comes with the term. As for the difference between indie-classical and more conventional presentations of new music, indie-classical concerts are not your typical new music concert in terms of venue (clubs), crowd (indie types) and performers (mix of indie and classical musicians). The repertoire is also different. In these concerts, more severe and established modernist works, like those of Lachenmann or Boulez, are infrequently heard. Such works do little to welcome popular genres, whereas indie-classical is premised on the embrace of popular styles. The minimalist rhythmic currents, lyrical melodic lines, sparse textures and spiky accents of that music can accommodate aspects of popular styles, including more pop-like vocals or electronic dance music beats. At the same time, the music has modernist bearings. It is committed to the harmonic, textural and rhythmic intricacies developed throughout the history of modernism, although it may not explore them in as extensive

[42] Ryan Hibbett, 'What is Indie Rock?', *Popular Music and Society*, 28/1 (2005), 55–77; Matthew Bannister, '"Loaded": Indie Guitar Rock, Canonism, White Masculinities', *Popular Music*, 25/1 (2006), 77–95, pp. 80–1; and Newman, 'Indie Culture', pp. 23–4.

ways as some composers have. I feel the need to make this point, as many people might not consider indie-classical works to be modernist, given the openness to popular styles and use of less astringent idioms. I would contend, though, that the music does fit into the history of modernism, especially considering that the affinities between popular genres and modernist idioms are, as I have argued, key to conceptions of new music today.[43]

The audience and cultural lines drawn by indie-classical works bring us to a related topic, that is, separation. Modernist music has often been depicted as being removed from public musical life. To recall, Adorno and Greenberg placed modernist arts in insular worlds of advanced and pure materials. On the performance and composition fronts, there have been such famous exits from the public stage as the closed recitals of Schoenberg's Society for Private Musical Performance and Milton Babbitt's call that composers withdraw into the protected sphere of university research. The new scene that we are discussing today makes no such grand isolationist claims. The scene stands apart, but not that apart. It may push away from mainstream popular culture, but it draws upon popular genres, a reliance that keeps it never too far away from mainstream popular culture. The use of those genres creates a closeness to popular culture, a nearness, though, that at the same time involves the drawing of lines of separation, those between the mainstream and indie culture.

It is this quality of being apart-but-not-so-apart that may be the form that separation takes in today's pluralist world. The kind of broad line stretched out by the indie/mainstream divide suits this space. It does not involve specific types of modernist arts, as with earlier modernist efforts of separation. It instead opens up to a range of genres. The emphasis on general and malleable qualities like innovation and unconventionality can apply to various genres. In addition, the line also depends on attitudes and taste, which are too changeable to demarcate rigid lines. Shaped by these qualities, the line made by the new scene is flexible enough to hold within the varied, shifting pluralist realm, yet firm enough to set apart a particular area, no matter how large and diverse that area proves to be.

I found myself in such a particular area at the Ecstatic Music Festival concert. The performance occupied a musical and cultural space that was removed from the mainstream, but not as remotely as most new music concerts are. By virtue of being rock music, the Deerhoof songs, even

---

[43] The analysis of indie-classical works is a topic for another essay. A compelling example of the mix of modernist and popular elements in that music can be found in *Planetarium*, a work jointly composed by Bryce Dessner, Nico Muhly and Sufjan Stevens.

though of a decidedly indie stripe, could bring in more mainstream listeners, in addition to all of the hipsters in the lobby. At the same time, the group's set kept the concert distinct from a standard new music presentation. Yet, as the organizers of the festival have realized, the new music and indie worlds can come together for an evening, and, beyond that one night, be part of a larger emerging scene. The festival concert that I attended and indie-classical works like *Planetarium* are part of a different conception of the new that is arising in the contemporary musical life. The new still has values of innovation, but it mixes them with values of inclusiveness and breadth. Also bringing new music and indie styles together are shared interests, particularly the lines of inquiry pursued by modernist works and, as observed over the preceding forty-some years, different types of popular music. In listening to the Ecstatic Music Festival concert, *Planetarium*, Sonic Youth, Public Enemy and Aphex Twin, what emerges is a modernism that has been transformed – a modernism that has been vitalized and expanded – by a growing proximity with popular music.

PART II

Rewriting modernism

6 Ritual and Eros in James Dillon's *Come live with me*

Michael Cherlin

> Come live with me and be my love,
> And we will all the pleasures prove,
> That Valleys, groves, hills, and fields,
> Woods, or steepy mountain yields.
>
> *Christopher Marlowe*

The divine presence was conceived as dwelling between the two cherubim. This biblical view was elaborated in the Talmud. The cherubim turn toward each other when Israel performs the commandments, but when they sin the cherubim turn their faces away from each other...

...show them the cherubim, which were intertwined with one another, and say to them: 'Behold! Your love before God is like the love of the male and of the female.'

Moshe Idel, Kabbalah & Eros

> But let the kirk-folk ring their bells,
> Let's sing about our noble sel's
> We'll cry nae jads frae heathen hills
> To help, or roose us;
> But browster wives an' whisky stills,
> They are the muses.
>
> *Robert Burns*

How is a tradition, any tradition, transformed? I find two wonderfully opposed models for tradition, the first in the writings of Walter Benjamin, in his 'Thesis on the Philosophy of History', and the second as formulated by Harold Bloom, in the *Anxiety of Influence*, and many subsequent writings.[1] Benjamin writes,

> There is a secret agreement between past generations and the present one. Our coming was expected on earth. Like every generation that preceded us, we have been endowed with a *weak* Messianic power to which the past has a claim. That claim cannot be settled cheaply.[2]

---

[1] Walter Benjamin, 'Thesis on the Philosophy of History' in *Illuminations*, ed. with an introduction by Hannah Arendt, trans. Harry Zohn (New York: Schocken Books, 1969), pp. 253–67. Harold Bloom, *The Anxiety of Influence: A Theory of Poetry*, 2nd edn (Oxford University Press, 1997).

[2] Benjamin, 'Thesis on the Philosophy of History', p. 254.

For Benjamin, each successive generation brings to fruition the unfulfilled prophecies of preceding generations. The works of earlier generations require and expect other, later works so that their implications may be realized. And so a 'weak Messianic power' is bequeathed to those who come later so that they may fulfil their obligations to those who came before. Benjamin's model is one of intergenerational interdependence.

Bloom's theory of influence is likewise a theory of intergenerational interdependence, but one with a profoundly different set of intergenerational relations. Indeed, I take Bloom's model to be the antithetical complement to Benjamin's. For Bloom, the 'strong poet' must develop strategies that will enable him or her to clear ground for new creativity. This requires a strong 'misreading' of the past, a creative engagement that allows the strongest poets (extendable to painters, composers or any creative thinker/maker) to influence our understanding of their precursors: rather than standing in the shadow of the precursor, the strong poet casts his or her shadow backwards.

To develop a different metaphor, we might think of Benjamin's model as a loving, intergenerational embrace, while Bloom's model is more like a wrestling match, kindred to the patriarch Jacob wrestling with the angel (Genesis 32: 22–32) so that he may secure the blessing.[3] With both models, we hold on to the past for dear life, whether in loving embrace or in a fight for our life.

Both Benjamin and Bloom emphasize the difficulties involved. For Bloom, only the strong poet can overcome the power of the precursor's poems by creating a new poetic vision. Moreover, like Jacob in the biblical story, in securing the blessing the wrestler is wounded for life. Benjamin, certainly thinking of the tragic difficulties of his own time and place, tersely states, 'that claim [of the past on the present] cannot be settled cheaply'.

My own model for tradition and its transformations is a dialectical opposition of both earlier models. In doing so, I draw a parallel between artistic traditions and the dynamics of a family, parents and children. The child who doesn't love his or her parents will face profound difficulties in becoming an adult for they are the chief models of what it is to be an adult. On the other hand, the child who doesn't resist the overwhelming influence of his or her parents will not be able to become his or her own person, and so he or she too will have difficulty in becoming an adult. To be healthy we need both 'weak Messianic power' and 'strong misreading'. Musical traditions are transformed by the same dynamics.

---

[3] Bloom invokes the story of Jacob at Peniel in many places. His essay 'Wrestling Sigmund' is an exemplary adaptation. It is included in *Poetics of Influence: New and Selected Criticism*, ed. with an introduction by John Hollander (New Haven, CT: Henry R. Schwab, 1988), pp. 213–34.

Twentieth-century musical modernism grows out of *and* reacts against its immediate precursors in late Romanticism. Schoenberg's precursors, Brahms and Wagner, are both embraced and resisted in his music. Stravinsky's precursors, Rimsky-Korsakov and Debussy among them, are similarly embraced and resisted. The same can be said for Bartók in his integration and resistance to tradition, including folk traditions.

The next generation of composers, Stockhausen and Xenakis, Carter and Babbitt among them, embraces *and* resists the innovations of those who came before, and so it goes. The traditions that James Dillon's *Come live with me* embraces and resists include the tradition that gave us the Hebrew bible, the traditions of erotic song and text setting in general, traditions of orchestration as well as rhythmic and harmonic language and the traditions of ritual that can be embodied in music. All of these have precursors in the modernism of previous generations. Dillon, like any composer worth our attention, brings both 'weak Messianic power' and 'strong misreading' to music. In 'Come live with me' the opposition includes the setting of its biblical text.

Born in Glasgow on 29 October 1950, James Dillon was raised as a Catholic. He served as an altar boy during his youth, and although any observance of Catholic orthodoxy has long lapsed in Dillon's life, a fascination with the sounds and structures of ritual along with a deeper sense of the unfathomable expanse and mystery of the cosmos and of being human within it remain fundamental to his musical imagination. Dillon is a secular composer whose works are infused with a spiritual sense of the strangeness of being.[4]

The sound of bells, so important in Catholic liturgy and ritual, had a particularly profound impact on young James, who found the complex partials and resultants of bell tones compelling. Bell tones have remained an important part of his musical imagination ever since. For example, many passages in his massive work for solo piano the *Book of Elements* mimic bell tones, these often evoking a ritualistic ethos. Bell tones are also a pervasive element of the even more massive *Nine Rivers*, a nine-movement work, each movement of which uses a distinctive ensemble – variously comprising percussion instruments, strings, winds, voices and electronics – and culminating in a confluence of the 'rivers' in a final movement named *Oceanos*. Bell tones are also fundamental to the acoustical and ritualistic properties of *Come live with me*.

---

[4] Special thanks to James Dillon for our many conversations about *Come live with me* and his other works. Many of the personal details of this chapter come out of those conversations. An earlier version of this chapter was originally presented in the symposium 'Transformations of Musical Modernism', Paris, France, 12 October 2011.

Composed from September to December 1981, *Come live with me* was conceived as a wedding present for Dillon's friends Roger Wright and Rosie Potter. The ritualistic aspects of the work, bell ringing in combination with other aspects of formal design, vie for pre-eminence with the work's other most salient aspect, that is, Eros. The second in a triptych of compositions dealing with Eros, in *Come live with me* Eros encompasses both devotional or spiritual love as well as sexual love.[5] Dillon would return to the erotics of musical expression in his 2004 opera *Philomela*; however, there the composer principally explores the dark side of erotic sexuality, devoid of anything we might recognize as spiritual love.

Come live with me is scored for mezzo-soprano, flute (piccolo, alto flute), oboe (English horn, oboe d'amore) piano and percussion.[6] One unique member of the percussion battery needs special mention. At some point prior to composing *Come live with me*, Dillon found a small metallic plate. Highly resonant, with a fundamental of C♯, this object, not originally intended as a musical instrument, became the core of the sonic world for *Come live with me*. The sum and difference tones derived from the C♯ bell partials inspired the work's harmonic language, and its potential for marking time in the strange and altered temporality of Eros became integrated into the fabric of the work. While found-object-as-musical-instrument is unique to this work in Dillon's catalogue, the idea of defining sound in a more encompassing sense than is suggested by conventional notions of pitch and timbre is another fundamental and pervasive aspect of Dillon's music. The 'grain of sound', the rosined bow scraping against the strings, the interaction of breath, oral cavity and musical wind instrument and sound as complex spectrum rather than fundamental frequency, is basic to James Dillon's way of thinking about music.

Dillon is an autodidact and avid book collector with wide-ranging and highly idiosyncratic interests, among them mysticism and esoteric writings within various traditions. Although Dillon does not have a background in Hebrew or Aramaic, the principal languages of Jewish esoteric writings collectively known as Kabbalah, *Come live with me* is one of two pieces inspired in part by Kabbalistic thought, the other being the solo piano piece *Dillug-Kefitsah* dating from 1976. *Dillug-Kefitsah* takes its name from a meditative technique developed by the thirteenth-century Kabbalist Abraham Abulafia. As described by Gershom Scholem, the great scholar of Kabbalistic thought, *dillug* and *kefitsah* involve a kind of 'jumping' or 'skipping' from one conception to another to create

---

[5] The other works in the triptych are *Who Do You Love* (1981) for voice, flute, clarinet, violin, cello and percussion and *A Roaring Flame* (1982) for female voice and double bass.
[6] All of Dillon's music is published by Peters Edition Ltd., London.

cross-associations not unrelated to later developments of free association used in psychoanalysis.[7] Key to the practice and concept is the transformation of normal consciousness into an altered state wherein things are perceived in a new way. Through *Dillug-Kefitsah* the scriptural text under contemplation takes on new meaning. In the piano piece the technique gives rise to the quick changes in musical texture and affect that comprise the work's sense of flow. In Dillon's evolution as a composer, *Dillug-Kefitsah* is a first step towards the reimagining of piano music that culminates in the *Book of Elements*, whose fifth and final volume was completed in 2002. There, the principles of *Dillug-Kefitsah*, unnamed as such, but arguably present, intertwine with the recurrent sounding of bells mimicked by the piano.

Come live with me, composed some five years after *Dillug-Kefitsah*, returns to a topic partially inspired by Jewish mysticism in its reimagining of an ancient Hebrew text.

One of the mysteries of music-induced ecstasies is its ability to profoundly alter our conscious state. In *Come live with me*, music-induced Eros – both spiritual and sensual – is our gateway to an altered state of being. The work is a setting of the first twelve verses of the second canticle of the biblical Song of Songs, whose translated text is shown in Figure 6.1.

As shown in the figure, Dillon used the Revised Standard Edition of the Bible as a reference while setting a transliteration of the original Hebrew. Both the transliteration and the translation are found in Carlo Suarès's book of Kabbalistic commentary on the poem, a book that Dillon consulted while composing the work.[8] Although James has cautioned me not to make too much of Suarès's commentary, his reading of the book seems to have influenced at least some of the musical imagery in the setting.

Suarès book, like Dillon's attitude toward the material, is highly idiosyncratic. Published originally in French in 1969 and in English translation in 1972, its full title, *The Song of Songs: The Canonical Song of Solomon Deciphered According to the Original Code of the Qabala*, gives a sense of the author's claims and attitude. Of course, there is no 'original code of Qabala' and so the claims are far-fetched to say the least. While not quite a piece within the pop-Kabbalah tradition, neither is Suarè's book part of the more learned commentaries on Kabbalah such as we find in Gershom Scholem or more recently Moshe Idel and many others. Nonetheless, it is

---

[7] Gershom G. Scholem, *Major Trends in Jewish Mysticism* (New York: Schocken Books, 1961), p. 135.
[8] Carlo Suarès, *The Song of Songs: The Canonical Song of Solomon Deciphered According to the Original Code of the Qabala* (Boston, MA: Shambala, 1972).

[1]I am a rose of Sharon, a lily of the valleys. [2]As a lily among brambles, so is my love among maidens. [3]As an apple tree among the trees of the wood, so is my beloved among young men. With great delight I sat in his shadow, and his fruit was sweet to my taste. [4]He brought me to the banqueting house, and his banner over me was love. [5]Sustain me with raisins, refresh me with apples; for I am sick with love. [6]O that his left hand were under my head, and that his right hand embraced me! [7]I adjure you, O daughters of Jerusalem, by the gazelles or the hinds of the field, that you stir not up nor awaken love until it please.	[8]The voice of my beloved! Behold, he comes, leaping upon the mountains, bounding over the hills. [9]My beloved is like a gazelle, or a young stag. Behold, there he stands behind our wall, gazing in at the windows, looking through the lattice. [10]My beloved speaks and says to me: "Arise, my love, my fair one, and come away; [11] for lo, the winter is past, the rain is over and gone. [12] The flowers appear on the earth, the time of singing has come, and the voice of the turtledove is heard in our land.

Figure 6.1 Song of Songs, Revised Standard Edition, second canticle, verses 1–12.

the book that Dillon referred to as he considered the biblical text, and its relevance to the music is an idea that we will return to shortly.

Another factor that informs Dillon's setting of the Song of Songs, and perhaps all of his musical compositions, is the composer's status as an 'outsider'. Dillon, the Scot, does not choose to set a Scots ballad, or text in Scots Gaelic, but rather an ancient Hebrew text – a language that he cannot read in the original. Of course, the Jew has long been recognized as Other, the perennial outsider inside European culture. Dillon, working within the tradition of European art music, is also an Other for a variety of reasons. His family left Glasgow when Dillon was ten years old, settling in Huddersfield, England. Dillon has told me that while there he stubbornly maintained his Glaswegian accent. As an adult Dillon moved to London, where he established himself as a pre-eminent figure in contemporary art music while remaining outside of the London music-making establishment. From 2007 to 2014, Dillon taught as my colleague at the University of Minnesota, and I can testify that he managed to maintain the status of an outsider in this new context (as I write, Dillon has resigned his position in Minnesota to return to London as a freelance composer without academic affiliation). Add to this that Dillon is a self-educated musician, working in an area where self-education is extremely rare. The closest parallel that I can think of is Arnold Schoenberg, who too was an autodidact. But Schoenberg did study briefly with Alexander Zemlinsky. Dillon has never studied composition in a formal context. His deep and wide-ranging knowledge of Western art music is mingled with a knowledge of other traditions, pop, folk and ethnic, creating a different attitude towards musical materials than one would usually find in conservatory or university-trained composers. Dillon's setting captures the strange otherness of the text itself, the otherness of erotic time-space and the strange paradox of the text's historical remoteness coupled to its sense of intimacy and immediacy.

The one musical precursor to *Come live with me* that Dillon singles out is Stravinsky's *Les Noces*. In addition to its obvious thematic affinity, it is clear that the ritualistic aspects of Stravinsky's piece resonated for Dillon. Stravinsky's fractured musical surface forms the musical analogue to a mosaic, evocative as a musical metaphor for the Eastern Church. Its musical tesserae, the mosaic's tiles, evoke the singing traditions of Russian Orthodoxy while simultaneously making its referents strange through their angular, incisive rhythms forged into asymmetrical patterns, by musical cross-cutting techniques that starkly juxtapose the musical tiles, and by contrapuntal juxtapositions that in certain passages place chanting voices at odds with one another. Of course, *Les Noces* also makes conspicuous use of bells, especially at the work's close and this became the inspiration for the final passages of *Come live with me*.

Yet another precursor work by Stravinsky is his setting of *Abraham and Isaac*. Like Dillon's *Come live with me*, Stravinsky's 'sacred ballad' is a reimagining of its Hebrew text, where the singing of the Hebrew is radically estranged from its varied Jewish modes of chanting. The text of Genesis 22: 1–19 is the story of God's command that Abraham sacrifice his son, Abraham's preparations for the sacrifice, God's forbidding that very sacrifice on seeing that Abraham is willing, the substitution of the ram for Isaac and then the blessing: 'I will multiply your descendants as the stars of heaven.' Although the two Hebrew texts, the one set by Stravinsky and the other set by Dillon, couldn't be more different in most respects, they share an intimate and loving scene between two persons. In contrast to the paradox of historical remoteness coupled with a sense of intimacy and immediacy that we find in Dillon's setting, Stravinsky keeps the events at a distance, emphasizing a diegetic mode of chanting the text rather than a mimetic presentation, an aspect of Stravinsky and Dillon that we will return to later in this chapter.

Dillon adapts these varied techniques derived from Stravinsky, but unlike countless other composers who have been influenced by Stravinsky's compositional voice, he manages to avoid surface characteristics that we would associate with Stravinsky. In fact, Dillon's various and varied composerly voices have very little in common with Stravinsky. Some of his very early music is reminiscent of Varèse, the influence of Messiaen is clear in some works, Xenakis had an obvious and profound impact on many works, but overall, Dillon's many voices remain his own. While Eros is arguably beneath the surface of the characteristic urgency that pervades *Les Noces*, Eros is unmistakably present in the Song of Songs – whether we take the erotics to be carnal, spiritual or both – and palpable in Dillon's setting.

Basing a piece on the sonic properties of a found object, integrating the ritualistic use of bells and reimagining Hebrew cantillation in the context of an esoteric reading of a canonical text celebrating Eros, all done by a composer who self-consciously plays outsider off insider within all the traditions that he evokes, might sound like the necessary ingredients for a postmodern aesthetic. But if by 'postmodern' we mean an ironic attitude towards musical materials that is self-consciously opposed to modernism, or if we mean an ahistorical attitude towards what otherwise might be understood as a richness of reference and historical depth, then the description doesn't fit. Dillon's music is a transformed modernism, and we need not add 'post' to our description.

Example 6.1 shows the first twelve bars of the piece. The Hebrew text in square brackets is the first verse of the second canticle: 'I am a rose of Sharon, a lily of the valleys.' Dillon's setting for both the first and second verses uses the same convention of placing the text within brackets – so we know that the music sets that text – but without the text being vocalized.

The very first sound, an incisive attack, particularly in the bass drum, bell and guiro, is a shattering of the silence that precedes it. The found-object-as-bell along with the other sounding percussion work together to effectively cover the initial entrance of the piccolo and oboe d'amore, the duet that emerges out of the shattering that opens the space of the piece. This duo, with various substitutions – oboe d'amore, oboe or English horn, in counterpoint with piccolo, flute or alto flute – will be a recurrent feature of the entire setting. The duet, with its combinations of normal tuning, bent pitches and occasional quarter-tones, creates an exotic soundscape where the counterpoint at times mimics an odd sort of heterophony, a combining of voices found in many folk traditions and a recurrent technique in many of Dillon's compositions. The double reed and flute are derived from ancient Eastern instruments, and both evoke pastoral associations appropriate to the imagery of the text. The sustaining breath of the woodwinds associates with the Hebrew word for breath, *ruah*, and its multiple meanings of wind, breath, spirit and soul.[9] The commentary provided by Suarès

---

[9] The Hebrew words *ruah elohim*, which appear in the first sentence of Genesis, have been variously translated including 'the spirit of God' (*The King James Bible*), 'a wind from God' (*Tanakh*. The Jewish Publication Society, 1999) and 'God's breath' (Robert Alter, *The Five Books of Moses: A Translation with Commentary* (New York: W. W. Norton, 2004)). The word *ruah* plays a major and varied role in Kabbalah including 'the *ruah ha-kodesh*, the "holy spirit", out of whom there speaks the voice and word of God' (Scholem, *Major Trends in Jewish Mysticism*, p. 111).

Ritual and Eros in James Dillon's *Come live with me*

Example 6.1   James Dillon: *Come live with me*, opening 12 bars: setting of 2.1, without vocalization (score pages 1–2).

interprets the biblical text as incorporating multiple, separate voices. The speaker in the first verse of the second canticle is identified as a personification of *Breath*. Within Kabbalistic writings, we find the idea that a

Example 6.1 (cont.)

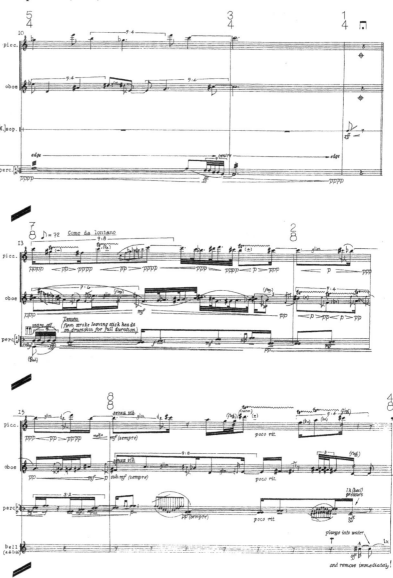

human soul can exist on multiple levels of reality, its singularity broken into a prism of differentiated manifestations or emanations.[10] Suarès draws upon this aspect of Kabbalah in his commentary for the first verse. 'I am a

---

[10] See for example Gershom G. Scholem, *On the Mystical Shape of the Godhead*, trans. Joachim Neugroschel (New York: Schocken Books, 1991), pp. 218 and 230.

rose of Sharon, a lily of the valleys' is paraphrased to have a radically different symbolic meaning: 'I am your body, depth of the upper Breath, Breath of the depth, double Emanation.'[11] The (male) *Lover*'s voice is identified with the second verse, 'As a lily among brambles, so is my love among maidens', paraphrased in Suarès as 'And you are these two Breaths, in existence and life, among unshaped substance.'[12] Given the prominence of the oboe–piccolo duet during the opening and in its variants throughout the work, the commentary seems pertinent to Dillon's setting.

It is only with the third verse that we hear the *Woman*'s voice, and this is the first verse that is vocalized in Dillon's setting (Example 6.2).

The setting of the third verse divides the four lines of the original Hebrew into 2+2, following the sense and syntax of the text. Bars 31–35 set the text translated in the Revised Standard Edition as follows:

> As an apple tree among the trees of the wood,
> so is my beloved among young men.

Bars 36–43 set the following two lines:

> With great delight I sat in his shadow,
> and his fruit was sweet to my taste.

The shift of meaning, from a metaphoric description of the beloved standing out and apart from his contemporaries in the first sentence to the delights of erotic pleasure – 'his fruit was sweet to my taste' – is well captured by Dillon's setting. The music lingers on the final word of the first couplet, *habaneem* [the young men], following the tradition in many kinds of chant, including Hebrew cantillation, where the final word of a poetic line is often embellished irrespective of its meaning. The musical shift from the first couplet to the second is a shift from diegesis to mimesis. The earlier bars proclaim the qualities of the beloved. The following bars, the halting, breathless triplets in the voice, mimicked by the oboe and piccolo in bar 38 (themselves imagined as emanations of the singer), are a stylized re-enactment of ecstasy.

The shift from diegetic presentation to mimetic enactment has conspicuous precursors in the late Baroque, Bach's *St Matthew Passion* being a touchstone in this regard, but it also has important antecedents in the musical modernism of the first half of the twentieth century. Stravinsky's dramatic works are particularly remarkable in this regard. Although most

---

[11] Suarès, *The Song of Songs*, p. 61.   [12] Ibid., p. 62.

Example 6.2 James Dillon: *Come live with me*, bars 31–43: setting of 2.3 (score pages 4–5).

of Stravinsky's *Les Noces* is a highly stylized mimesis – an acting out of the wedding preparations and celebration – the text and music does occasionally shift into a diegetic mode. For example, the third scene (Rehearsal Figure 65) opens with the chorus singing descriptive prose. In Stanley Applebaum's translation,

Ritual and Eros in James Dillon's *Come live with me*

Example 6.2 (cont.)

Just as one sees in the sky the white moon and the sun, thus the princess lived in the palace, lived with her old father, and she was happy beside her father and mother.[13]

[13] Igor Stravinsky, *Les Noces* (Mineola: Dover Publications), p. xix.

The music then returns to mimetic mode as the bride-to-be sings, 'Bless me father, I am leaving.'[14] Similar shifts from one mode to the other are also woven into the fabric of Part II, the wedding feast. Whereas the shifts from diegesis to mimesis in *Les Noces* are relatively rare and arguably subtle, the technique is highly conspicuous in Stravinsky's *Oedipus Rex*. There, Stravinsky contrasts the speaking narrator, in diegetic mode, with the singing chorus and soloists whose music is a highly stylized mimesis. Within *Oedipus Rex*, the narration is used in conjunction with the sung music to distance the musical enactment of the story, as though it too is a story being told rather than directly expressed and experienced as in 'realistic' theatre. Stravinsky uses similar techniques in *The Flood*, to similar ends. Stravinsky's *Abraham and Isaac*, although integrating some aspects of mimesis, tilts towards a diegetic presentation, emphasizing the remoteness rather than immediacy of the story. The shift from diegesis to mimesis in Dillon is used to the opposite affect, giving the expression of erotic love an intensified immediacy.

While it is easy to imagine the ecstatic state as being purely sexual in nature – or obversely as being purely spiritual as in the Greek concept of *agape*, so fundamental to Christian theology as well as Rabbinic Judaism – a more nuanced reading unifies the sexual and spiritual, bringing a concept of Eros that interconnects carnal with supernal. Such is the approach of Moshe Idel in his book *Kabbalah and Eros*. Although Idel's 2005 study post-dates Dillon's composition, his inclusive understanding of Eros better captures what is expressed in Dillon's setting than giving a reductive interpretation of either purely spiritual *agape* or purely sexual Eros.

> I propose to distinguish among three terms that will serve us throughout the following analyses. *Agape*, a term which means disinterested love, will designate a spiritual attraction to either God or human beings, an attitude which is devoid of a libidinal urge, hetero- or homoerotic. *Eros* will denote a complex of feelings ... that inform the drive to establish sexual or emotional contacts, corporeal or spiritual, between two entities, in which at least one of them attracts the other ... Though sexuality may be an important part of erotic discourses as defined above, it is only one aspect of its much more variegated nature.[15]

In this sense, and perhaps in this sense only, a musical precursor to Dillon's *Come live with me* is found in Arnold Schoenberg's *Verklärte Nacht*. There,

---

[14] Ibid., p. xix.
[15] See Moshe Idel, *Kabbalah and Eros* (New Haven, CT: Yale University Press, 2005). Idel defines his approach towards Eros on page 7, developing this theme throughout the book's study of specific texts within the Kabbalistic tradition.

Hishbaati Etkhem Benot Yerushlom
Bi'tsebaot
(I adjure you, O daughters of Jerusalem,
by the gazelles)

Hishbaati Etkhem Benot Yerushlom Bi'tsebaot
Aw B'aylot Hassehdèh Im Taayro We'im Teoreroo
(I adjure you, O daughters of Jerusalem,
by the gazelles or the hinds of the field,
that you stir not up nor awaken)

Hishbaati Etkhem Benot Yerushlom Bi'tsebaot
Aw B'aylot Hassehdèh Im Taayro We'im Teoreroo
Et-Ha'ahevah Aad Shetehhfats
(I adjure you, O daughters of Jerusalem,
by the gazelles or the hinds of the field,
that you stir not up nor awaken love
until it please.)

Figure 6.2 Textual setting of 2.7, transliteration along with the RSE translation.

Eros in its purely sensual aspect is evident in abundance, yet spiritual transformation, the heart of Schoenberg's moonlit *Verklärung*, is unmistakable.

The ritualistic aspects of Dillon's setting are emphasized particularly in the seventh and ninth verses. The adjuration of the seventh verse is set in three parts. Each part commences at the beginning of the verse and each progresses further than the last, literally reiterating what had come before until the full verse is completed only with the third iteration. The text for the accruing fragments is shown in Figure 6.2. Example 6.3 shows the music for the third, final and complete iteration of the text.

The opening fragment is set vocally in a broad declamatory style that is juxtaposed against the nearly chaotic activity in the instrumental ensemble. It is as though the oath resists what William James characterized as the 'blooming, buzzing confusion' of nature. The voice, though nearly overwhelmed, holds firm against the world's hubbub. The final word of the fragment, *Bi'tsebaot* (translated here as gazelles), is highly ornamented, reimagining the melismas so characteristic of traditional cantillation.

After the reiteration of the first fragment, the continuation of the verse is preceded by a short interlude in the ensemble, allowing us to focus on the instrumental voices. The next fragment of the text, including the injunction 'that you stir not up nor awaken love' (literally 'not/never to awaken and never to arouse'), is declaimed more quickly and leads directly into the third iteration of the adjuration.

In the third iteration, a grand pause separates the injunction 'never to arouse' from its crucial exception, desired love. In contrast to what came

Example 6.3 James Dillon: *Come live with me*, bars 98–166: setting of 2.7 (score pages 17–20 (third and full iteration)).

before, the ensemble seems to attend to the singer's words as the woodwinds drop out for the first part of the phrase. The final word, *Shetehhfats*, literally a future tense 'that she will desire', receives special setting, a long

Example 6.3 (cont.)

vocal melisma complemented by melismatic writing in the woodwinds, who join the singer to close the verse.

Figure 6.3 is a schematic for the setting of the ninth verse (page 22 of the score is reproduced in Example 6.4).

Example 6.3 (cont.)

The words to the left of the slash mark (/) are all set to the same vocal music, *portamenti* in close pitch-space. The first iteration, *Domeh Dodi* (My beloved), is accompanied by bells, piano and oboe, and with each subsequent reiteration one of the instruments is removed, so that the final iteration, *Ha'hhalonot* (at the windows), is set by the voice alone. The words to the right of the slash mark are set in a descending sequence of variants of the same idea: six iterations of the same note, each of which is

Example 6.3 (cont.)

followed by a downward *portamento*: the respective initial pitches are B5, then G5, then F♯5, then E5.

The work ends with Dillon's setting of the twelfth verse: 'The flowers appear on the earth,/ the time of singing has come,/ and the voice of the

Domeh Dodi / Li'tsvi Aw Le'oofer
(My beloved / is like a gazelle,
or a [young] stag)

Ha'ayaleem / Hineh-Zeh Aomed
(young [stag]) / Behold, there he stands)

Ahhar Ke'tel' / noo Ma'shghiahh Min-
(behind our wall, / gazing in)

Ha'hhalonot / Mi'tsits Min Ha'hhrakeem
(at the windows, / looking through the lattice.)

Figure 6.3 Schematic for the setting of the ninth verse (page 22 of the score).

turtledove /is heard in our land.' The text evokes images of springtime, nature's rebirth out of winter's sleep, a time of joyous singing heard through the voice of the turtledove. Careful readers of the Jewish Bible will recognize how exceedingly rare such naturalistic imagery is, all the more striking for being so. In Dillon's setting, the verse becomes the final sanctification of the ritualistic celebration that is the piece (see Example 6.5). The text is introduced by three bars of percussion alone, the only time in the setting that we hear the percussion isolated. The alto flute anticipates the entry of the voice with G octaves marked *o Zag hareet*, the ululation commonly used in Arab countries to express celebration, particularly at weddings. (It is worth noting that the Song of Songs is important in Islamic tradition as well as Judaism and Christianity.) Ululation is also integrated into the vocal line as the celebratory text unfolds. The wind parts waver between heterophony and true polyphony; the piano introduces a bell motif at bar 230 (C–A–G♯–G♭–F–B, all doubled at the octave, here filled in with inner voices, but later reduced to the octaves) that will further emerge in the song's coda. At the completion of the verse's text, beginning in bar 234, the vocalist sings five iterations of the syllable A, each set the same way, grace note C5 descending to D♭4. This added text, vocal sound supplanting vocalized words, a stylized version of the cooing of the turtledove, marks and celebrates Eros. The work ends with five tollings of the found-object-as-bell, all but the last followed by a variant of the same six-note formula in the piano – C–A–G♯–G♭–F–B – each more expanded than the last, and each supported by a low C pedal, 'difference tone' in the piano. In a work that hovers between ritual and Eros, *Come live with me* ends with a ritualistic bell ringing. But that ringing signals a consecration of Eros that fuses body and spirit.

Earlier on, we considered the connection between the bell ringing that closes *Come live with me* and that which closes Stravinsky's *Les Noces*. The Stravinsky connection is striking because both works combine ritual and Eros, so salient in Dillon's piece. With the importance of ritual being so

Example 6.4 James Dillon: *Come live with me*, bars 176–191: setting of 2.9 (score page 22).

attenuated in our contemporary lives, music that is ritualistic has been quite rare – Boulez's *Rituel* is an obvious exception. A larger frame of reference, however, would bring us to a consideration of the erotics of

Example 6.5 James Dillon: *Come live with me*, bars 213–250: setting of 2.12 (score pages 25–9).

music. Almost always a presence in popular music, Eros has been conspicuously absent in most discussions of musical modernism and its later offshoots. Yet a super-charged eroticism is essential to many landmark

Example 6.5 (cont.)

works of the early twentieth century: Debussy's *Pelléas et Mélisande* and *Prélude à l'après-midi d'un faune*, Schoenberg's *Verklärte Nacht*, *Gurrelieder* and *Pelleas und Melisande* and Berg's *Wozzeck* and *Lulu* just to name some obvious examples. It is difficult to generalize, but it seems safe to say that in the post–World War II period Eros is not particularly

Example 6.5 (cont.)

salient in the vast majority of art music (popular music is another story!). To make a short list of some major figures, I do not associate Stockhausen, Boulez, Nono, Ligeti, Xenakis, Carter or Babbitt with the musical expression of Eros. Some aspects of Berio might make an exception that proves

Ritual and Eros in James Dillon's *Come live with me*

Example 6.5 (cont.)

the rule. It is impossible to pinpoint where Dillon's sensitivity to musical erotics comes from. He knows the music of the early twentieth century well, but he also grew up knowing the music of the Rolling Stones, to name just one group important in Dillon's musical evolution who are obvious

Example 6.5 (cont.)

masters of musical eroticism in the world of popular music. And then again, perhaps because his atypical musical education never separated musical activity from the rest of life, there is nothing to cause this most essential aspect of our being human to be omitted from our making of music.

7 Montage in modernity

Scattered fragments, dynamic fragments

Jean-Paul Olive

Montage, fragment and shock

A central and problematic process of modern art and a corrosive agent of artistic form, montage spread through the art of the twentieth century as an invasion of fragments imported from empirical reality. Questions about the borders between art and life – a problem that has haunted avant-garde movements – are in practice almost always based upon the presence of montage techniques and accompanying heterogeneous elements. However, by means of this act of transgression, exceeding the domain of pure aesthetics with this approach to literality, the work, according to Adorno, thus runs a risk: '*realia* – foreign in the sense that, from outside the fraying process, they have landed in the field of art works – these *realia* are potentially saved by being endowed with meaning at the same time as they clash head-on with the traditional meaning of works of art.'[1] Furthermore, in as much as it is based on shock, montage incurs another risk: when the shock has waned, montages turn back into simple, indifferent matter and – after initially having been so explosive – their relevance is cancelled out and becomes simply historic. For Adorno, such dilemmas haunt contemporary art, and montage remains a practice that is impossible to ignore, because of the diversity of its operations and techniques. Certainly, this kind of assessment is even more convincing since the use of digital tools (integrating a number of montage operations) has become common practice. For some thinkers – notably in critical theory, and more particularly Adorno and Benjamin – this state of affairs is linked to the fate of human experience.

According to Françoise Proust, who takes up Walter Benjamin's thought, the modern present is characterized by 'the dislocation of unity of experience, the impossibility of any of the three syntheses, that is, precisely and simply the explosion of experience'.[2] The speed of data that

---

[1] Theodor W. Adorno, *L'art et les arts*, trans. Jean Lauxerois (Paris: Desclée de Brouwer, 2002), p. 71.
[2] Françoise Proust, *L'Histoire à Contretemps: Le Temps Historique Chez Walter Benjamin (Passages)* (Paris: Éditions du Cerf, 1994), p. 21.

consciousness has to face, the breaking up of activities and information and the violence of situations modern human beings are confronted with, all lie at the origin of the shocks that consciousness is forced to absorb – a situation that replaced a mode of existence based on experience and transmitted traditions. The philosophies of the early twentieth century – those of Husserl or Bergson – have attempted to grasp this phenomenon, to understand it, to take the measure of its consequences. According to F. Proust, 'consciousness is no longer able to register each piece of information in its singularity, to store its specific content in the intended place in memory, and to keep it in its continuous arrangement. It has become incapable of living every single experience and preserving a living memory of it: a whole series of data is pushing violently into disorder against consciousness, which breaks up and explodes.'[3]

In particular, because all events have become blows, shocks, traumas, the question of the fragment correlates to modernity, and the fragment is its particular mode of expression. For this reason, Walter Benjamin generally considered that ruin is the very state of modern things. But at the same time Benjamin has taught us that modernity also has the effect of making conscious this state of affairs, and perhaps even of countering it. Indeed, tradition has tended to neutralize every event by incorporating it into a continuity, by naturalizing and transforming it into second nature. The question of the fragment – and therefore of montage – thus presents a strong ambivalence which also constitutes its interest; and it is this ambivalence that leads to the necessity of recasting the fragment in a wider context in relation to what surrounds it, in every particular configuration a work presents, embedded in the creative project of an artist.

Montage, history and time

Despite some divergences, Adorno and Benjamin shared a conception of the work that thoroughly takes into account the fractures of modernity; for Adorno, modern works could only be created in response to the phenomenon of shock, this being characteristic of modern times. In his famous publication *Philosophy of New Music*, the philosopher clearly notes that Schoenberg as well as Stravinsky – even though they are opposed on many points – developed their composition in response to shocks that strike both the subject and the tonal language of tradition. The explosive experience of modernity (which, as seen in Benjamin, cannot any longer bring about a 'synthesis', at least in the classical sense of the word) is matched by an art

---

[3] Proust, *L'histoire à contretemps*, p. 21.

that shatters itself and cannot be satisfied any more with a unified appearance. This accords the question of montage a particularly important position for Adorno, for whom 'in terms of [its] microstructure all modern art may be called montage'. Refusing to consider montage simply as a technical innovation, Adorno considers its source as the 'antithesis to mood-laden art', as a 'protest' against subjectivization to the extent that the inclusion of materials unrefined by any personal input calls into question the producer subject. The destructive character of montage in relation to the work is thus underlined several times: 'Montage is the inner-aesthetic capitulation of art to what stands heterogeneously opposed to it. The negation of synthesis becomes a principle of form.'[4]

The understanding of montage occurs in Adorno in the context of the logic of decomposition characterizing modern art; the characteristics of the modern work – hermeticism, fragmentation, the loss of coherence of meaning along with rationality and the importance of technique – are the concretization of its ambivalent refusal in the face of the movement to reification, which art integrates as much as other spheres of human activity. Adorno's way of addressing montage takes this element into account: 'Artworks, however, that negate meaning must also necessarily be disrupted in their unity; this is the function of montage, which disavows unity through the emerging disparateness of the parts at the same time that, as a principle of form, it reaffirms unity.'[5] From this quotation, one understands that Adorno's critique is focused less on the crisis of the traditional principle of unity brought about by montage than on the problems posed subsequently by the structuring principle of modern works.

Indeed, for Adorno, the only way to consider the problem of montage theoretically is to include it in the larger one of the articulation of the work, and thus within the question of the relationship between detail and whole. If the work is above all a process – that is to say, a phenomenon in progress – it achieves its real and profound expression only through the intensity of the relationships that the parts maintain among themselves and with the whole. For Adorno, the whole, as a synthesis of scattered elements, cannot be reduced to the result of an authoritarian decision which would constrict the dispersed fragments according to an external plan, a kind of administering of the material. And for their part, rather than being inert or dead data, the parts are 'centers of energy that strain towards the whole on the basis of a necessity that they equally perform'.[6]

---

[4] Theodor W. Adorno, *Aesthetic Theory*, ed. Gretel Adorno and Rolf Tiedemann, trans. Robert Hullot-Kentor (London and New York: Continuum, 1997), pp. 154–5.
[5] Adorno, *Aesthetic Theory*, p. 154.   [6] Adorno, *Aesthetic Theory*, p. 178.

This is evident in this dynamic, even dialectical relation, which is also a complex relation without preliminary models, inscribed in the problematics of the fragment, inseparable from the modern work. Adorno has thus endeavoured to think about the question in a particular way, perhaps influenced in this by the medium of music: trying to understand how and under what conditions scattered fragments – resulting from the splitting up of the phenomenal world and of the existing materials – have a chance of becoming dynamic fragments, of speaking again within a coherent work, without, for all that, closing up into a totality with a false and systematic façade. The book about Mahler, on which I would like to pause for a while, is an example of such an attempt.

The example of Mahler

At the end of the 1950s, at a time when the European musical avant-garde was beginning to identify with the tendency towards a generalized serialism, Adorno paradoxically wrote a book in which he expertly analyses the work of the Austrian composer Gustav Mahler, whom he passionately defends. At that time, Mahler was frequently criticized by modern musicians; the presence of largely outdated material in his works, the use of banal elements borrowed from popular music and the presence of stylistic turns that were already old-fashioned in his own time – all these features distanced Mahler from post-war composers. A reputation for kitsch and sentimentality hovers over his work, which the avant-garde would have liked to classify under the category of a quaint post-romanticism. Why did Adorno, who engaged the avant-garde in this debate – notably with the question of the neutralization of material and of musical time – defend Mahler at this very time by demonstrating in a remarkable book (which is also a method) that such an approach to composition was a burning issue?

It is precisely the question of the fragment that is central to his philosophical undertaking. For Adorno, traditional cultivated music – whose model is linked to the Classical style – was characterized by its act of closure, by the fact that its 'economic principle . . . its kind of determination, exhausts itself in exchanging one thing for another, leaving nothing behind. It "comes out" but has no outcome. Anything new that it cannot wholly assimilate it shuns.'[7] If one may say so, that is music's tautological character, a unity and a closed perfection, which it shares, Adorno suggests, with non-contradictory philosophical systems.

---

[7] Theodor W. Adorno, *Mahler: A Musical Physiognomy*, trans. Edmund Jephcott (University of Chicago Press, 1992), p. 14.

Mahler brings this type of construction to a crisis point by welcoming into his music heterogeneity and diversity in the guise of the scattered fragments included in his symphonies: the remains of old waltzes and old-fashioned Ländler, repeated faded old tunes, fanfares and worn-out military marches fill his music like so many visions of a village from the past. Nature itself, so important to the soul of the Viennese composer, also finds here its mode of expression. But, make no mistake, for Mahler this is a matter of seizing again what Adorno calls 'the unregulated voices of the living'. What needs to be understood is that these inserted fragments in Mahler – those expressing the presence of nature as well as reminiscences of the popular world – are never the agent of meaning fixed once and for all (in an ontological way) but are always presented as something produced, preformations laden with the history that presided over their creation.

Adorno suggests Mahler's strategy is one of resistance in view of the historical and socio-cultural tendency towards neutralization of musical material; and because this music is also a resistance to ideological and systematic thinking, Adorno interprets it as being a music of ruin. Thus Adorno compares Mahler's music to Freud's cathartic method, because both destroy the conventional appearance of culture by bringing into appearance the fragments of strata beneath the phenomenal world: 'After the destruction of a musical culture debased to ideology, a second whole is shored up from the fragments and scraps of memory. In it the subjective organizing power allows the return of culture, which art opposes but cannot eradicate.'[8] By reactivating these fragments – which become for him the means to make the traditional material of tonality speak again – Mahler, according to Adorno, can hope to transform them into the 'explosive matter of utopia'.

It is not, however, the mere presence of these materials that ensures the work's dynamism. Only the contact between the characteristic detail and the movement of the whole is capable of transforming these elements; if the characteristic detail is fit to gather the perceptible intensity that the abstract construction had neutralized, it nevertheless remains incapable of bringing this meaning to incandescence on its own. For Adorno, 'the music does not therefore find its peace in details that, though charged, are merely accumulated and mutually indifferent. Rather, the less the form is substantially prescribed, the more insistently it is sought by compositions that begin with the unprotected individual figure.'[9] It is by means of a renewed relationship between form and unique details that the composer from Vienna carries out a profound critique of musical language in his symphonies, which, like huge rivers, carry along the particular without destroying its uniqueness.

[8] Adorno, *Mahler*, p. 39.   [9] Adorno, *Mahler*, p. 49.

In order to fully comprehend the reach of Mahler's music, at least two characteristics of the utmost importance have to be taken into account. The first is the fact that the material – and the fragments carried within Mahler's symphonies truly are material – is not inert in itself; as Adorno says, the material contains the history of musical language. Even for the philosopher, it is the place that it occupies in musical language that transcends its simple existence. Hence, it is here that history, with all its frailties and possibility of being so easily lost, forgotten or repressed, animates the fragments of the past, provided that the composer is sensitive to their intensity. The second characteristic is musical time, which, with Mahler, is set up in a dynamic and open duration, not compressed by a pre-established pattern, a novelesque and epic time that gives way completely to the dimension of becoming. Only placement in dynamic time, within a dialectical rather than schematic form, prevents the fragment here from falling infinitely into the undifferentiated and prevents it from becoming obsolete.

Some musical models of the post-war period

If Mahler, as a composer from the end of the tonal system, has no direct heirs, the problematics opened up by his composition, notably the problematics of the fragment, have been taken up and reflected upon by several musicians. Among the post-war composers who integrated this question of the fragment into a more general problematics of musical time, I would like to consider the case of three later musicians, each in their way providing equally critical models of behaviour with respect to composition.

Without doubt, one should cite first the case of Bernd Alois Zimmermann. For Zimmermann, music is, in its essence, determined by the nature of the time in which it is inscribed. According to the composer, it also has to do with a profound antinomy. Because of the extreme organization of time in musical composition, time is overcome and brought into a transcendent order. In music, 'real' time (in Ezra Pound's sense) comes about only through the order of unfolding 'apparent' time. Hence, for Zimmermann, music is precisely the place where the relationship of humanity to time may express itself; music grants the inner perception of ordered time in which human experience finds profound expression, an order which 'invests humanity in its essence and brings time to consciousness as a profound unity'.[10]

---

[10] Bernd Alois Zimmermann, 'Intervalle et temps' in Philippe Albéra (ed.), *Bernd Alois Zimmermann* (Contrechamps 5) (Lausanne: Édition L'Age d'Homme, 1985), pp. 32–5, p. 35.

We know that Zimmermann did not hesitate to create multiple stylistic borrowings, ranging from simple audible quotations to more complex procedures that could hide the source of the integrated fragments: the *Requiem for a Young Poet* (1967–69), the Cello Concerto, the opera *Die Soldaten* (1958–60) and of course the *Music for the Suppers of Ubu Roi* (1966) multiply heterogeneous materials and, at times, do not shrink from raw and violent contrasts. Elements from the world of jazz (essentially free jazz), old forms and materials from the past sit next to atonal or serial writing in a large number of works. But most important is doubtless the fact that the heterogeneous fragments, far from being considered inert objects, take their place in a true conception of time. Carl Dahlhaus attempted to summarize this conception by using the category of 'layers of time', a phenomenon accounting for the fact that the multiple voices of a musical work express different times. The importance of techniques and procedures based on quotation, collage and montage – a set of processes Zimmermann called 'stylistic pluralism' – has to do, for him, with the idea of the sphericality of time. According to Dahlhaus, the historical before and after are forcibly assembled by Zimmermann in the simultaneity of a single work: they are, so to speak, 'superimposed'. The concept of stylistic pluralism and the idea of sphericality of time in Zimmermann's musical poetics are complementary sides of the same coin. Without going into the details of the music here, we can nonetheless note in Zimmermann's music the presence of a cluster of specific tensions resulting in stylistic breaks, triggered by montage processes. This situation refers, for this composer, to the idea of an active simultaneity of past and present, and more widely, to an inner simultaneity of epochs. Such organization of the musical fabric in temporal, superimposed, active layers is, of course, reminiscent of some late remarks by Walter Benjamin on the explosive power of the past in his *Theses on the Philosophy of History*.

For another post-war composer, the Hungarian György Kurtág, the question of the fragment plays out in a different way. István Balázs noted that the struggle with time is perhaps the fundamental problem of Kurtág's entire work: time in *What Is the Word*, a work composed on Samuel Beckett's last text, is time that does not contrive to be given over to duration, a time that remains 'faced with' subjectivity and that appears disquietingly behind the surface of the music. According to Balázs, what emerges in an expressive manner in such a piece 'is the desert of human life, of history's private existence, of a kind of paralysis forbidding the human a truly human existence'.[11] Equally, in the *Kafka Fragments*, a work written in 1986 for

---

[11] István Balázs, 'But, chemin, hésitation' in Philippe Albèra (ed.), *György Kurtág: Entretien, Textes, Écrits sur son Œuvre* (Geneva: Contrechamps, 1995), pp. 173–83, p. 183.

soprano and violin, the cycle of brief pieces only maintains its coherence on the verge of a dispersal that constantly threatens the composition's unity. The work incorporates different genres evoked through the use of banal styles: waltzes, sentimental dances, gypsy violin and so on, these forms lending a particular character to the work, halfway between the reminiscence of daily triviality and disquieting fantasy.

Splinters, memories, fragments, pieces 'in memory of' or as 'tributes to': as these terms may indicate, the production of this Hungarian composer is full of references to the past, be it near or distant, historical or personal. In fact, Kurtág's writing is haunted by the problematics of memory; Philippe Albéra claims that 'this is why it tends to re-composition: paraphrase, quotation and self-quotation, developments starting from a musical idea, from a piece in the repertoire, from a "stolen" or "found" object; but also filtering, dilution, reduction to the essential'.[12] Yet, as is the case with Zimmermann, Albéra is right to specify that what matters most of all in this kind of writing is the subtle and profound manner in which the multiple relations are put into place: 'if the work is weaving multiple links – some obvious, others more hidden – it is not in the form of accumulation, but of an unveiling, a laying bare'.[13]

If – as with Mahler and Zimmermann – the questions of the fragment and of musical time are merging here, then it is through the use of brief, aphoristic, extremely articulated forms during which the past recovers an expressive and unsuspected charge. This is because in Kurtág's writing, elements of the past are not dead objects available like goods on the shelves of a shop; the elements of the past are ghosts, phantasms that are still alive and were waiting for us to look at them to take on life again. Françoise Proust wrote that 'it is only by interweaving the thread of the new with the fabric of the old that the present may be the object of an experience, and be lived as such';[14] indeed, it seems that this is what the Hungarian composer manages almost magically: 'the material with the most worn-out appearance, be it an interval, a scale or a melodic formula, gains a kind of innocence, as if the composer was rediscovering initial meaning and original power.'[15] But we have to add that this power given to the fragments of the past represents only one side of Kurtág's music; the other side is expressed through the fractures, the cracks in the construction, through the strangeness of the articulation, through all the operations that transform what appears to be questioned.

---

[12] Philippe Albéra, 'Avant-propos' in *György Kurtág: Entretien, Textes, Écrits sur son Œuvre* (Geneva: Contrechamps, 1995), pp. 7–10, p. 8.
[13] Ibid. [14] Proust, *L'Histoire à Contretemps*, p. 60. [15] Albéra, 'Avant-propos', p. 8.

The fragment is presented in an equally questioning way in the last model I would like to consider here: Luigi Nono. The last creative period of the Italian composer is characterized by particular attentiveness to listening, to searching for a new dimension of perception; the composer regarded this dimension of listening as a form of resistance to the deterioration of hearing tied to the violence of advanced capitalist society. For the composer, listening is a privileged connection which fuses the interior and exterior worlds, a position certainly not far from Adorno's criticism of the phenomenon of the decline of listening. His last works, moreover, are designed to rekindle this dimension of listening, built on the edge of silence, like dynamic and fragmentary constellations actively integrating the dimensions of cessation, interruption and silence.

A strong political involvement in the 1960s – characteristic of Nono – gave way over the years to an attitude of retreat that was not a disengagement, but which must have seemed to the composer to be the only behaviour still possible to safeguard the musical dimension in the face of a tide of noise of all kinds, flooding over individuals in the course of everyday life. It has rightly been said that the spatial configuration of Venice could have influenced Nono's thinking, and it is true that the universe of the last works, especially *Prometheus*, with its multiple sound levels punctuated with silence, is close to the insular atmosphere of the city of the doges. Yet the fragmentation of these works goes beyond this single geographic reference.

Thus, in the string quartet *Fragmente – Stille, An Diotima*, written in 1980, Nono invokes around fifty fragments from Hölderlin's poems which he records in the score above the staves, although these texts are not to be spoken or sung. In fact, the text fragments are meant for the performers with the aim of improving their 'intuitive understanding'. The music itself is designed to be fragmentary, constantly interrupted, whether by silence or by sustained notes brought about by a series of pedal points of different lengths. The pedals are 'spaces' designed to be fully occupied by the musicians of the quartet, who take on Hölderlin's text. As Nono writes, 'The pedal points are constantly to be taken in with a free imagination: as dream-like spaces, as sudden ecstasy, as inexpressible thoughts, as calm breathing, and as the silence of "timeless song"'.

Perhaps most impressive, on hearing the quartet *Fragmente – Stille*, is this double position one can feel in its presence: on the one hand, one gets the sense of a splitting up in the composition that is constantly suspended or interrupted, but at the same time, on the other hand, the fragments foreground their dynamism so intensely that they paradoxically carry on beyond the pauses and silences, without discontinuity. A community of thought and intention thus seems to link, across time, *Fragmente – Stille* with the last quartets and sonatas of Beethoven. Beethoven's late works are indeed characterized by caesurae and sudden interruptions through fragmentation, whose importance Adorno notes: 'This sheds light on the paradox that late Beethoven is called both subjective and objective. Objective is the fractured landscape, subjective: the only light in which it glows.'[16]

In *Fragmente – Stille*, the role of Hölderlin's text fragments is decisive, in the sense that Nono established a new kind of relationship between music and text; for the benefit of the musicians, Nono specifies this relationship at the beginning of the score: 'The fragments of Hölderlin's text must sound in your hearts! Never trivially or literally, but from the most subtle part of you, from the interior.' These texts are thus given in order to permeate, in their fragmented way, the musical texture – as Nono designates them, 'multiple fragments and the silence of other spaces, other skies, in order to find in other ways the possibility of not bidding farewell to hope'. The work is full of multiple references – from the *scala enigmatica* of Verdi's sacred works to the quotation of a piece by Ockeghem – but they are barely recognizable. Like the text fragments, quotation here remains within an inner and secret universe in order to avoid any recovering, any reification.

With Nono, as much as with Zimmermann or Kurtág, the fragmentary is presented as a resistance to systematic or all-encompassing composition, and as a reflection on a dimension of the perceptible that rejects evidence of a world already fully established and settled in. With these composers the fragment is not conceived as an inert object that can easily be taken over; while defying the fetishism of the commodity, it pulsates on the contrary with a subterranean dynamism, charged with history, as a cluster of tensions in its relation to the work's entirety, but all the while refusing its closure, its confinement.

Faced with a breaking-up into dead objects inflicted by a semi-mercantile culture, the few processes briefly described here are characterized by what could be called rescuing the fragment. And if modernity has well and truly settled accounts with ideas of totality and system, rendering fragmentation and division inescapable, rescuing the fragment might still be part of its 'unfinished project', harbouring considerable and perhaps still unsuspected issues. Seizing the scattered fragment in its fatal downfall to give it back the spark of its dynamic content, and releasing it from its petrification to allow it to express its temporality – here we have quite a musical and aesthetic agenda; in its relationship to time and utopia, we are also undoubtedly dealing, in the wider sense, with an agenda that is ethical and political.

---

[16] Adorno, *Aesthetic Theory*, p. 93.

8 Transformations of appearance

Suddenness and the modernist fragment

Marion Hestholm

> Many works of the ancients have become fragments. Many modern works are fragments as soon as they are written.
>
> *Friedrich Schlegel*[1]

This chapter will suggest an approach to the musical fragment and the fragmentary writing of modernist composers by way of applying a concept from philosophy, a concept expressed by the metaphor of 'appearance'. My approach will be phenomenological in the sense that it will focus on the *experience* of the fragment, rather than historical and hermeneutical analysis. The concept of appearance or semblance has always been ambivalent in colloquial language and in aesthetic theory; it has been associated with deception and superficiality, as something that hides the true essence of a thing. In music, appearance is connected to the moment – and related to the dichotomy between whole and part – where the whole stands for the depth and truth, whereas parts and details are seen as surface and embellishment. This picture of the part–whole relationship is already put into question in romanticism, and it is further challenged in modernism. The idea of appearance, then, is relevant to understanding the continuity between romanticism and modernism; indeed, the way in which we understand and value appearance plays a part in the transformation of musical modernism.

The problem of formal realization comprised a key issue in the musical aesthetics of the twentieth century, in the course of which composers of all orientations investigated the dynamics of fragmentary writing as they developed new solutions to the problem of form. This cross-stylistic interest in the fragment can be understood as a general attraction towards what David Metzer calls 'the fragmentary state' – where 'state' means 'the shaping of the musical language of a work so as to emulate a specific ideal'.[2] This accounts for the fact that fragmentary writing is found in the works of

---

[1] Friedrich Schlegel, *Philosophical Fragments*, trans. Peter Firchow (Minneapolis, MN: University of Minnesota Press, 1991), p. 21.
[2] David Metzer, *Musical Modernism at the Turn of the Twenty-First Century* (Cambridge University Press, 2009), p. 8.

composers of otherwise dissimilar aesthetic orientations. One advantageous feature of fragmentary writing is that it allows the incorporation of snippets from historical works into new ones. While the uncompromising complexity of mid-century serialism generally failed to meet the public's desire for beauty, composers of the late 1960s found a way of referencing a historical idea of beauty within new music – without letting go of complexity – by quoting fragments from the past in montage works. However, quotations were not applied as mere ornaments to soften serialist austerity; the emergence of montage aesthetics signalled a shift in priorities from coherence to momentariness. This technique has recurred across artistic genres throughout modernism and postmodernism, and the interest in works of the past seems as strong as ever among artists today.

In aesthetic theory, the modernist and postmodernist affinity with quotation and reference has been subject to various interpretations. The explanations generally pertain to artists' historical and cultural context, assuming that twentieth-century artists are using bits and pieces of existing works to deconstruct and parody works of the past, as a more or less deliberate endeavour to enact a 'loss of meaning'. This loss of meaning and alienation is due to radical changes in people's lives, brought on by industrialization, the technological revolution and the two World Wars, all taking place within a time span of seventy years. Other interpretations of the modernist technique of quotation and reference seem to allow a more positive motivation, understanding quotation as a play with connotations and memories, a comment upon, or even honouring and celebration of, works of the past. In this manner, art becomes self-reflective and the autonomy of art is put into question. In *Philosophy of New Music*, Adorno writes about Stravinsky: 'The music about music lets it be understood that it is no microcosm complete in itself but rather the reflection of the broken and depleted ... Parody, the fundamental form of music about music, means to imitate something and through imitation ridicule it.'[3] Adorno distrusts Stravinsky's distancing of himself from his material, seeing this operation as a symptom of shallow parody. However, in discussing Mahler's music, Adorno associates references and 'fractured form' with a unique treatment of obsolete material (describing the Scherzo from Mahler's Ninth Symphony, which Adorno declares to be the first example of musical montage), allowing that this might be the best means of transcending the reification of this material in an authentic way.[4] Either way, Adorno treats fragmentary music as something that withdraws meaning, destabilizes

---

[3] Theodor W. Adorno, *Philosophy of New Music*, trans. and ed. Robert Hullot-Kentor (Minneapolis, MN: University of Minnesota Press, 2006), p. 137.

[4] Theodor W. Adorno, *Mahler. A Musical Physiognomy*, trans. Edmund Jephcott (University of Chicago Press, 1992), p. 32.

aesthetic autonomy, parodies and makes art self-reflective. Accordingly, quoted fragments and references are used as a means to make a statement about extra-aesthetic matters, often thought to reflect alienation and the collapse of what Lyotard called the 'grand narrative'[5]. This view resonates in aesthetic theory throughout the twentieth century, in both Renato Poggioli's and Peter Bürger's classic theories of the avant-garde, in writings on postmodern intertextuality and in Linda Hutcheon's book on parody, viewing parody as the spirit of twentieth-century art by and large: 'Parody links the modern to the post-modern, James Joyce to Salman Rushdie, Pablo Picasso to Cindy Sherman, Sergei Prokofiev to Luciano Berio.'[6] Correspondingly, the understanding of twentieth-century art is thought to be dependent on the recipient's awareness of the references that the work contains, and the ability to read it in terms of deconstruction, parody, commentary and so on. By contrast, the momentary experience and the immediate aesthetic effect of such fragments has been given less attention by theorists, even though momentary experience – especially in the case of music which unfolds in time – represents an essential factor of the work's effectiveness.

Interpretation based on the assumed intention and referential meaning of quotations and references may no doubt provide important perspectives, which, retrospectively, may influence a listener's experience of the work in question. But if taking pleasure in fragmentary pieces relied essentially on the listener's ability to decipher the origin and meaning of quotes and references, and on 'catching the statement', this would require an analytical listening mode and the effect of such works would be reserved for a marginal group of listeners. If the enactment of meaninglessness, irony, parody and deconstruction were the final purpose of avant-garde techniques of montage, quotation and reference, its effect would be dated and its potential soon depleted. It would then be fair to say that the avant-garde really did bring on its own destruction, which seems to be Peter Bürger's conclusion on the matter of the historical avant-garde.[7] Bürger's account is mainly based on Benjamin's and Adorno's writings on early

---

[5] In *The Postmodern Condition* (*La Condition Postmoderne: Rapport sur le Savoir*, Paris: Les Editions de Minuit, 1979), Lyotard coins the term 'grand narrative' to designate the stories a culture tells about itself as a means to maintain stability and order, and observes that society, in the course of the twentieth century, is increasingly characterized by incredulity towards these grand narratives.

[6] Linda Hutcheon, *A Theory of Parody: The Teachings of Twentieth-Century Art Forms* (New York: Methuen, 1985).

[7] In *Theory of the Avant-Garde*, Peter Bürger presents 'shock' as the main purpose of avant-garde art; shock brought on by the refusal to provide coherence and meaning, and in turn make the recipient put into question his or her 'life praxis'. (*Theory of the Avant-Garde*, trans. Michael Shaw (Minneapolis, MN: University of Minnesota Press, 1984), p. 80.) Although Bürger's account of the historical avant-garde to a great extent can be ascribed to Adorno, one should

twentieth-century avant-garde. Adorno views montage as the defining feature of the avant-garde and relates montage to shock: the principle of montage was conceived as an act against a surreptitiously achieved organic unity; it was meant to shock. Once this shock is neutralized, the assemblage once more becomes indifferent material; the technique no longer suffices to trigger communication between the aesthetic and the extra-aesthetic, and its interest dwindles to a cultural-historical curiosity. However, the techniques and approaches that typically are traced back to Dadaism and surrealism, like montage, juxtaposition, quotation and automatism, still thrive in various forms and continuously develop today within all art genres. In the realm of music, this can be seen in the works of an older, established generation of composers such as Salvatore Sciarrino, Helmut Lachenmann, Hans Zender, Dieter Schnebel, Wolfgang Rihm and James Dillon, as well as in works by the younger generation that includes Matthew Herbert, Francois Sahran, Johannes Kreidler, Jennifer Walshe, Natasha Barrett and Lars Petter Hagen – evidence enough that composers today still rely on the aesthetic value of these creative techniques. I will suggest that the resilience of these techniques owes much to the fact that they continue to carry great aesthetic potential in their creation of intense 'moments' in addition to, and regardless of, the outcome of retrospective analysis of the references that they contain.

Modern moments

The technique of fragmentary writing provokes some remarkable consequences in terms of temporality. The *moment* is central to modern aesthetic consciousness regardless of genre, whether this moment is labelled as 'epiphany', 'aesthetic ecstasy', 'aesthetic appearance', 'aphorism' or 'pure instant'– concepts that all indicate culminating points of expressive or dramatic intensity. As Berthold Hoeckner points out, the musical moment is paradoxical in taking place 'at the intersection between part and whole in the material realm, and between instant and process in the temporal realm',[8] and the ability to understand the relationship between these parameters has often been a measure of musical education and social status. While unrefined listeners may enjoy particular moments of larger works, the appreciation of beautiful passages is not qualified and complete

---

be aware that it is but one of several possible interpretations of Adorno's rather dense and, at times, paradoxical argument.
[8] Berthold Hoeckner, *Programming the Absolute: Nineteenth-Century German Music and the Hermeneutics of the Moment* (Princeton University Press, 2002), p. 5.

unless it is the product of the capacity to perceive the whole, as Adorno argues in the following, much-quoted, passage in *Aesthetic Theory*:

> Some measures in Beethoven sound like the sentence in *Elective Affinities*: 'Like a star, hope shot down from the sky'; thus in the slow movement of the Sonata in D minor op. 31, no. 2. One only has to play the passage in the context of the whole movement and then alone in order to hear how much it owes its incommensurability, its radiance beyond the structure, to that structure. The passage becomes tremendous because its expression transcends what precedes it through the concentration of a cantabile, humanized melody. It is rendered individual in relation to, and by way of the totality; it is its product as well as its suspension.[9]

Adorno convincingly articulates the necessary and logical relationship between 'tremendous passages' and the whole. The celebration of the awareness of overarching structures seemed to him to have a pedagogical, if not a moral, foundation. Adorno had a clear conception of 'structural listening' as superior to 'atomistic listening', the former implying an ability to perceive the relationship between part and whole and the latter described as the mere consumption of culinary moments. Nevertheless, Adorno did acknowledge that musical Bildung not only meant the ability to perceive music as a meaningful whole but also included the sensitivity to particular beautiful passages. Works of modernism, however, accord a higher priority to the moment as an individual unit. Modernist listeners no longer – at least not in the manner of classical or early romantic listeners – expect the last part of the work to be a logical consequence of the first part of the work; Adorno's 'structural listening' or, for that matter, Furtwängler's concept of 'Fernhören' (informed by the structural theory of Heinrich Schenker) does not find its object in contemporary symphonic writing.

Today, the preference for intense moments is still often associated with shallowness and even hedonism, and a symptom of degeneration; nevertheless, instead of Jean Paul's condescending comparison of the concentration span of 'the people' to that of cattle,[10] we now relate the attention patterns of modern listeners to the experience of information overload and the immediacy of access – via the internet – to any tune, work, article or debate we wish to explore or browse. One may safely say that any aesthetic experience (any experience) that requires a long span of concentration comes under threat today. However, what is at stake here is not so much a question of the changing (or, indeed, deteriorating)

---

[9] Theodor W. Adorno, *Aesthetic Theory*, ed. Gretel Adorno and Rolf Tiedemann, trans. Robert Hullot-Kentor (London and New York: Continuum, 1997), p. 280.
[10] Quoted in Hoeckner, *Programming the Absolute*, p. 5.

attention patterns of the modern listener – as Adorno thought – as it is a question of the potential of the moment, and our interest in understanding the moment through analytical investigations, both hermeneutical[11] and phenomenological.

Appearance

The literary critic and philosopher Karl Heinz Bohrer wrote extensively about the moment of aesthetic appearance in 1981, in a collection of essays subsumed under the title *Suddenness (Plötzlichkeit)*, which Bohrer defines as 'a temporal modality ... understood ... as an expression and a sign of discontinuity and nonidentity, as whatever resists aesthetic integration'.[12] An important point in Bohrer's analysis is his discussion of a central concept in philosophy and aesthetic, that is, appearance (*Schein*). He examines the history of the concept as it is discussed in aesthetic theory, and finds that appearance, or semblance, from the earliest aesthetic writings, has been an object of suspicion and distrust as that which cloaks, and falls short of the essence and truth. This understanding can be traced back to Plato's theory of the Ideas versus their reflections.[13] Continuing his examination of the truth/appearance dichotomy, Bohrer finds that the late eighteenth-century aesthetic debate about 'the beautiful' also judged appearance to be deceptive and empty in comparison to truth. He further references the treatment of appearance in more recent theory, 'in the critique of "commodity aesthetics"'[14] with reference to Adorno and the writers influenced by him. Appearance was accorded some positive value, however, by Friedrich Schiller, in conceptualizing the immediate presence of beauty in art, in his 1795 essay 'On the Aesthetic Education of Man'. Here, Schiller rescues the concept of 'beautiful appearance', *although* it cloaks the truth. Kant, for his part, absolves semblance in poetry in his

---

[11] Hoeckner offers an extensive hermeneutical approach to the moment of German music in his *Programming the Absolute*. Although his investigations do not include examples from high modernism, the discussions provided on the musical moment, and the discourses of the moment in aesthetic literature, are helpful in this context.

[12] Karl Heinz Bohrer, *Suddenness: On the Moment of Aesthetic Experience*, trans. Ruth Crowley (New York: Columbia University Press, 1994), p. vii.

[13] Plato's theory of Forms presents non-material abstract forms (or ideas) as possessing the highest and most fundamental kind of reality, rather than the material world of change known to us through sensation. Plato's view also had implications for art: in the *Republic*, Plato declared the painters were three times removed from reality, since the painter imitates the reflection (i.e. the visible object, appearance) of the Form or Idea. Plato also disdained poets and rhetoricians because they betrayed reality (i.e. the Forms/Ideas) for the sake of creating an effect.

[14] Bohrer, *Suddenness*, p. 113.

Critique of Judgement, since poetry makes no claim to truth anyway. Nonetheless, Bohrer points out, both Schiller and Kant sustain the pejorative view of appearance, because they uphold the dualism between appearance and truth and define appearance as opposite to truth, or essence.

Bohrer points to Friedrich Nietzsche for the first radical revision of the concept of appearance, because Nietzsche is able to separate appearance from its morally superior companion, truth. Nietzsche brings about a historical change in the concept of appearance, by ridding it of the ambivalence and tension between the claim to truth and the objection that appearance exists only for effect. In fact, Nietzsche insists, 'one can no longer think of a metaphysical referent in connection with appearance';[15] instead, he introduces ideas of 'pure appearance' and 'appearance of appearance'. To Bohrer, Nietzsche's rehabilitation of the concept of appearance is vitally important to how we understand the position of art; building on Nietzsche's insight in *The Birth of Tragedy*, Bohrer writes that freeing appearance from a metaphysical referent can 'provide a new point of departure for supporting the position of aesthetic autonomy'.[16]

I find Bohrer's understanding of appearance illuminating when attempting to conceptualize the musical moment, and this concept of appearance sheds light on important aspects of the modernist musical fragment. Treating the fragment as appearance (Schein) temporarily liberates it from its referential significance and exposes music's unique way of producing meaning celebrated by the romantics. Thus, I will suggest that the understanding of the modernist fragment may throw modernist aesthetics of music into relief.

The fragment as experiment

In the early Romantic era, artists had already proclaimed the potential of the fragment, which was thought to be imperfect when complete, and incomplete when perfect. Friedrich Schlegel, a master of fragments and aphorisms, famously stated that a 'fragment, like a miniature work of art, has to be entirely isolated from the surrounding world and be complete in itself like a porcupine'.[17] Fragments were part of the romantic fascination with ruins, as architectural structures that suggested a greater completeness that only the imagination could fill, and the aesthetic of the fragment, moreover, allowed the threat of chaos to be presented within the frames of

---

[15] Friedrich W. Nietzsche, *The Birth of Tragedy*, trans. Clifton Fadiman (New York: Dover Publications, 1995), p. 139.
[16] Bohrer, *Suddenness*, p. 114.   [17] Schlegel, *Philosophical Fragments*, p. 45.

a conventional formal symmetry.[18] Music, and especially instrumental music, enjoyed a special position, as a model to other art forms. This was due to music's perceived meaninglessness – that is, music's freedom vis-à-vis referential meaning, as described in Novalis's proposal for a new kind of literature:

> Tales, without logic, nevertheless with associations, like *dreams*. Poems – simply *sounding well* and filled with beautiful words – but also without any sense or logic – at most single stanzas intelligible – they must be [?] like mere broken pieces of the most varied things. At best, true poetry can have an *allegorical* sense on the whole, and an indirect effect like music, etc.[19]

As much as praising music, this passage could serve as an honouring of the fragment, which allowed for a more spontaneous creativity, unbound by formal restrictions and expectations. Rosen writes, 'The technique of the fragment . . . allowed the artist a partial detachment of his work from reality, made a much more freely conceived relationship possible. What poets and painters envied was the freedom of music to manipulate its own forms and symbols, apparently without reference to a reality outside itself.'[20] Thus, the romantic aesthetics of the fragment did not only herald a turn away from the closed work – it also implied the awareness that the fragment as form accommodated music's way of making sense. The fragmentary state of modernism can, then, trace its prehistory to eras long preceding the pursuits of deconstruction and postmodern irony. This, I will argue, comprises one of the key transformations of musical modernism in recent decades: rather than being defined within a narrow historical model as a movement that rejects the past, modernism emerges in terms of innovative practices that allow composers to draw out connections to much earlier music.

Modernist fragments: the abandoned, the homeless and the abducted

The fragmentary becomes a key category for twentieth-century artists facing what Adorno describes as the crisis of meaning production, or

---

[18] Schumann's *Kinderszenen* provides an emblematic case. The last piece, 'Der Dichter Spricht', is an epilogue of sorts: the child has fallen asleep ('Kind in Einschlummern' precedes it) and Schumann stages himself as 'Der Dichter' – which reflects his idea of kinship between the arts – the poet who thinks out loud, so to speak. By staging himself in the title, Schumann also steps out of the piece; he recognizes a distance between himself and the work. The piece contains an abundance of fermatas and ritardandos within only twenty-six bars, centered around a dreamy recitative. This piece shows how far the romantic fragment could go in dissolving structure.

[19] Novalis, quoted in Charles Rosen, *The Romantic Generation* (Cambridge, MA: Harvard University Press, 1995), p. 75.

[20] Rosen, *The Romantic Generation*, p. 78.

what we, in a less dramatic (but also less salient) wording, may call a crisis of the idea of continuity – a crisis that had already emerged in romanticism and became more fully reflected in the 1890s, in the music of Mahler and Ives. The illusion of an adequate presentation of meaning, from then on, could only be maintained in individual moments. To Adorno, the fragment is that part of totality which resists totality, and as such – in line with his negative dialectics – Adorno found that the fragment reinvested art with truth content. To Maurice Blanchot, on the other hand, the fragment exists beyond a possibility of a whole, 'like a piece of meteor detached from an unknown sky'.[21] Either way, the fragment stands in a relation to something outside itself; it is never alone.

One may outline three main categories of musical fragments. The first category comprises works that for some reason remain unfinished either because the composer died or because, for other reasons, he or she had to abandon the work. In some cases, these works have been finished by later composers, either as performing versions completed in a style as close as possible to the style of the composer, or as recompositions (such as, e.g., Schubert's Tenth Symphony – finished by Berio in his 'Rendering'). In this category, we also find works that are left unfinished because the work itself seems to reject completion, as if it carries an immanent impossibility. This seemed to be the case, for example, with Schoenberg's opera *Moses und Aron*.[22]

The second category includes musical motives, lines and sections that present themselves as fragmentary in that they are created as open and ambiguous fractions rather than closed and defined units. Works by Luigi Nono and György Kurtág present this type of fragment – without any identifiable home surrounding or original context, they are 'fragments of nothing' and appear homeless.[23] This type of fragment relates to Blanchot's 'piece of meteor', and the composer's creative task is to endow the fragment with a marked potential – to make it point beyond itself in its state of incompleteness.

The third kind of fragment is quotation and reference, a more or less identifiable part abducted from an existing work in which it filled a specific function. This kind of fragment may be recognized and even identified by the listener, but it may also be experienced merely as a vague hint of something unidentified but somehow familiar. At any rate, this kind of

---

[21] Quoted in Metzer, *Musical Modernism*, p. 105.
[22] In *Moses und Aron*, Schoenberg takes what might be called the problem of representation to its limits. The opera raises the question as to whether the unrepresentable, the absolute, or God, can be represented. Due to the impossibility of the opera's ambition, it must necessarily remain a fragment, however, a 'fulfilled fragment'.
[23] The term 'fragments of nothing' is coined by David Metzer in *Musical Modernism*, p. 108.

fragment carries connotations from its original context, by virtue of which it explicitly points beyond itself; the composer's creativity lies in the process of selection, and recontextualization.

Here, I will examine a specimen of the latter – the abducted fragment – in particular, namely the opening motive of the second movement of Beethoven's Sixth Symphony quoted in what must be called a musical montage classic: the third movement of Berio's *Sinfonia*, 'In ruhig fliessender Bewegung'. This particular moment in Berio's montage will be discussed with particular regard to temporal aspects, examining how a small musical moment that, in its original context, participates in a continuous flux, becomes a 'now' in the context of the later montage, and to what extent this 'now' contains referential meaning.

Pastoral: Scene am Bach/In ruhig fliessender Bewegung

The fragment under discussion here is the 'Szene am Bach' clarinet motive from Beethoven's *Pastoral* Symphony, as it appears in Berio's *Sinfonia* (Example 8.1):

In Beethoven's symphony this brief motive is the first part of the second movement's main theme, comprised of softly undulating six-note figures. In its original context, this section primarily functions to establish the pastoral atmosphere: an unassuming clarinet figure accompanied by strings.[24] The motive is a small part of a peculiar theme that begins with a series of phrases that are so modest they could be taken to be middle-voice accompaniment figures – almost as if Beethoven had forgotten to write down the main theme for his movement. The theme points forward to more eventful parts; it establishes a certain atmosphere and has a particular role in the symphony's teleological line of development.

In Berio's montage, the motive is subject to several operations, the effect of which will vary according to the listener's familiarity with the references that are contained in the movement and this section in particular. We may

Example 8.1   Beethoven, *Pastoral* Symphony, 2nd movement (Szene am Bach), clarinet motive (bars 69–70).

---

[24] Berio in fact quotes the Beethoven theme as it appears in the recapitulation part of the *Pastoral* movement (as shown in Example 8.1), but this has no significance to the present argument.

Transformations of appearance

describe these operations and their effects, assuming, for now, that the listener is somewhat familiar with the canon of Western art music, and the connotations accumulated through a common reception history. I will focus here on those that are easy to perceive, independently of any retrospective scrutiny and analysis:[25]

- When Berio places the clarinet motive from Beethoven's *Pastoral* in a quiet section surrounded by rather noisy and contrasting excerpts from Hindemith, Mahler, Globokar and Beckett, he elevates certain of its attributes (ethereal, serene, and enchanting) while suppressing others (e.g. the earthy and traditional) that might in turn have come forward in other contexts.
- When Berio quotes Beethoven's clarinet motive, he evokes the entire *Pastoral* by association. However, by being quoted (or pointed at) by Berio, we hear Beethoven via Berio, that is, as Berio hears Beethoven. Although the fragment is recognizable, we now hear it 'as new'.
- Being separated from the context in which it served a musical-syntactical function, the fragment appears to preserve only its semantic, or connotative, meaning. In effect, the fragment demonstrates music's 'own peculiar way' of signification by largely invalidating those otherwise recognizable qualities that music shares with verbal language – namely, syntax and a certain grammatical logic.
- The Beethoven fragment attains a specific kind of referentiality; the motive is chosen as an emblem of the *Pastoral* Symphony as well as for its other connotative abilities, that is, the evocation of nature, tranquility, ease, harmony and so on.

Relating this moment to Adorno's description of the beautiful passages in Beethoven (see above), one could say that the 'Szene am Bach' motive is rendered individual in relation to the totality of Berio's movement, in that it is fairly easy to discern 'as quotation', compared to many of the other quotations in this movement. One could hardly say, however, that it is the product, or the suspension, of that totality, at least not in the way that Adorno had in mind. While this motive takes a natural part of the *Pastoral* movement's syntactical and architectural logic, its relation to Berio's totality is that of a visitor from the past. It is a surprise, in terms of its familiarity. In its original context, however, Beethoven's clarinet motive does not strike us as a moment charged with

---

[25] Other operations are most likely to be recognized only with retrospective analysis: taking part in a multilayered web of signification – voiced over by the recitation of text from Samuel Beckett, new (referential) meaning results from the juxtaposition with other composers' voices and intentions indicated by the neighbouring fragments. Through an act of quotation, Berio enters a dialogue with Beethoven, that might even change the way we listen to the *Pastoral* Symphony.

meaning; it attains this potential by force of Berio's reuse. Its relation to Berio's totality is rather different from that logical and reciprocal relation that Adorno saw as a precondition for what he calls the 'schöne Stellen' (see above). It is still a beautiful moment – and, in my view, more intensely so, than in its original context. How does this new potential arise?

The 'now' – the moment of aesthetic appearance

Bohrer's rehabilitation of the concept of appearance is significant to how the *Pastoral* fragment may be explained and understood, and I will argue that it offers a viable approach to the aesthetic experience of the fragmentary works of modernism, and how these works evoke emphatic moments. To Bohrer, the fragment – with its high degree of momentary character and resistance towards aesthetic integration – represents the aesthetics of suddenness, and as such stands in a certain relation to the Sublime.[26] In the context of musical montage, suddenness relates to the change of temporality brought on by the fragment's separation from a whole. The new capacity of the *Pastoral* fragment discussed above indicates that something changes in our experience of this excerpt when it appears as a fragment – and this change cannot be exhaustively explained by the mechanisms of intertextual references; nor can the new intensity of the clarinet motive simply be reduced to the joy of recognition. Rather, it has to do with the change of status from part of a teleological development to fragment; it entails a shift from being a part of a continuous flow to becoming a 'now'. When Berio borrows this small motive from Beethoven's *Pastoral*, the fragment is liberated from its original formal function as a symphonic theme; it now 'goes nowhere'. The appearance of the Beethoven motive now has no musical-syntactic justification. We get no warning of its appearance; it is suddenly upon us. Likewise, after its statement, the motive is left to linger; it lacks future. The motive is deprived of, or rather, liberated from, the surroundings so habituated in the ears of those familiar with Beethoven's symphony.

In his elaborations on suddenness, Bohrer draws on Nietzsche's phenomenology of appearance as presented in *The Birth of Tragedy*, where Nietzsche identifies the Dionysian energy of art as that in which

---

[26] Bohrer does not, in this discussion, define the Sublime and the Beautiful as mutually exclusive. Rather, he seems, in line with Schopenhauer, to view the two as related and the difference between them to be a matter of degree rather than kind. After all, the view of the Sublime and the Beautiful as antithetical was not established until the 1700s, first voiced in the writings of Edmund Burke's *A Philosophical Enquiry into the Origin of Our Ideas of the Sublime and Beautiful* (1756).

the power of life breaks through the balanced and orderly Apollonian form. By means of the artistic principles of the Dionysian and the Apollonian, Nietzsche defined the specific affective mode of aesthetic appearance and the psychological effect of the aesthetic-rhetorical epiphany. Nietzsche famously stated that existence can only be justified as an aesthetic phenomenon, and his impulse to separate out the concept of the 'appearance of appearance' arose from aesthetic experience. He explains this apparently tautological concept by referring to the aesthetic perception that dreams leave behind in the dreamer. 'Just as we have a sensation glimmering through the dream reality that it is mere appearance, we enjoy the illusory nature of poetry.'[27] But reality itself, according to Nietzsche, *is appearance*, and art – which reflects this appearance – is the appearance of appearance. When 'danger' and 'terror' occur in this double illusion, we take pleasure in it, because we are aware that it is just an illusion. Nietzsche holds that pleasure in illusions, or a 'primordial desire for mere appearance' is elaborated as a law of human psychology, irrespective of historical context. Nietzsche reverses the metaphysical priorities: neither being nor truth, but rather appearance occupies the pre-eminent place of existential experience; in Plato's terms, Nietzsche wants to reach not the Ideas, but their reflections.

Bohrer traces Nietzsche's interest in the pathos of the sudden, terrifying appearance back to the rhetorical tradition and the concept of the Sublime developed from Longinus and, later, in Burke's aesthetic theory. In his description of rhetoric, Longinus in fact places emotional effect over truth: the orator's ability to bring the audience to ecstasy was valued over his ability to persuade. Bohrer observes an affinity between the arguments of Longinus and Nietzsche: the former regards the 'dazzling effect of the sublime' as opposed to merely rhetorical effect; the latter holds that the ecstasy of Dionysian appearance should not be jeopardized by the 'lethargy' of Apollonian appearance – that is, by such elements as plot development, character representation and psychological refinement.

Fragmentary writing disregards the concerns of plot and character development, or, in music, large-scale form and thematic development. Fragmentary writing can mimic the dream-narrative, which operates beyond formal considerations, as Nietzsche describes it in *The Birth of Tragedy*:

> The beautiful appearance of the dream-worlds, in creating which every man is a perfect artist, is the prerequisite of all plastic art, and, in fact, as we shall see, of an important part of poetry too. In our dreams, we delight in

---
[27] Bohrer, *Suddenness*, p. 124.

the immediate apprehension of form; all forms speak to us; none are unimportant and none are superfluous.[28]

To Bohrer, the valuation of art as appearance makes an argument against the prevalent understanding of the avant-garde and modernism; viewing avant-garde art as resting on a shock effect that becomes ever more difficult to obtain, Bohrer sees something else in avant-garde art. In reference to Nietzsche's Dionysian aspect of art, Bohrer argues as follows:

> To date, we have failed to examine this dimension of depth in the avant-garde, say in Duchamp's provocation, because it was classified too early as formalist anti-art and was relegated to an objective history of art and style and to the idea of art prevalent in those disciplines. We might still discover that Duchamp's laughter has never yet been heard. Shock is disturbing not only because it provokes us but also because of the up to now unknown aspects of what it expresses, an aspect that confuses us. Shock is not a matter of ever more eccentric new eccentricities; it is a result of contents of consciousness that have not yet been processed. Otherwise what the avant-garde originated would become a mere craft. Duchamp's cynicism lies in his epistemological wit. It is the same cynicism as that of Heinrich von Kleist, of Oswald Wiener, of Kurt Schwitters. It is yet to be realized in the mind of the academic disciplines and, in all of our minds.[29]

Bohrer defines the emphatic moment as that which presents 'the unknown' – regardless of style and formal innovation. The innovative impulse is wit, which breaks through convention and expresses itself in the moment, which accommodates the unknown, the new, the not yet understood:

> Especially montage, as we know, has uncomfortably prevented that comforting synthesis, that direct interpretation of meaning. For that reason scholars have largely explained the enigmatic character of modern art by recourse to the aesthetic accomplishments of those formal means thanks to which a large segment of the public can still exclaim, half a century after the appearance of the first products of modernism: I don't understand it![30]

Instead of shock, then, Bohrer sees the moment, or the 'now', as the defining feature of avant-garde art, since the 'now' opens to the unknown. Montage presents its own constructedness, its own fabrication; fragmentary writing does not present itself to the listener as the product of any discernible causal chain, structural necessity or teleological process. It presents no musical-syntactic 'argument'; rather, the elements are chosen primarily for their immediate, individual appearance. Rather than

---

[28] Nietzsche, *The Birth of Tragedy*, p. 2.   [29] Bohrer, *Suddenness*, p. 78.   [30] Ibid.

emerging from any rational logical necessity, it evolves much like the way elements of dreams appear by force of the dreamer's unconscious, affective motivation. The borrowed fragments may imply snippets of development, direction or tonal argument that they have been part of in their original context; in the Beethoven quotation in Berio traces of development are displayed, but not acted upon – they are not granted any significance for the further unfolding of the montage.

Wit and 'the new' versus irony and convention

To Bohrer, then, it is not through its formal innovations per se that the avant-garde provided the new, but through epistemological wit that breaks through cultural norms and that can be interpreted as the realization of the emphatic moment:

> This epistemological wit at this emphatic moment originates when an observer or reader is put into a perceptual situation where the unique character of what he or she sees or reads shakes up the dominant perceptual norms and values.[31]

While irony is a socially mediated attitude which depends on cultural norms, wit, to Bohrer, is subjective and breaks through cultural norms in a subversive, dangerous way. In this line of thought, it is not the manipulation of references that makes up the striking moments in Berio's montage, since references rely on cultural norms. Rather, it is Berio's wit, manifested in the way in which the fragments are allowed to appear for no evident reason – appearing *as appearances*. Likewise, it is not the identification and analysis of references that makes the listener decide whether or not the music is valuable to her or him, because aesthetic judgement begins to take place in a pre-theoretical intuitive phase: 'The aesthetic-evaluative reaction that finally produces a value judgement is not an analytical act; it is always a synthetic act that is simply performed in different phases', in which the first phase is 'an intuitive, imaginative decision in which we enter into a basic value relationship before we arrive at any intellectually justifiable judgement'.[32] Rejecting the idea that the innovation of the avant-garde lies in its development of shocking techniques, Bohrer also invalidates Peter Bürger's suggestion that the neo-avant-garde (or postmodernism) is void of sense, because it attempted to repeat the project of the avant-garde. If wit is the innovative force that broke ground for the new in the avant-garde of the early twentieth century, this could, in principle, also apply to the

[31] Ibid.   [32] Ibid., p. 80.

'avant-garde' of romanticism, or, for that matter, innovation in any historical epoch. Wit is 'what fits the moment',[33] and, indeed, wit is what fits the fragment; the fragment accommodates wit, or the modern impulse, as Schlegel observed in Fragment 24 of his *Aetheneum Fragments*, quoted at the beginning of this chapter.

Although the *Sinfonia* movement is a unique and unusual example in its comprehensive use of quoted fragments, it shows some general mechanisms that also apply to other, quite different instances of fragmentary writing. One composer who explored fragmentary writing was Luigi Nono, whose string quartet *Fragmente – Stille, An Diotima* has become a modernist classic. As David Metzer recounts from a pre-concert talk Nono gave before its performance,[34] Nono was concerned to distinguish the fragment from the aphorism; the fragment should always remain open, as 'moments' of 'potential' and 'possibilities', and not self-contained, like the aphorism.[35] Once the quiet atmosphere of the work is established, each sound produced by the string instruments appears with intense and transparent materiality. To Nono, the nature of the interaction between the fragments should be one of succession and proliferation rather than development,[36] and he rejected the idea of a large-scale coherent unity. Another composer responsible for a modern classic of fragmentary writing is György Kurtág: when Kurtág sets fragments from Kafka's notebooks and diaries, he musically enacts various states of mind expressed in the text. Apart from their instrumentation, Kurtág's Kafka fragments have too little in common concerning musical material to evoke the unified whole of a song cycle. The trembling voice, and the precipitous bowing and nervous pizzicati of the violin in the fragment *Eine Lange Geschichte* evokes the intensity of the moment related in Kafka's words:

> Ich sehe einem Mädchen in die Augen, und es war ein sehr lange Liebesgeschichte mit Donner und Küssen und Blitz. Ich lebe rasch.[37]
>
> (I look a girl in the eye and it was a very long love story with thunder and kisses and lightning. I live fast.)

Describing the overwhelming plenitude experienced in a moment, Kafka's note could in itself serve as a good metaphor for the potential of the fragment. Since the fragment remains open, unfinished and inconclusive it can accommodate the utopian.

---

[33] Ibid., p. 78.   [34] Metzer, *Musical Modernism*, p. 111.   [35] Ibid., p. 112.   [36] Ibid., p. 113.
[37] Quoted in Christopher Cook, 'Programme note: Kafka Fragments: Text and Translation', available at: http://www.barbican.org.uk/media/events/10292kafkafragmentsforweb.pdf (accessed 9 March 2015).

These different examples of the modernist fragment all seem to obtain a certain status, by force of their separation from 'the whole' – whether that whole is an actual work (as with the abducted *Pastoral* motive) or the *possibility* of a whole (as in the homeless fragments of Kurtág/Kafka and Nono/Hölderlin). When the (idea of a) whole withdraws, the fragment becomes the locus of existential experience. The fragment is displayed as *pure appearance*; its function is in the moment, with no obligations towards the large-scale architecture. In this state, the unassuming *Pastoral* motive attains an intense, but nonreferential meaning when it appears in Berio's *Sinfonia*. In this perspective, we may say that Berio stages Nietzsche's 'world of mere appearances' in his *Sinfonia* movement. Rather than viewing the fragment as a symptom of modernism's withdrawal of meaning, it may be seen as the archetype, or indeed, *appearance* of musical meaning. The modernist fragment does not draw its force from the idea of essence or totality; rather, it is true by force of being the appearance of appearance. Likewise, the intense moments, 'schöne Stellen' or epiphanies, of fragmentary music do not come about as reward for the listener's apprehension of totality; their logic does not rest on continuity or causality, and they ignore dichotomies such as depth versus surface, or truth versus appearance. Rather, they appear suddenly. What is required from us listeners, then, is not so much the ability of perceiving overarching structures, as the capacity to remain sensitive to the moment – and thus, to the new and unknown.

9 Rethinking Boulez

Schemes, logics and paradigms of musical modernity

Edward Campbell

Midway through the second decade of the twenty-first century, Pierre Boulez, as the sole surviving member of the serial generation of composers that came to prominence after World War II, remains for many the elder statesman of European musical modernism. His longevity and continued prominence notwithstanding, the cultural status of post-war European modernism has long been uncertain. For Richard Taruskin, the movement was nothing more than an aesthetic epiphenomenon of the Cold War;[1] Benoît Duteurtre celebrated a 'Requiem for an Avant-Garde',[2] in which Boulez featured prominently, and even the sympathetic Arved Ashby, who highlighted 'the pleasure of modernist music', could not help but note that 'Babbitt, Boulez, Varèse and Stockhausen [were] close to becoming irrelevant at the turn of the twenty-first century'.[3]

Whatever the views of his critics, Boulez, like Nono, Pousseur and Stockhausen and later Berio, Ligeti and Xenakis, to name only some key figures, belongs to an intermediate generation of composers that sit between the early modernists, Debussy, Schoenberg, Berg, Webern, Stravinsky and Bartók, and the post-serial generation that have made musical modernism at the end of the twentieth and beginning of the twenty-first century a multiple phenomenon that is irreducible to any one compositional tendency. In this historically central position, he has been well placed to observe and comment on the transition from late romanticism to early modernism, on the shift from early modernism to the post-war serialism of his own generation and finally on the transformed

---

[1] Richard Taruskin, *Music in the Late Twentieth Century: The Oxford History of Western Music*, 5 vols. (Oxford University Press, 2010), vol. V, pp. 18–22.
[2] Benoît Duteurtre, *Requiem pour une avant-garde* (Paris: Robert Laffont, 1995).
[3] Arved Ashby, 'Intention and Meaning in Modernist Music' in *The Pleasure of Modernist Music: Listening, Meaning, Intention, Ideology* (University of Rochester Press, 2004), p. 36. Susan McClary stated in 1989 that the music of the avant-garde has 'been heard by few and has had next to no social impact. It is the last hurrah of a historical bloc that lost its hegemonic grip on culture at the turn of the century' (Susan McClary, 'Terminal Prestige: The Case of Avant-Garde Music Composition', *Cultural Critique*, 12 (1989), pp. 57–81, p. 64). McClary recontextualizes her comments in her chapter in this volume.

understanding of serialism from the 1950s to the changed circumstances of the 1980s and 1990s.

Transformations of musical modernism notwithstanding, Boulez is characterized by Henri Pousseur as, of all the post-war generation, the one who remained the most enduringly connected to the 'grammatical formulations' of the 1950s, still finding in them new possibilities for development.[4] Indeed, Boulez is generally portrayed as having essentially been faithful to the principles of mid-century musical modernism. Given the frequent equation of high modernism and the nascent serialism of the 1950s, it is noteworthy that uncertainty regarding the precise role of the series in Boulez's works from the 1970s onwards has to some extent been dispelled by recent scholarship. Erling E. Guldbrandsen concludes that the place of the series has been overstated in the literature on Boulez. Looking specifically to *Pli selon pli*, a work which the composer began in 1957 but which he continued to work on and revise intermittently until 1990, Guldbrandsen shows that the serial language was transformed radically during this period. So much did Boulez develop his materials in original and unexpected ways that what appears in the final versions of scores such as *Improvisation III* bears little direct relation to the serial procedures employed at the outset.[5] At the same time, Jonathan Goldman notes that while Boulez's later works are marked by greater interest in questions of perceptibility, he remains faithful to serial thinking in *Répons* and 'realizations of serial matrices abound' in *Dérive I* and *Mémoriale*.[6]

Acknowledging the continuous but transformed nature of Boulez's modernity, I set out in this chapter to explore his identification with the modernist paradigm and his rejection of others. This is followed by a summary and discussion of how the concept of musical modernism punctuates Boulez's early writings and how the positions set out there are to some extent modified or even transformed in his statements from the 1980s and 1990s. The final section of the chapter looks to how the philosophical work of Gilles Deleuze and Félix Guattari, as well as that of Alain Badiou, provide alternative ways of conceptualizing the composer's trajectory.

---

[4] Henri Pousseur, *Musiques Croisées* (Paris: L'Harmattan, 1997), p. 165.
[5] See Erling E. Guldbrandsen, 'Casting New Light on Boulezian Serialism' in Edward Campbell and Peter O'Hagan (eds.), *Boulez Studies* (Cambridge University Press, 2016, forthcoming).
[6] Jonathan Goldman, *The Musical Language of Pierre Boulez: Writings and Compositions* (Cambridge University Press, 2011), p. 98.

Aspects of modernism

In her 1995 study of IRCAM, Georgina Born lists six characteristic features of musical modernism, characteristics that indicate succinctly that Boulez is a modernist composer. The claim that modernism is 'a reaction by artists against the prior aesthetic and philosophical forms of romanticism and classicism',[7] while not respecting the complex positions of early modernists such as Schoenberg, is clearly the case with early Boulez. To take only some of the clearest examples, aspects of a negational aesthetic are glimpsed in the *Sonatine* for flute and piano (1946) to the extent that it is written against the grain of early twentieth-century French chamber music; the four movements of the Second Piano Sonata (1948) attempt to explode traditional musical forms, and the works of the early 1950s, *Polyphonie X* and *Structures I*, unleash the negational impulse with unprecedented vigour in confounding the kinds of relationships that had formerly linked the separate musical parameters within a unified whole. Indeed, the very notion of the composer's subjectivity is negated in the algorithmical processes of *Structures Ia*.[8]

An interest in 'new media, technology, and science' is again apparent with Boulez from his early attentiveness to Cage's prepared piano, his brief involvement with Pierre Schaeffer and *musique concrète* and, over a longer period, a fascination with the combination of electronics and live performance that, while not a permanent feature in his composition, is nevertheless found in *Poésie pour pouvoir* (1958), *Répons* (1981/5), *Dialogue de l'ombre double* (1984), ... *explosante-fixe* ... (1991/3) and *Anthèmes 2* (1997). We can add to this, the importing of conceptual terminology from the scientific domain and, perhaps above all, the foundation of IRCAM.

The importance of theory for modernist composers[9] is confirmed by Boulez's voluminous writings, from the articles of the late 1940s and 1950s dealing most importantly with the legacy of his immediate predecessors, the setting out of the post-war challenges and the nuts and bolts of the new serial technique, to articles, occasional pieces, endless interviews and the significant achievements of the Darmstadt and Collège de France lectures. Born identifies 'a rhetoric of progress, constant innovation, and change' at the heart of modernism,[10] an element that is found throughout Boulez's

---

[7] Georgina Born, *Rationalizing Culture: IRCAM, Boulez, and the Institutionalization of the Musical Avant-Garde* (Berkeley, CA: University of California Press, 1995), pp. 40–1.
[8] See Edward Campbell, *Boulez, Music and Philosophy* (Cambridge University Press, 2010), pp. 38–47.
[9] Born, *Rationalizing Culture*, p. 42. [10] Ibid., p. 43.

writings and which, more importantly, is put into practice in all of his compositions, in which no piece replicates exactly what has been achieved by a previous one, but is always an attempt to do something new, something different, albeit that certain techniques and habits for generating material and producing compositions are retained or developed.[11] Born's charge that modernist composers are wilfully obscure and that they set out to alienate audiences needs to be much more nuanced.[12] While it is far from established that Boulez and his contemporaries wanted their compositions to be inaccessible to listeners, the radical estrangement experienced by many cannot be denied and it is clear that the price of innovation has often been severely diminished perceptibility, audibility and communicability. Nor can it be denied that Boulez's more technical writings, such as the Darmstadt lectures, have not always been transparent.

Born identifies within modernism an 'oscillation between rationalism and irrationalism, objectivism and subjectivism' that resonates forcefully with the dialectic of Boulez's composition. In terms of the irrational, there is the oft-cited call for a music that is 'collective hysteria and magic, violently modern – along the lines of Antonin Artaud' and his identification of the organization of delirium, as an imperative for 'effective art'.[13] As for the rational, there is his penchant for deduction in musical composition, the citation of the philosopher Louis Rougier and those paradoxical passages where he states that deduction should not be equated solely with rationality, and where he envisages the possibility that it can be 'highly illogical or irrational' and disruptive in effect.[14] Born's observation that modernist artists often have 'ambivalent relations with popular culture'[15] is clearly the case with Boulez. While we might be tempted to conclude that there is no ambivalence in Boulez's generally poor opinion of popular culture, the actuality is not necessarily so simple. David Schiff, for example, describes *Le Marteau sans maître* as

> remotely jazzy and vaguely oriental, rhythmically frantic yet emotionally cool. It was atonal, but without the angst of most of the atonal music I knew. Heard today, it might seem quintessentially fifties – a vodka martini set to

---

[11] For an extended discussion of Boulez's ideas on the philosophy of history, historicism, evolution, revolution and necessity see Campbell, *Boulez, Music and Philosophy*, pp. 47–56.
[12] Born, *Rationalizing Culture*, p. 44.
[13] Pierre Boulez, *Stocktakings from an Apprenticeship*, collected and ed. Paule Thévenin, trans. Stephen Walsh (Oxford: Clarendon Press, 1991), pp. 54 and 43.
[14] Pierre Boulez, *Leçons de musique (Points de repère III)*, collected and ed. Jean-Jacques Nattiez (Paris: Éditions Christian Bourgois, 2005), pp. 92–3.
[15] Born, *Rationalizing Culture*, p. 44.

music, with instrumentation not far from what you would hear on a Chet Baker record or, with those bongos, a hi-fi demo.[16]

If we recognize something of Boulez in each of these characteristics of musical modernism, it is equally the case that postmodernism in none of its multiple theorizations seems to fit the bill. While Boulez has not addressed the principal exponents of postmodernism explicitly in his writings and interviews, we can infer his most likely responses to their positions easily enough. Defined as the end of the avant-garde, in which the innovative possibilities within modernism are now exhausted, Boulez clearly disagrees. He is no more convinced by the related view that postmodernism indicates the end of the idea of history as a succession of novelties, understood as the new, and he reiterates the importance 'of novelty, in the sense of renewal', and of 'grammars' that are constantly transformed, in a conversation published in 2014.[17] While Boulez has not addressed explicitly the hypothesis of Jean-François Lyotard that postmodernism marks the end of metanarratives or the grand modernist narratives, it is clear that his agreement with the philosopher's later recasting of the debate in the musical sphere must be at best partial.

For Lyotard, who is ultimately unconcerned with designations such as 'modern' and 'postmodern' in relation to new music, the crucial point of commonality linking Boulez and John Cage is precisely the continued 'emancipation of sound matter',[18] and he goes so far as to suggest that their seemingly conflicting desires, to let sounds be (Cage) and to organize several aspects of sound (Boulez), are facets of a shared project. Boulez's numerous dismissals of Cage's compositional activity indicate that he is not in agreement with Lyotard on this point.[19]

While Boulez's view of musical history and his theory of musical creativity are not unilinearly progressive in direction, they nevertheless harbour an underlying historicism and sense of progress, though with certain caveats.[20] Once again, he refuses the idea that we can speak of more recent music as 'better' than what has gone before while allowing that it has 'another kind of complexity', and he is equally unwilling to argue for

---

[16] David Schiff, 'Unreconstructed Modernist', *The Atlantic Monthly* (September 1995), 104–8, p. 104.
[17] Pierre Boulez, Jean-Pierre Changeux and Philippe Manoury, *Les Neurones enchantés* (Paris: Odile Jacob, 2014), pp. 58–9. See also pp. 60–2.
[18] Jean-François Lyotard, 'Musique et postmodernité', *Surfaces*, 6/203 (v.1.0F – 27 November 1996), 4–16, p. 10.
[19] Boulez, Changeux and Manoury, *Les neurones enchantés*, p. 150.
[20] For a more detailed discussion, see Campbell, *Boulez, Music and Philosophy*, pp. 47–56.

the superiority of the European tradition over musical traditions from elsewhere.[21]

In contrast with the modern, postmodernism often signals that it is no longer mandatory to 'forget' the past, and eclecticism and the mixing of styles and genres is now valued. Elements from older works can be cited within a new composition and the old division of culture into high and low, elite and popular is abolished in favour of their interaction and the promotion of heterogeneity and pluralism. Nothing here has any place in Boulez. While for Charles Jencks, in a postmodern age many styles are simultaneously acceptable and 'all fashions are in fashion',[22] in Fredric Jameson's view postmodernism is a kind of 'aesthetic populism'.[23] Boulez's rejection of this kind of thinking is evident *avant la lettre* in the article 'Stravinsky Remains' (1953), where, while analyzing rhythmic structures in *The Rite of Spring*, he laments that it was not Stravinsky but 'jazz, with its single poverty-stricken syncopation and invariable four-beat bar, that was able to take the credit for rhythmic renewal in music'.[24] In discussion with Deliège over twenty years later he states that elements from the past can only be integrated into contemporary composition 'in the most abstract terms'.[25] Finally, postmodernism demands communicability and one of its most highly prized aspirations is the desire to end elitism and a certain hermeticism. While communicability has been an important consideration for Boulez at least from the 1970s onwards, this has not necessarily been at the expense of complexity.

Notions of modernism in early Boulez

In a number of passages in his early writings, Boulez looks to the work of previous composers in relation to romanticism and modernism. In 'Trajectories' (1949) he commends Mussorgsky's poetics as having had an explosive impact on romanticism and he praises the modernity of his great opera *Boris Godunov*.[26] While accepting that 'morphological innovation' is more advanced in Schoenberg than in Debussy, he suggests that Schoenberg's music, particularly *Pierrot Lunaire*, does not achieve 'a modern dialectic of poetic expression' since it fails to break free from a

---

[21] Erling E. Guldbrandsen, 'Pierre Boulez in Interview, 1996 (I) Modernism, History and Tradition', *Tempo*, 65/255 (2011), 9–16, pp. 14–15.
[22] Charles Jencks, *What is Post-Modernism?* (Chichester: Academy Editions, 1996), p. 58.
[23] Fredric Jameson, *Postmodernism, or, The Cultural Logic of Late Capitalism* (Durham, NC: Duke University Press, 1991), p. 2.
[24] Boulez, *Stocktakings*, p. 56.
[25] Pierre Boulez, *Conversations with Célestin Deliège* (London: Eulenburg, 1976), p. 25.
[26] Boulez, *Stocktakings*, p. 196.

sensibility inherited directly from Wagner and Brahms.[27] Webern's music, in contrast, is described in 'Incipit' (1952) as 'the threshold'.[28] In an encyclopaedia entry on Schoenberg (1961), he writes of his 'post-romantic aesthetic',[29] while in 'The Current Impact of Berg' (1948) he expresses some concern that the romantic aspect of Berg's style is being used as 'the starting point' for a return to Wagnerism, a move he believes is anachronistic and an unacceptable 'capitulation'.[30] It is worth noting in this regard that while the young Boulez sees Schoenberg and Berg as implicated within German romanticism, Adorno already identifies the autonomy of the modernist aesthetic in the music of Wagner and Brahms which may be said, in different ways, 'to turn in upon itself'.[31]

A second tendency in Boulez's early writings sees him look beyond the musical domain and begin to think in terms of a more expansive, multidisciplinary modernism in which the discoveries of writers and artists are as significant for music as the innovation of composers. The first explicit reference to the 'modern', which appears in his first published article 'Proposals' (1948), asserts, as noted earlier, that 'music should be collective hysteria and magic, violently modern – along the lines of Antonin Artaud',[32] an insight shared not coincidentally in the same year as the composition of the explosive Second Piano Sonata.

In 'Current Investigations' (1954), a particularly important article in which Boulez attempts to come to terms with the unintended and unwanted results of the early musical experiments undertaken by the new generation of composers, he notes a certain kinship between modern painting and modern music and wonders how to escape monotonous abstraction and 'sterile mannerism'.[33] This is a decisive moment in his development when he accepts that there had for a short time been an overemphasis upon technique, which he recognizes within his own work, and he moves in consequence from the systemic rigour epitomized by the algorithmic *Structures Ia* (1951) and *Polyphonie X* (1950–1) to reintegrate aspects of freedom and choice within composition, a new stage in his creative practice that begins with *Le Marteau sans maître* (1953/5).

Articulating the need for a new musical poetics, 'a new way of listening', he notes that music has not advanced as far as poetry and that neither Mallarmé's 'Un coup de dés' nor Joyce's great works have musical equivalents, and it is clear that he is looking to literary modernism for the renewal

---

[27] Ibid., p. 202–3.   [28] Ibid., p. 215, p. 175, and p. 303.   [29] Ibid., p. 287.   [30] Ibid., p. 187.
[31] Max Paddison, *Adorno's Aesthetics of Music* (Cambridge University Press, 1993), pp. 221–2; Theodor W. Adorno, *Sound Figures*, trans. Richard Livingstone (Redwood City, CA: Stanford University Press, 1999), p. 131 and p. 187.
[32] Boulez, *Stocktakings*, p. 54.   [33] Ibid., p. 16.

he believes music requires.[34] This is primarily evident in the area of musical form where even the most significant modern compositions continue to embody 'a general concept of form' that is as old as tonality itself.[35] This tendency surfaces again in 'Sound and Word' (1958), where he highlights the slowness of music's development in relation to the other arts, the great impact of poetry on the development of music from the end of the nineteenth century and the fact that those writers who have experimented with language, specifically Mallarmé and Joyce, have had the greatest impact on musicians.[36] These are indeed two of the most important artistic figures he looks to in the composition of the never-completed Third Sonata for Piano (1955–57) with its great Mallarméan *Constellation-Miroir* as well as *Pli selon pli* (1957–90), which, with its three *Improvisations sur Mallarmé*, forms a portrait of the poet.

Boulez's most extended reflection on modernism in his early writings appears in 'Corruption in the Censers' (1956), where he suggests that 'a Debussy-Cézanne-Mallarmé axis' might be set up 'as the root of all modernism',[37] a thought that is motivated by a growing appreciation that modernism is more than the violence of 'surface shocks' and that it comprises more subtle subterranean forces.[38]

Acknowledging the difficulty of capturing precisely the nature of Debussy's modernism, he cites Baudelaire, for whom modernism 'is the transitory, the fugitive, the contingent, one half of art, of which the other half is the eternal and the immutable',[39] and the sources of Debussy's modernism are identified as Mussorgsky and painters and poets such as Manet, Whistler and Verlaine. For Boulez it is feasible that visual art and literature enabled music to escape from Wagnerism and to some extent facilitated Debussy's 'radically new aesthetic consciousness' and 'hitherto unknown "modern" sensibility' which has become 'the pre-condition for all subsequent development'.

Before closing this survey of Boulez's early engagement with the concept of the modern, it is important to note an unequivocal rejection of the term 'avant-garde' in relation to his own project. The term is first mentioned in 'Possibly ...' (1952), where his dodecaphonic contemporaries are dismissed as 'absurdly conservative' and as 'sit[ting] enthroned like fat idiots to the greater glory of the *avant-garde*'.[40] While Bartók pleases the '"reasonable" avant-garde',[41] Berg appeals to those who merely flirt with the notion.[42] Apart from these occasional mentions, the term 'avant-garde' does not seem to have been particularly important for Boulez in the late

---

[34] Ibid., p. 18. [35] Ibid., p. 18. [36] Ibid., p. 39–40. [37] Ibid., p. 20. [38] Ibid., p. 21.
[39] Ibid., p. 24. [40] Ibid., p. 111. [41] Ibid., p. 241. [42] Ibid., p. 249.

1940s and 1950s. In conversation with Pierre-Michel Menger in the late 1980s, he states that he did not like the term and that the question of whether he had ever been 'part of an avant-garde movement' had 'never preoccupied' him.[43]

Boulez in the 1980s and beyond

By the 1980s and 1990s, the situation of new music was very different from that of the 1950s and the modernist narrative, in both its Schoenbergian and post-war manifestations, was seriously in question. In the presentation 'Classique-Moderne'[44] (1996) Boulez now defines the concept of the 'modern' in relation to the 'classical'.[45] While the classical indicates stability, the modern is inextricably linked to 'movement', 'transition', 'insecurity' and the uncertainty of working with things that are not otherwise established or validated. As in his earlier texts, the notions of evolution, possibly even that of progress as well as technical expertise, and a serious commitment to research and experimentation are identified as 'the exterior signs of modernity', and he questions how the concepts of modernity and classicism might be linked.[46] For Boulez, it comes down to the absolute dependence of form and style upon the musical idea and the reciprocal dependence of the musical idea upon form and style. With the passing of commonly held musical forms such as sonata form or fugue, forms that were both strict enough to be 'recognizable' and 'supple' enough to allow the composer a significant degree of freedom, 'grammatical hierarchy' and the unequivocal functions of the tonal system have been dissolved and relational ambiguities have multiplied. Addressing what are evidently 'postmodern' or neo-classical options, Boulez argues that the alternative to modernity is the resort to belief in a musical 'golden age', the conviction that music history is already accomplished and a consequent refusal of exploration. This, he suggests, leaves only the option of employing musical models in one of

---

[43] Pierre-Michel Menger, 'From the Domaine Musical to IRCAM: Pierre Boulez in conversation with Pierre-Michel Menger', trans. Jonathan W. Bernard, *Perspectives of New Music*, 28/1 (1990), 6–19, pp. 16 and 12.

[44] The text 'Classique-Moderne' was presented by Boulez in the symposium 'Der klassizistische Moderne in der Musik des 20. Jahrhunderts' on 26 April 1996 in Basel. See Pierre Boulez, *Regards sur autrui (Points de repère II)*, collected and ed. Jean-Jacques Nattiez and Sophie Galaise (Paris: Éditions Christian Bourgois, 2005), pp. 469–73. Arnold Whittall, who also participated in the symposium, theorized later that Boulez's trajectory is marked by the turn 'from Utopian avant-gardism to [a] more pragmatic modern classicism' (Arnold Whittall, 'Boulez at 80: The Path from the New Music', *Tempo*, 59/233 (2005), 3–15, p. 5).

[45] Boulez, *Regards sur autrui*, p. 470.   [46] Ibid., p. 471.

three ways, which he terms the 'serious conceptual approach', 'artisanal application' and 'ludic distortion'.[47]

Boulez provides only abstract definitions of these three approaches and he gives no worked-out examples of the composers and compositions he has in mind. With the 'serious conceptual approach' the model is dominant and the composer's ideas are subjected to an alien and extraneous constraint; with 'artisanal application' the 'contours of the model' are taken up superficially and imitated literally, producing what Boulez dismisses as 'an empty, meaningless shell' and no more than a 'stylistic envelope'; with 'ludic distortion' the model is taken as a 'stylistic object' that can be distorted in a self-evidently ludic way.[48] Recognizing clear differences between approaches, in all three cases the model is unabsorbed and maintains its autonomy in the face of what Boulez dismisses as 'clever, mannered or degenerate copies'. In place of models, 'example' is preferable in that it offers possibilities for 'observation, deconstruction, reevaluation and deduction'. In terms of historical reference, he admits that 'everything [and anything] can be transformed', but that it must be done without using 'literal examples' and, where classicism seems to represent unacceptable memory, modernism is ultimately reaffirmed as the kind of Klee-based 'amnesia' or forgetting that he first set out in the 1950s.[49]

Boulez tells us exactly the kind of example he favours in his Collège de France lectures from 1983–5, where he looks to Stravinsky's *Les Noces* (1914–23) and the *Symphonies of Wind Instruments* (1920), works in which musical form results from the permutation and return of recognizable sections. He notes, in particular, how Stravinsky succeeded in transforming the ancient forms of the litany and the verse response couplet into an entirely new concept, in which formal development is paradoxically produced through formal return, in a thematicism that is based upon modified repetition.[50] This kind of thinking is evident in the verse–response form of Boulez's *Rituel in memoriam Maderna* (1974–5), which is made up of fifteen sections, in which the even-numbered are verses and the odd-numbered are responses. Developing the idea further, *Transitoire VII* from … *explosante-fixe* … (1991/3), which is formally much more elaborate than *Rituel*, has ten individually characterized ideas, occurring variously from one to six times in the course of the movement. The sections are permutated in such a way that it is impossible to predict in advance which one will follow any other.[51]

---

[47] Ibid., pp. 471–2.   [48] Ibid., p. 472.   [49] Ibid., p. 473. The brackets are mine.
[50] Boulez, *Leçons de musique*, pp. 232 and 276.
[51] See Campbell, *Boulez, Music and Philosophy*, pp. 206–9.

In the talk 'Moderne/Postmoderne'[52] from 1987, Boulez tackles the oft-made charge that the modernists from the 1950s extinguished creative vitality through 'excessive dogmatism'.[53] He argues that a period of rigorous, even rigid discipline was necessary in order to 'relaunch modernity' in the midst of the 'shipwreck of ... archaic neo-classical tendencies', an over-reliance on instinct and a superficial bricolage-like approach to musical language. Having said this, he attempts in this talk, to demonstrate how some of the key ideas from the 1950s became less rigid and over time came to pervade 'every element of the language'.[54]

In doing so, he takes the example of Ligeti's *Trio* for violin, horn and piano (1982), with its reintegration of some traditional features. He contrasts the 'severity' of Berio's *Sequenza I* for flute (1958) with *Sequenza VIII* for violin (1976), a piece that is based on open strings, that employs repetition in ways that were excluded in the 1950s and that centres on particular polar pitches. Finally, he compares his own *Domaines* (1961–8) and *Dialogue de l'ombre double* (1985), highlighting the relative rigidity of the former piece with the freer expansion of the same material in *Dialogue*, in which six strophes played by a live performer alternate with five transition sections (transitoires), that are pre-recorded and diffused by loudspeaker. While each of the strophes is based on a unique musical idea, the transitions combine different ideas, with the result that, by means of fairly simple differentiations, the piece is more clearly articulated.[55]

Boulez suggests that these works are musically coherent in terms of language and expression, the 'dogma' of the 1950s having been 'dissolved'. In response to the criticism that he and other modernist composers have abandoned their earlier 'more aggressive positions', Boulez argues that if more recent compositions have returned to elements that were previously unacceptable, for example, the 'ostinati, mouvement perpetuels and repeated notes' in Ligeti's *Trio*, this is possible because they have been rethought in a new context.[56]

Further consideration of musical modernity in the changed circumstances of the 1980s is given in 'Contemporary Music and the Public', a dialogue with Michel Foucault from 1983. In the course of their exchange, Boulez acknowledges that the musical sphere is divided up into many separate subcultures or 'circuits', and he recognizes, perhaps surprisingly, that contemporary music is merely one musical circuit and, as such, 'does

---

[52] The text 'Moderne/Postmoderne' was presented by Boulez in Bordeaux on 12 May 1987. See Boulez, *Regards sur autrui*, pp. 474–80.
[53] Ibid., p. 474.   [54] Ibid., p. 475.   [55] Ibid., pp. 475–9.   [56] Ibid., pp. 475–6.

not escape ... the faults of musical society in general'.[57] While this statement may lull us into thinking that he is promoting a rather pragmatic, even postmodern stance, he goes on to reject any kind of musical pluralism, liberalism or 'eclectic ecumenism', making a stark contrast between 'musics which bring in money and exist for commercial profit' and those 'whose very concept has nothing to do with profit'.[58] Modernity is now defined as the 'technical superiority we possess over former eras in being able to recreate the event', a situation that is equated to 'Plato's cave: a civilization of shadow and of shades'.[59] Audience incomprehension, as before, is attributed to 'laziness, to inertia, to the pleasant sensation of remaining in known territory', and Boulez reiterates the view that audiences will only develop 'deep understanding' of works through repeated exposure and listening.[60]

The Boulezian diagonal

While this chapter has been concerned up to this point with the exploration of Boulez's modernism from primarily music theoretical perspectives, we turn now to how Boulez's theory and practice assume a significant place in the conceptualizing of musical modernism in the philosophical domain, through the work of Deleuze, Guattari and Badiou. In *A Thousand Plateaus*, Deleuze and Guattari, drawing on Boulez, conceptualize the role of every great composer in terms of the invention of a diagonal, a 'transversal line', a deterritorialization.[61] In this respect, the Viennese school (presumably the second) is cited as exemplifying this kind of diagonal move which produces 'a new system of territorialization'.[62] While this kind of movement is not unique to modernity and is simply the way that all innovative musicians operate, for Deleuze and Guattari, it marks, among other things, the shift 'from harmonic closure to an opening onto a polytonality or, as Boulez will say, a "polyphony of polyphonies"'.[63]

Despite Boulez's undoubted prominence in *A Thousand Plateaus*, where a number of his theoretical terms form the starting points for philosophical reflection, the theory of modernism that is found there makes little explicit reference to his work. For Deleuze and Guattari, 'if there is a modern age, it

---

[57] Michel Foucault and Pierre Boulez, 'Contemporary Music and the Public', *Perspectives of New Music*, 24/1 (1985), 6–12, p. 7.
[58] Ibid., p. 8. [59] Ibid., p. 9. [60] Ibid., p. 10.
[61] Gilles Deleuze and Félix Guattari, *A Thousand Plateaus: Capitalism and Schizophrenia*, trans. Brian Massumi (London: Athlone, 1988), p. 296.
[62] Ibid., p. 297.
[63] Gilles Deleuze, *The Fold: Leibniz and the Baroque*, trans. Tom Conley (London: Athlone, 1993), p. 82.

is ... the age of the cosmic',[64] an age focused exclusively on technique and *'material-forces'*, and where 'material is a molecularized matter' that must harness the 'forces of the Cosmos'. Where, after Klee, 'visual material must capture nonvisible forces' and render them visible, modern philosophy, after Nietzsche, elaborates 'a material of thought in order to capture forces that are not thinkable in themselves'. Forms, matters and themes are relinquished in favour of 'forces, densities, intensities' and Cézanne is identified as the visual artist who first makes such forces perceptible.

The question of molecular, cosmic forces is one of guaranteeing the consistency or consolidation of material, and Debussy is credited as having molecularized 'sound matter' and with having harnessed 'nonsonorous forces such as Duration and Intensity'. It is 'the age of the Machine', exemplified by Varèse's dream of a machine that can molecularize 'sound matter, and harnesses a cosmic energy'. The modern creative figure is 'the cosmic artisan' who 'connects a material with forces of consistency or consolidation'[65] and the modern is identified as that moment when 'matter has been sufficiently deterritorialized that it itself emerges as molecular'. To this degree, the reconfigured concept of the Boulezian diagonal symptomizes the modern for Deleuze and Guattari with its cosmic transversality.

In *What Is Philosophy?* (1994), Deleuze and Guattari provide a more contracted account of musical modernity in which it relinquishes

> projection and the perspectives that impose pitch, temperament, and chromaticism, so as to give the sonorous plane a singular thickness to which very diverse elements bear witness: the development of studies for the piano, which cease being just technical and become 'compositional studies' (with the extension given them by Debussy); the decisive importance assumed by the orchestra with Berlioz; the rise of timbre in Stravinsky and Boulez; the proliferation of percussive affects with metals, skins and woods, and their combination with wind instruments to constitute blocs inseparable from the material (Varèse); the redefinition of the percept according to noise, to raw and complex sound (Cage); not only the enlargement of chromaticism to other components of pitch but the tendency to a nonchromatic appearance of sound in an infinite continuum (electronic or electroacoustic music).[66]

While presenting a number of characteristics of musical modernism, Deleuze and Guattari acknowledge the multiple nature of the modern and the impossibility of encapsulating it within any singular definition or of attributing it to any one personality. Despite justifiably limited reference

---

[64] Deleuze and Guattari, *A Thousand Plateaus*, pp. 342–3.   [65] Ibid., pp. 345–6.
[66] Gilles Deleuze and Félix Guattari, *What Is Philosophy?*, trans. Graham Burchell and Hugh Tomlinson (London: Verso, 1994), p. 195. Translation modified by the author.

to Boulez in this regard, it is nevertheless an arguably Boulezian modernity that is theorized where the key figures, Debussy, Varèse, Cézanne and Klee, are all of great importance for Boulez's own articulation. Even the caveat issued in relation to the territorialized nature of found objects in Cage's works for prepared piano seems to echo something of Boulez's eventual distrust of the American composer's music.[67] It would be a mistake, however, to argue for the exclusive priority of any one musical figure, and the cosmic quality of Deleuze-Guattarian modernity demonstrably owes more to Stockhausen, Varèse and Messiaen than to anyone else.

Boulez and the Schoenbergian event

An alternative conceptualization of musical modernity is presented in *Logics of Worlds*, the second volume of the epic *Being and Event*, where Alain Badiou fleshes out what he terms 'A Musical Variant of the Metaphysics of the Subject'.[68] Summarizing briefly, Badiou's philosophy posits that innovation is a phenomenon that occurs with the irruption of an event, an event being the appearance of something that was previously unnoticed or uncounted within a situation. This event reveals a new truth and concomitant with its irruption is the formation of a new subjectivity. The new subject, however, is not to be confused with any historical personage and the subject of a truth is someone who is faithful to the truth that has appeared with the irruption of the event. Events in this way then create worlds and the 'subject is an indirect and creative relation between an event and a world'.[69]

While acknowledging that an event cannot be equated with a single author or work, Badiou identifies the appearance of a musical event in Germany at the beginning of the twentieth century which, for pragmatic reasons, he terms 'the Schönberg event' or better the 'serial event' and which is to do with 'the possibility of a sonic world no longer ruled by the tonal system'. This 'event' is represented by a 'trace' which is 'what allows itself to be extracted from Schönberg's pieces' as the means for organizing the twelve-pitch classes in post-tonal ways that avoid the hierarchical prescriptions of tonal organization. It becomes clear fairly quickly that the musical world elaborated by Badiou, initially identified with early twentieth-century Austro-German music, would be better termed modernism. Significantly, 'the trace of the event is not identical' to either

---

[67] Deleuze and Guattari, *A Thousand Plateaus*, p. 344.
[68] Alain Badiou, *Logics of Worlds: Being and Event (II)*, trans. Alberto Toscano (London: Continuum, 2009), pp. 79–89.
[69] Ibid.

dodecaphonic or serial technique but instead takes the form of the statement that 'an organization of sounds may exist which is capable of defining a musical universe on a basis which is entirely subtracted from classical tonality'.

What Badiou calls 'the body' is all those musical compositions that 'attempt to construct a universe conforming to the imperative harboured by the trace'. The subject, in this instance, is 'the becoming of a dodecaphonic or serial music, that is of a music that legislates over musical parameters',[70] and Badiou reads the history of post-tonal music between the seemingly arbitrarily chosen *Variations* for Orchestra by Schoenberg (1926) and Boulez's *Répons* (1981–84) as one which 'treats a sequence of problems, comes up against obstacles ("points" ...), extends its domain, fights against enemies'. This history, he claims, is 'coextensive with the existence of a subject' which realizes the consequences of the trace, in this case 'a new imperative for the musical organization of sounds' in a body of musical works.

The radically different serial possibilities pursued by Berg and Webern, along with all other 'openings' and 'discontinuities', are incorporated within the subject 'serial music'. In a clearly Boulez-influenced reading, Berg is described as 'an inspired negotiator of openings to the old world', while 'Webern is only interested in points' and in 'irrevocable choice'.[71] Badiou acknowledges rather obviously that neither the rhythmic and durational developments of Stravinsky, Bartók and Messiaen nor the timbral innovations of Debussy and Varèse are 'incorporated in dodecaphonic or serial music', factors that are undoubtedly inconvenient for his hypothesis, since Boulez, who qualifies as perhaps the most faithful subject of this 'event', draws as much on these composers and their innovations as on the Viennese.[72] Badiou knows nevertheless that Boulez has not followed Schoenberg slavishly and that his fidelity to the 'truth' of the event was maintained not through the triumphal academicizing of dodecaphony, as with Leibowitz (another Boulezian trope), but rather through explicit opposition to, or a further radicalizing of, Schoenberg.[73] Ultimately, the serial event goes well beyond dodecaphony and subsumes within itself the experiments undertaken in all of the other parametric domains, and Boulez, according to Badiou, has worked to incorporate music in France into this new subjectivity,[74] employing in the process both an initial 'dose of terror' and increasing compositional freedom.[75] Indeed, in a passage that calls to mind Boulez's 'Corruption in the Censers' (1956), Badiou

---

[70] Ibid., p. 81. [71] Ibid., pp. 83–4. [72] Ibid., p. 82. [73] Ibid., pp. 84–5. [74] Ibid., p. 86.
[75] Ibid., p. 87.

reflects thus: 'for, as Saint-Just asked: "What do those who want neither Virtue nor Terror want?" His answer is well-known: they want corruption – another name for the failure of the subject.'[76]

For Badiou, neither the serial subject, which he thinks of as having been 'unpromising... for at least twenty years', nor any musical pluralism holds the key to the current situation.[77] Despite the seeming exhaustion of the serial event, as with all events whose possibilities are limitless, it is always open to the prospect of being taken up again at some future moment or of being re-articulated within a new musical current.

Concluding reflections

While Born's criteria place Boulez clearly in the modernist camp, the composer's own early statements align him with a more circumscribed modernism. His later statements seemingly acknowledge greater latitude in the musical situation of the 1980s and 1990s, but, while ostensibly distancing him from any dogmatic modernism, much of the substance of his earlier position is seemingly intact. Arnold Whittall's concept of modern classicism is an important contribution in exploring the distinctiveness of Boulez's later position and it provides a productive alternative to Helmut Lachenmann's arguably less benign judgement, whereby the transformation in the work of many of the post-war generation turned the one-time 'prospectors for gold' into mere 'jewellers'.[78] It is interesting to note in this respect that for Lachenmann and Brian Ferneyhough, two very different composers, whose work is equally radical and distinctively modern, it is Boulez's early, Artaudian works that contain the greatest transformative potential. Taking a rather different view, Michaël Levinas judged in 1993 that the one-time conflict between serialism and spectralism now seemed artificial[79] and that Boulez's recently performed version of ... *explosante-fixe* ... demonstrated the possibilities of a renewed concept of polyphony and the productive mix of acoustic instruments and real-time electronic transformation of sound.[80]

In terms of the philosophical perspectives, Badiou's view of Boulez as the faithful subject to a serial event is not without its merits, despite the potential violence that is done to modernist multiplicity for the sake of a neat philosophical scheme. In the arbitrariness of its historical

---

[76] Ibid., p. 88.   [77] Ibid., p. 89.
[78] Helmut Lachenmann, *Écrits et entretiens* (Genève: Contrechamps, 2009), p. 196.
[79] Michaël Levinas, *Le compositeur trouvère: écrits et entretiens (1982–2002)*, collected and ed. Pierre A. Castanet and Danielle Cohen-Levinas (Paris: L'Harmattan, 2002), p. 120.
[80] Levinas, *Le Compositeur Trouvère*, p. 221.

periodization, it poses questions as to the extent to which Schoenberg's work actually does mark the irruption of a new event or whether Schoenberg himself is merely yet another faithful subject witnessing to a much older Bach/Beethoven/Brahms/Wagner event. While both possibilities have their merits, 'Schoenberg is Dead' notwithstanding, Boulez's work in a number of respects may be read as continuing that of Schoenberg, though it is clear that this is only part of the picture. Even if Webern's importance for the Darmstadt generation can be subsumed within a Schoenberg event, as Badiou would have us do, Debussy's innovations in the realms of form, texture and timbre, Stravinsky's significance for rhythm, duration and instrumentation and Varèse's idiosyncratic conceptions of sound and space make clear that musical modernity emanates from multiple evental irruptions of arguably equal importance. Badiou's focus on Schoenberg in the naming of the event perhaps restores the parameter of pitch as the dominant musical value over all others.

Boulez's concept of the diagonal becomes, in the hands of Deleuze and Guattari, the image of musical modernity around which the advances of Cézanne, Debussy, Stravinsky, Varèse, Klee, Cage, Boulez and others are assembled, albeit that it is described *à la Stockhausen* in terms of a cosmic transversal. This Deleuze-Guattarian version of musical modernity has much to recommend it in its gathering of abstract values from the spheres of music and visual art. Less selective and lopsided than Badiou's account, it recognizes the multiplicity of lines of force that together form the modern.

Where Deleuze and Guattari use the term 'modern' with a tentativeness that makes clear that this is no terminological panacea, Jacques Rancière, without discussing music to any significant degree, goes beyond the modern and postmodern in favour of an aesthetic regime of art, a much more inclusive category in which the aesthetic production of the twentieth and early twenty-first centuries can be grasped as a more unified phenomenon, though it is doubtful that this is his intention.[81] Adorno in the *Philosophy of New Music* (1949) had set out an oppositional dialectic of Schoenberg and Stravinsky, a dialectic in which Schoenberg fares better than his Russian counterpart and in which a musical remainder is always the case.[82] In a similar way, the young Boulez advocated the necessity of pursuing the implications of dodecaphony while avoiding what he saw as the regressive characteristics of neoclassicism, a judgement which not only leaves a

---

[81] See Jacques Rancière, *The Politics of Aesthetics: The Distribution of the Sensible*, trans. Gabriel Rockhill (London: Continuum, 2004).

[82] Theodor W. Adorno, *Philosophy of New Music*, trans. and ed. Robert Hullot-Kentor (Minneapolis, MN: University of Minnesota Press, 2006).

seemingly non-modern remainder in the work of Stravinsky but also that of Schoenberg.

Whether we think of Boulez as a modernist, a modern-classicist, a faithful subject to a serial event or a cosmic artisan tracing a new diagonal, this array of views reaffirms the provisional nature of our historical categories and suggests the possibility that serial and post-serial music may be considered in ways that move beyond the concept of the modern. While Deleuze and Guattari, and Badiou concur with Boulez on a number of points, it is Rancière's retracing of the territory normally occupied by the modern and the postmodern that most readily acknowledges the exclusions that each concept enacts. It is a stance that perhaps finds a musical corollary in Wolfgang Rihm's reflections, which set out what musical modernity can be today in its dizzyingly multiple forms.[83] That Rihm's mélanges and syntheses are by no means the only way forward is clear, for example, from the work of Claus-Steffen Mahnkopf, who theorizes and practices a 'second-modernity' as the Hegelian overcoming [Aufhebung] of both musical modernity and postmodernity.[84]

In the midst of this ongoing activity and reflection, Boulez's compositions and theoretical writings provide an invaluable sense of modernity as something that is dynamic and transformative. The ongoing activity of innumerable composers suggests that the paradigm, far from having exhausted itself, continues to be significant in the production of music and music theory that is innovative and surprising. The events celebrating Boulez's ninetieth birthday in 2015, in a range of musical centres around the world, provide opportunities for new generations of composers and conductors, such as George Benjamin, Matthias Pintscher and Jörg Widmann, to express their respect, admiration and gratitude to Boulez for his efforts, and this alone is evidence enough that the work goes on.

---

[83] Wolfgang Rihm, *Ausgesprochen: Schriften und Gespräche*, ed. Ulrihc Mosch, 2 vols. (Mainz: Schott, 2002). See vol. I, p. 36.

[84] See Klaas Coulembier, 'Multi-Temporality: Analysing Simultaneous Time Layers in Selected Compositions by Elliott Carter and Claus-Steffen Mahnkopf', unpublished PhD dissertation, University of Leuven (2013), pp. 157–8.

10 Remembrance and prognosis in the music of György Ligeti

Peter Edwards

There is little repetition in the oeuvre of the Hungarian composer György Ligeti (1923–2006). The expressive contrasts are vast and there are few conventions by which to gain a sense of orientation. Yet a sense of stylistic continuity can be detected in the transitions or transformations that his compositional development might be said to perform, and in the characteristic play between past and present and association and prognosis, which seek reconciliation in the ear of the listener. References to the past are abundant, sometimes explicit but often concealed, sometimes reminiscent of a stream of consciousness, at other times frozen into stasis and pushed to the brink of silence. Yet the listener gains little from striving to disentangle these indices, for the signs and signals of the past in themselves point to their own fragmented, withdrawn or concealed state as a condition of their existence.

Any attempt to explain the pastness in Ligeti's music in abstract terms detracts from its most alluring quality: the manner by which the music acknowledges its own self-production in response to the past and the contradictions that this incurs. For the listener it is not a question of what is or is not heard in terms of musical content, but the patterns and processes by which the music achieves its otherness in response to the past. This is perhaps the root of the ever-increasing popularity of Ligeti's music. For this music, with its profound diversity, confounds classification: each work challenges perception and interpretation in new ways. Moreover, the broad trend away from structural analysis and the excavation of rigorous precompositional systems that characterize the early reception of post-war musical modernism in Central Europe and towards critical musicology, strategies of listening and philosophical aesthetics casts the rich multiplicity of the music in a whole new light. Previously unexplored qualities of Ligeti's music are now receiving attention as a result of these transformations in scholarly work on musical modernism, contributing to a level of interest in his music that shows little sign of abating.[1] So how might we

---

[1] Two recent studies featuring Ligeti's music highlight this trend. David Metzer (*Musical Modernism at the Turn of the Twenty-First Century* (Cambridge University Press, 2009))

begin to understand the appeal of the music, the modes of listening to it and the ambiguities with which we are confronted in attempts to 'read' Ligeti's oeuvre? A brief examination of selected works invites interpretation from the perspective of how the past is enacted in the present in Ligeti's music.

In the orchestral work *Atmosphères* (1961), famed for its inclusion in Stanley Kubrick's *2001: A Space Odyssey* (1968), a multitude of past musical styles are transformed and concealed. Seemingly representative of the high-modernist values of aesthetic consistency and rigorous constructive principles, the work subverts the canonic style of renaissance counterpoint, transforming it into a supersaturated echo of an entire epoch. The chromatic strands that participate in the countless layers of the canon, spread over several octaves, effectuate an irreversible process of change. The inner life of the work teems with energy – the complex polyphonic weave can be felt but is not heard directly.[2] Subtle changes in orchestration and instrumentation transform the texture – the chiaroscuro effect altering the perspective on the massive sound object as it is gradually unveiled and one sound event melts into another. In the surging flow of events, occasional moments of orchestral colour and intervallic transparency recall the music of Debussy. The work labours forward, weighing the burden of history, as if it were the echo of the entire polyphonic tradition sounded out simultaneously. The excess of expression inters its inner workings in a web so dense that only the contours of sound shapes are perceived.

The expressive identity of *Atmosphères* can be better comprehended in light of a subsequent work which creates an even greater sense of stasis: the organ piece *Volumina* (1961–2). Ligeti describes the piece as consisting of the 'remains of the entire organ literature. Somewhere you can feel certain baroque figurations, albeit digested whole, Liszt and Reger and the Romantic sound of the organ also play a part subliminally.'[3] Yet here there is no supersaturated canon as in *Atmosphères* and no clear musical

---

advocates an approach to compositional states, shifting emphasis from musical material to composition and the ideals and idioms which inform the creative processes of composers (see p. 10). The lament is one such ideal discussed in relation to the music of Ligeti (Chapter 4). Amy Bauer examines the fundamental significance of the lament in Ligeti's music as emblematic of the paradoxical, expressive power of the past in the present. Her extensive study brings new insight to the deep critical significance of Ligeti's involution with the past throughout the vast span of his oeuvre. Amy Bauer, *Ligeti's Laments: Nostalgia, Exoticism and the Absolute* (Farnham: Ashgate, 2011).

[2] The gradual crescendo onset of the melodic strands and their sheer number make it impossible to hear the voices individually or 'directly'. See Jonathan W. Bernard, 'Voice Leading as a Spatial Function in the Music of Ligeti', *Music Analysis*, 13/2–3 (1994), 227–53, pp. 228–9.

[3] Ove Nordwall, *György Ligeti: Eine Monographie* (Mainz: Schott, 1971), p. 129 (my translation).

language on a constituent level to give rise to the sculpted sound: the graphic score defines only the sound on a gestural level, as shapes, spaces and densities. The impression is again of the sedimentation of tradition, and in this case an imagined, never-ending reverberation that hangs in a room after all of the music once performed there has ceased to be played. *Volumina* refers to the void that remains, an articulation of the negation of the past. The music does not express the past in any direct form; it articulates the paradoxical nature of its own position in relation to its past, as Ligeti suggests when he refers to the 'great works by Bach like the Passacaglia [being] present, but very, very hidden', perhaps in some psychological state.[4] The expressive force of *Volumina* does not lie in any explicit celebration of the allusions to which Ligeti refers. Instead, his comments address the consequences of history, which are digested whole into the fabric of the work in its dialogue with tradition. This is not about the musical materials of tradition, but the reception of the organ sound – the augmentation of a moment in Bach's Toccata and Fugue in D minor or Reger's Passacaglia in D minor as the keys are released and the cathedral is filled with reverberating dissonances as the chords envelop one another.

The material is no longer simply the notes on a constituent level, but the very performance space itself and the patina of age. It is the overloaded memory of all that has come before: unable to sift through the overwhelming back catalogue of history, it conscientiously forges a futile attempt to not forget, and to acknowledge, the debt it owes. *Volumina* expresses the success of its own failure, for it draws its energy from remembering, yet prerequisite to remembrance is forgetting. In articulating the overabundance of memory, the work offers a critique of the kind of history that might lead us to believe that we might truly become archivists of our past and make sense of the teleological culmination and consequences of such a history. However, such a process would no longer be remembrance. The most supreme of all archives, the internet, accumulates where the mind differentiates, and failure to differentiate or sift through the sheer wealth of information brings about the effects of data smog – a symptom of a world in which the presence of all data becomes overwhelming and impossible for the subjective mind to reconcile.[5] For only against that which is forgotten does that which is remembered stand out, and what is remembered is not controlled by the will, but is contingent on forces much greater

---

[4] Péter Várnai, Josef Häusler, Claude Samuel and György Ligeti, *György Ligeti in Conversation with Péter Várnai, Josef Häusler, Claude Samuel and Himself* (London: Eulenburg Books, 1983), p. 105.

[5] David Shenk describes this effect in his book *Data Smog: Surviving the Information Glut* (New York: Harper Collins, 1997).

than the self. As the counterpart to remembering, forgetting becomes concealment – that which is necessarily absent in order that the narratives of memory can establish any sense of order. In both *Volumina* and *Atmosphères*, overabundance becomes a sign of concealment, reminding us of our inability to perceive all with which we are confronted. As a result, these works resist the listener's attempts to 'read' them – the past is purposefully hidden in overabundance. It is this concealment and absence that offers the point of departure for an expression that exists as a semblance of that which has come before. Instead the listener can only surrender to the open horizons that the works offer.

The musical theatre works *Aventures* (1962) and *Nouvelles Aventures* (1962–5) are plays of associations in a different way. The indecipherable phonetic librettos build on a mimetic impulse and encompass a vast range of human affects.[6] The sounds are alienated from their semantic context, removed from the human condition which they articulate and recompose as expressive states. The eruptions and dramatic gestures are perhaps familiar, yet a new musical imperative arises from the relationships that evolve between expressive conditions as the works unfold; rather than develop in any linear fashion, expressive states become like coordinates in a reference system.[7]

The states in *Aventures* are suggested in the score with remarks such as 'aggressivo', 'with longing' (*mit Sehnsucht*) and 'contemptuous laughter' (*geringschätziges Lachen*), characters which correspond to the associations that they elicit in a listener. The first scene fluctuates between 'excitedness', 'longing', 'joyfulness', 'irony', 'sadness' and 'aggression'. These states nevertheless remain correlative to an underlying expression of angst.[8] The series of expressions presented in the first scene lay the foundation for the initiation of a formal process that sees the sound layers applied in various combinations and superimpositions, each state returning to be embellished at greater length later on. The pedal clusters at the beginning return at the end of the first scene and at various stages throughout the work, offering an underlying tension and backdrop to the onset of varying expressive characters. The ecstatic breathing effects of the first bars also return in an altered state in bar 89. The depth of the form derives from the differing proximity of the expressive states to the central angst trope.

---

[6] See Bauer, *Ligeti's Laments* for a close reading of the opening scene of *Aventures* (pp. 44–55).
[7] Martin Zenck, 'Auswirkungen einer "musique informelle" auf die neue Musik: Zu Theodor W. Adornos Formvorstellung', *International Review of the Aesthetics and Sociology of Music*, 10/2 (1979), 137–65, p. 161.
[8] Ibid., p. 158.

A fitting analogy is found in Bergson's notion that laughter is not an expression of joy but a form of suppressed angst, and therefore correlative.[9]

The stream-of-consciousness-like expressive states in the opera *Le Grand Macabre* (1974–77, revised 1996) are not unrelated to the recomposed affective associations of *Aventures*. One expressive type intersects another, building relationships between contrastive characters that are correlative to the underlying 'fear of death' in the opera. As we follow the people of the gluttonous world of Breughelland, they display varying levels of concern with a threat made to their existence, from mockery to deep-seated angst. Their capriciousness is reflected in the divergent musical expressions. Ligeti refers to the contrasting expressive states of *Le Grand Macabre* as 'leit-characteristics',[10] marking a contrast to the kind of motivic development associated with Wagner's leitmotifs. The roles and their arias exhibit a vast expressive range, from sardonic indifference and humorous sarcasm (Piet the Pot) to neurotic anxiety (Gepopo); the way these highly distinctive roles are aligned like expressive coordinates provides the momentum in the unfolding drama. Moreover, the 'leit-characteristics' of the vocal parts and the orchestral score engage with and transform past expressive models, numerous references to which are found in remarks in interviews and in the form of verbal comments and notation in the source sketches: from Machaut, Beethoven and Mahler to Ives, Schwitters, Scott Joplin and Ella Fitzgerald.[11] Some references feature as overt, albeit harmonically distorted, citations. Yet many remain hidden from the listener. Astradamors's 'mad baroque aria'[12] and Gepopo's coloratura bravura – intended to outstrip the most demanding of Mozart's and Rossini's arias[13] – verge on becoming connotative references but are at the same time the withdrawn, personal reminiscences of the composer. And while the allusions to Monteverdi's baroque trumpet fanfare in *L'Orfeo* are suggested in Ligeti's car horn prelude, the abstract quantity of any affinities is difficult to determine.

In *L'Orfeo*, shrill natural baroque trumpets mark the commencement of a grand spectacle. In Ligeti's opera, the car horns elicit a sense of urban decay, cacophony, chaos and irony, as they deliver a postindustrial answer to Monteverdi's trumpets. There are further subtle connections between the preludes of Ligeti and Monteverdi. Ligeti calls for twelve differently

---

[9] Ibid., p. 159.   [10] Várnai et al., *György Ligeti in Conversation*, p. 120.
[11] The Sketches for Ligeti's *Le Grand Macabre* are housed at the Paul Sacher Foundation in Basel.
[12] As described in the score at rehearsal 161.
[13] Peter von Seherr-Thoss, *György Ligetis Oper Le Grand Macabre: Erste Fassung: Entstehung und Deutung: von der Imagination bis zur Realisation einer musikdramatischen Idee* (Eisenach: Wagner, 1998), p. 300.

pitched car horns, four for each of the three players, two in hand and two on the floor to be played by each foot. The first horn is pitched highest, while the twelfth is lowest and the rest are distributed accordingly: the first percussionist plays the high-pitched horns, the second percussionist the mid-range horns and the third percussionist the lowest-pitched horns, while the third percussionist's horn in the right hand should be higher than the first percussionist's horn held in the left hand.[14] This division of register loosely corresponds with the division of Monteverdi's toccata into *Alto e Basso* (third, fourth and fifth partials above the fundamental), *Quinta* (fourth to eighth) and *Clarino* (eighth and above). Also, Ligeti's request for twelve horns of different pitches would seem to signal the influence of serialism, perhaps connoting an attempt to bring the consequences of the recent musical past to bear on Monteverdi's toccata. The strong downbeat, the semiquaver repeated notes and the duration of both Ligeti's and Monteverdi's toccatas, all strengthen a sense of affinity between the two works. Moreover, the trumpets in Monteverdi's *L'Orfeo* perform the specific function of signalling the start of the opera and are not called on again. Ligeti's car horns do feature once more, but only to provide a short interlude between the first and second scenes. Heard in isolation – Ligeti's prelude is sometimes performed as a concert work in its own right – the idea that the prelude refers to Monteverdi might seem obscure to some listeners. However, performed in the context of the opera, with the curtain rising as the prelude comes to an end, its hidden legacy is rendered more ostensible.

The listener, preoccupied with the classification of references to the past, remains detached from the dramatic nucleus of the opera and the relationships that develop between contrasting expressions, both within the work and with other works. The contours of this underlying musico-dramatic form and the correlation of states is reflected in the draft sketches for the opera, which suggest the stream of consciousness at work in its creation. The musical sketches have all the hallmarks of 'continuity drafts', sketches created rapidly during a short space of time, in order to capture the dramatic essence of the form of the entire work, before the sections are then filled out in greater detail.[15] The stream of consciousness accentuates

---

[14] Score p. 1.

[15] I examine the form of the opera and present an analysis of the continuity drafts found among Ligeti's sketches in Peter Edwards, *György Ligeti's Le Grand Macabre* (Farnham: Ashgate, 2016, forthcoming). Ligeti spent more than a decade considering ideas for the opera. However, the continuity drafts represent a method with which to assimilate the dramatic contours of the music and the leit-characteristics in a burst of creativity, along the same lines that Donizetti approached the composition of his operas, as described by Luca Zoppelli in 'Processo

and conceals its past, and to become attuned to the opera we too must become sensitive to the temporality of this process. Just as we remember and forget, so too the opera conceals and reveals to varying degrees an awareness of its own past, embedded in the conception of the dynamic musical form.

In a later work, the Violin Concerto (1989–93), the listener is again met with the stream of memory and a boundless fluctuation between expressions. The narrative of memory arranges the contrasts around the constituted identity of the piece, and it is through this identity, by way of empathy with the stream of remembering, that our own associative mind might follow the trajectory of the unfolding vision. Ligeti has cited his influences across genres and epochs; yet the means are clearly transcended by the overall form, which is closer to the kind of musico-dramatic forms of *Aventures* and *Le Grand Macabre* than the fixed forms of the classical concerto. The opening portamento violin harmonics perform a dramatic core – an ephemeral shimmering expressive theme – which dissipates into the background to re-emerge at various points. A range of expressive contrasts is offset against the violin portamento, which resonates in the ear, recalling instances of the effect in past works. Only here the portamento is not simply an effect: it is a primary motif, an orientating coordinate.

The portamento effect can be traced to its earliest usage in Rimsky-Korsakov's 'Demonic Carol' from the suite *Christmas Eve* (1895), where it is performed by the cellos. The technique subsequently features in Ravel's *Rapsodie espagnole* (1908), before it is revisited in Stravinsky's *The Firebird* (1910) (for two bars before Figure 1).[16] While previously this feature was used sparingly as an effect in the context of Ravel's impressionism and Rimsky-Korsakov's and Stravinsky's more vigorously contrastive colouristic harmonies, it is transformed by Ligeti into a significant structuring element, as if it were the augmentation of a fragmented memory suspended in time. The effect makes sense in a whole new way, emerging and fading into concealment. The portamento is transformed into an expressive focal point, informing the intervallic material on which the concerto is based and also translating into the scordatura tunings of the second solo violin and viola, which draw support from naturally tuned ocarinas and horns along the way.

compositivo, "furor poeticus" e Werkcharakter nell'opera romantica italiana: Osservazioni su un "continuity draft" di Donizetti', *Il Saggiatore Musicale*, 12/2 (2005), 301–38.

[16] Richard Taruskin, *Stravinsky and the Russian Traditions: A Biography of the Works through Mavra*, 2 vols. (Berkeley and Los Angeles, CA: University of California Press, 1996), vol. I, p. 311.

The ocarinas in the second movement (bar 75) wake further associations. Their entry recalls the Bolivian flute motif from Harry Partch's 'The Quiet Hobo Meal' (Act II of *Delusion of the Fury: A Ritual of Dream and Delusion*).[17] This striking moment of clarity nevertheless merges into the harmonic and expressive context of the movement and of the Violin Concerto as a whole. The folky whole-tone flavour of the initial violin melody in the movement, echoed by the ocarinas, connects the disparate sounds as the relationships between the expressions evolve. Whatever residue of allusions to past expressions we may trace in the Concerto, their sedimentation cannot be extricated from the new, emergent formal hierarchies within which they become sealed and concealed. Even the opening bars of the first movement, as it commences with the solo violin alone rapidly alternating between open A- and D-string harmonics, recall the single note and single interval entries in several of Ligeti's prior works, including the Cello Concerto (1966), *Lontano* (1967), both movements of the Double Concerto (1972) and the first movement of the Hamburg Concerto (1998–9, rev. 2003). Yet to the listener, these familiar incipient characteristics are soon engulfed by a new narrative of remembering.

Ligeti's Trio for Violin, Horn and Piano (1982) represents yet another vision of memory, a vision of the past that provoked critical reaction in the wake of its premiere in some quarters for its overt debts to the classical-romantic tradition and especially the works of Brahms, Beethoven and Schumann (the subtitle is 'Hommage à Brahms').[18] The homage displays a consistency and clarity of memory, with room for melodic expansion, sonority and formal cohesion. Above all the instrumentation renders tangible the influence of Brahms's Horn Trio Op. 40. Yet the memory is distorted; despite the lucidity of vision, the representation is of the shadowy trace of Brahms and Beethoven. The very opening, a distorted rendition of the *Lebewohl* motif from Beethoven's Op. 81a, *Les Adieux* Sonata, signals that this is a transition into unfamiliar territory, in which what might on the surface appear familiar becomes the tangible absence of the original.[19] Even the form of the Trio reflects a sense of lack or loss and comprises a critique of the act of recollection and the inability of the mind to conjure forth true repetition. The first movement, the Andante, closes with a recapitulation of the *AB* section, and, as Amy Bauer points out, this apparent retreat into the classical ternary form was likely more shocking than skewed references to Beethoven. Yet subtle differences in voicing,

---

[17] Harry Partch, *Delusions of the Fury*, for voices and large ensemble. First recording available as *Delusions of the Fury*, Innova Records B000035X6C (1999).
[18] For an analysis of the Horn Trio see Bauer, *Ligeti's Laments*, pp. 160–74.
[19] See Bauer, *Ligeti's Laments*, p. 161.

register and muted horn and violin confer 'a strange sublimity on the return of *A*'.[20] Moreover, as Bauer argues, the repeated *A* section engages with the paradoxical nature of classical ternary form and its inevitable inability to fulfil its original function of introducing the movement's themes and harmonic tensions.[21] By shrinking from the task and receding into the background as a shadow of itself, the repeated *A* section acknowledges the contradiction immanent in its own self-production, and even becomes an analogy for understanding the Trio as a whole. For the expression of modernist melancholy and lacking surpasses the echoes of what once was, underlining the insufficiency of memory and the illusion that any kind of revisitation might be possible. Any criticism of retrospective tendencies that the piece triggered following its premiere is challenged by the critical sentiment of the music, which not only underlines 'the pure difference that separates *A* from *A*'[22] but also draws on the contradiction it contains as a creative impulse. The memory of the past becomes only as true as its constitution in the present.

This brief encounter with Ligeti's oeuvre identifies the past in the music as one of three things: as saturated present, as associative stream and as vivid, yet contorted reminiscence. In *Atmosphères* and *Volumina* the overabundance of the past becomes a frozen, augmented moment; in *Aventures, Nouvelles Aventures, Le Grand Macabre* and the Violin Concerto the flux of states seeks narrative consolidation; and with the Horn Trio we hear an extended, distorted vision of remembrance. Yet each is contained in the other. Each exhibits a fragmented past accessible only by memory. And all rely not on the abstract materials of the past but on a creative impetus drawn from the contradictory nature of any attempt to disengage the past from the remembering present. It is this contradiction that is etched into the expressive identity of much of Ligeti's music. The weaknesses of an objective signification of the past are exposed by their fragmentation, a fragmentation emphasized in the frozen moment of subjective memory – a memory stream mirrored in the music and in the listener. Allusions to the past point to structures and conditions beyond the individual, but even these are subsumed into Ligeti's personal style, their fragmentation and indeterminacy emphasized by their concomitance with other expressions. The music cannot be considered either a subjective expressive impulse or an objective reification of the cumulative consequences of an abundant past, for it is in the process of transition between the two that the music comes into being. It does not exhibit pure subjective

---

[20] Ibid., pp. 165–6.   [21] Ibid., p. 166.   [22] Ibid., p. 165.

urgency or objective force, but is drawn from the recognition of its self-production in response to the past.

The spatially conceived formal structures and the expressive coordinates therein are perceived as coherent as a response to past music, not in terms of abstract qualities or the gradual permutation of rules of musical languages, but in the wake of historically contingent expressive faculties. Ligeti describes this developmental progress of form in the following way: 'by involuntarily comparing each new aspect that enters our consciousness with those aspects already experienced, and by drawing conclusions from this comparison about what is to come, we pass through the construction of the music as if it were present in its entirety. It is the interaction of association, abstraction, remembrance and prognosis which elicits in the first place the nexus of relations that makes the conception of musical form possible.'[23] Not only are works constituted in the ear of the listener by way of the correlations between the aspects or parts of a composition, or expressive states, and the relationship of these states with the whole, but also by the involuntary predictions the listener makes in comparing the works to other works and potentially the entirety of music history. Form takes the guise of memory; the contours of the musical landscape take form as a result of the differentiation of explicit and hidden connections to the past. Yet the motives for what is remembered or forgotten are, as Freud describes in *Psychopathology of Everyday Life*,[24] the result of processes hidden from us. Forgetting and the failures of memory, and the unconscious, provide the necessary dynamic for form to emerge. The narratives that arise are differentiated against that which is suppressed.

The dynamic through which we identify with the music elicits a sense of familiarity that requires no validation through 'reading'. The creative impetus is not one that conceives abstract moments, autonomous works or eternal monuments from the associations or experience of the composer. Instead, the music draws on what lies behind the identifying features that the mind so readily acknowledges. This is the imprint of a memory in flux. The Heraclitean stream that flows in the music also flows in us: it is in affinity with the dynamic of remembrance and forgetting that our listening is intensified.

Sometimes we can still divine the signs and traces of the past, and sometimes these are covered over or sedimented beyond recognition. As

---

[23] György Ligeti, 'Form' in Ernst Thomas (ed.), *Darmstädter Beiträge zur Neuen Musik* (Mainz: Schott, 1966), pp. 23–35. English translation in Ruth Katz and Carl Dahlhaus (eds.), *Contemplating Music: Source Readings in the Aesthetics of Music* (Stuyvesant: Pendragon Press, 1992), pp. 781–95. Here p. 783.

[24] Sigmund Freud, *Psychopathology of Everyday Life* (Seattle: Pacific Publishing Studio, 2010).

a consequence, we detect a sense of loss or nostalgia for that which is unknown. Something is withdrawn and remains beyond reach. Yet this ambivalence is nonetheless accompanied by an affirmative sense of new, indeterminate and emergent meanings. The presence of memory and the surrealist stream is here more intense even than in the music of Stravinsky, and Ligeti's allusions to the past, even when sometimes exposed, hang in the balance to a greater degree: the presentation of fragments is countermanded by the prospect of their dissolution into an absorptive, voluminous background. This is not a straightforward presentation of the memory, but the memory's critical awareness of its remembering – forgetting is an immediate and inevitable prospect. It is on the basis of this understanding that the expressive force of the music is minted. Ligeti's music seems to act upon the past and alter its character. The past is mediated, but the trace elements of which this past might consist are second to the creative force of the memory in itself – its self-awareness of its own role in the alteration of the past. In this resistance to closure memory redeems its fingerprint, its style – style measured not according to self-contained, closed, identifying features, but by the idiosyncrasies and gradually evolving manner of responding to the past. This awareness of self-production contends just as much with what is remembered as with what is forgotten. In this engagement with history, memory mirrors history: remembrance is, as Benjamin pointed out, history's vocation, not discrete or autonomous history, but history mediated in the present.[25] In Ligeti's music, with its submerged, sedimented content, and its absence and concealment, it is not the de facto past but the expression of the dynamic of the remembering and forgetting memory that remains.

[25] Walter Benjamin, 'Über den Begriff der Geschichte' in *Gesammelte Schriften*, Rolf Tiedemann and Hermann Schweppenhäuser, 7 vols. (Frankfurt am Main: Suhrkamp, 1974), vol. I, p. 695 and 1231.

11 Valentin Silvestrov and the symphonic monument in ruins

Samuel Wilson[1]

> In the ruin history has physically merged into the setting. And in this guise history does not assume the form of the process of eternal life so much as that of irresistible decay.
>
> Walter Benjamin[2]

Andreas Huyssen has suggested that ruins capture a quality immanent to the character of modernity. For Huyssen, to speak of the 'authentic ruin' is not to talk about the ruin's ontological essence but of the ruin 'as a significant conceptual and architectural constellation that points to moments of decay, falling apart, and ruination already present in the beginning of modernity in the eighteenth century'.[3] This notion of immanent decay is pre-echoed in the writing of the sociologist and philosopher Georg Simmel, who saw the ruin as a provocative reminder of the immanence of the decay of things, independent of any externally imposed force. He wrote that 'the ruin strikes us so often as tragic – but not as sad – because there is not something senselessly coming from outside but rather the realization of a tendency inherent in the deepest layer of existence of the destroyed'.[4]

It goes without saying that the conditions of modernity – and now our 'late' modernity – do not only impact architecture but all modern artistic and cultural practices, music included. In light of this, it is my suggestion that the aesthetics of ruins might tell us about the conditions of music in our recent modernity. Drawing on Huyssen's insight that ruins reveal

---

[1] This chapter developed out of work originally undertaken for my doctoral thesis. Samuel Wilson, 'An Aesthetics of Past–Present Relations in the Experience of Late 20th- and Early 21st-Century Art Music', unpublished PhD dissertation, Royal Holloway, University of London (2013). This project was generously supported by the Arts and Humanities Research Council (UK). I am grateful to Julian Johnson for his supervision of this project, and indebted to Professors Johnson and Erling E. Guldbrandsen for their invaluable comments and editorial work.

[2] Walter Benjamin, *The Origin of the German Tragic Drama*, trans. John Osborne (London: Verso, 2003), pp. 177–8.

[3] Andreas Huyssen, 'Nostalgia for Ruins', *Grey Room*, 2 (2006), 6–21, p. 9.

[4] Georg Simmel, 'The Ruin' (1911) in *Georg Simmel, 1858–1918: A Collection of Essays, with Translations and a Bibliography*, ed. Kurt H. Wolff and trans. David Kettler (Columbus: The Ohio State University Press, 1959), pp. 259–66, p. 263.

something immanent to conditions of modernity and its culture, I suggest that these conditions are foregrounded not only in monumental architecture but also in monumental music. As is demonstrated below, this may be underlined by exploring conceptual points of contact between these two arts.

Musical works have become understood increasingly as performing socio-cultural practices beyond the 'purely musical' – practices of subjectivity, gender, nationalism, nature, desire, Otherness, sexuality, orientalism and selfhood, to name but a few.[5] Music has brought to life and enabled us to habituate diverse subjectivities, and relationships between subjects and worlds. But what would happen if the modern work was a ruin of its former self – how would it then relate to these historical practices and performativities, if only to evoke traces of musical practices now passed over and decayed? What would this mean for transformed approaches to the comprehension, meaning and significance of musical modernism?

Simmel called the ruin 'the site of life from which life has departed'.[6] Past ways of living through music reverberate through some works of late twentieth-century music – and one such work I discuss in detail in this chapter: Valentin Silvestrov's single-movement Symphony No. 5 (1982). In works like this we hear, through music, past ways of living as remote and now departed. Crucially though, this decay does not mean such works are without expression or meaning – just as, in the architectural ruin, the departing of previous inhabitants and crumbling of architectural forms does not make these forms meaningless in the present; ruins may, on the contrary, make apparent cultural and ideological priorities of past eras, priorities now seen to be abandoned or transformed. The ruined factory is a monument to concrete but now abandoned or transformed practices of production and instrumentality – and is, potentially, a site that as such contests the post-Enlightenment myth of rational 'progress'.[7] Ruination is

---

[5] It would be impossible to include an exhaustive list of such studies here, but some indicative works include: Susan McClary, *Desire and Pleasure in Seventeenth-Century Music* (Berkeley and Los Angeles, CA: University of California Press, 2012); Susan McClary, *Conventional Wisdom: The Content of Musical Form* (Berkeley, CA: University of California Press, 2000); Mark Evan Bonds, *Music as Thought: Listening to the Symphony in the Age of Beethoven* (Princeton University Press, 2006); Scott Burnham, *Sounding Values: Selected Essays* (Farnham: Ashgate, 2010); and Julian Johnson, *Webern and the Transformation of Nature* (Cambridge University Press, 2006). In light of such scholarship, I explore a treatment of 'selfhood' in Alfred Schnittke's music in Samuel Wilson, 'After Beethoven, After Hegel: Legacies of Selfhood in Schnittke's String Quartet No. 4', *International Review of the Aesthetics and Sociology of Music*, 45/2 (2014), 311–34.

[6] Simmel, 'The Ruin', p. 265.

[7] Dylan Trigg, *The Aesthetics of Decay: Nothingness, Nostalgia, and the Absence of Reason* (New York: Peter Lang Publishing, 2006). See in particular pp. 218–21, pp. 212, and 132.

a process that may lead to new and significant aesthetic possibilities, new relationships to the material that stands as ruin. Silvestrov's Symphony No. 5 underscores the processes whereby an aesthetic of ruination is operative within music.

The Ukrainian composer Valentin Silvestrov (b. 1937) described his Fifth Symphony as a 'post-symphony'.[8] This symphony is monumental, but not unproblematically so. I will suggest that his symphony, as 'post-' to the canonic symphonies of the past,[9] elicits experiences and creates meanings analogously to processes that take place on one's contact with ruins of great former monuments. His 'post-' is neither a rejection of nor a 'comment on' the symphonic tradition. It is, instead, a remembering of what *was*, particularly of former ways of living practices, values and aesthetics through music.[10]

Silvestrov's musical language in this single-movement symphony evokes traces of the past, particularly of a late-romantic soundworld and of past symphonic structures. Critics have cited 'allusions to Bruckner and Mahler, alongside the German romantic tradition: Schubert and Schumann', although Silvestrov by no means provides listeners with specific citations.[11] Svetlana Savenko has added that one hears a type of "maximalism" in Silvestrov's music, in contradistinction with "the Romantics of the past".[12] While retaining a sense of monumentality, the orchestration, nonetheless, in the manner of some of Mahler's works, 'approach[es] chamber-music procedures' (to borrow a phrase from Adorno on Mahler).[13] Silvestrov provides us in this symphony with a 'game of infinitesimal details that make the texture more diversified'.[14]

---

[8] Silvestrov quoted in Svetlana Savenko, 'Valentin Silvestrov's Lyrical Universe' in Valeria Tsenova (ed.), *Underground Music from the Former USSR* (Amsterdam: Harwood Academic Publishers, 1998), pp. 66–83, p. 75.

[9] Peter Schmelz notes that the theme of 'ending' is one of Silvestrov's preoccupations. His Third Symphony (1966), for example, 'carried the subtitle "Eschatophony" [*Eskhatofoniya*]'. Peter J. Schmelz, 'What Was "Shostakovich", and What Came Next?', *The Journal of Musicology*, 24/3 (2007), 297–338, pp. 329–30. Paul Griffiths writes of the Fifth that it 'seems to begin where a slow movement by Bruckner, Tchaikovsky or Mahler might have ended, and then to go on ending'. Paul Griffiths, *A Concise History of Western Music* (Cambridge University Press, 2006), p. 312.

[10] For a detailed investigation of Silvestrov's 'post-' style, as indicative of its late twentieth-century Soviet cultural context, see Peter J. Schmelz, 'Valentin Silvestrov and the Echoes of Music History', *The Journal of Musicology*, 31/2 (2014), 231–71.

[11] Ibid., p. 246.   [12] Savenko quoted in Ibid., p. 246.

[13] Theodor W. Adorno, *Mahler: a Musical Physiognomy*, trans. Edmund Jephcott (University of Chicago Press, 1992), p. 53.

[14] Levon Hakobian, *Music of the Soviet Age 1917–1987* (Stockholm: Melos Music Literature, 1998), p. 311.

Example 11.1 Valentin Silvestrov, Symphony No. 5, figs. 10–12 (upbeat to bar 73–88), reduction.

There is a frequent splitting of orchestral sections and a passing and colouration of melodic lines. The fragmented, expressionistic character at the opening leads to a sweeping melody in the first violins at figure 10 in the score (upbeat to bar 73, presented in reduction in Example 11.1). Two harps accompany this, contributing to a texture reminiscent of the Adagietto from Mahler's Fifth Symphony, to a melody that, in repeatedly reaching upward before descending, is itself evocative of the opening theme from the last movement of Mahler's Ninth.

This musical language conjures the monumental symphonies and orchestral works of the late nineteenth century. More specifically, associations of romanticism bring about a constellation of concepts including the ruin and the fragment. I explore these concepts first, as well as the notion of the music monument. Second, the ruination of these monuments is considered. The dialectics of nature and culture are central to the processes of ruination, dialectics that are also key to much monumental symphonic writing. This connection is explored here. Third, and finally, having outlined the musical monument and its ruination, the place of subjectivity is considered. This concerns both its place in the musical 'space' – a space that collapses around it – and its relation to the historicity of performing subjectivities musically.

Monuments and ruins

Ruins were part of the palette of romantic artistry – an aesthetic legacy that is still pertinent to Silvestrov's 'neo-romanticism'.[15] The romantic concept of the fragment 'is clearly influenced by the contemporary taste for ruins', Charles Rosen points out.[16] But the ruin exceeds the mere fragment. As Michel Makarius puts it,

---

[15] Silvestrov has himself referred to his music using this term (Savenko, 'Valentin Silvestrov's Lyrical Universe', p. 70).
[16] Charles Rosen, *The Romantic Generation* (Cambridge, MA: Harvard University Press, 1995), p. 92.

> [the] ruin conjures up absence. And yet in the same breath one might say that
> the presence of a ruin creates a world with colors, atmosphere, and ghosts
> of its own, tearing itself off the past like a page ripped from a calendar. Hence
> the ruin is more than a fragment.[17]

The association of fragment with ruin which Rosen highlights is called upon in Silvestrov's work. However, it is not only through the presentation of musical fragments that the ruin is evoked; we are not presented merely with a fragmented musical object. In addition to fragmentation, one hears *processes* of ruination playing out – and this is crucial to the transformation of the ruin that I explore here. 'Ruins are processes as much as objects.'[18] These are processes, I argue, that play out in the aforementioned dialectic of nature and culture and, in addition, in the construction and ruination of the musical space.

One observes in Silvestrov's work a critical sensitivity to history and memory, and to the institutional dimension of art. The symphony, as a genre or idea, is taken as a space of memory, one that has now abandoned older modes of subjective habitation and musical expression; new significance, however, is found in remembering past expressivities. Institutionally, as 'post-symphony', the work sits in critical relation to the roles played by the symphony as a canonic form, as an institutionalized site of Western art music. The treatment of this musical space is also highly particularized historically; the contours of a late romanticism are evoked but again exceeded through the terms of a late modernity. And thus one charts one possible historical-aesthetic transformation of musical modernism.

Silvestrov's work is a ruin – or, rather, it elicits aesthetic experiences through processes analogous to those elicited by ruins. However, the adoption of this view requires a historical-aesthetic foundation: an examination of musical monuments. One could cite various 'musical monuments' from music history. The reception history of J. S. Bach provides two ready examples: in Johann Nicolas Forkel's 1802 biography of Bach, the author called for public performances of Bach's works in order to 'raise a worthy monument to German art'[19] (a monument of musical performance). The complete Bach edition, launched in 1850 by the Leipzig

---

[17] Michel Makarius, *Ruins*, trans. David Radzinowicz (Paris: Flammarion, 2004), p. 147.
[18] Andreas Schönle, *Architecture of Oblivion: Ruins and Historical Consciousness in Modern Russia* (DeKalb: Northern Illinois University Press, 2011), p. 8.
[19] Forkel quoted in Lydia Goehr, *The Imaginary Museum of Musical Works: An Essay in the Philosophy of Music*, revised edn (Oxford University Press, 2007), p. 205. See also Alexander Rehding, *Music and Monumentality: Commemoration and Wonderment in Nineteenth-Century Germany* (Oxford University Press, 2009), p. 19.

Bach Gesellschaft to mark the Bach centenary, could be understood in terms of its status as a musical and national monument (a monument of music publication), as has recently been the case in Alexander Rehding's *Music and Monumentality*.[20]

These are not the types of monuments that I focus on here. Instead, I explore ways in which monuments shape modern subjectivities and what happens when these monuments become ruined. Monuments, writes Marita Sturken, 'have been constructed throughout history to signify a sense of permanence'.[21] This is one of their central features: their highlighting of something past as somehow relevant to the present, and their ability to make us remember, in a certain way, events or values – indeed to help select what is worth collectively remembering. Since Alois Riegl's highly influential 1928 essay on 'The Modern Cult of Monuments',[22] the historical dimension has become seen to be a crucial element in the discussion of monuments. Riegl argued that, in contrast with monuments that were intentionally constructed, some monuments garnered monumental status over time: 'the traditional, intentional monument could be distinguished from the historical monument, which acquired its monumental status specifically through the passage of time.'[23]

As Rehding points out, Riegl denied that musical works could be monuments.[24] However, I concur with Rehding's argument that Riegl's thoughts on the monument do have a bearing on music.[25] What the monument and the musical work concept share – as Sturken notes in reference to the former – is a striving for a 'sense of permanence'.[26] In musical and artistic terms, this supposedly permanent – imaginary museum[27] – collection of musical works has a label, that is, 'The Canon'. With the ontological change and emergence of the work concept around 1800, 'a musical work became something which, because of its special transcendental nature, could be repeated without becoming out-dated'.[28] This sense of permanence remains significant even in contemporary musical society; Giles Hooper has rebuffed postmodern assertions to the contrary, recently restating that

---

[20] Rehding, *Music and Monumentality*, p. 144.
[21] Marita Sturken, 'Monuments – Historical Overview' in Michael Kelly (ed.), *Encyclopedia of Aesthetics* in *Oxford Art Online* (accessed 4 September 2012).
[22] Alois Riegl, 'The Modern Cult of Monuments: Its Character and Its Origin' (1928), trans. Kurt W. Forster and Diane Ghirardo, *Oppositions*, 25 (1982), 21–51.
[23] Sturken, 'Monuments', summarizing Riegl.
[24] Riegl, 'The Modern Cult of Monuments', p. 21.
[25] Rehding, *Music and Monumentality*, p. 155.   [26] Sturken, 'Monuments'.
[27] Goehr, *The Imaginary Museum of Musical Works*.
[28] Willem Erauw, 'Canon Formation: Some More Reflections on Lydia Goehr's Imaginary Museum of Musical Works', *Acta Musicologica*, 70/2 (1998), 109–15, p. 109.

a canon of classics is still operative within the world of art music. He notes that 'an analysis of research interests, undergraduate taught modules and research grant recipients across the Anglo-American sector would most likely reveal that the "hegemony" of Western "high-art" canonic repertoire remains rather more resilient in practice than reports of its imminent or actual collapse tend to suggest in theory'.[29]

In the crystallization of their permanence, musical works, like monuments, serve to embody values and concretize socio-cultural practices. Philip Bohlman suggests that, due to complicities between ideologies and musical canons, musical works are 'the manifestations of political and ideological principles, such as greatness, genius, importance to a social group or class of society, etc'.[30] Similarly, monuments are

> a form of pedagogy; they instruct on historical values, persons, and events, designating those that should be passed on, returned to, and learned from. Some monuments speak the language of celebration, while others indicate codes of nobility, valor, sacrifice, and heroism.[31]

Monumental symphonies, like monumental architecture, provide a public form of social performance – performances of selfhood and society, for instance. The 'Heroic' dialectical becoming of some of Beethoven's works provides a well-known example of this musically immanent function.[32] Similarly, the symphony in the nineteenth century was a space for an imagined reconciling of the dialectic between subject and state, 'of reconciling personal autonomy with social order'.[33] Musical monuments thereby enabled the learning and practice of particular subjectivities. Monuments inscribe social values; musical monuments perform values and discipline conditions mediative of (musical) experience. Potentially, with the ruination of the musical work, and the decay of the structures by which a musical monument(ality) takes form, comes a reformulation of these musical values and performativities. To say that Silvestrov's symphony is a ruin of past symphonic monuments is, crucially, to suggest something about musical experience: within this work one hears the ruination and transformation of conditions through which (musical) experience is

---

[29] Giles Hooper, *The Discourse of Musicology* (Aldershot: Ashgate, 2006), p. 26.
[30] Philip V. Bohlman, 'Epilogue: Musics and Canons' in Katherine Bergeron and Philip V. Bohlman (eds.), *Disciplining Music: Musicology and Its Canons* (University of Chicago Press, 1992), pp. 197–210, p. 201.
[31] Sturken, 'Monuments'.
[32] For a classic characterization, see Scott Burnham, *Beethoven Hero* (Princeton University Press, 1995); Janet Schmalfeldt, *In the Process of Becoming: Analytic and Philosophical Perspectives on Form in Early Nineteenth-Century Music* (Oxford University Press, 2011) for a recent discussion.
[33] Bonds, *Music as Thought*, p. 63.

mediated in our late modernity. And it is in this aspect that this ruin acts as a distinctly modern, critical musical ruin; it proffers an object that immanently problematizes the musical, institutional, disciplinary context in which it appears.

Relationships between Silvestrov's symphony, history and musical modernism can perhaps be better understood with reference to what Svetlana Boym has termed 'off-modernism'. The term *off-modern* invokes 'a tradition of critical reflection on the modern condition that incorporates nostalgia'.[34] Boym suggests that off-modernists often appear in contexts that are seemingly 'marginal or provincial with respect to the cultural mainstream'.[35] This rings true for Silvestrov's symphony, caught as it is between the spheres of Soviet Russian music making (Shostakovich) and memories of the Austro-German symphonic tradition. Silvestrov's reaction to the latter differs markedly from, say, that of Alfred Schnittke, who in his Symphony No. 3 – completed one year before Silvestrov's – explored a polyglossia of musical references and historical influences.[36] Silvestrov's strategy, in contrast, explores the paradoxes of a present shot through with the past; with the off-modern, 'reflection and longing, estrangement and affection go together', suggests Boym.[37] The off-modern's characteristic marginality is here as much historical (temporal) as it is geographical (spatial). Exploring a hazy space between the modern and the postmodern, the off-modern 'take[s] a detour from the deterministic narrative of twentieth-century history';[38] it resists dominant historical narratives and the idea of forward-driven progress. Yet, at the same time, it does not commit to a historical time that supersedes the modern. Silvestrov's symphony evokes the musical language of the late romantics – of late Mahler, Bruckner and so on – but does not commit to this expressive vocabulary; this musical language is neither enclosed entirely within an inaccessible past nor is it within the immediate reach of the present. 'The off-modernists mediate between modernists and postmodernists, frustrating the scholars.'[39]

Nature and culture

The interrelationship between nature and culture is central to the aesthetics of the ruin. The dialectics of 'nature' and 'culture' are pertinent to much romantic symphonic writing also. It is through these common terms that process of musical ruination becomes possible. Mahler's musical

---

[34] Svetlana Boym, *The Future of Nostalgia* (New York: Basic Books, 2001), p. xvi.
[35] Ibid., p. xvii.
[36] Alexander Ivashkin, *Alfred Schnittke* (London: Phaidon Books Ltd., 1996), pp. 163–4.
[37] Boym, *The Future of Nostalgia*, p. xvii.   [38] Ibid., pp. xvi–xvii.   [39] Ibid., p. 31.

language provides an excellent example of a nature–culture dialectic at work musically, weaving together the pastoral and 'natural' (folk music, the Ländler, hunting calls, birdsong) with the urban and 'cultural' (art music, the Viennese Waltz, a markedly human presence).[40] Silvestrov also makes reference to both past cultural forms and the natural. Svetlana Savenko has commented that the 'natural and the cultivated in this symphony are not confronted at all but closely blended, with one growing out of the other and dissolving in it'.[41] The latter is most readily evident in the appearance of both symbols of the natural (pastoral topical devices such as drones and horn calls) and in some 'extra-musical' techniques (audible breath sounds produced by the winds and brass). The relationship between ideas of nature and culture is also crucial in the aesthetics of ruins. This dialectic thus provides a crucial juncture between the monumental symphony and the monumental ruin.

Georg Simmel's 1911 essay 'The Ruin' is a far-reaching and, as Huyssen has pointed out, overtly romantic analysis of what makes ruins evocative.[42] Simmel suggests that this culture–nature dialectic is central to the aesthetic of the ruin: ruins play between the categories of man and nature, foregrounding the return of the one into the other. Simmel saw architecture as a dialectical art drawing together man and nature. It was, for him, a counterbalancing of the 'will of the spirit' and 'the necessity of nature', 'in which the soul in its upward striving and nature in its gravity are held in balance'.[43] This, he claimed, distinguished it from the other arts, in which natural laws are 'made dumbly submissive' to the human side – composition and invention – the result of which, if achieved correctly, would absorb and hide the natural within it.[44] Architecture, in contrast with the other arts (Simmel cites poetry, painting and music), uses nature's laws to win over and determine itself, leading to 'the most sublime victory of the spirit over nature'.[45]

This 'sublime victory' is potentially also the case in musical contexts: what of Wagner's *Tristan und Isolde*? Its opening motif provides surely the most prototypical image of the will of the spirit reaching upwards, a rise in tension against the force of gravity, a desire for resolution and hence a victory of the spirit over nature, a victory which – paradoxically – draws on the laws of nature in achieving this goal. The prelude to *Das Rheingold*,

---

[40] In his *Mahler's Voices*, Julian Johnson considers relationships between these 'natural' and 'cultural' (or 'human') features. Julian Johnson, *Mahler's Voices: Expression and Irony in the Songs and Symphonies* (Oxford University Press, 2009). See in particular p. 54.
[41] Savenko, 'Valentin Silvestrov's Lyrical Universe', p. 75.
[42] Huyssen, 'Nostalgia for Ruins', p. 16.   [43] Simmel, 'The Ruins', p. 259.   [44] Ibid.
[45] Ibid.

built over a monumental E-flat overtone series, provides another excellent example of the upward striving of the spirit as determining itself over nature; yet, at the same time, this is a goal achieved through nature – an overtone series is employed in service of this goal. A shared aesthetic framework appears to underpin both a romantic musical aesthetic and Simmel's architectural aesthetic. Silvestrov's neo-romanticism evokes this legacy in its response to the musical and historical conditions of late modernity.

An upward striving defines the heartfelt theme that appears in the strings from figure 10 (bar 73), shown in reduction in Example 11.1. This thematic material is of structural importance, appearing towards the end of the symphony in something akin to a moment of recapitulation. The melody revolves around a series of small descents and greater leaps upwards, a continual rise towards an apex. Once this is achieved (bar 85) cluster material almost immediately intervenes into the texture (bar 86, fig. 12) and, as an apparent result of this, fragments of the melody material appear across the orchestra (and are no longer limited to the strings). A tritone movement in the bass (A to E-flat), dissonant to the third-related sequential movement established so far, parallels this interjection and affirms its otherness. The melody then returns (bar 94) but without the impassioned strength it had before.

This rising movement – especially when considered as dramatically 'at odds' with another force (the cluster material's intervention) – can be understood as drawing on a late romantic musical palette and alluding to a soundworld that evokes a notion of 'spirit'. It provides the semblance of a subjective, expressive voice. The string writing and the harps' accompanimental figures too evoke, in the manner of the Adagietto from Mahler's Fifth, the 'presentation of an overtly "authentic" voice'.[46] But a dialectic is at work here: the melody also emphasizes the 'naturalness' of this expression, growing and overcoming gravity through balance, proportion and structuring through sequence. Despite these potentially 'natural' qualities, the melodic materials' spirited, expressive qualities are foregrounded – especially prominently in the theme from figure 10 onwards, given its character of continually reaching upwards. A 'sublime victory of the spirit over nature' is embodied dialectically; the laws of nature – of a nature that is nonetheless culturally mediated – enable an expressive subject to speak through and over it.

[46] Johnson, *Mahler's Voices*, p. 115. Regarding Julian Johnson's concept of 'voice', as expressive presence in music, see pp. 3–17.

For Simmel, nature connoted an inescapable gravity – a return to the earth – as opposed to the upward spirit of the will: 'what has led the building upward is human will'. The ruin, however, brings the powers of the human will into question; what gives the ruin 'its present appearance is the brute, downward dragging, corroding, crumbling power of nature'.[47] The neo-romantic character of Silvestrov's melodic material carries with it potential associations of the will of the spirit; other materials (drones, horn calls and breath-like phrasing) are heard as inscriptions of the natural. (Yet, as the prefix 'neo-' suggests, these romantic associations are not reproduced unproblematically; in line with the off-modern, paradoxically they are both affective and estranged.) Expressive structures built up through the dialectical relationship between spirit and nature are immanent to both music and architecture.

This dialectic of spirit and nature – a dialectic embodied in the first theme – collapses as the movement ends. Rather than affirmation, we hear negation, comparable to that which Adorno proposed as occurring at the end of Mahler's Sixth Symphony.[48] More precisely, in terms of ruination, and in a manner akin to Simmel's dialectics of ruin, nature's gravity reclaims the symphonic architecture built above and through it. Three complementary features give rise to this ruinous process: (1) musical motion is suspended as increasing focus is brought towards musical stasis and associations of the timelessness of nature. The first feature thus concerns *musical time*. (2) Structural processes supplement this stasis, processes themselves situated within the symphonic space. The music exemplifies the 'downward dragging, corroding, crumbling power of nature' as a collapse occurs in the structural background; the symphonic space embodies a process of ruination. This second feature thus concerns the structuring of the *musical space*. (3) The last feature foregrounds neither from time nor space but *musical symbolism (semiotics)* – in particular, musical connotations of Nature. To give one prominent example, figures reminiscent of 'horn calls' – figures closely aligned historically with the natural and the pastoral – are heard in a series of motives based on fifths. These three dimensions together act towards the dual character of the ending's material, processually embodying and symbolically confirming the ruination of symphonic architecture. Each of these three aspects will now be explored in detail.

(1) Stasis – timelessness and the ahistorical – has often been considered a hallmark of musical constructions of nature; stasis may provide a kind of mythic time that goes beyond that which is humanly experienced. As Julian Johnson puts it,

[47] Simmel, 'The Ruins', p. 261.   [48] Adorno, *Mahler*, p. 138.

Nature music, in its apparent self-containment and avoidance of linear motion, seems to suspend time. In this it seems to offer an analogy for our experience of spaciousness in which there is little or no movement. Space without perceived directed movement appears timeless.[49]

Static material enters intermittently throughout Silvestrov's symphony, often coexisting simultaneously with other material. Most prominently, pauses in melodic phrasing, in which phrases stand still, 'outside' of time, become particularly prominent in a passage starting at figure 34, but are not limited to this section. From the passage that follows figure 34, static bars of 'inserts' prolong moments in the unfolding of the music. Furthermore, each of these inserts is filled with sustained pitches in the strings and downward flourishes in the first harp (Example 11.2). Such stasis is symbolic of the static qualities heard in the work more generally, a characteristic that has led Savenko to call this a 'static composition'.[50]

Example 11.2 Valentin Silvestrov, Symphony No. 5: first harp, bar 300.

This stasis becomes exceptional towards the end of the symphony. It is in the closing passages that stasis, and a collapse of spirit into timeless nature, becomes foregrounded. Harmonic stasis is heard, first, in the slowing and final suspension of harmonic movement and, second, through a chromatic saturation of the pitch space. (This fall into suspended temporality is rhetorically confirmed by downward sweeping gestures carried across the strings, for instance triggered at bar 797 (fig. 94) and bar 802.) Wind and brass players supplement these associations of the natural in the use of their instruments; the immediate physicality of nature is heard when air is blown through their instruments without producing pitch (e.g. in bars 810–812). These qualities mediate a construction of nature that then itself decays into a natural state – silence – in which human activity is apparently absent.

(2) A large-scale structural descent precedes this final array of sonic imagery; the gravity of nature drags downwards before it is made audibly present on the semantic surface. From figure 90 onwards one hears a familiar melody, though one now characterized by descent. Its upward leaps do not contradict this – they are octave displacements that descend again, thus reconfirming downwards motion. As can be seen from the

---

[49] Johnson, *Webern and the Transformation of Nature*, p. 232.
[50] Savenko, 'Valentin Silvestrov's Lyrical Universe', pp. 75–6.

Example 11.3 Valentin Silvestrov, Symphony No. 5, figs. 90–92 (upbeat to bar 758–777), reduction.

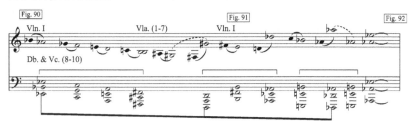

Example 11.4 Valentin Silvestrov, Symphony No. 5, bar 772 to end, reduction.

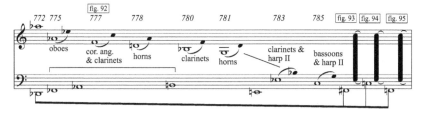

reduction (Example 11.3), this line in the violins and violas revolves around a central A-flat/G-sharp. This is important for two reasons. First, it stabilizes the descent, giving it a centre of 'gravitational pull'.

Second, those instants when the A-flat/G-sharp centre is settled upon momentarily tell us something crucial when the bass is considered also: it suggests an underlying harmonic coherence to this extended passage that is itself constitutive of a descent, a huge structural exhalation. This can be observed in the semitone movement embedded in the line of those instruments given the role of the bass, the double basses and the cellos (players 8–10): E-flat, at figure 90; D-natural, in the bass below the G-sharp just before figure 91; and, finally, D-flat, beneath the high A-flat preceding figure 92. It should also be noted that this bass is related to that heard originally supporting the melody at figure 10. Unlike the earlier bass, this motion is made by minor thirds (not major thirds, as earlier). These collections are shown bracketed in the background diagrams.

(3) Arriving at figure 92, the ear is led by a descent at a surface rather than the background level. A series of fifths, so important to the rising contour of the original melody at figure 10 (Example 11.1), becomes the basis of a sequence of motifs that fall away. The instrumentation of these is spread across the orchestra and is generally doubled in the strings (Example 11.4). (Indeed, the rising fifth motif is pre-echoed earlier in the movement, prominently in the cor anglais and first clarinet at bar 346.)

Despite the foregrounding of the fifth motif's descent, harmonic processes play a role too, with this movement being echoed at a larger level in the bass: a D-flat moves to an F-sharp, and then a C-natural to an F-natural, which brings the symphony to a close.

This should not be seen as a moment of resolution; instead it further illustrates the ruination of symphonic architecture at work in the symphony, its process of self-negation. The long-range bass movement D-flat (C-sharp) to F-sharp, while reminiscent of a large-scale structural resolution, does not affirm any real closure. This is surprising as this contradicts F-sharp major's earlier establishment as a centre with strong tonal tendencies. Indeed, an extended passage appears (from fig. 20 onwards) that, for the most part, appears in this key. A key signature even appears for the first time, of six sharps. However, at the end of the movement, this return to material reminiscent of F-sharp is quickly undercut by the re-emergence of cluster material (included in the reduction at figs. 93–95). In addition, a movement by a fifth in the bass – C-natural to F-natural – mirrors the D-flat (C-sharp) to F-sharp movement, but a semitone 'out'. This large-scale gesture is also submerged in a chromatically saturated texture and, furthermore, is unmoored from the strings' material, still connotative of F-sharp, that sits above it. Both 'cadences' show through, but lose their functionality, written over as structures of closure. And, as has already been outlined above, the material that envelops this problematic articulation of the musical space connotes imagery of a myriad and timeless nature – a state beyond the realms of human experience and the reaches of its agency.

Subjectivity and musical space

Musical structure has often been conceived of in spatial terms. Indeed, explicitly architectural frameworks have enabled some such conceptualizations.[51] Such musical spaces may become subject to decay and ruination, and it is the spatial towards which we now turn.

This connection between musical structure and (architectural) space is a long-standing one. The composer Johann Mattheson, for instance, suggested architectural imagery as a means by which one might conceive of musical structure. He suggested that composers should properly order 'all the sections and elements in the melody, or in an entire musical work,

---

[51] Bonds locates this tendency as becoming widespread in the second quarter of the nineteenth century. Mark Evan Bonds, 'The Spatial Representation of Musical Form', *The Journal of Musicology*, 27/3 (2010), 265–307, p. 268.

almost in the manner in which one arranges a building and sketches out a draft or an outline, a ground-plan'.[52] Hegel, in his *Philosophy of Fine Art*, compared music and architecture on the basis that both must follow the natural laws of structure, proportion and balance.[53] Such long-standing connections between music and architecture – between a temporal art (music) and its spatial (architectural) conception – are reaffirmed by the widespread romantic notion of architecture as 'frozen music'.[54] More generally, as Mark Evan Bonds has pointed out, spatial and temporal conceptions of musical form often work in conjunction, drawing on one another. 'Form is both a [temporal] process and a [spatial] structure, and accounts of form routinely acknowledge this dual nature.'[55]

These conceptual legacies – whereby music is spatially conceived – provide the foundations of the ruination of musical spaces. 'In its common usage, "ruins" are often enchanted, desolate spaces, large-scale monumental structures abandoned and grown over. Ruins provide a quintessential image of what has vanished from the past and has long decayed', writes Ann Laura Stoler.[56] The ruin is a decayed architectural space. But what kind of 'enchanted space' does the *symphonic ruin* offer a listening subject?

Legacies of musical, structural space are evoked in Silvestrov's symphony – although, like a ruin, they appear as 'large-scale monumental structures abandoned and grown over' (as Stoler puts it). Svetlana Savenko's observation that 'one can easily discern in his symphony the contours of sonata form' is important here;[57] these 'contours' are more of a compositional inclination than affirmed means by which normative symphonic space (and temporality) is articulated. Points of structural reference are not taken as concrete boundaries so much as evocations defined by semi-permeability. Notably, the appearance of melodic material in the strings at bar 727 (fig. 87, Example 11.5), material outlined originally (albeit in a slightly different form) at bar 73 (fig. 10, Example 11.1), can be heard as a moment of sonata-like recapitulatory return. However, this is a return that

---

[52] Mattheson quoted in Bonds, 'The Spatial Representation of Musical Form', pp. 268–9.
[53] Georg W. F. Hegel, *The Philosophy of Fine Art*, trans F. P. B. Osmaston, 4 vols. (London: Bells and Sons, 1920), vol. III, p. 346.
[54] More recently, Holly Watkins has considered changes in musical and architectural space in early twentieth-century Vienna, in light of Schoenberg's music and Adolf Loos's architecture. Holly Watkins, 'Schoenberg's Interior Designs', *Journal of the American Musicological Society*, 61/1 (2008), 123–206.
[55] Bonds, 'The Spatial Representation of Musical Form', p. 266.
[56] Ann Laura Stoler, 'Imperial Debris: Reflections on Ruins and Ruination', *Cultural Anthropology*, 23/2 (2008), 191–219: p. 194.
[57] Savenko, 'Valentin Silvestrov's Lyrical Universe', p. 76. Savenko notes that while sonata form is evoked – and despite the fact that sonata form is a processually driven form – temporal development is eschewed in the name of stasis.

Example 11.5 Valentin Silvestrov, Symphony No. 5, returning melody, first violins, from bar 727 (fig. 87).

Example 11.6 Valentin Silvestrov, Symphony No. 5, first clarinet's solo line, bars 611–615.

is announced dramatically rather than emerging teleologically (as the result of an unproblematic tonal framework). This markedly subjective material returns, but through neither triumph nor overcoming. Past formal archetypes show through (sonata form); these formal spaces, however, are not inhabited by concurrent subjectivities, as they once were.

Fragments of subjectively allusive material appear within the musical space, returning often, although quickly dissipating. No-longer-present subjectivities are evoked but do not inhabit the musical space as such. This can be heard, for example, in moments of 'subjective' intervention, when markedly soloistic – often melodic – material enters, which bear traces of past ways of 'doing' musical subjectivity. (This 'trace' recalls Adorno's observation that the *sedimentation* of past subjective appearances is always present in musical material inherited from previous generations.[58]) An entry of the first clarinet, starting at the upbeat to bar 612, provides an excellent example. Here, Mozartian embellishments appear in descending phrases reminiscent of classical cadential approaches, but these never resolve in terms of classical syntax (Example 11.6). These return again and again, interspersed with smudged dissonant clusters in the strings; these are modified in response to the soloist, but they never achieve consonance with them. (Indeed, these interactions make up a significant portion of the work, a passage of almost one hundred bars, from bar 607 (fig. 75) to approximately bar 700.) Furthermore, a performance note instructs that the soloist 'should sound as if from afar, now approaching, now moving away (with careful observance of dynamic nuances)', further distancing the embellished material from being situated unproblematically within the musical space. As such, traces of past

---

[58] Max Paddison, *Adorno's Aesthetics of Music* (Cambridge University Press, 1993), p. 93.

subjectivities show through the musical material. These appear as palimpsests, however, written over and never fully present: literally written over where orchestral timbres appear in superimposition over the clear articulation of individually expressive, soloistic moments; and problematically present where subjective materials appear fragmented and unable to act in the form of an expressive whole.

Something similar can be said of the means by which expression is articulated instrumentally within the musical space. Traces of a romantic use of a soloist are called on at bar 703. Importantly, this is the moment when the impassioned thematic material that appeared in the strings returns for its 'recapitulation'. This return is preempted by the entry of fragments of this melody by a solo violin, this material being explored across far-reaching leaps upward in a high tessitura. This recalls a romantically idiomatic use of a solo violin, acting first as an expression of individuated agency, one whose material is then taken into the orchestral texture wholesale. This subsumption of the soloist's material occurs principally at bar 727 and is confirmed in being echoed by soloistic entries in the brass from 743 onwards. Inscribed into the symphony's orchestration, as a material being, are aesthetic legacies going beyond the immediate yet that are nonetheless entangled with it. It is in both the drawing upon these inherited habitations of the musical space and their transgression that the ruination of symphonic architecture becomes audible.

In the ruin, subjectivity's presence is problematic; in Silvestrov's symphony we hear an echo in its absence. Traces of the past are audible both moment to moment (as, for instance, in the clarinet's Mozartian embellishments) and in the structuring of symphonic space at a larger, abstracted level. A sustained episode of this problematic subjective presence appears in a passage that revolves around fragments of melody in the solo piano, starting at bar 479 (Example 11.7). This is marked *lontano*. A performance instruction also accompanies the piano part at this point – 'Piano: very gentle and delicately, as if from afar' – something immediately suggesting

Example 11.7   Valentin Silvestrov, Symphony No. 5, bars 479–483, beginning of the piano's solo material.

questions of presence and absence in a very literal sense. The background to this solo is relatively sparse and static. Three elements define this texture: clusters that appear in the strings, breath sounds in the winds and brass and fragments of previously heard harmonic colours in the pitched percussion. The piano's phrases appear homeless among the orchestral textures, which themselves intercede and discolour the piano's line through dissonance, or sit beside it, suggesting neither dialogue nor synthesis with it. The resonance at the end of the piano's final melodic fragment (which begins on the upbeat to bar 494) is followed by these three orchestral elements heard simultaneously, a kind of dissonant reverberation as all that remains of it in a now empty (static) space (fig. 64).

This dialectic of presence and absence also appears at the level of structure. As already observed, principles of sonata form are recalled but not enacted wholesale. More fundamentally, Silvestrov repeatedly evades objects of clear experiential focus – melodic figures, for example, rise up and quickly dissipate. In particular, a swirling (often descending) figure is present throughout much of the work. It is given particular prominence in the first harp from fig. 34 onwards (as cited in Example 11.2). However, it appears in a constellation of multiple variants, without an archetypical identity – recalling Adorno's view of Mahler that he conceived of 'theme as gestalt'.[59] This swirling figure's presence is never affirmed and as such it avoids being arrested in any single immediate moment; it appears instead only in 'echoes of music history',[60] echoes of a past sound – of Mahler, Bruckner, Schubert and others – which is itself absent. This musical material is given an aura of being out of reach: 'Aura, from the Hebrew word for light, was defined by Benjamin as an experience of distance, a mist of nostalgia that does not allow for possession of the object of desire.'[61] Many of the materials that make up Silvestrov's work appear and dissipate such as to never guarantee their ontological firmness.

Such features within the musical space point to a dialectic of presence and absence; past subjectivities may no longer inhabit this space as they have done historically, yet their traces are crucial to the evocativeness of the symphonic ruin. Beyond the relatively autonomous space of the work one may observe traces acting at another level, the historical and institutional: a canon of past works leaves its mark on our experience of the symphony in the present. While Silvestrov may have dubbed his Fifth

---

[59] Adorno, *Mahler*, p. 88. [60] Schmelz, 'Valentin Silvestrov and the Echoes of Music History'.
[61] Svetlana Boym summarizing Benjamin on *aura* in *The Future of Nostalgia*, p. 45.

Symphony a 'post-symphony', it is the composer's words on another one of his 'post-' forms – the 'postlude' – that sheds light on this matter:

> [The] 'Postlude' is conceived of as the act of gathering resonances, as it were – or else as the form which supposes the existence of some text which, without being included into the given text, is in some way connected with it. Thus, the form is open – though not, as would be more usual, at the end, but at the beginning.[62]

The form of the postlude, in other words, suggests a relation to something outside of itself. (This it shares with the romantic fragment.) Yet, at the same time, it is this very absence that defines the identity of the work as a postlude. This absence of the work's determining feature is critical to the post-symphony also: the reverberation of the musical canon fills symphonic space, although it is not present as such. Silvestrov said that his Fifth Symphony was 'something not so much beginning, as responding to something already uttered'.[63] Past forms – such as the 'cadences' at the end of the work – are remembered within the space, but are not (unproblematically) operative in articulating the musical space of the work. Indeed, Peter Schmelz has recently suggested that Silvestrov's heightened suspension of a romantic harmonic palette is central to his *neo*-romanticism (a tendency most clearly exposed in the composer's postludes).[64]

Georg Simmel insisted that, for the ruin to be evocative, enough must remain of the original form for there to be a visible relation between spirit and nature – forms engendered by a dialectic of spirit and nature must still remain perceptible. In his architectural terms he wrote that, for this reason, the 'stumps of the pillars of the Forum Romanum are simply ugly and nothing else, while a pillar crumbled – say, halfway down – can generate a maximum of charm'.[65] Silvestrov's Symphony No. 5 presents us with an audible equivalent to the visibility of the architectural ruin. We see in the traces of past forms, past musical structures and subjectivities relationships between each and the others that no longer function as they once did. This symphony is itself monumental – drawing on the romantic symphonic tradition – while at the same time the ruination of symphonic monuments of the past is made audible. However, the traditions that are

---

[62] Silvestrov quoted in Hakobian, *Music of the Soviet Age 1917–1987*, p. 310.
[63] Silvestrov quoted in Peter J. Schmelz, *Such Freedom, If Only Musical: Unofficial Soviet Music during the Thaw* (Oxford University Press, 2009), p. 261.
[64] Schmelz, 'Valentin Silvestrov and the Echoes of Music History', p. 270.
[65] Simmel, 'The Ruins', p. 265.

'ruined' are not negated, no longer relevant or concealed in an inaccessible past. As Svetlana Boym puts it, the 'ruin is not merely something that reminds us of the past; it is also a reminder of the future, when our present becomes history'.[66] The musical ruin prompts us to consider the continual transience of the conditions through which modern experience is mediated.

---

[66] Boym, *The Future of Nostalgia*, p. 79.

PART III

Replaying modernism

12 Playing with transformations

Boulez's Improvisation III sur Mallarmé

Erling E. Guldbrandsen

I have never been quite convinced by the way the story of 'high modernism' has generally been told. More often than not, it has been a saga of radical ruptures and new starts – a 'progress narrative' involving limitless constructivism and the increasing rationalization of musical language and compositional technique. In short, the simplest historiographical tropes seem to have prevailed. Moreover, technical analyses of the music in question often fail to account for the actual listening experience. The hegemonic language of structural analysis and modernist historiography from the last fifty-odd years falls short of the musical imagery, poetic sensuality and strangeness present in works by Messiaen, Stockhausen, Ligeti, Xenakis, Berio, Saariaho or Sciarrino.

Even though the general textbook image of European post-World War II modernism as a predominantly rationalist era of strictly 'logical' composition is gradually changing, it appears to be changing rather slowly. During the last six decades, mainstream structural analyses of music by Pierre Boulez (b. 1925) – a prominent figure in post-war modernism and a co-founder of the so-called 'total' serialist composition – seem to have taken for granted a certain notion of serialism that emphasizes the need for structural unity and rational compositional control. To a surprising extent – aside from certain valuable exceptions in more recent decades – the general analytical literature on Boulez's music resorted to a terminology of such concepts as structural coherence, unity, consistency, order, strictness, rigour, discipline, deduction, logic, necessity and rational compositional control. I call this the 'unity and control model' of serialism.[1]

A similar idea informs readings of Boulez's theoretical writings, from *Relevés d'apprenti* to *Leçons de musique*.[2] This lopsided understanding of

---

[1] See references in Erling E. Guldbrandsen, 'New Light on Pierre Boulez and Postwar Modernism: On the Composition of "Improvisation I–III sur Mallarmé"' in Søren Møller Sørensen (ed.), *In the Plural: Institutions, Pluralism and Critical Self-Awareness in Contemporary Music* (University of Copenhagen, 1997), pp. 15–28.

[2] Pierre Boulez, *Relevés d'apprenti* (Paris: Seuil, 1966), English: *Stocktakings from an Apprenticeship*, collected and ed. by Paule Thévenin, trans. Stephen Walsh (Oxford: Clarendon Press, 1991); *Penser la musique aujourd'hui* (Genève: Gonthier, 1963), English:

serialism was intertwined with the hard-core structural analysis of 'formalist' musicology from the 1950s onward.[3] Closely related to the 'unity and control model' of serialism is the often unmentioned historiographical figure who construes post-war high modernism as a break with the past – one that tries to obliterate any traces of the classic-romantic tradition of Western art music.

It is true that Boulez's own rhetorical strategies as theorist and polemicist have themselves contributed to the rationalist optics that has governed our picture of Boulez the composer. Boulez even emphasizes 'coherence' and 'control' in his articles on compositional technique, particularly the earlier ones, though his texts are undoubtedly ambiguous on this point. From the start he also signals the presence of other aesthetic and artistic influences on his compositional thinking, and especially the powerful inspiration of poetry and literature, visual arts and architecture, and non-European musics. These sources of inspiration indeed appear to mark the stylistic and aesthetic surfaces of works throughout his oeuvre, from the gestural eruptions of the *Second Sonata* (1948) and the estranged orientalism of *Le Marteau sans maître* (1955) to the suggestive archaism of *Rituel* (1975), the introverted murmurings of *Dialogue de l'ombre double* (1985) and the austere darkness and grandeur of the ostensibly hypermodern live-electronic surfaces of *Répons* (1981–4). Far from communicating a cold and calculated 'rationalism', his works come forward as poetic statements, ringing through the echo chambers of orchestral labyrinths and evoking – as it were – fictitious imageries of forgotten rituals and futuristic splendour.

From early on, too, Boulez noted an unpredictable dimension to his serialist procedures. Though it is hard to distinguish between earlier (generative) and later stages in his compositional process, given his constant back-and-forth movement between them, an irruption of free elements characterizes both. On the one hand, Boulez makes striking free aesthetic choices in later phases of his musical articulation, constantly moulding and rephrasing his final textures.[4] On the other hand, even more interestingly, the serialist procedures that he develops in the early stages of the compositional process – inside his very laboratory of technical generation – are

Boulez on Music Today, trans. Susan Bradshaw and Richard Rodney Bennett (London: Faber and Faber, 1971); *Points de repère* (Paris: Éditions Christian Bourgois, 1985); *Jalons (pour une décennie)* (Paris: Éditions Christian Bourgois, 1989); *Regards sur autrui (Points de repère II)*, collected and ed. Jean-Jacques Nattiez and Sophie Galaise (Paris: Éditions Christian Bourgois, 2005); *Leçons de musique (Points de repère III)*, collected and ed. Jean-Jacques Nattiez (Paris: Éditions Christian Bourgois, 2005).

[3] See Joseph Kerman's diagnosis of Western musicology and structural analysis in his seminal *Musicology* (London: Fontana Press, 1985).

[4] See Erling E. Guldbrandsen, 'Casting New Light on Boulezian Serialism' in Edward Campbell and Peter O'Hagan (eds.), *Boulez Studies* (Cambridge University Press, 2016, forthcoming).

marked by an intentional renunciation of compositional predictability and control.

Unpredictability and free choice do not stand in opposition to his serialist writing (as in commonplace dichotomies of strictness 'versus' freedom); rather, they are constitutive conditions for the workings of the system itself. In my view, the non-rationalist leanings that work at the centre of his compositional practices have been largely underestimated in the analytical and historical renderings of what Boulezian – and indeed, European – high modernism was, or is, all about.[5] In Boulez's case, one might label these leanings a 'poetics of practical musicianship and taste', one that forms an indispensable criterion for his compositional choices. Also, over the past four decades, the interplay between his work as an orchestral conductor and his modes of compositional writing has become increasingly apparent. I suggest that these experiences have contributed to a new take on musical articulation, phrasing and form in his compositions after the mid-1970s, as well as his later revisions of earlier scores.[6]

In this chapter, I will take my examples from Boulez's 'Improvisation III sur Mallarmé – A la nue accablante tu'.[7] The piece is the fourth and the longest of the five movements in *Pli selon pli – portrait de Mallarmé* for soprano and orchestra, which stands as a milestone in Boulez's development as a composer.[8] While other movements of *Pli selon pli* have been more widely analyzed, the grand and complex 'Third Improvisation' still awaits an in-depth international study.[9] I will here consider different kinds of 'transformations' that can be traced in the long-term process of composing, playing, recording, revising and re-recording this movement in the years from 1959 to 1983 and onward. One by one, in a kind of generalist effort, I

---

[5] See Erling E. Guldbrandsen, 'Pierre Boulez in Interview, 1996 (Parts I–IV)', *Tempo*, 65/255–58 (2011).

[6] See Erling E. Guldbrandsen, 'Modernist Composer and Mahler Conductor: Changing Conceptions of Performativity in Boulez', *Studia Musicologica Norvegica*, 32 (2006), 140–68.

[7] First version (composed 1959), Universal Edition, London 1963, withdrawn; second version, Universal Edition, London 1983 (the score says 1982, but the publication date appears to be late 1983 – see Dominique Jameux, *Pierre Boulez* (Paris: Fayard, 1984), 400–1).

[8] *Pli selon pli – portrait de Mallarmé* (composed 1957–60; 1962; 1982–3; 1989), London: Universal Edition.

[9] Brief accounts include Raphaël Brunner, 'L'"Improvisation III sur Mallarmé" de Pierre Boulez: Éléments pour une mise en perspective', *Dissonanz/Dissonance*, 50 (1996), 4–14; Luisa Bassetto, 'Orient – Accident? *Pli selon pli*, ou l'"eurexcentrisme" selon Boulez' in Pierre Albèra (ed.), *Pli selon pli de Pierre Boulez: Entretiens et etudes* (Genève: Éditions Contrechamps, 2003), pp. 37–44; and Arnold Whittall, '"Unbounded visions": Boulez, Mallarmé and Modern Classicism', *Twentieth-Century Music*, 1/1 (2004), 65–80. 'Improvisation III', along with the rest of *Pli selon pli*, is analyzed across 630 pages in Norwegian in my dissertation, *Tradisjon og tradisjonsbrudd: En studie i Pierre Boulez: Pli selon pli – portrait de Mallarmé*, unpublished PhD dissertation, University of Oslo (1995) (published Oslo: Scandinavian University Press, 1997).

will address the following five kinds of 'transformations' that are at large in the musical becoming and understanding of this particular movement:

1. Performative transformations: revisions of the score from 1959 to 1983
2. Generative transformations: from serial structures to musical form
3. Transformations of Mallarmé's poetics into music
4. Transformations of Mallarmé's poem into music
5. Historiographical transformations of current images of post-war modernism

From the outset, these five points will be discussed chronologically – although the first one, labelled 'performative transformations', inevitably intersects with all of the other ones by invoking a deeper level of methodological impact throughout the following discussion.

Performative transformations: revisions of the score from 1959 to 1983

As is well known, Boulez frequently rewrites his scores as seemingly unending 'works in progress' – a phrase he borrowed from James Joyce's original publication of the novel *Finnegans Wake* as a *feuilleton* under the title 'Work in progress'. As a conductor, Boulez likewise frequently offers new performances and recordings of the same 'canonical' works of the twenty-first, twentieth and late nineteenth centuries, including his own. While his presentation of Webern's complete works, for instance (recorded 1967–72), set a new standard in the structural understanding of this music at the time, in the 1990s he eventually re-recorded it all, with a strikingly new take on the romantic gestural agogics of Webern's music.[10]

Far from setting him apart from the common practices of Western art music, this process of incessant reinterpretation actually ties Boulez quite closely to the classic-romantic tradition. Though this is not the place to dig into recent reconstructions of the concept of the artwork, suffice it to say that the idea of *Werktreue* – emerging around 1800[11] – has been challenged by the growing scholarly conviction that the musical work of art was never really considered a closed entity, like a marble sculpture or printed book, but instead was always regarded as something in need of constant renewal. (Of course, sculptures and books are likewise subject to new readings and interpretations.)

---

[10] See *Webern Complete Works*, opp. 1–31, Sony Classical, recorded 1967–72; and *Complete Webern*, Deutsche Grammophon, recorded 1992–6.

[11] Lydia Goehr, *The Imaginary Museum of Musical Works* (Oxford: Clarendon Press, 1992).

Boulez's 'Improvisation III' was written in 1959 and revised mainly in 1982–83, producing two 'completed' versions of the musical score. In addition, non-printed amendments have appeared outside the processes of completing (1959) and revising (1983) the work, probably during rehearsals at different occasions over the past five decades.[12] Amendments aside, there are significant differences between the two main versions of the score, a few of which I shall mention here.

In the 1959 version, the piece opens with four distinct musical episodes. After a brief statement in two harps (the first episode), the soprano delivers a long vocalize passage (the second episode) on the vowel 'A', which is the first word of the text that Boulez sets here ('A la nue accablante tu'). Then comes a brief passage in the mandolin, guitar and cowbells (the third episode), followed by a rapid exchange in two xylophones (the fourth episode). Together, these four textures (pp. 1–2 in 1959) constitute what I label 'Episodes I' (see Table 12.1, below). Another aspect of the 1959 version is its reliance upon an open form, comprised of several variants or *ossia* textures, among which the performers – or the conductor – can in principle choose freely over the course of the performance. Thus only a limited portion of the written material will actually be performed on any given occasion.

The musical contrasts among the four initial episodes are striking, and related episodes return in the piece's middle and ending sections ('Episodes II' and 'Episodes III', respectively). Remarkably, Boulez made two recordings of the 1959 version, thereby confirming its authoritative work status, only to then withdraw the score completely. I present an overview of the main formal sections in the 1959 and 1983 versions in Table 12.1.

In 1983, not least the exposition ('Episodes I') has been profoundly changed. Several parts have been added and the formerly distinct, four episodes have been merged into a much more continuous musical flow. Added material is mostly played by instruments with sustained notes (trombone, five violoncellos, three double basses), as opposed to the predominantly attack-resonance instruments of the other textures (harps, mandolin, guitar, xylophones, other percussion). Moreover, all of the traits associated with the 1959 'open form' have been abandoned in 1983.

---

[12] Minor revisions were made during Boulez's recording of the piece in 1969 (with Halina Lukomska and the BBC Symphony Orchestra). Further changes were made during his recording with Phyllis Bryn-Julson and the BBC Symphony Orchestra in London in 1981, resulting in deviations between these two recordings of the 1959 score. The 1983 version was recorded by Boulez in 2001 (with Christine Schäfer and the Ensemble InterContemporain), again with deviations from that score.

Table 12.1

	1959			1983	
	Text	Pages		Text	Pages
Episodes I	'A–'	1–2	Episodes I	Verses 1–8	1–7
Alpha	No text	3–21	Alpha	Verses 9–14	8–16
			Alpha (cont'd)	No text	17–31
Interlude	Verse 1	22–24	Interlude 1	Verse 1	32–35
Episodes II		24	Episodes II		36–37
Beta	Verse 2	25–34	Beta	Verse 2	38–57
Gamma	Verse 3	35–48	Gamma	Verse 3	58–84
			Interlude 2 (new)	Verse 4	84–87
Episodes III		49	Episodes III		88–90

In addition, a lot of new text has been accommodated in the work. In the place of the opening vocalize, all fourteen verses from Mallarmé's sonnet have been added, and a flute quartet now accompanies the voice in a new kind of heterophonic texture in an expanded musical exposition. Throughout this new exposition, the musical phrasing has been changed and the transitions have become more fluid, amid much more ornate musical figuration. In the first harp episode on page 1 of the 1959 version (Example 12.1a), there are a relatively barren six attacks, compared to the flurry of notes we find in the 1983 version (Example 12.1b).

The very few 'structural' notes from 1959 have been enriched by repetitions, arpeggios and 'diagonal' gestures in the 1983 version. The same goes for the revised episodes for voice, for mandolin and guitar and for xylophones. This enrichment of texture is, broadly speaking, the way Boulez generally works when he revises and expands on his earlier pieces, and he has wrought similar changes in the middle and final sections. To sum up, the opening section sees a profound transformation from its 'punctualist' articulation and early 'French-Russian' episodic form (in 1959) to processes of more gradual musical transitions (in 1983). The earlier episodic form was possibly related to the influence of Messiaen's conception of musical form or to Stravinsky's musical cells in *The Rite of Spring*; Boulez's revisions, on the other hand, appear to reflect the more 'Austro-German' approach to continuous formal processes that characterizes the later stages of his development as a composer.

I refer to this as a 'performative transformation', since I suggest it can partly be seen in light of Boulez's experiences as an orchestral conductor through the 1960s and 1970s. His abandonment of open form may be read as a quite pragmatic decision. In an interview with Boulez that I attended in

Playing with transformations

Example 12.1a '"Improvisation III", harps, page 1, first version'.

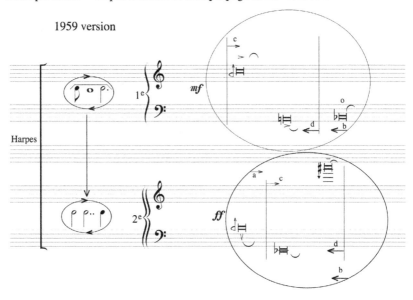

Example 12.1b '"Improvisation III", harps, page 1, revised version'.

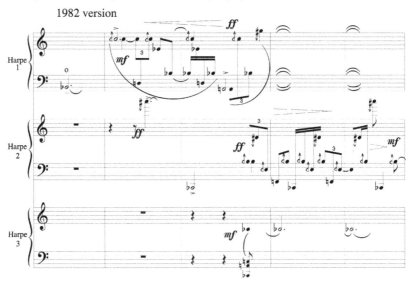

London in 2011, he stated clearly and simply that in this case 'the conductor's experience overruled the composer's experience'.[13] His practical

---

[13] Author's notes from the Southbank Centre in London, 1 October 2011.

experiences with a broadening repertoire, in tandem with his increasing focus on musical perception in his writings of the late 1970s and onwards, likely motivated the stylistic changes he made in the later version of 'Improvisation III', and in other pieces. In the early 1950s, Boulez was mainly analyzing and conducting recent scores by composers like Webern, Stravinsky and Messiaen, as well as his own work and that of the composers of his generation.[14] In the following decades, though, he gradually immersed himself more deeply in the Austro-German repertoire of early modernist and even late romantic music. The general trajectory went back in time from then-contemporary scores to the music of Berg, Debussy and Wagner.

A similar transformation – or broadening of scope – took place in his theoretical writings. In his early articles, he distanced himself from Berg as the 'romantic Viennese' in favour of Webern (in 1948, Boulez wrote that certain traits of Berg's *Lyric Suite* 'spring from the bad taste of romantic effusion carried to the point of paroxysm').[15] Later on, however, he came to appreciate Berg's 'organic' compositional procedures,[16] as well as the long-range musical processes of the late Wagner, which he compared to the writing style of Proust. Whereas Wagner himself called his *Tristan* music 'die Kunst des Überganges', Theodor W. Adorno later referred to Berg as 'der Meister des kleinsten Überganges'.[17] In addition, in Boulez's theoretical output there is a gradual shift of perspective from an early focus on problems of compositional technique (in the early 1950s) to an increasing interest in questions of musical form and text–music relations (in the late 1950s), then in musical performance and aesthetics (the 1960s) and then in issues of musical perception contemporary with the founding of IRCAM and the Ensemble InterContemporain in the late 1970s and articulated throughout his lectures at the Collège de France between 1976 and 1995. With his increasing commitments as a conductor in the 1960s and 1970s (particularly with the BBC Symphony Orchestra, the New York Philharmonic and the Wagner Festival in Bayreuth), there is a decline in his commencement of new compositions. But it is during this time – up to the beginnings of *Répons* (in 1980) and the revision of

---

[14] Jésus Aguila, *Le Domaine musical: Pierre Boulez et vingt ans de création contemporaine* (Paris: Fayard, 1992).
[15] *Stocktakings of an Apprenticeship*, p. 185 (*Relevés d'apprenti*, p. 238).
[16] *Boulez on Music Today*, pp. 71–3 (*Penser la musique aujourd'hui*, pp. 79–80). See also his affirmation of the composer in the articles on Berg from 1977 to 1979 (in *Points de repère*), and later in his Collège de France lectures (in *Leçons de musique*).
[17] Letter to Mathilde Wesendonck, 29 October 1859, in *Richard Wagner: Briefe* (Stuttgart: Reclam, 1995), p. 365. Theodor W. Adorno, *Alban Berg: Der Meister des kleinsten Überganges* (Frankfurt am Main: Suhrkamp, 1995).

'Improvisation III' – that his compositional style gradually changes, and his revisions of earlier scores come to almost outshine the production of completely new works.

However, this narrative, suggesting a linear historic development in Boulez's conception of musical phrasing and form – from Webernian pointillism and French-Russian episodic form towards Austro-German flow and Wagnerian gradual transitions – may very well be too simple and straightforward to account for the intertwined complexities of the actual historical facts. Notably, Boulez deplored Webern's excessively 'compartmentalized forms' and instead sought an imagined future music which Jonathan Goldman summarizes as follows: 'Its forms would be more Debussian than Webernian, since Boulez admires the formal unanalyzability of certain pieces by Debussy' (such as *Jeux* for orchestra).[18]

Upon closer examination, we find that both tendencies coexist (in palpable tension) in Boulez's large-scale pieces, and oppositional thinking – between Schoenbergian 'organic' continuity and Stravinskian 'segmented' episodes – is too blunt an instrument to account for the third way for which Boulez seems to be searching. Lastly, the transition from the micro-level of the series to the macro-level of musical form became a pressing compositional issue very early on in his career. Towards the mid-1950s, Boulez already appears to reject direct deductions from series to form. Still, things are not always as clear-cut as one might hope. Instead of continuing to speculate in the abstract, then, let us look a bit more closely at 'Improvisation III'. Interestingly, in the 1959 version there is already considerable suppleness to the musical phrasing and form, not least in the long sections that have been labelled *Alpha, Beta* and *Gamma* in the composer's sketches (I will retain those names here). We see that these long sections, with their more flexible phrasing and general sinuosity, are *not* changed much from the 1959 version, which already had this quality of overall musical flow.

In the respective long sections, we hear a flexible play with elastic musical phrases and a flowing continuity to the musical development. When we analyze them in turn, we find that, for all of their suppleness, they were generated using a rather crude and mechanical process that seems to contradict the pseudo-'romantic' allure of the result. In what follows, I shall briefly recapitulate the main steps in the generative process of these weighty musical sections, or what I earlier referred to as a 'transformation' from (tiny) serial structures to (large-scale) musical form.

---

[18] Jonathan Goldman, *The Musical Language of Pierre Boulez: Writings and Compositions* (Cambridge University Press, 2011), p. 48.

Example 12.2 'Basic figures'.

♪ ♩ ♩. ♩

Example 12.3 'Permutations and multiplications'.

1 3 2 4	x4	=	4 12 8 16
3 2 1 4	x2	=	6 4 2 8
1 4 3 2	x3	=	3 12 9 6
1 2 3 4	x1	=	1 2 3 4

Generative transformations: from serial structures to musical form

I will present the generative process behind Alpha, Beta and Gamma in nine steps, referring to Boulez's very brief description in *Boulez on Music Today* (pp. 135ff), supplemented by my studies of his sketches at the Paul Sacher Foundation.

Step 1. The generation starts with the extremely basic figures of 1, 2, 3 and 4 (Example 12.2), represented in durations.

Steps 2–3. The order of these four numbers is freely permutated and placed into a table (Example 12.3, left column). Notably, these free permutations have decisive musical consequences later in the process. Multiplications over the permutation '4–2–3–1' produce an expanded table (Example 12.3, middle column).

The important point, methodologically speaking, is that each group of numbers now comes to represent a durational series of musical notes (Example 12.3, right column). This is the Columbi egg – the brilliant yet simple idea – underpinning Boulez's method since 1951 at least: in his serialist structures, he supplants the pitches, durations, dynamics and so on with abstract numbers, and instead of working with his musical material directly, like Schoenberg and Webern did, he manipulates the numbers to produce this material.[19] One might say that the overall modernist tendency towards abstraction reaches its peak at this point.

Steps 4–5. Superposition and displacement. Next, the four durational series are superimposed in a durational grid, producing a kind of four-part

---

[19] Robert Piencikowski seems to have been the first researcher to pinpoint this carrying principle in Boulez's technique. See, for example, 'Nature morte avec guitare' in Josef Häusler (ed.), *Festschrift Pierre Boulez* (Mainz: Schott, 1985), pp. 66–81.

Playing with transformations

Example 12.4 'Superposition and displacement'.

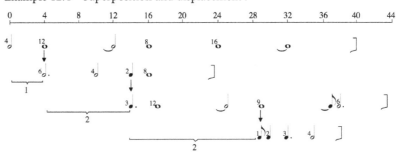

Example 12.5 'Reduction of polyphony'.

polyphony. The entrance of each new part in Alpha is then postponed (as Boulez describes it) by 'observing the distances 1-2-2 as their linking principle'.[20] (In Beta and Gamma, in turn, the linking formulae are 2-2-1 and 2-1-2, according to the sketches.) In Alpha, this means that the second group (6, 4, 2, 8) will enter after one duration is presented by the first group (4, 12, 8, 16); the third group (3, 12, 9, 6) will enter after two durations of the second group; and the fourth group (1, 2, 3, 4) will enter after two durations of the third group. The result is the table of superimpositions given in Example 12.4.

Steps 6-7. Reduction of polyphony. Instead of exposing this polyphony directly, the four voices are then reduced to a single part ('reduction' being another typical trait of modernist formalism, on a par with 'abstraction'). Only the last part to enter is exposed at any given time, and the deleted parts are indicated by grace notes (Example 12.5).

As a result, only one part is presented at any one time. The reduction produces the following Alpha series, according to Boulez's sketches (Example 12.6).

In the 1959 score, this little series is extended over more than four minutes of musical time, filling the entire Alpha section. In fact, the

---
[20] *Boulez on Music Today*, p. 135.

Example 12.6 'Alpha series'.

Example 12.7 'Beta series'.

Example 12.8 'Gamma series'.

fourteen 'main notes' of this series are directly represented by the fourteen static chords that one can readily hear in the winds and strings. The 'grace notes' of the series are turned into brief staccato chords, vividly marking the shifts in the aforementioned progression of the static chords. Thus this durational row, generated by the crude arithmetic manipulations that I have presented, is almost directly responsible for the temporal process of the grand Alpha section at the macro-level of musical form. The first stages of this procedure are presented in *Boulez on Music Today*, but true to form, Boulez does not show it all. The sketches reveal a considerable amount of free choice throughout this procedure, not least in subsequent stages of composition that are not mentioned in the book.

Steps 8–9. After several additional superimpositions, reductions and other amendments, the durational series for the Beta and Gamma sections come out as shown in Example 12.7 (Beta) and 12/8 (Gamma). In Examples 12.6–8, as well, I have entered the rehearsal numbers from the musical score of 1983 (see numbers framed in squares).

The entanglement of Boulez's generative techniques (of which I have only shown the beginnings here) leads to the following question: is the large-scale form actually determined directly by these mechanical procedures? Certainly the durational grid is mechanically produced, generating 'automatic' results whose proportions and order of elements must have been unforeseeable at the start. However, the sketches reveal how Boulez subsequently changes the durations at free will. Some of them are multiplied by four, some by eight and others again by sixteen, something that changes the internal proportions. On a principal level, the question of musical form cannot in any case be reduced to a spatial representation of sections in a durational grid. The formal process is a result of the actual interplay among the textural elements over musical time. Likewise, we must distinguish between the generation (*production*) of the elements and their placing *(mise-en-place)* throughout the piece.[21] Astonishingly, here we see that not only the durational grid but also the placing and superimposition of the four distinct groups are strictly regulated by the generative mechanics (the four groups being comprised of 'harps', 'voice', 'mandolin/guitar' and 'xylophones').[22] Nevertheless, free choice is in play on every level. First, the generation of the piece's 'timeline' itself inevitably depends on an abundance of minor choices that are freely made during the process. Second, the ensuing musical result depends not least on the musical gestures, phrasings, textures and articulations that are painted onto the mechanically framed canvases, as it were, thereby transforming the formal process into an expressive musical result.

We are therefore forced to rethink the relation between the micro-level of the series and the macro-level of musical form, as well as the 'transformation' from one to the other. Charles Rosen has briefly discussed this relation with regard to the piece *Structures Ia* (1951): 'The musical events created by the interaction of the series do not in fact constitute a musical form, if by "form" we mean strictly a temporal order of events in which the order itself has an expressive significance.'[23] This is clearly the case with 'Improvisation III' as well, despite the drastic developments in Boulez's rethinking of musical form from 1951 to 1959.

If Boulez makes many free choices during his generative processes, he makes even more in the final forming of his stylistic surfaces during the later phases of composition. Regarding the early phase of arithmetical generation, it is crucial to realize that the results of the procedures are

---

[21] Boulez stresses this distinction in *Boulez on Music Today*. See also Pascal Decroupet, 'Comment Boulez pense sa musique au début des années soixante' in Pierre Albèra (ed.), *Pli selon pli de Pierre Boulez: Entretiens et etudes* (Genève: Éditions Contrechamps, 2003), pp. 49–58.

[22] The musical textures for each group are generated separately (cf. 'production'), whereas their 'placing' (cf. 'mise-en-place') is regulated by the mechanical grid and is furthermore transformed in the sketches labelled 'Sectionnements polyvalents'. The generative sketches of material for the four groups ('harps, voice, mand/guit/cowbells, xyl') are collected in separate folders that Boulez labels 'Bulles de temps', 'Echiquiers', 'Paranthèses' [sic] and 'Hétérophonies', respectively. This goes for the aforementioned groups in Alpha, Beta, Gamma and the 'Episodes I–III', whereas the rest of the parts (mainly soprano, winds and strings) are generated independently. Furthermore, the sketches to 'Interlude 1 and 2' are found in the folder named 'Enchaînements multiples'. See *Sammlung Pierre Boulez*, film 137 (n.d.), pp. 325–477, mainly.

[23] Charles Rosen, 'The Piano Music' in William Glock (ed.), *Pierre Boulez: A Symposium* (London: Eulenburg, 1986), pp. 85–97, p. 94.

largely unpredictable at the start, and in Boulez's texts, the dimension of 'the unpredictable' (*l'imprévisible*) is underlined from early on. These texts have been widely read and referenced but still manage to leave few apparent traces in the analytic interpretations of his music. Strictly morphological analyses have prevailed instead, setting serialist music apart – as it were – from the musicological practices of music analysis, listening and 'criticism' (in Joseph Kerman's sense of the word) that have developed in most other fields of music study over the last three or four decades. However, there is no obvious reason to treat post-war modernist pieces completely differently from all other kinds of music. It goes without saying that modernist pieces are also written mainly for performance and listening. The question of musical relevance (or, as Schoenberg once put it, of 'what it is') needs to be raised for them as well vis-à-vis the painstaking analyses of how their structures 'were made' (as Schoenberg said). Moreover, without falling into the trap of 'intentional fallacy', it is of interest to see what Boulez says about analysis himself. While he always requires analyses to be technically penetrating and sound, he also preserves an untainted space for non-rationalist, non-controlled dimensions that he variously labels, for example, the 'non-formulated' (*l'informulé*, with reference to Adorno) or the non-analyzable (*l'inanalysable*).[24] The motivations for such a choice of words bring me to my next 'transformation': the aesthetic transformation of Mallarmé's poetics into a veritable world of new procedures for musical composition.

Transformations of Mallarmé's poetics into music

Along with Boulez's concepts of the unforeseeable (*l'imprévisible*) and the 'non-analyzable' (*l'inanalysable*), there is the Mallarméan concept of *l'anonymat* – the anonymity of the author's voice, which allows the voice of the compositional subject to step back and 'give away the initiative to the words'.[25] In the case of Boulez, this would probably mean giving away the initiative to the procedures of serialist composition, and he says as much during his work on *Pli selon pli* (1957–62). In 1960, for example, he writes thus:

> The great works of which I have been speaking – those of Mallarmé and Joyce – are the data for a new age in which texts are becoming, as it were, 'anonymous', 'speaking for themselves without any author's voice'. If I had to

---

[24] Pierre Boulez, 'L'informulé', *Révue d'ésthetique: Adorno*, 8 (1985), 25–30.
[25] Stéphane Mallarmé, 'L'Œuvre pure implique la disparition élocutoire du poète, qui cède l'initiative aux mots' in *Œuvres Complètes* (Paris: Pléiade, 1989), p. 366.

name the motive underlying the work that I have been trying to describe, it would be the search for an 'anonymity' of this kind.[26]

Boulez apparently encountered these ideas by reading Jacques Schérer's publication of Mallarmé's 'Book', *Le 'Livre' de Mallarmé*, in 1957. He seems to reference Schérer's preface more closely than the actual text by Mallarmé (which is little more than an amalgam of scattered notes and sketches). The ideas presented by Schérer struck Boulez 'as a revelation', even though he had been a passionate reader of Mallarmé's poems since the late 1940s.[27] The ideas he found in *Le 'Livre'* inspired his ideas about open form (first realized in his *Third Sonata* and rephrased in his essay 'Alea' in 1957). He also formulated notions about 'the unforeseeable' and the renunciation of total serialist 'control' from very early on. In his article 'Possibly... ' [*Éventuellement...*] from 1952, Boulez writes, for example, 'From the prescriptions we have been examining in detail arises the unforeseen.'[28] In 1957, he writes in 'Alea', 'In my experience it is impossible to foresee all the meanders and virtualities in the material with which one starts.'[29] Much later, Boulez admitted that his search for an 'anonymity' for the composer's voice mainly applied to the structural results of serial generation, whereas the final articulation of that material was always clearly marked by his own, highly profiled musical choices.[30] In my view, this fact should encourage analysts to go not around but into, through and beyond the technicalities of serialist procedures in their efforts to understand this music.

Mallarmé famously considered the poem to be not a fixed result but a strategy for reading.[31] In this sense, reading a poem almost amounts to rewriting it, presenting a striking parallel to the act of interpreting a score by playing it. Applied to serialist composition, this idea would involve a shift in perspective from regarding the work as a fixed result to regarding it as a performative procedure – for playing, for analytical interpretation, for further compositional writing. This idea of an always-unfinished 'unfolding' lies, as far as I can see, at the heart of Boulez's construal of musical composition, revision, conducting and playing, and it directly informs the conception of *Pli selon pli – portrait de Mallarmé*. The notion of 'fold' or

---

[26] 'Sonate, "que me veux-tu"' [1960], English edition; *Orientations* (London: Faber and Faber, 1986), p. 154 (*Points de repère* (Paris: Éditions Christian Bourgois, 1985), p. 175).

[27] Pierre Boulez and Célestin Deliège, *Par volonté et par hasard* (Paris: Seuil, 1975), p. 64; Erling E. Guldbrandsen, 'Pierre Boulez in Interview, 1996 (III) Mallarmé, Musical Form and Articulation', *Tempo*, 65/257 (2011), pp. 11–21), p. 13.

[28] Boulez, *Stocktakings*, p. 133 (*Relevés*, p. 174).   [29] Boulez, *Stocktakings*, p. 29 (*Relevés*, p. 45).

[30] Guldbrandsen, 'Pierre Boulez in Interview, 1996 (III)', pp. 11–12 and 17–18. See also Guldbrandsen, 'Casting New Light on Boulezian Serialism'.

[31] Mallarmé, *Œuvres Complètes*; Jacques Scherer, *Le 'Livre' de Mallarmé* (Paris: Gallimard, 1957).

pli, taken as an incessant unfolding or 'becoming', is not coincidental here. The Mallarméan impulse may also represent additional motivation for Boulez's use of Joyce's concept of a 'work in progress' and points towards the French textual theory – *théorie du texte* – that would later be developed by Gilles Deleuze, Jacques Derrida and Roland Barthes in the disciplines of philosophy and literary criticism. It is interesting to note that Boulez anticipated Derrida's reading of Mallarmé in *La dissémination* (1972), for example, by at least fifteen years. While it could be argued that Boulez, during the early 1950s, installed himself within the French structuralist movement that was so characterized by classic 'oppositional' thinking, it would be a mistake to overlook his gradual undermining of dichotomies in general and his movement in the direction of post-structuralist thinking.[32] The influence of Mallarmé's poetics means that we ought to rethink the aesthetic base of Boulez's serialism from its very beginnings. His serialism is basically a set of procedures for generating structural 'raw material' from which he can later choose freely. Then follows his artistic formation, articulation and rephrasing of the musical surface. Whereas the result of the generative processes may be unpredictable at the outset, Boulez intervenes and makes free aesthetic choices during the compositional process.

If the Mallarméan impulse is manifest primarily in a musical performativity of free choices, it also prompts the introduction of non-European stylistic elements into Boulez's scores. His choices of instruments and twisting of idiomatic modes of playing are topics that remain to be systematically studied.[33] Luisa Bassetto suggests that the treatment of the voice in 'Improvisation III' recalls the mode of sung declamation characteristic of Japanese *nō* theatre; likewise, the striking glissando entrances of the flutes invoke the traditional flute playing of eighth-century Japanese court music, as it is described to us. The sonorities of his wooden percussion can be associated with Mexican xylophone playing, and his treatment of the harps – with their microtone tuning, 'guitarist' style of playing and absence of traditional arpeggios – evokes playing techniques from Peru and Bolivia. Following Raphaël Brunner, Bassetto claims that this is far from a simple indulgence in musical exoticism or 'orientalism' on Boulez's part. Though the elements are highly stylized, they are also confronted with Western

---

[32] While Goldman (2011) primarily sees Boulez as structuralist and gives documentation for such a reading (see pp. 18–30), Edward Campbell discusses Boulez's relation to post-structural thinkers such as Deleuze and Foucault: Campbell, *Boulez, Music and Philosophy* (Cambridge University Press, 2010).

[33] Brunner (1996) and Bassetto (2003) discuss these aspects of Boulez's music in some detail. Campbell (2010), pp. 23–25, presents Boulez's early interest in music ethnology as influenced not least by André Schaeffner.

generative techniques at the highest level of abstraction – contradictions that are taken directly into the music itself. Also, there are instances of outgoing melodic gestures and 'romantic' phrasing in the cello and trombone, particularly in the Beta and Gamma sections (see for instance the cello solo after rehearsal number [35] in the 1983 version of the score). To sum up, examples concerning Boulez's moulding of sounding surfaces and modes of playing fit quite well into the dynamics of what I have here labelled the 'performative transformations' of his compositional writing. Concerning the striking use of distinctive instrumental sounds and 'formants' directly related to the ingenious pattern of phonemes in Mallarmé's sonnet text, I refer to the closer study presented in my book on *Pli selon pli*.[34] This brings me to the fourth kind of 'transformations' in this chapter.

Transformations of Mallarmé's poem into music

Many of Boulez's works have remained incomplete, partly because the material has continued to grow due to generative techniques that seem to multiply their own elements, and partly because he may have always intended to revise the musical form and rephrase the surface after 'testing' his works in performance. Processes of ongoing revision and expansion can be associated with works stretching from *Douze notations* (1945) to *Dérive II* (2006).[35]

Accordingly, 'Improvisation III' started out in 1959 with an approximate length of less than sixteen minutes (the duration is 15:51 in Boulez's 1969 recording), only to be expanded to well over eighteen minutes (18:29) in his 1981 recording and to just over twenty-one minutes (21:09) in 2001. Notably, these expansions are mainly confined to the material in the opening section of the piece. Had they also been applied to the main sections of the movement (such as Alpha, Beta and Gamma), the revised work might very well have been much longer. As for serial generation, the sketches to 'Improvisation III' contain material for several further sections (Delta, Epsilon, Zeta, Eta and so on), suggesting that the original plan may have been to transform not just verses 1–3 (Alpha, Beta, Gamma) but all

---

[34] Guldbrandsen, *Tradisjon og tradisjonsbrudd* (1995/7), pp. 351–7.
[35] This list only hints at the many revisions that have been going on for decades: *Douze notations pour piano* (1945) – *Notations I–IV* (1977–80) – *V* (1997); *Le visage nuptial* (1946; 1953; 1986–9); *Livre pour quatuor* (1954–65–); *Le troisième sonate* (1955–7; 1963–); *Figures-Doubles-Prismes* (1957–8; 1963; 1965–8; 1988); *Éclat* (1965) – *Éclat/Multiples* (1966–70–); *Livre pour cordes* (1966–8; 1988); *cummings ist der Dichter* (1970; 1986);... *explosante-fixe*... (1972–4) – *Mémoriale* (1985) – *Anthèmes* (1991–2) – *Anthèmes 2* (1997); *Répons* (1980–4–) – *Dérive* (1984) – *Dérive II* (1988, 2002, 2006); *Dialogue de l'ombre double* (1983–5; 1985–95); *Incises* (1994; 2001) – *Sur Incises* (1996–8).

fourteen verses of Mallarmé's sonnet into like sections. With fourteen such sections, Boulez might easily have ended with a movement of one and a half hours in duration – and this, again, to occur within the frame of the larger, five-movement work that was the entire *Pli selon pli*.

In 1959, Boulez obviously had to pause his generative processes – or excesses – after the third verse of the sonnet ('verse' is here equivalent to 'line'). Then in 1982 he added the fourth verse, 'Par une trompe sans vertu', in a section inserted towards the end of the piece. Then came the addition of all fourteen verses of sung text on top of the existing musical textures. In this way, single phonemes, words and verses and complete renderings of the sonnet proliferate simultaneously on different levels of the musical unfolding – 'pli selon pli' – and create a *mise-en-abyme* structure of unprecedented formal complexity (the spiral or the labyrinth might be suitable metaphors for the ensuing result). In this dialectical play, there seems to be no synthesis or final closure. The Mallarméan concept of mobility (*mobilité*) deconstructs the opposition between *écriture* and performance (between vision and listening, or space and time) by ascribing to the poetical text a double existence, one split between the written signs on a page (like Mallarmé's labelling of the poem as a 'constellation') and the sonic performance of those signs (like Mallarmé having his poems read, as in a musical performance).

The complexity of musical form clearly takes its rationale from Boulez's express interest in the formal structure of the sonnet itself, *in casu* the poem 'A la nue accablante tu'.[36] This late sonnet (completed in 1895) is arguably one of the most equivocal and enigmatic poetic texts that Mallarmé ever published, in terms of its semantic meaning, its pattern of phonetic play and its finely calculated and irreducible ambiguity of grammatical syntax. The reader cannot even determine with certainty the grammatical subject or object in the single long sentence that runs without stop through the sonnet.[37]

The formal, phonetic, syntactic and semantic ambiguities of this poem were to a large extent retained and even reinforced in Boulez's music by 1959, not least through all of the different – and mutually exclusive – alternatives and *ossias* in the score. This plenitude of trajectories represented an extremely rich combinatory set of possible choices. As this open form was transformed into a fixed version in 1982–83, moreover, things were not simplified, as one might have expected. On the contrary, when most of the *ossia* textures were reused and integrated in the new score, they

---

[36] Mallarmé, *Œuvres complètes*, p. 76.
[37] Robert Cohn, *Towards the Poems of Mallarmé* (Berkeley, CA: University of California Press, 1980), pp. 229–36; Jean-Pierre Richard, *L'univers imaginaire de Mallarmé* (Paris: Seuil, 1961), pp. 276ff; Michel Butor, 'Mallarmé selon Boulez', *Melos*, 28 (1961), 356–59.

Playing with transformations

produced an increased multiplicity of possible readings of the text–music relation on several new levels.

In 1959, Alpha, Beta and Gamma clearly constitute the main sections of the movement in question, and only the first three of the sonnet's fourteen verses are sung. In 1983, a new section is introduced ('Interlude 2' – see Table 12.1 above), presenting verse 4, the music of which is nothing other than the *second variant* of verse 1 from 1959, now furnished with the text of verse 4 instead of verse 1. In addition, the complete sonnet text is sung at a comparatively high speed during 'Episodes 1' and well into the first half of the Alpha section. This new text presentation arrives in two parts. First, the soprano sings verses 1–8 (the sonnet's two quatrains), accompanied by the four flutes, followed by an interlude comprised of expanded versions of the earlier episodes for two xylophones, for two harps and for mandolin, guitar and cowbells. Second, the soprano sings verses 9–14 (the sonnet's two tercets), supported by various instrumental textures. Then, from 'Interlude 1' onwards, the soprano starts from verse 1 again and much more slowly works her way to verse 4.

With its initial vocalize on the vowel 'A', the entire 1959 piece can – on one level – be heard as a single, vastly prolonged elaboration of the sonnet's very first word (and the first letter of the alphabet), or, indeed, of the dark phoneme 'a', which is the central vowel in the poem. On another level, the 1959 version falls largely into three parts, clearly gravitating around the Alpha, Beta and Gamma sections, each of which corresponds structurally to one sonnet verse (in fact, Alpha is without text, and verse 1 is dislocated to 'Interlude 1'). The piece thereby corresponds to the sonnet's first three verses, and a tripartite form ensues.

In contrast to all of this, the 1983 version falls more clearly into two parts, like the sonnet's form, as divided between quatrains and tercets. With the new installation of verse 4 (in 'Interlude 2'), the musical form turns in the direction of representing the first four verses of the sonnet, or, indeed, the four strophes of the complete sonnet form as such – thereby miming the direct rendering of sonnet form in the two preceding movements: 'Improvisation I & II'. Furthermore, the insertion of all fourteen verses at the start is – astonishingly – placed across the otherwise deep-structural divide between 'Episodes 1' and the Alpha section. This placement of the text completely disregards the constitutive logic of the musical structures that underlie these fourteen verses, since the four episodes of the former 'Episodes 1' were constructed with methods that differ completely from those that generated the Alpha textures.[38] Hence Boulez obviously

---

[38] See sketches, 'Sectionnements polyvalents', 'Bulles de temps', 'Echiquiers', 'Paranthèses [sic]' and so on.

does not care much about the earlier, generative 'construction', or the problem of 'structural unity', when he sets out to recompose his own piece. He deliberately ignores the generative deep structure in the rephrasing of the musical surface. As a consequence, by adding the complete fourteen verses in this manner, another level of complexity is reached in the interplay between poetic and musical text.

How do all of these complexities come across to the listener? Arguably, the text and music are perceived less as a set of structural labyrinths than as a directly accessible musical-rhetorical flow.[39] In his conversations with Deliège, Boulez proposes two opposite readings of the text–music relation in *Pli selon pli*: the music may represent a 'complete osmosis' or (at the same time) a 'complete transformation' of the poetic text.[40] This is a fairly good account of what happens in 'Improvisation III'. On the one hand, in both versions of the piece, the formal, syntactical and phonetic patterns of the poem are – so to speak – retained and analyzed by the music in a kind of 'complete osmosis' of the text. On the other hand, precisely by being extremely 'true' to its formal structure, the poem is also transformed into something completely different. This forms a paradox – at one and the same time, there is a 'complete osmosis' and a 'complete transformation' of the text.

At this point, a thematic reading of the semantics of Mallarmé's sonnet and Boulez's interpretation of it might contribute to our discussion of the text–music relation. The connections go from the sonic renderings of consonants and vowels – not least of the more significant phonemes (*a, b, u, ab, ba, tu,* etc.) and their ingenious distribution throughout the poem – to the readings of the poem's ambiguities in syntax and poetic meaning and their transformation into Boulez's highly differentiated orchestration of the formal elements of the music. On a semantic level, as is often the case in Mallarmé, nothing actually happens within the scenery that the poem suggests. His text is centred around a 'nothingness' or an absence. In a kind of failed Odyssey of modern poetry or art, the 'abolished' shipwreck, with its muted horn and its broken, 'phallic' mast, has gone under, leaving behind little more than some whitish foam among the floating wreckage in the dark waves, conjuring the image of a muted siren, once perhaps deadly but now probably drowned or in any case no longer singing. This absence at the poem's centre evokes the similar function of the poem as 'centre and absence' in the music, particularly

---

[39] The formal process of the piece is described through auditive categories of musical listening (articulation, phrasing, timbre, allure, density, gesture, texture and so forth) in Guldbrandsen, *Tradisjon og tradisjonsbrudd* (1995/7), chapter 4, pp. 381–506.

[40] *Par volonté*, pp. 121–8.

in the 1959 version.[41] The truly vertiginous play between textual and musical meanings I have elaborated on elsewhere, particularly in two of the chapters in my 1995/7 book on *Pli selon pli*.[42]

Historiographical transformations of current images of post-war modernism

Finally, the analytical findings and aesthetic readings that I have very briefly presented here also call for a historiographical revision of the current image of what Boulezian serialism of the 1950s (and later) was and is all about, including the dimensions of compositional unpredictability and free choice. As far as I can see, the full methodological consequences of these findings, regarding the interpretation of Boulez's poetics, his compositional proceedings and the historiographical understanding of his role in high modernism in post-World War II Europe, still remain to be developed. Boulez's frequently repeated suggestion to break with tradition by 'burning down the library every day', thereby forgetting the past, must of course be read metaphorically (in one case, he refers to René Char's poem 'La bibliothèque est en feu'),[43] whereas the idea of modernist rupture, conversely, is historiographically difficult to maintain.

The concept of the musical work, as it has been active in Western art music since at least 1800, carries the constitutive implication that a work has to be played in always new versions. Boulez undoubtedly inscribes himself into this tradition, both as a composer and as a conductor.[44] Also in this regard, we cannot sustain the notion of a clear-cut modernist 'rupture' with tradition. Boulez's practice of making free choices in the course of his musical composition only ties him more firmly to that same tradition, pointing back to the early German Romantic philosophers and to Immanuel Kant's concept of the aesthetic judgement – as presented in his *Critique of Aesthetic Judgment*, all the way back in 1790. Two centuries later, in 1986, in Boulez's significant article 'The System and

---

[41] See Boulez's references to Henri Michaux at the time he completes the first version of *Pli selon pli*, in 'Poésie – centre et absence – musique (Poésie pour pouvoir)' (written in 1958). *Points de repère*, pp. 183–200.

[42] See Guldbrandsen, *Tradisjon og tradisjonsbrudd* (1995/7), chapter 3, pp. 251–380, and chapter 5, pp. 507–88.

[43] See Boulez's statement: 'Je pense qu'on doit mettre le feu à sa bibliothèque tous les jours, pour qu'ensuite la bibliothèque renaisse comme un phénix de ses cendres, mais sous une forme différente. Pour moi, ce qui est intéressante, c'est justement de ne pas être étouffé par la bibliothèque.' Goldman, Jonathan, Jean-Jacques Nattiez and François Nicolas, *La Pensée de Pierre Boulez à Travers ses Écrits* (Paris: Delatour, 2010), p. 250.

[44] See Guldbrandsen, 'Modernist Composer and Mahler Conductor'.

the Idea' (*Le système et l'idée*), he writes that the system of generative procedures is nothing more than a crutch (*une béquille*), a help for the imagination in order to get started.[45] By this accounting, he requires serialist writing only to furnish him with the raw material of structural objects, and then in the next round he chooses from these objects. And what does he choose? 'I choose', says Boulez in 1986, 'what I judge to be good, beautiful, necessary'.[46] To some music historians, this kind of statement may still come as a surprise. In a conversation in Paris in 1996, Boulez confirmed this point at several instances, however; here is one of them:[47]

> E. Guldbrandsen: Mr. Boulez, this is not the picture of serialism that has survived in normal, ordinary textbooks, and not even in the general output of musicological analyses of your work ... Everybody seems to talk about some kind of logical positivism of composition.
>
> P. Boulez: Yes! But I mean, that is exactly the point where they are totally wrong. Totally wrong!

According to the findings above, we must abandon the 'unity and control model' of serialist composition and allow – or persuade – formalist music analysis to be integrated into a much wider perspective on interpretation, or, indeed, on criticism. In Boulez's case, the modernist project is obviously carried by a fundamental poetical vision – one that includes notions of free aesthetic choice and of the reinterpretation of the musical past. There is a need to look and see how he actually reads poetry, how he regards painting and architecture, how he listens to non-European musics and how he conducts musical works from the great Western tradition of the last 150 years, in order to understand his music more richly. And in order to grasp what happened to Central European art music in the precarious decades after World War II, we need to open up the full context of the performative, aesthetic and cultural dimensions that made this music necessary – or at least, possible – thereby paving the way for new musical experience.

---

[45] 'Cela revient à considerer le système comme une aide, une béquille, un exitant pour l'imagination', *Jalons*, p. 378. Reprinted in *Leçons de musique*, p. 407.

[46] *Jalons*, p. 378: 'Je choisis, donc je suis; je n'ai inventé le système que pour me fournir un certain type de matérieau, en moi d'éliminer ou de gauchir ensuite, en function de ce que je trouve bon, beau, nécessaire'.

[47] Guldbrandsen, Erling E., 'Pierre Boulez in Interview, 1996 (II) Serialism Revisited', *Tempo*, 65/256 (2011), 18–24, p. 23.

13 Performance as critique

Arnulf Christian Mattes

idiom | ˈidēəm |noun:
   ORIGIN late 16th cent.: from French *idiome*, or via late Latin from Greek *idiōma 'private property, peculiar phraseology'*, from *idiousthai 'make one's own'*, from *idios 'own, private'*.

Introduction

When speaking of performance practice in the context of musical modernism in the twentieth century, the official story usually begins with the post-war era and the International Summer Courses for New Music at Darmstadt. Driven by an ideology of progress and anti-romantic objectivism, the Darmstadt movement's systematization of expressive features as serial parameters diminished the role of the performer as an interpreter. The performer's interpretive freedom was thus confined to executing meticulously detailed prescriptive scores. The early post-war reception of Anton Webern as a proto-serialist lay the foundation for an understanding of musical modernism during the subsequent decades. Boulez's famous proclamation 'Schoenberg est mort', in 1951, was as influential as his recordings of the music of the Schoenberg school, which, more than all of the compositional manifestos, emphasize the distance between pre- and post-war performance practice and its cultural understanding.[1]

---

[1] Boulez's recording of Schoenberg's *Die Jakobsleiter* illustrates the aesthetic and historical distance between post-war reception and performance practice of pre-war modernism: see Jennifer Shaw, 'New Performance Sources and Old Modernist Productions: *Die Jakobsleiter* in the Age of Mechanical Reproduction', *The Journal of Musicology*, 19/3 (2002), 434–60. A further debate arose following the publication of Peter Stadlen's 'performance scores' of Webern's *Variations for Piano*, Op. 27, in 1979, inciting a reassessment of Webern's expressive qualities in the light of nineteenth-century, 'romantic' performance traditions. The literature on changing performance styles during the twentieth century has since increased immensely, from early examinations such as Robert Wason's 'Webern's "Variations for Piano", Op. 27: Musical Structure and the Performance Score', *Integral*, 1 (1987), 57–103 to more recent contributions, see Daniel Leech-Wilkinson, 'Musicology and Performance' in Zdravko Blazekovic (ed.), *Music's Intellectual History: Founders, Followers and Fads* (New York: RILM, 2009), pp. 791–804.

Adorno played an active role in the Darmstadt movement, as an invited lecturer of several courses during the summer courses in the 1950s and 1960s and, of course, as author of influential, albeit controversial, books such as *Philosophy of New Music*, published in 1949. Adorno's critical theory has left an indelible mark on both the academic debate and public opinion of modernist music up to the present day. Much less known is that his engagement with the music was deeply rooted in his encounter with the musical culture of Vienna in the 1920s, to which he was introduced by his composition teacher Alban Berg and the violinist Rudolf Kolisch. Adorno's intimate reflections on the musical practice and its practitioners he met in Vienna remained unknown until the 1980s, following the posthumously published collection of notes and lecture manuscripts on the topic. In many ways, Adorno's fragmentary 'Theory of musical reproduction' is a document of pre-war musical practice and its ideological and philosophical premises.[2] The main informant and closest collaborator during the years Adorno collected his thoughts on musical performance and interpretation, from the 1920s to the late 1940s, was Rudolf Kolisch. Adorno's reflections on musical performance are orientated around adequate modes of score reading, described as a quest for the origin of musical signs, and the nature of musical gesture. His questions imply an urgent need for interpretation in an age in which subjectivity and individual freedom of expression had increasingly become suppressed by a modern, rationalized society. Adorno's questions to the performer suggest this modernist fear; his critique of performance practice in 'Theory of musical reproduction' corresponds with his theses on the dialectic of Enlightenment which informed his critique of Schoenberg's twelve-tone method in *Philosophy of New Music*.

This chapter is intended as a contribution to the more recent discussions of musical modernism that include the discourse on pre-war performance, a field that has flourished as a result of the availability of musical performances contained in reissued historical recordings. This focus offers a corrective to the narratives of musical modernism that promote composer-oriented perspectives, and as a result the distinctions between the different agents – composer, performer and critic – become more transparent. Moreover, the examination of pre-war performers such as Kolisch highlights the cultural difference between post-war and pre-war generations of performers, as their views on the musical expression of 'being progressive' were forged by quite different critical responses to diverging cultural challenges.

---

[2] Theodor W. Adorno, *Towards a Theory of Musical Reproduction*, ed. Henri Lonetz, trans. Weiland Honban (Cambridge: Polity Press, 2006).

Adorno raises these crucial questions: What is the task of the performer? Is an 'expressive' performance always the same as an adequate interpretation of the score? Or would it be better to *read* music rather than *make* music? The topos of 'falling silent' linked to this final question in particular is prominent in Adorno's well-known essays on musical listening as well as in his lesser-known notes on musical interpretation. Adorno's critique of musical performance became increasingly pertinent with the rise of the technically accomplished performance star in America during the 1930s and 1940s. Along with the 'fetishization of surface' came a 'regression in listening' and the loss of 'the capacity for conscious cognition of music'.[3] If any performer can be said to have put Adorno's polemical statements into practice, it has to be the Viennese violinist Rudolf Kolisch. A considerable number of recordings from live concerts and broadcasts have once again become accessible in recent years, making it possible to reassess the performance theory of the Schoenberg school, which Adorno draws on in new ways in his own theory of musical performance and interpretation.[4] In this chapter, the issues addressed by Adorno are discussed, taking selected recordings of Kolisch as a point of departure. As leader of the internationally renowned Kolisch Quartet in the late 1920s and during the 1930s, he applied the Schoenberg school's aesthetics in his performance practice, which became known for idiomatic 'otherness', interpretive rigour and opposition to 'beautiful tone'.[5]

Kolisch shared the fate of his mentor Arnold Schoenberg, as well as Adorno and other Viennese peers who were forced to emigrate to America in the 1930s. Eventually settling in Madison, Wisconsin, Kolisch became an 'outsider' in American musical life, a position which brought him even

---

[3] Max Paddison, 'Performance and the Silent Work', *Filigrane: Musique, esthétique, sciences, société*, http://revues.mshparisnord.org/filigrane/index.php?id=147 (accessed 27 May 2011).

[4] In 1992, archiphon released the remastered 1936/7 private recordings of Schoenberg's four String Quartets with the Kolisch Quartet (ARC 103/4), followed by recordings of the Kolisch Quartet playing Schubert (ARC 107), and Mozart (ARC 108). In 2003, archiphon continued its series with *Kolisch in America*, presenting archive recordings made at the University of Wisconsin, including Kolisch's recordings of the violin sonatas Beethoven and Schubert (ARC 130/1 and 132). In 2003, Music & Arts issued the CD-box set *In Honor of Rudolf Kolisch (1896–1978)*, including the complete 1950 Dial recordings of works of Schoenberg, Berg and Webern, and previously unreleased broadcast performances, 1940–67. In 2012 audite released the CD-box set *The RIAS Second Viennese School Project* (audite 21.412), which presents recordings of Schoenberg, Berg and Webern made between 1949 and 1965 by musicians invited by Hans Heinz Stuckenschmidt, the editor of new music at the RIAS in occupied West Berlin, and Josef Rufer, the Schoenberg student, theorist and conductor.

[5] The most comprehensive discussion of the Schoenberg school performance theory is found in Markus Grassl and Reinhard Kapp (eds.), *Die Lehre von der musikalischen Aufführung in der Wiener Schule: Verhandlungen des Internationalen Colloquiums Wien 1995* (Vienna, Cologne and Weimar: Boehlau Verlag).

closer to Adorno, with whom he had become acquainted during his stays in Vienna as a student of Alban Berg and Eduard Steuermann from 1925 to 1926.[6] Adorno and Kolisch developed a close friendship, which lasted until Adorno's death in 1969. The philosopher and the performer engaged in a rich correspondence, in which they discuss upcoming projects, manuscripts for new articles and books or reviews of recent performances and recordings. Following World War II, Adorno invited Kolisch and other members of Schoenberg's circle to give lectures and courses for the group of young composers and performers gathered at Darmstadt.[7] Adorno used this occasion to rearticulate his enormous collection of notes, short essays and aphorisms in a more systematic manner as 'a theory of musical reproduction/theory of true interpretation'.[8] This treatise can be read as Adorno's reflections on the relationship between performance and interpretation, and its critical, historical status. Adorno addresses the question of interpretation from different angles, including modes of writing, reading and performing music. Kolisch's interpretations of the works belonging to the Viennese tradition made a huge impression on Adorno. To Adorno, Kolisch performed the critical potential of the ideas and values inherent in works by composers ranging from Beethoven to Schubert and Schoenberg. Accordingly, Adorno referred to Kolisch's interpretations in his theory of performance, which at the same time was a critique of contemporary performance culture.

One priority in this chapter is to reach a deeper understanding of the reciprocal relationship between Adorno's theory of musical interpretation and Kolisch's performance practice. In this way, Adorno's assessments of

---

[6] Stefan Müller-Doohm, *Adorno: A Biography* (Cambridge: Polity Press, 2009), pp. 86ff.

[7] A full record of Kolisch's correspondence is kept with the Kolisch papers at Harvard, to which the author was granted generous access by the staff during a research stay at Houghton Library in autumn, 2010.

[8] Drawing on his knowledge of the oral *Aufführungslehre* during his stay in Vienna in the 1920s, Adorno further developed the Schoenberg school's ideas on performance in collaboration with his friend Kolisch during the 1930s and 1940s. However, Adorno and Kolisch's book on performance and interpretation was never completed. Adorno's notes were edited posthumously by his wife Gretel Adorno and published in 2001: Theodor W. Adorno, *Zu einer Theorie der musikalischen Reproduktion* (Frankfurt am Main: Suhrkamp, 2001). Hermann Danuser's article, published in 2003, initiated the scholarly reception of Adorno's theory on musical interpretation. See Hermann Danuser, 'Zur Haut zurückkehren: zu Theodor W. Adornos Theorie der musikalischen Reproduktion', *Musik & Ästhetik*, 7/25 (2003), 5–22. Kolisch's notes on a theory of performance remain unpublished and are kept at Harvard Houghton library as part of the Kolisch papers. A series of interviews with Kolisch on topics based on the lectures and sketches left from his courses at Darmstadt from 1953 to 1956 was put on tape in 1978, and published as Rudolf Kolisch, *Rudolf Kolisch: Zur Theorie der Aufführung* (Musik-Konzepte 29/30), ed. Heinz-Klaus Metzger and Rainer Riehn (Munich: edition text+kritik, 1983).

Kolisch's interpretations can be put to the test: what procedures does Kolisch employ in rising to the task of the performer as described in Adorno's theory? A closer look at Kolisch's recordings of Schoenberg's *Phantasy* for violin with piano accompaniment and Beethoven's Violin Concerto gives some insight into the 'anti-culinary' features of Kolisch's particular musical idiom that attracted Adorno's critical ear. Ultimately, though, this chapter aims to contribute to the reassessment of a particular performance style which fashioned itself in opposition to the 'streamlined' production of the 'beautiful tone' and the notion of the perfect performance. To Kolisch, as to Adorno, musical interpretation, including all its stages – from composing to reading, performing and eventually listening – is a deadly serious human practice, in a historical situation where only art has the power to resist the total rationalization and commodification of all areas of human expression. To me, Kolisch's recordings become particularly engaging in light of Adorno's theory of interpretation. This does not mean that we must listen to Kolisch as Adorno might have heard and understood him. This chapter will by no means suggest the possibility of an ideal interpretation existing in the past, providing a final answer to the questions posed at the outset. On the contrary, this chapter is an attempt to understand the particularity of a historical performer's idiom – which evolved from a specific historical situation – and why it might still attract the attention of the present-day listener.

Towards origin: idiom and interpretation

For Adorno, Kolisch was the epitome of an artist with transformative powers. According to Adorno, Kolisch achieved a 'totally new type of presentation (Darstellung)', a new mode of interpretation

> which does not originate from sound, which does not originate from the coherence of the surface, which does not originate in the brilliance and dexterity of the presentation, but is created instead by the cognitive comprehension of musical relationships, and most of all, the knowledge of all the structural and spiritual moments beneath the surface. One might suggest that you were the first to fully achieve the cognitive comprehension of interpretation, and as a result interpretation has become profoundly changed, transformed.[9]

---

[9] Theodor W. Adorno, 'Rede zu Rudolf Kolisch's 60: Geburtstag', *Musiktheorie: Zeitschrift für Musikwissenschaft*, 24/3 (2009), 238–40, p. 239 (my translation). Adorno delivered this speech on 20 July 1956 at the Internationalen Ferienkurse für Neue Musik in Darmstadt. It was kept on tape in the Kolisch collection at Harvard and published for the first time in printed form in *Musiktheorie* on the initiative of Anne C. Shreffler. Shreffler led a graduate seminar on 'The

Adorno's 'theory of musical reproduction/true interpretation' can be read as the philosopher's attempt to apply his dialectical critique of art – art being the residue of its mimetic origins – within a rationalized, modern world and within contemporary performance practice. A performer's interpretation renders truth only when it retrieves the transformative powers residing in the musical work, turning affirmative illusion into the expression of the repressed origin: 'The task of musical interpretation is to transform the idiomatic element into the neumic by means of the mensural. "The origin is the goal. Thesis of my book."'[10]

Adorno qualifies the dialectical movement between the three 'elements' of the musical text – the 'idiomatic', the 'neumic' and the 'mensural' – with a reference to Kraus's aphoristic notion 'The origin is the goal', from the journal *Die Fackel* of 1910. To Kraus, true creative art and language have the same origin, nature and goal: the expression of nature. Neither art nor language should be used as an 'instrument', and no 'ornament', no matter how modern or popular its effect might be, could cover the lack of a genuine, ethically driven, creative imagination. *Fackel* reader Arnold Schoenberg's famous aphorism 'Art is the outcry of those who partake of the fate of mankind' (*'Kunst ist der Notschrei jener die an sich das Schicksals der Menschheit erleben'*)[11] echoes Kraus's notion of art as rejection. Schoenberg's aphorism conveys in concentrated form the Viennese modernist's discontent with the instrumental use of art as comfort and the commitment to art as an expression of human nature. Yet, according to Adorno, only by 'immersion' within the objectified structures of the musical work can the emphatic subject transcend its cognitive limits in a kind of 're-creative', mimetic act, and thereby activate the faculties of imagination. The dialectical movement between the elements of the written musical language, the 'neumic' and the 'mensural',[12] and the 'sonic element' of musical language involving the 'idiomatic', indicates what is at stake when a performer attempts to unravel the nexus of meaning in a musical work. To Adorno, the truth of a work is never given as an absolute, but always 're-produced' in the subject's engagement with the musical structure of a particular work. The task of the performer is to trace the gestural origins of these structures. This process of immersion in musical

---

Second Viennese School's Theories of Performance' at Harvard University in the fall semester, 2005–6.

[10] Adorno, *Towards a Theory of Musical Reproduction*, p. 67.

[11] Arnold Schoenberg, 'Aphorismen', *Die Musik*, 9/21 (1909/10), 159–63, p. 159. (The first draft from 1910 is kept at the archive of the Arnold Schoenberg Center, Vienna.)

[12] Adorno traces the mimetic origins of musical notation from the 'mensural' to the 'neumic', drawing on Riemann's *Handbuch der Musikgeschichte*. See Adorno, *Towards a Theory of Musical Reproduction*, pp. 57ff.

structure requires in equal degree the cognitive understanding of the immanent logic of 'mensural signs' and the bodily engagement with the gestural and sensuous surface. A performer's interpretation always already involves internalized stylistic conventions, articulated as a socially and culturally conditioned 'dialect'. The individual mode of expression is closely related to how, where and when a performer learns technical skills and acquires her or his specific set of performance habits. What Adorno calls the 'idiomatic' element is always an inevitable precondition of performance, allowing individual response and intuitive realization of musical gestures. The idiomatic provides the performer with a kind of prefigured set of metaphors and schemes, enabling the reading and articulation of musical gestures 'spontaneously' and providing a basis for the modification of musical gestalts and figures in terms of the nuances of melodic inflexion and prosodic articulation, which are not determined on the mensural level in notation. In this way, the dialect of the performer is an inevitable precondition for idiosyncratic musical expression.

From dialectics to dialect: performing Schoenberg's *Phantasy*

During the late 1940s and throughout the 1950s, Kolisch, with support from his friend Adorno, made several attempts to re-emigrate to Germany. Yet his applications for vacant positions as violin professor at a number of German music academies were turned down. Settling in Darmstadt for a shorter period, he organized several concert tours for 'Amerika-Häuser'.[13] He taught at the music school and gave lectures and recitals at the Internationale Ferienkurse in Darmstadt.[14]

The *Phantasy* for violin with piano accompaniment Op. 47, composed by Schoenberg in 1949, represents, together with Schoenberg's String Trio Op. 45, a cornerstone in Rudolf Kolisch's repertoire during the post-war years. For Kolisch, the style and structure of this work was much more familiar than for most of the younger violinists who encountered Schoenberg's music for the first time following World War II. A comparison of two recordings produced in 1953 in the studios of RIAS, the West Berlin-based radio station, highlights principal differences of style and expressivity between the Viennese 'Schoenbergian' and a young

---

[13] Amerika-Häuser (America Houses) were information centres and cultural meeting places, established by the US Information Service in Western Germany and Austria after World War II.
[14] Thomas Schäfer, 'Zwischen Schönberg und Stockhausen: Rudolf Kolisch bei den Internationalen Ferienkursen' in Rudolf Stephan, Lothar Knessl, Otto Tomek, Claus Trapp and Christopher Fox (eds.), *Von Kranichstein zur Gegenwart* (Stuttgart: DACO, 1996), pp. 104–11.

Hungarian virtuoso keen to engage with challenging new music: Tibor Varga epitomized what Kolisch opposed, that is, the 'romantic' virtuoso's straightforward display of 'beautiful tone'.[15] The listener is immediately struck by the potency and guttural resonance of Varga's sound. From the very beginning, Varga's tone encourages the listener to visualize the energetic sweeps of the down-bow strokes with which he carries out the initial rhythmic motive. Varga takes full advantage of the friction of the bow hair, and the powerful resonance of the violin's G-string, in order to realize the idiomatic-expressive potential of the introductory gesture. One is reminded of a work that would otherwise probably not be associated with Schoenberg's *Phantasy*: Ravel's *Tzigane*. Varga's Hungarian background is perhaps also brought to bear on his performance style: the influence of the culture of Gypsy violin music formed part of his 'idiomatic identity'. Varga seems to revel in every tone and attributes to the melody a persistent espressivo character by virtue of extensive vibrato and portamento articulation. Varga radiates a sense of idiomatic confidence, which draws the listener's attention to the display of instrumental *virtú*. His performance of the opening gesture immediately promises the kind of satisfaction achieved by full control of the breathtaking musical and technical challenges. His dramatic transitions from dolce to furioso that follow the opening gesture merge with an exotic flair of otherness, recalling the *Tzigane*-character, with associated affects of the unconventional and indomitable. For the listener familiar with this kind of repertoire, the *Tzigane* conveys the topos of the *Stegreifgeiger*, the instinctive natural talent that woos the audience with irresistible charm, breathtaking dexterity, fiery rhythms and exotic melodies.[16] Vargas's Hungarian origin makes the proximity to this vernacular musical tradition plausible but, for Kolisch, it represented a trivial, culinary culture of instrumental music he wanted to bury once and for all.

Compared to Varga, Kolisch's recording sounds ascetic, and at the same time full of frantic activity. Kolisch suppresses the contrasts implied by the juxtaposition of textures and common stylistic topics, and instead exaggerates the melodic flow by moderating the divergent characters of melodic gestalts and textural sections. Although linear and goal orientated,

---

[15] Rudolf Kolisch (vl.) and Alan Willman (pn.), recorded in 1953 (disc 2, track 36, 8'28"); Tibor Varga (vl.) and Ernst Krenek (pn.), recorded in 1951 (disc 1, track 27, 10'40"), both on *The RIAS Second Viennese School Project* (audite CD 21412, 2012). Further recordings of the *Phantasy* by Kolisch are collected on archiphon (ARC-WU45). Among them are Kolisch's performances with Eduard Steuermann, 15 August 1954 (9'23"), and Else Stock, 26 July 1953 (7'52"), recorded at the Internationale Ferienkurse in Darmstadt.

[16] Robert Orledge, 'Evocations of Exoticism', *The Cambridge Companion to Ravel* (Cambridge University Press, 2002), pp. 27–46.

Kolisch's flow halts somehow. There is little sense of pleasure in his restrained mode of swelling and receding, between the violent pace of musical rapids and peaceful meandering. Kolisch's focus is the economic connection of tones, and motivic units. The same restrained use of affect-evoking means is particularly evident in moments of emphasis and expansion within and between phrase trajectories. Large intervallic leaps are articulated in the least dramatic way possible. Each tone is clearly articulated, yet in a manner that is far from as emotionally charged as in Varga's performance. Kolisch's phrases do not dwell on immediately satisfying moments of closure and recollection; instead, they seem driven by a relentless will to move on, anticipating the future, to 'function' as subordinated in larger thematic units. In this way, Kolisch mimics the unrest, the demand for continuation, inherent to the form as a whole as it unravels, becoming a 'compositional problem'. At the same time, Kolisch's pursuit of the work as it grows from its parts to an organic whole somehow lacks the feeling of relaxation and intensification, as might be expected of organic phrasing and naturally arched melodic inflection. Kolisch consequently avoids portamenti, and it seems as if he carries out any kind of 'sound-accompanying' gestures with great control, avoiding any impression of virtuosic showmanship. Stylistic tropes, such as the waltz, seem to remain beyond Kolisch's imaginative scope. Neither does he make artificial pauses; caesurae are kept to a minimum duration.

Do all these restrictions of expressive means render Kolisch's interpretation more comprehensible than Varga's? What is left once the 'beautiful tone' is expunged? How does Kolisch compensate? How does he intend to convince the listener, if he does not seek to seduce them? At first glance, Kolisch's economical interpretation expresses a lack of confidence in the inner logic of progression. Paradoxically, Varga's performance seems much more self-confident in all its rhetorical eloquence. The affective content of Kolisch's performance emanates from the problem of continuity and coherence; the anxiety of 'athematic form' has to be eradicated, at all costs. Varga does not seem to have such anxieties. To Kolisch, the anxiety for dissolution belongs to the existential foundation of the Viennese culture with which he identified. The thematic principle belongs to the core of the Viennese compositional tradition. Any threat of disintegration would jeopardize the tradition derived from Schoenberg's 'new music'.

One has to recall that Varga, at the time he performed the *Phantasy*, had already studied and performed another of Schoenberg's American works. In 1949, Varga gave the European premiere of Schoenberg's Violin Concerto. In 1951, he performed the same work with the BBC

Symphony Orchestra in London, with reviews praising the 'full, secure tone and effortless technical mastery'.[17] Schoenberg comments on a tape recording of Varga's performance of his Violin Concerto in remarkably enthusiastic words:

> It really sounds as if you have known the piece for 25 years, your rendering is so mature, so expressive, so beautifully shaped. I must say that I have never yet come across such a good performance without having myself helped with every detail. The fact that you discovered all this for yourself is not only evidence of your outstanding talent; it gratifies me, besides, in that it shows me how distinctly my music can speak to a true musician: he can know and understand me without explanations, simply through the medium of the written notes.[18]

Obviously, the composer viewed Varga's performance as a more than acceptable interpretation, confirming for him that his concerto could be understood by this gifted musician 'simply through the medium of the written notes' and apparently without a thorough knowledge of the 'Viennese performance tradition'. Moreover, to Schoenberg, Varga's reading of his score was by no means inferior to that of other performers (such as Kolisch), who had 'been helped with every detail' by the composer.

Listening to Kolisch's recording of the *Phantasy* with Varga's 'mature, expressive, and beautifully shaped' performance style in mind, Kolisch's rendition might appear dry and inflexible, certainly not emotionless, but preoccupied with structural transparency. As indicated earlier, Kolisch's goal was to develop a 'tone', in the sense of 'prose-like' melodic inflection of a fundamentally different quality compared to what has been considered 'beautiful' in the musical culture he was a part of. Drawing on Schoenberg's principles of motivic comprehensibility and 'musical prose', Kolisch developed a speech-like practice of phrasing analogous to prosodic segregation, 'miming' modes of inflection and accentuation comparable to verbal arguments, questions, statements and so on.[19] To achieve the coherence of motivic units within thematic gestalts, and to avoid shifts of positions, open strings and 'glissandos' within coherent phrases, Kolisch developed a specific fingering technique.[20] His idiosyncratic technique of musical articulation was developed according to the principles of thematic

---

[17] See the review of Martin Cooper from 1951, 'Triumph for the Violin: Tibor Varga's Schoenberg'. Scan of newspaper clipping (Arnold Schoenberg Archive Vienna).
[18] Schoenberg to Tibor Varga (letter), 27 June 1951, Houghton Library, Harvard University.
[19] Kolisch, *Zur Theorie der Aufführung*, pp. 86ff. See also Károly Csipák, 'Sehr schnelle Reflexe: Erinnerungen an das Kolisch-Quartett', *Musica* (1986), 518–24, pp. 523f.
[20] Kolisch, 'Religion der Streicher' in *Zur Theorie der Aufführung*, pp. 116ff.

composition. This might have made it difficult for him to approach Schoenberg's *Phantasy* from a different angle, as is suggested by Regina Busch.[21] Kolisch always emphasizes the linear flow and the tendencies of isolated melodic gestures as they become coherent thematic gestalts.[22] Does he achieve this intention of thematic-motivic *Vergeistigung* to such a degree that he somehow gets stuck in the structural, cognitive side of the work? Varga on the other hand seems almost to surge from gesture to gesture, impression to impression, relying on the effect of the moment, connecting one phrase to another through a chain of loose associations. In this way, by residing at the surface, Varga's *Phantasy* also fails to make the dialectical turn, in his case the turn from the sensuous to the cognitive.

One conclusion might be that the performances resist comparison. Kolisch, with his emphasis on the motivic-thematic structure, makes his interpretation of this work sound more cognitive. Varga's interpretation, on the other hand, is comparably more sensuous, 'culinary' and at the same time more daring, imaginative and thus engaging. Both interpretations mark a certain stage in the quest for 'ideal interpretation'. As such, both of these performances leave the listener in a 'state of dissatisfaction', to borrow Hullot-Kentor's expression, instead providing motivation for new interpretations which might express the 'desire for the particular'.[23]

Interpretation as revolution: Beethoven's Violin Concerto

Alongside Schoenberg, Beethoven also featured at the core of Kolisch's repertoire. Kolisch's string quartet became famous for its performances of Beethoven quartets played by heart – a result of the use of cut and pasted scores, whereby each member of the group knew and analyzed not only their own part but also the parts of the others.[24] While he never recorded

---

[21] In 1965, Kolisch was asked to give an analysis of the *Phantasy* in addition to a performance he gave in London. The note Kolisch probably used for his speech consists of a synoptic list of features taken straight from Adorno's *Interpretationsanalyse* given as a talk in 1961 of the same work. Whereas Adorno stresses athematic features in the *Phantasy*, Kolisch's performance once more reveals his persisting commitment to thematic principles. See Regina Busch, 'Thematisch oder athematisch?', *Mitteilungen der internationalen Schönberg-Gesellschaft*, 3–4 (1989), 5–9.

[22] Arnold Whittall's reading of the String Trio, Op. 45 also suggests a latent thematicism in Schoenberg's late works, which should not be overshadowed by the shattered turmoil of their surface. See Arnold Whittall, 'Schoenberg and the "True Tradition": Theme and Form in the String Trio', *Musical Times*, 115/1579 (1974), 739–43.

[23] Robert Hullot-Kentor, 'Right Listening and a New Type of Human Being' in *Things beyond Resemblance: Collected Essays on Theodor W. Adorno* (New York: Columbia University Press, 2006), pp. 193–209, p. 208.

[24] Christoph Wolff, 'Schoenberg, Kolisch, and the Continuity of Viennese Quartet Culture' in Reinhold Brinkmann and Christoph Wolff (eds.), *Music of My Future: The Schoenberg Quartets and Trio* (Cambridge, MA: Harvard University Press, 2000), pp. 13–24.

any Beethoven quartet with the Kolisch quartet, Kolisch took every opportunity to perform and record Beethoven's Violin Concerto and the Violin Sonatas in the post-war years.

Beethoven's Violin Concerto had a special place in Kolisch's life: in 1922 he performed the work arranged for chamber orchestra, together with Reger's Violin Concerto. Schoenberg was engaged as conductor.[25] In 1954, during his stay at Darmstadt, Kolisch's Parisian friend René Leibowitz asked him to perform the violin concertos of Schoenberg and Beethoven, with Kolisch as soloist and Leibowitz as conductor. Kolisch responded immediately to Leibowitz's request:

> The Beethoven Concerto would interest me especially, as it has been completely distorted by tradition. You should be aware of the fact that a correct performance would cause an upheaval. I would have to know far in advance, as I have to work on it again (the last time I played it was with Schoenberg!), especially on the cadenzas, which I have lost. I had discovered that Beethoven himself had written cadenzas to an arrangement of the piece, which he made for two pianos, and I arranged them for the violin, this I would have to do again. They are worlds away from the conventional cadenzas and quite interesting (with timpani participating).[26]

Kolisch and Leibowitz had to wait another ten years before the plans with Leibowitz became a reality in 1964, when Hans-Jörg Pauli invited Leibowitz to produce a recording of Beethoven's Violin Concerto with the Radio Orchestra Beromünster.[27] During the preparations, Kolisch informed Adorno about his project: 'For the time being, I am working with the Beethoven Concerto, which has become totally removed from the realm of music at the hands of the "Entertainers", and is petrified in this condition (reinforced by the conformity of their "individual" rubati).'[28]

Tempo was always a crucial interpretive concern for Kolisch. For him, Beethoven's metronome markings were an integrated part of the composer's works, and as such had to be respected by a performer, even in works which lacked explicit markings.[29] With some rare exceptions, the general

---

[25] The programmes of Kolisch's concerts in Vienna and Frankfurt are kept at the Kolisch papers (Houghton Library, Harvard University).

[26] Kolisch to René Leibowitz (letter), 24 November 1954, Houghton Library, Harvard University.

[27] The author was given generous access to Leibowitz's correspondence with Pauli, which is kept at the Paul Sacher Stiftung, Basel, including details of the production with Radio Beromünster. A recording of the broadcast production is available on demand from the SRF-archive. Kolisch was in possession of a copied tape, which is kept at Harvard Houghton Library.

[28] Kolisch to Theodor W. Adorno (letter), 19 January 1962, Houghton Library, Harvard University (my translation).

[29] Rudolf Kolisch, 'Tempo and Character in Beethoven's Music', trans. Arthur Mendel, *The Musical Quarterly*, 29/2 (1943), 169–87 (part 1); 29/3 (1943), 291–311 (part 2).

custom from the beginning of the Concerto's performance tradition has been to follow much slower tempi than those suggested by Kolisch, especially for the first and the second movement, despite one exception – the famous recording by Heifetz and Toscanini from the early 1940s, which applied tempi quite close to the range suggested by Kolisch. Even so, Leibowitz used every opportunity to promote their 'revolutionary' project. In 1960, the year before he recorded all nine Beethoven symphonies with the RCA orchestra, Leibowitz published his article 'How to Interpret Beethoven' in Sartre's famous journal *Les Temps modernes*,[30] asking Kolisch to edit it. In this polemical essay against interpretive 'sloppiness', Leibowitz promoted his and Kolisch's ideas on interpreting Beethoven and posed the rhetorical question as to whose recordings of the Beethoven symphonies should be considered the primary reference for the audience. Adorno, having received Leibowitz's recordings, immediately wrote an enthusiastic review:

> The so-called *Werktreue* is turned by Leibowitz into something different, in a similar way to the Beethoven interpretations of the Kolisch quartet, something radically modern. This is what makes his performances incomparable ... Moreover, these [performances] will grant [the listener] something that they do not expect, or even do not want at all: an introduction to the new music in the spirit of the greatest achievements of the tonal age.[31]

The élan of Leibowitz's recordings and his rising reputation as conductor gained the attention of the producer Hans Jörg Pauli, who was at the time affiliated with Radio Beromünster.[32] Pauli, who was also a musicologist with a particular interest in Luigi Nono, showed genuine interest in the cause of Kolisch and Leibowitz and their attempt to 'actualize' the Beethoven performance tradition. Besides the performance of the Concerto, Kolisch and Leibowitz were given the opportunity to present their ideas in a radio interview, where they described concrete analytical examples of how their performance deviated from the 'trivializing tradition'.[33] To Kolisch and Leibowitz, the exclusivity of their 'reference recording' of Beethoven was a major concern. Accordingly, Leibowitz and Kolisch considered

---

[30] René Leibowitz, 'Comment interprète-t-on Beethoven?', *Les Temps Modernes*, 175 and 176 (1960), 630–46.
[31] Theodor W. Adorno, 'Beethoven im Geist der Moderne. Eine Gesamtaufnahme der neun Symphonien unter René Leibowitz' in Rolf Tiedemann and Klaus Schultz (eds.), *Musikalische Schriften* (Frankfurt am Main: Suhrkamp, 2003), pp. 535–8.
[32] Thomas Meyer, 'Zum Tod von Hansjörg Pauli', *Dissonanz/Dissonance*, 98 (2007), 46-7.
[33] Rudolf Kolisch and René Leibowitz, 'Aufführungsprobleme im Violinkonzert von Beethoven', *Musica*, 33/2 (1979), 148–55, p. 148.

Schneiderhan's 1962 recording of the Concerto, including his use of Beethoven's cadenza, as a rival project, one that might have the potential to jeopardize their own 'revolutionary' project.[34] Only after Leibowitz had had the opportunity to listen to Schneiderhan's recording were their anxieties dispelled, as they noticed the inclusion of an adapted version of the piano cadenza:

> Heard the Schneiderhan recording recently ... You can relax! ... the performance is conventional, maybe even less interesting than the usual ones. The first movement comes with the common faults (the vagueness of the tempo is outraging). The second movement falls asleep ... and the third could wake up nobody. We still have to carry out our 'revolution'![35]

A more detailed comparative analysis with the orchestral score might illustrate the rigour of Leibowitz's extraordinary control as a conductor and his attempts to prevent the orchestra falling back into conventional patterns of tempo modification. Any 'intuitive' idiomatic gesture or any 'natural' choice of tempo and tempo modification was subject to a painstaking, critical assessment. Beethoven's resistance to 'stylized idiomatic patterns' (*Manieren*)[36] – considered second rate – and learned conventions was precisely the element in his music that Kolisch and Leibowitz wanted to bring to the fore through an insistence on the rhythmical-metrical rigour of the tempo. The motto was '*Grösste Strenge – Höchste Freiheit*'. Kolisch's goal with his performance was to convey how Beethoven composed 'against' the instrument even in the Violin Concerto. Even the most self-evident melody, texture or rhythm carries a sense of unrest and uncertainty with it, a sense of resistance against conventional modes of execution, which is composed into Beethoven's music. A performance which pursues Beethoven's musical 'character' should feature this inner tension; the conflict between the rhetorical meaning of the figure and its structural meaning as a motive should become transparent. Crucial to Kolisch is the recognition that this unrest and uncertainty is an inherent part of the 'object' – Beethoven's work – and that non-idiomatic features should not be overshadowed by the 'beautiful tone'.

---

[34] Wolfgang Schneiderhan, Eugen Jochum and the Vienna Philharmonic Orchestra (Deutsche Grammophon CD: 447 403-2, 1995).

[35] Leibowitz to Rudolf Kolisch (letter), undated (probably from April 1964), Houghton Library, Harvard University (my translation).

[36] Siegfried Mauser, 'Zum Begriff des musikalischen Charakters in Beethovens frühen Klaviersonaten' in Otto Kolleritsch (ed.), *Beethoven und die Zweite Wiener Schule* (Studien zur Wertungsforschung 25) (Wien: Universal, 1992), pp. 190–202.

Transformation instead of adaptation: the Beethoven Cadenza

To Kolisch, there never was an alternative to the incorporation of Beethoven's cadenza, written by the composer for the piano version of the Violin Concerto.[37] Unlike Schneiderhan, Kolisch refused to make any idiomatic adaptations of the cadenzas, making it clear to Leibowitz that he preferred the unplayable passages in particular. To understand Kolisch's interpretive choices, one has to consider some features of the cadenza, which are indeed remarkable. Beethoven's cadenza in the piano version of the Violin Concerto lasts for 141 measures, making it one of the most extensive he wrote. It begins with the harmonic and thematic material from the Concerto's development section, featuring the timpani motive. Kolisch's notion of the cadenza as second development is reflected in the identical length in terms of numbers of measures, and the identity of character of the start of the cadenza, with its rough, unpolished 'war music' of the orchestral passage at the first development section, where thematic material was presented by the timpani motive. The virtually endless series of chromatic figures in the transitional passage of the cadenza increases the intensity, culminating in a fermata and anticipating the sudden shift of tempo with the 'piu vivace' of the 'Marcia' section. Here the timpani finally come to the fore, emphasizing the martial affect of this part. The dotted rhythm and double stops of the second part emphasize to an even greater degree the 'war music' character of the march section.[38] What follows is far from a moment of relaxation. On the contrary, the passagework demands the listener's attention. The manner of figuration is dazzling and idiomatically integrated when performed on the piano. In Kolisch's version for the violin it becomes a hysterical notion: the simultaneous execution of chromatic triple-figuration with percussive double stops exceeds the technical possibilities of the violin. Kolisch attributes to the whole passage a sense of risk, balancing 'on the edge' of an abyss of fiasco. Concluding with trills and fermatas, the main theme features at full strength, and, after another extended, slightly relaxed, diminishing passage of embellished octave doublings, the final trills signal the transition back to the coda, which, in this case, presents the lyrical second theme with the most tender of dynamics.

Despite the fact that both Kolisch and Schneiderhan take Beethoven's cadenza as their point of departure, the contrast between them is striking: Schneiderhan shortens Beethoven's cadenza considerably and adapts its

---

[37] Kolisch to Leibowitz (letter), 24 November 1954.
[38] Mai Kawabata, 'Virtuoso Codes of Violin Performance: Power, Military Heroism, and Gender (1789–1830)', *19th-Century Music*, 28/2 (2004), 89–107.

proportions in accordance with the norms of a 'tasteful' cadenza in the classical tradition, following the model of Joachim and Kreisler. Schneiderhan's cadenza is virtuosic in the traditional sense: the virtuoso plays with the themes, blends dexterity with fantasy in a tasteful manner and avoids the excessive use of chromatic slides, which sound idiomatic in the piano version, but monstrous when literally transferred to the violin (as in Leibowitz's transcription). Moreover, Schneiderhan polishes the rough accentuations and turns the awkwardness of Beethoven's 'musical prose' into smooth, effortless parlance. What Kolisch commissioned from Leibowitz under the preparation of their broadcast was something else: a note-by-note transcription of Beethoven's piano cadenza, which would have been considered by most violinists to be 'unplayable'. Kolisch took the opposite position, as illustrated in a concise note by Kolisch scribbled underneath an awkwardly pianistic combination of double stopping and trills in his autograph copy of Leibowitz's transcription: 'Gerade möglich, was sie interessant macht' ('almost impossible to play – this is what makes it interesting').[39]

Kolisch's literal and unabridged reintegration of Beethoven's cadenza into the Concerto's structure suggests that Beethoven turned towards the sonata principle and thematic integration in this work. However, put to the empirical test of source critical analysis, Kolisch's intention comes into conflict with Beethoven: the cadenza was composed with the idiomatic requirements of the piano version in mind. Beethoven never composed another version for the violin. Lack of empirical proof became a moment of opportunity for Kolisch. His retrospective extrapolation of integrative principles exaggerates not the historical, but the 'cognitive' (*geistige*) proximity between Schoenberg and Beethoven, at the same time that it increases the distance between Beethoven and Mozart, the great model of Beethoven's early concertos. What might be the consequence of this kind of 'actualization'? What is gained and what is lost? Bringing Beethoven's structures closer to Schoenberg's 'new music' might ensure the legitimacy of Schoenberg's 'revolution by virtue of evolution'. On the other hand, Kolisch's 'new interpretation' of Beethoven, rendering every melody thematic, every figure motivic, suppresses an essential part of the concerto understood as a genre – the play with extra-musical topics and characters. Beethoven's violin should sing cantabile, not emulate 'musical prose'. The lyricism of the instrumental melodies in the Concerto, its most prominent

---

[39] Several original sketches of this transcription are kept in the Leibowitz collection at the library of the University of Bologna. Further copies are kept at the Paul Sacher Stiftung in Basel and at the Harvard Houghton Library.

characteristic feature, loses its magic in Leibowitz's forced orchestral accents and Kolisch's 'motivically integrated' solo line. In Kolisch's interpretation, the serenity of the pastoral character, counterbalanced by the subdued, stylized echo of martial rhythms in Beethoven's Concerto, becomes a 'battle of the material'. Ironically, Leibowitz's almost obsessive pursuit of control over the orchestra leads to a loss of the same on Kolisch's part: in the end, Kolisch's weakened stamina ends up leaving the quest for a historic 'reference-recording' – that might convey the revolutionary Beethoven in the spirit of Schoenberg – sound more like a desperate struggle against total physical and mental exhaustion.

The radical difference between Kolisch's performance and more recent, modern attempts to reinstate Beethoven's cadenza in the violin version of the work is suggested by Gidon Kremer's 1992 recording with Harnoncourt.[40] Kremer opted for a different strategy in rendering the 'unplayable' piano version of Beethoven's cadenza more 'tasteful', though with an odd mixture of commitment to HIP and postmodern playfulness: his recording of Beethoven's cadenza includes a duet between violin and piano. Kremer openly refers to the original piano version and combines the sound worlds of both versions. Moreover, the distribution of the parts allows Kremer to concentrate on playing with different shades of expression and a smooth flow of articulation in the violin part, avoiding awkward, 'unplayable' passages. Yet, the sudden entrance of the piano is awkward, an intrusive element which does not fit into the whole: the violin concerto's domain seems violated, and its very raison d'être is undermined. What should be the display of violinist bravura, culminating in the cadenza, eventually leads to the paradoxical situation whereby the violin seeks assistance from the piano in order to finish the cadenza.

Transformative interpretations, transformed traditions

Adorno's apparently biased praise of Kolisch raises certain questions, considering the controversial aspects of Kolisch's interpretations. Adorno did not agree with Kolisch's apparently rationalistic theory of tempo and the typology of musical characters in Beethoven. Even for Adorno, it is not evident that any of Kolisch's attempts to overcome the second nature of his 'idiomatic self' necessarily lead to the origin, the true nature of the musical work. There is always the danger of establishing new idiomatic habits and conventional mindsets. The truth of Kolisch's recording of the Beethoven

---

[40] In 1992 Kremer recorded the Violin Concerto with the Chamber Orchestra of Europe, conducted by Nikolaus Harnoncourt (Teldec CD: 9031-74881).

Violin Concerto or his recordings of Schoenberg's *Phantasy* is conveyed not so much in their status as authentic 'reference recordings', but rather as polemic comments on the 'streamlining con brio', the contemporary 'state of the art' in modern performance practice. Both Kolisch and Leibowitz followed Adorno's maxim that truth is expressed only as polemics. Kolisch's 'new interpretation' transforms Beethoven's work into 'new music'. To achieve this goal he sacrificed the 'beautiful tone', a move that left him an outsider in a modern musical culture that celebrated the virtuoso culture of the past and with it the affirmative stance towards the role of art as entertainment in society.[41] Kolisch's resistance to the 'beautiful tone' pushed him further, and in some cases over the edge, in denying idiomatic comfort. Accordingly, Kolisch's fidelity to the work acknowledged the limitations of cognition, as revealed in the moment the subject really attempts to immerse itself in the object. To Adorno, nobody came closer than Kolisch to true interpretation, for the reason of his unconditional renouncement of conventional 'means of expression' and his submission to the structure of the work. On the other hand, the examples of Kolisch's interpretations of Beethoven's Violin Concerto and Schoenberg's *Phantasy* convey the struggle in Kolisch's analytical mind in his pursuit of control, and his 'anxiety of relaxation', '*loslassen können*'. There are moments when Kolisch's intentional rationality leaves him blind to the non-intentional logic of the work's subcutaneous structures.

In retrospect it might seem as if the impact of Kolisch's quest for origin and transformation of the idiom – as attested to by Adorno in relation to Kolisch's performances – never extended beyond a small, exclusive group of dedicated 'new music' followers. Kolisch himself never aspired to entertain the 'masses' as a famous virtuoso; nor did he establish a 'school' as a teacher. His domain was the intimate, 'vergeistigte' realm of chamber music, in which he achieved considerable success with the Kolisch quartet during the late 1920s and 1930s. He was clearly aware of his responsibility as a mediator of Schoenberg's ideals, taking any opportunity to share his knowledge about Schoenberg's views on performance, gained through numerous rehearsals in the 1920s with the composer present. His approach to communicating the motives behind his interpretive choices and instrumental techniques involved the intense reading and rehearsing of scores, to begin with as the leader of his own string quartets (*Wiener Streichquartett, Kolisch Quartett, Pro Arte Quartett*), and in his later years as a teacher at masterclasses in Madison, Boston and Mödling.

---

[41] Theodor W. Adorno, 'Kolisch und die neue Interpretation' in Rolf Tiedemann and Klaus Schultz (eds.), *Musikalische Schriften* (Frankfurt am Main: Suhrkamp, 2003), pp. 460–2.

Today, the idiosyncratic features of Kolisch's performance style might sound closer to the preferences of 'modern' modes of listening. It is perhaps no longer the case that Kolisch's interpretations still grant the listener an 'unexpected, even unwanted' experience of the Viennese tradition, as Adorno suggested. On the other hand, we may well still experience Kolisch as a contemporary idiom that sounds 'foreign' and is resisted by 'genuinely undialectical ears'.[42] The virtuosic performance of new music is no longer a utopian dream, as it was for Schoenberg. Today, performances of Webern and Schoenberg (or Boulez, Stockhausen, Nono etc.) are at the same level of quality as performances of Beethoven or Mozart. Moreover, performers have gained specialist competence in the performance of twentieth-century musical styles. The 'reconstruction' of a performance tradition of the Schoenberg School since the early 1990s would seem to correspond with this trend, complementing technical perfection with 'historically informed' faithfulness to the score. However, a present-day performer inspired by Kolisch's performance practice would no longer rely on a repertoire of styles, topoi and gestures, internalized and naturalized, as a more or less 'tacit' performance tradition, helping the performer to 'add to' and 'fill in' the 'empty spaces' left open by the notated signs. Re-listening to historical recordings of Kolisch, with Adorno's dialectical critique in mind, provides a discomforting narrative on modern performance practice and its concepts of perfection and faithfulness. Kolisch's approach represents a culturally contingent musical dialect. At the same time, he takes a still-relevant critical position on the history of interpretation of 'new' music', expanded into the progressive interpretation of the tradition from Beethoven to Schoenberg. Not least, his unique idiom resists being consumed by the major narrative of musical modernism induced by post-war ideologies of musical progress.

---

[42] Hullot-Kentor, 'Right Listening and a New Type of Human Being', p. 207.

14 'Unwrapping' the voice

Cathy Berberian and John Cage's Aria

Francesca Placanica

Dearest John
> Life is a fountain?
> Did your 'Aria + Fontana' [sic] for Swedish TV and they say it's a WOW – also Flower + Widow for the radio.
> They love you here in Sweden and in Denmark and me, too
> Life isn't a fountain?
> Cathy[1]

With these words Cathy Berberian addressed John Cage in a postcard sent to Stony Brook from Stockholm on 25 November 1965, informing the latter of the success of *Aria with Fontana Mix* for Swedish TV and of the positive reception of her radio broadcasts of *A Flower* and *The Wonderful Widow of Eighteen Springs*. This correspondence, which could be interpreted as a deliberate act of self-fashioning on Berberian's behalf, is one of numerous testimonies to the friendship and collaboration between Berberian and John Cage, underlined by the familiar terms of her reference to *Aria*, a work which the two friends had successfully produced seven years earlier. By 1965, Berberian was recuperating after her divorce from Luciano Berio, while intensifying her independent and fruitful collaborations with Bruno Maderna, Sylvano Bussotti and Cage himself. The friendship between the two American artists had begun in late 1958 in Milan and was sealed by their creative collaboration on *Aria* in 1958–59.

According to David Osmond-Smith's detailed study of her early career, *Aria* was a turning point for Berberian as it had an immense impact on her artistic development.[2] The creation of *Aria* was, prima facie, a landmark in

---

[1] Cathy Berberian to John Cage (postcard), item 56:4:2, John Cage Archive, Northwestern University Library (Evanston, IL).
[2] David Osmond-Smith, 'The Tenth Oscillator: The Work of Cathy Berberian 1958–1966', *Tempo*, 58/227 (2004), 2–13, reprinted in Pamela Karantonis, Francesca Placanica, Anna Sivuoja-Kauppala and Pieter Verstraete (eds.), *Cathy Berberian: Pioneer of Contemporary Vocality* (Farnham: Ashgate, 2014), pp. 19–31.

the vicissitudes of Berberian's private and professional lives. However, in many ways, the work was a reciprocal investment, on the one hand, in the fashioning of Berberian's New Vocality, and on the other, in the recognition of Cage's compositional praxis into the realm of vocal performance.

This chapter begins exploring Berberian's act of liberation and self-determination undertaken with *Aria* and describes the work as emblematic of the revolutionary transformations of vocal performance in late modernist music. Without aiming to provide a definitive account of *Aria* either from Berberian's or Cage's perspective, I will illustrate the principal milestones of the collaborative act behind the composition and probe how the work sparked novel approaches for both Berberian's and Cage's performance aesthetics. It is sufficient to note at this point that Berberian's experience with *Aria* galvanized her creative approach to vocal performance, later summarized in her 'manifesto' on New Vocality, a working practice that contributed radically to the transformation of attitudes towards vocality in avant-garde composition.[3]

In *Aria*, possibly for the first time in Western art music, 'unmusical' noises produced through vocal emission as well as by the singer's body were introduced into a composition. At the same time, phonemes and words, as well as vocal styles, were conceived as an entity per se, a far cry from the linearity of a written text or the constraints of the word–music relationship typical of conventional vocal forms. By loosening the mark of things, and allowing detachment between signifiers and signifieds, wandering and interacting freely in the playground of the composition, vocal noises were turned into 'vocality', thus disrupting their dramatic interdependence with text and authority. Berberian registered this invention in her essay manifesto 'The New Vocality in Contemporary Music' (1966).[4]

> What is the New Vocality that appears so threatening to the old guard? It is
> the voice which has an endless range of vocal styles at its disposal,
> embracing the history of music as well as aspects of sound itself; marginal
> perhaps compared to the music, but fundamental to human beings. Unlike
> the instrument, which can be locked up and put away after use, the voice is
> something more than an instrument, precisely because it is inseparable from
> its interpreter. It lends itself continuously to the numerous tasks of our
> daily lives: it argues with the butcher over the roast beef, whispers sweet words

---

[3] Cathy Berberian, 'La nuova vocalità nell'opera contemporanea', *Discoteca*, 62 (1966), 34–35; reprinted (trans. Francesca Placanica) as 'The New Vocality in Contemporary Music' in Karantonis et al., *Cathy Berberian*, pp. 47–50.

[4] Berberian, 'La nuova vocalità nell'opera contemporanea', p. 47.

in intimacy, shouts insults to the referee, asks for directions to the Piazza Carità, etc. Furthermore, the voice expresses itself through communicative 'noises', such as sobs, sighs, tongue snaps, screams, groans, laughter.

In an interview released in 1972, Berberian acknowledged Cage's influence on her invention of the New Vocality; however, when asked to define it she stated that it was actually 'a continuation of the original, old vocality, like Monteverdi's', and traced the substantial interaction between words and music back to the birth of *recitar cantando* and *seconda prattica*.[5] This reference to *seconda prattica* indicates the creative approach expected of singers to music and composition rather than to musical material: singers in Monteverdi's time had a sufficiently grounded cultural background to be able to improvise *fiorituras* in order to embellish the piece, and were therefore required to 'compose' their own performances more or less extemporaneously, a creative attitude that was crucial in the New Vocality.[6]

In short, Berberian charged the performer with the responsibility of finding a vocality that 'would do something' immanently, participating in the creative act throughout its utterance. In framing Berberian's New Vocality within the tenets of performance studies, Pamela Karantonis has defined Berberian's newly coined notion of avant-garde voice as a 'performative vocality':[7]

> for singers who can *do something* with both the sound and the textual/theatrical element. She [Berberian] suggested an alternative artistry based on intelligent and conceptual risk-taking at the live moment of singing, speaking and gesturing.

By freeing the voice from the 'impasse' of conventional operatic aesthetics,[8] such as timbre, volume, virtuosity and tonal beauty, singers would be able to create their own niche independently by placing themselves entirely at the service of their performance:

> For this reason the singer today can no longer be just a singer. Now the boundaries of interpretation, like those of the arts, are no longer clearly defined – and performers in one field violate the territory of others. (Brecht-Weill demanded actors who could sing, Schoenberg wanted singers

---

[5] Charles Amirkhanians, *Other Minds: Cathy Berberian on KPFA's Ode to Gravity Series* (MP3 audiofile), 1 min. 31 sec., 1 November 1972, 'RadiOM.Org/Interviews', http://rediom.org/berberianOTG.php (accessed 24 July 2010).

[6] Berberian, 'La nuova vocalità nell'opera contemporanea', p. 49.

[7] Pamela Karantonis, 'Cathy Berberian and the Performative Art of Voice' in Karantonis et al., *Cathy Berberian*, pp. 151–68, p. 153.

[8] Michelle Duncan, 'The Operatic Scandal of the Singing Body', *Cambridge Opera Journal*, 16/3 (2008), 283–306, p. 283.

who knew how to act.) The New Vocality affirms that there should be singers who are able to act, sing, dance, mime, improvise – in other words, affect the eyes as well as the ears. [I] propose the artist as a universal fact and the voice as part of the living body, acting and reacting.[9]

This attitude towards physicality and its expression paved the way to a completely different experience compared to avant-garde aesthetics, and the way vocality had been interpreted by composers throughout the century.

There is colourful evidence that the New Vocality found its roots in Berberian's eclectic performing talents. Berberian studied and performed as a dancer and an actress, though opera singing remained her predominant interest, which she pursued in Milan in the late 1940s thanks to a Fulbright scholarship, at a time when the cultural life of the city was cautiously – even suspiciously – opening up to stimuli injected by the European avant-garde. Married to Berio a few months after the two met, Berberian contributed actively to his early compositions for the radio and contributed material to his tape works for voice, even though she maintained a sceptical attitude towards the principles of the avant-garde. And yet, the involvement of the couple in the endeavours of the *Studio di Fonologia Musicale* soon made Berberian's interaction crucial for the international artistic collaborations that unfolded around its nine oscillators, and that made their apartment in Via Moscati a crucible for international composers and technicians attracted by the new studio.[10] Berio's and Berberian's hospitality and their generous dinners created an atmosphere of cordiality and involvement. All composers stopping off in Milan to undertake work at the studio enjoyed an Armenian meal at the generosity of Berberian, who not only cooked for them but strove to create a warm sense of companionship.[11] In addition, Berberian became more and more

---

[9] Berberian, 'The New Vocality in Contemporary Music', p. 49.
[10] The Parisian experience was keenly pursued by Pierre Shaeffer (1910–95), who in 1951 set up the *Groupe de la recherche de musique concrète* (GRMC), which later became a stable department of the RTF (Nicola Scaldaferri, *Musica nel laboratorio elettroacustico* (Lucca: Libreria Musicale Italiana, 1994), p. 22). Meyer-Eppler (1913–55), Robert Beyer (1901?) and Herbert Eimert (1897–1972) can be considered to be the forces behind the Studio für Elektronisches Musik in Cologne, which on 18 October 1951 broadcast their early electro-acoustic experiments together with lectures by Herbert Eimert, Robert Beyer and Friedrich Trautwein (1888–1956), the inventor of the Trautonium. As researchers and lecturers, the group was vitally linked to the Darmstadt summer course, with the occasional involvement of Varèse, Stockhausen and others.
[11] Along with Berio, active early on in the Studio di Fonologia were musicologists Roberto Leydi, Luigi Rognoni and the then director of technical services at RAI, Alfredo Lietti. Marino Zuccheri, a technician at RAI who was very sensitive to musical issues, was proposed as collaborator and was significant in helping the composers realize their ideas on the equipment (Scaldaferri, *Musica nel laboratorio elettroacustico*, pp. 64–6).

indispensable as a translator who made conversations and the exchange of ideas possible.[12]

Although Berberian was crucial to the intellectual exchange taking place around the table, she was left out of 'important' discussions. Her place was not in the studio, but in the kitchen, where she would sit apart, sometimes in the company of Luigi Nono's wife, Nuria Schoenberg.[13] Those were the years that Berberian had spent away from the stage after giving birth to her child Cristina, and that Osmond-Smith illustrates quite effectively as follows:

> By now, she was eager to return to live performance. For both Berio and Berberian, this was a turning-point. Berio was insistent that she should 'decide between babies and singing', and Berberian chose singing. That choice being made, Maderna did everything he could to help.[14]

Maderna secured Berberian a guest appearance in a 1958 concert of the 'Incontri musicali' season in Naples, where on 17 June she performed Stravinsky's *Pribaoutki* and Ravel's *Trois Poèmes de Stéphane Mallarmé*.

The making of *Aria*

In the same year, John Cage participated in the Darmstadt summer courses, and immediately afterwards was invited to Milan by Berio. Cage stayed not far from Via Moscati and regularly joined the Berios for meals, where Berberian, acting as interpreter, facilitated dialogue between the two composers. Cage's time spent with the Berios was fondly remembered by Berberian when early symptoms of the impending crisis that would break their marriage were emerging.

> John's presence in Milan – for the two-and-a-half months that he was there – I think it was two-and-a-half – I can't remember exactly but it seems like that – were for me, and for Luciano too at that time, a period of such serenity. [Cage's aforementioned *Aria* is played in the background here.] He radiated serenity and he gave it to us. And all of our tensions when we were with him seemed to – melt away ... and he had this smile that wasn't ever artificial. It's not an artificial smile that he has. It's a very peculiar smile because it has his tongue halfway out like – like a dog's you know and his eyes crinkle up and this serenity sort of opened up his face – that smile. And we all worked – all the people around him felt like better people when he was there. That's a nice way to leave people, don't you think? If we could all say that [laughing].[15]

---

[12] Osmond-Smith, 'The Tenth Oscillator' (2014), p. 23.
[13] Marie-Christine Vila, *Cathy Berberian Cant'atrice* (Paris: Fayard, 2003), p. 62.
[14] Osmond-Smith, 'The Tenth Oscillator' in Karantonis et al., *Cathy Berbarian*, p. 22.
[15] Cathy Berberian, 'Cathy's Solo Talk Show' (1979), produced by Frans van Rossum and Frits Bloemink, audio material digitized by Joes Roelofs and edited by John Knap for CD (2010).

Cage used Milan's soundscape as the basis for an electro-acoustic composition that would replicate methodologies applied to his first electro-acoustic work, *Williams Mix* in 1952. He performed it on Italian television in a quiz show in which he participated as a competitor expert on mycology.[16] *Fontana Mix* had its own life before Cage went on and composed *Aria* as a playful homage to Berberian. The singer thus described the inspiration that engendered both *Fontana Mix*, the prime example of Cage's indeterminacy poetics, and its subsequent vocal juxtaposition, *Aria*:

> He found a boarding house run by a lady called Fontana, then he would come to have each meal with us, and we would host him to help him save some money, but also because he was very nice. My part-time helper was called Fontana, and John's favorite wine was Fontanafredda, Barolo of Fontanafredda, which we used to buy at a wine seller at the corner of the street, called Fontana. Moreover, he [Cage] was an expert on mycology, and he found a bookshop with many books on mushrooms, whose owner was called Fontana. So, with all these coincidences, he called his work *Aria for Mezzo-Soprano and Fontana Mix*.[17]

While spending time together, Berberian would imitate singers of renown and perform funny vocal noises to entertain the American composer and, above all, her little daughter Cristina, who was five years old at the time. Berberian would vocally mock the procedures used in the studio to record and combine the recordings made, a feature of her 'vocal clowning' that Cage particularly endorsed, as it displayed the flexibility and multiple nuances of Berberian's voice. In her own words:

> So he decided to compose this work, for me and with me, so he asked me to . . . search for things in the Russian and in the Armenian languages. Then he searched in our books for French and Italian things. I remember that he found some Russian words in a book of mine by Pushkin, I mean, included in a Russian grammar book, 'How to Learn Russian', and there was a text in Russian. I got the Armenian words from some songs . . . I don't remember . . . That was a work made of five languages.[18]

While working on *Aria*, Berberian presented Cage with a selection of vocal styles on which he drew, using his chance system. The final score displayed

---

Special transcript by Pamela Karantonis in *Cathy Berberian Pioneer of Contemporary Vocality*, pp. 33–44, p. 40.

[16] Richard Kostelanetz, *Conversing with Cage* (New York: Routledge, 2003), p. 114.

[17] Cathy Berberian, unedited interview with Silvana Ottieri, tape 9 side A (Milan, 1981). See Francesca Placanica, 'Cathy Berberian: Performance as Composition', unpublished Master's thesis, Southern Methodist University (Dallas, 2007), p. 34. Translations from the Italian are by the author.

[18] Ibid.

a formidable combination of styles and colours, which challenged Berberian and stimulated her to practise in order to accomplish the composer's prescriptive intentions. All different vocal styles were juxtaposed in sequence, leaving the singer no 'chance to breathe or think about the following one'.[19] Berberian experimented with the 'friendly freedom'[20] of spacing out her voice flexibly and engagingly, using the whole gamut of colours and styles which she equally and unconditionally loved, ranging from jazz to bel canto, from *Sprechgesang* to a mocking quotation of Marilyn Monroe and of Marlene Dietrich. In Berberian's words:

> It was an impressive idea, and at that time, when I saw it, it seemed even impossible [to sing], so I needed a while. For example, the first year, the first four sheets of the piece – which consisted of two open pages each – were supposed to last a minute each, I mean, thirty seconds each sheet. Instead, I needed three minutes to sing them in, rather than in two, because my reflexes were not yet sharp enough and not accustomed to that speed. Today I can sing the whole piece in four minutes rather than in ten. Moreover, there were cues, some little signs, where I could add an extra-musical noise to my liking. Sometimes I would snap my fingers or stomp my foot, or would shout a lacerating scream, or an Indian noise; in short, it was up to me. There was also the barking of a dog.[21]

Berberian's account of her imprimatur of the linguistic fashioning of the composition illustrates the undoubted weight and awareness of her contribution. Moreover, the information she provides on the performance practice and timing of the piece remain valuable historical evidence and a source for later generations of performers approaching the composition:

> We premiered it in Rome, in the foyer of the Eliseo for the Academia Filarmonica Romana. It was a whole programme featuring Cage's music, in which I think Luciano played the piano. After the concert there was a debate, and the audience was inflamed, I can't tell you: after I finished *Fontana Mix* there was chaos! Then, during the debate, a woman got up – Ah! I had to be the interpreter, because the questions were posed in Italian, and I had to translate them for Cage into English, and then translate his answer from English to Italian again. Well, this woman got up and said:
> 'Mister Cage, how could you allow that lady to do so many obscene things?'
> 'That lady' was I, who was the interpreter! I got stuck for a minute, thinking: 'That lady?' I was like ... Finally, I translated to John and he, very calm and tranquil, kept quiet for half a minute, then he said:

---

[19] Ibid.
[20] Luciano Berio, interview in Carrie de Swaan, *Music Is the Air I Breathe* (documentary), dir. Carrie de Swaan (Amsterdam: Swaan Produkties, 1995). I report Berio's words literally, since in the excerpt he speaks in English.
[21] Cathy Berberian, interview with Silvana Ottieri; Placanica, *Cathy Berberian*, p. 34.

> 'There was a village, and in this little village there was a beautiful girl, sixteen, seventeen years old, so beautiful that there was no man from six to sixty years old that did not desire her. She was stupendous, splendid. One day, this girl went down to the small lake of the village, took off her clothes, dived into the lake, and ... the fish were frightened!'
>
> The silence that followed that sentence was fabulous ... then naturally a big applause ... There was a big silence first, perhaps because they were expecting a much more obvious ending, but that story forced them to think! I have always found this thing fabulous.[22]

The following summer, Berberian's performance of *Aria* at Darmstadt made a great impression on her audience: 'Everyone was astonished by the possibilities of the voice.'[23] A generation of young composers attending the Darmstadt summer courses started to think of Berberian's voice and charismatic stage presence as a flexible instrument for their compositions, impressed not only by her vocal qualities but by the full range of her performance abilities:

> All the invention in the use of my voice, that I had inside, would never pop out without Cage's composition. Some aspects came out with that work, but then Sylvano [Bussotti] found other ones; naturally Berio put my voice to the service of the enormous amount of music that he had inside, and so I gave him everything I had. By the time of *Aria with Fontana Mix* I was like a 'wrapped' instrument. Nobody really knew what was inside, and he [Cage] opened the package and started toying with some of the strings. But there were levers, buttons; there were lots of other things in this instrument.[24]

Aria: the score

The Henmar Press copy of the score of *Aria*, dedicated exclusively 'To Cathy Berberian' (while the future Peters score would be dedicated 'To Cathy and Luciano Berio') preserved in Cristina Berio's private archive in Los Angeles (CBLA), shows Berberian's own lead and coloured pencil markings juxtaposed to the coloured indications functioning as keys to different vocal styles.[25] The latter reproduced a unique mapping of vocal styles suggested by Berberian, and which eventually crystallized in the published version of *Aria*. In the preface to the work, Cage acknowledges

---

[22] Ibid., p. 35.
[23] Ibid. It is interesting to point out that Berberian recounts this exact story in *Cathy's Solo Talk Show*, which shows that she was used to 'performing' her stories or favourite anecdotes, as if they were a script, fashioning her divadom and feeding the aura that surrounded her *persona*. Cathy Berberian, 'Cathy's Solo Talk Show', p. 40.
[24] Ibid.
[25] John Cage, *Aria* (New York: Henmar Press, 1958). Cathy Berberian's personal score preserved in her private archive in Los Angeles.

Berberian's vocal choices and invites future interpreters of the piece to lace their performances with vocal styles that best suit their voices.

> The *Aria* may be sung in whole or in part to provide a programme of determined time-length, alone or with the *Fontana Mix* or with any parts of the *Concert*.
>
> The notation represents time horizontally, pitch vertically, roughly suggested rather than accurately described. The material, when composed, was considered sufficient for a ten minute performance (page = 30 seconds); however, a page may be performed in a longer or shorter time-period.
>
> The vocal lines are drawn in Black, with or without parallel dotted lines, or in one or more of 8 colors. These differences represent 10 styles of singing. Any 10 styles may be used and any correspondence between colour and style may be established. The one used by Miss Berberian is Dark Blue = jazz; Red = Contralto (and Contralto lyric); Black with parallel dotted line = Sprechstimme; Black = dramatic; Purple = Marlene Dietrich; Yellow = coloratura (and coloratura lyric); Green = folk; Orange = oriental; Light Blue = baby; Brown = nasal.
>
> All aspects of a performance (dynamics, etc.) which are not notated may be freely determined by the singer.
>
> The black squares are any noises ('un musical' [sic] use of the voice, auxiliary percussion, mechanical or electronic devices). The ones chosen by Miss Berberian in the order they appear are: tsk tsk; footstomp; bird roll; snap, snap (fingers), clap; bark (dog); pained inhalation; peaceful exhalation; hoot of disdain; tongue click; exclamation of disgust; of anger; scream (having seen a mouse); ugh (as suggesting an American Indian); ha ha (laughter); expression of sexual pleasure.
>
> The text employs vowels and consonants and words from 5 languages: Armenian, Russian, Italian, French, and English.[26]

Noteworthy is the freedom assigned to the interpreter of the piece, a structural component of the work. In this very performance score, Berberian marked each black square with a gesture or an unmusical noise drawn in red ink. The procedure adopted by Cage and Berberian in the making of *Aria* must have been similar to the one at which Berberian hints in a 1971 letter, in which she gives Cage 'her vocal measurements'.[27] This was when Cage's *Song Book* had just seen the light of the day, and Berberian was possibly preparing her customized approach to the songs for the Holland Festival a year later. In the 1971 letter, Berberian sketches her range and lists a number of vocal styles that suit her best, a vocabulary that

---

[26] Ibid., p. i.
[27] Cathy Berberian to John Cage (letter), 1971[?], item 56:4:4, John Cage Archive, Northwestern University Library (Evanston, IL). The letter is very possibly associated with the composition of *Song Books* (Solos for Voice 3–92), 1970.

was the acid test of her subjective response to lifelong favourites and also reflected the contemporary vocal congeries to which she was exposed, imitating Joan Baez, Milizia Korgues, Sarah Vaughan, Chaliapin (doing either the Flea or Faust), Clara Cluck singing opera ('Caro nome'), Marilyn Monroe, Marlene Dietrich, Betty Boop, old-fashioned 'hill-billy' repertoire, Russian gipsy vocals, Gladys Swarthout, Callas, Sicilian peasant song and Mary Garden's rendition of 'Dépuis le jour'. 'I'm willing to try anything. The only thing I can't do is whistle ... The repertory of noises I can do? My god, I don't know – again, I'll try anything!'[28]

However, one of the most important aspects of *Aria* lies in the fact that it was conceived to be an independent piece for solo voice, which could have its own life, away from the purposes of *Fontana Mix*. As proven by the works of Nono, Berio and Stockhausen, up to that point, the voice in electro-acoustic composition was used as a 'device', an experimental tool to be fashioned in the studio. The process of emancipation that Cage and Berberian's collaborative undertaking allowed in vocal terms gradually became a metaphor for her social conquest and paved the way for the singer's career as an independent interpreter.[29]

The affinity that Berberian's performance of *Aria* had with the sensibilities of a Darmstadt audience stimulated Luciano Berio to deploy his own response to Berberian's recently 'unwrapped' instrument.[30] However, the singer also lent her voice and extraordinary performance skills to the realization and dissemination of the works of a whole generation of composers, regularly performing in vocal lecture recitals in Darmstadt, and incorporating those works into her more or less conventional recital settings. Her interpretive devices became embedded in the performance practices of those works, leaving an indelible mark as well as a burden for future performers. For instance, Berberian's masterful performance of *A Flower* by Cage, with her own percussive accompaniment on the closed piano lid, compelled any subsequent interpreter to emulate and expand her innovation and to incorporate the percussive part into their performances along with their vocal line.[31] Berio's *Folk-Songs*, all conceived entirely for Berberian's flexible voice, later required four singers to perform, while many of Bussotti's stage works, deliberately conceived and constructed for Berberian's dramatic and vocal qualities, were not performed for a long time after her death.

---

[28] Ibid. [29] Osmond-Smith, 'The Tenth Oscillator' (2014), p. 23.
[30] After *Aria* Berio composed for Berberian *Thema (Omaggio a Joyce)*, *Circles*, *Epifanie*, *Visage*, *Sequenza III*, *Folk songs* and *Recital I (for Cathy)*.
[31] Karantonis, 'Cathy Berberian and the Performative Art of Voice', pp. 163–4.

On the personal and artistic level, *Aria* was an epiphanic *medium* through which Berberian realized her own release from cultural and social constraints. Settling in Milan immediately after the war, she was surrounded by the conservative views of the city of La Scala, and by a strong anti-capitalist and chauvinist intellectual lobby that was then synonymous with anti-Americanism. Furthermore, she was also a 'Turk in Italy' and, although a classically trained singer, she apparently lacked the characteristic of 'la voce'.[32] According to Berberian's mentors, in fact, her voice was 'troppo piccola', not powerful enough to be considered suitable for opera, the only possible outlet for a talented singer in Italy. Given all these factors, Berberian created her own game, devised her new set of rules and was able to pursue her performing avidity by devising creative ways of interacting with vocal performance.

On the one hand, Cage can be credited with triggering Berberian's extraordinary contribution to twentieth-century vocal output, legitimizing her position as the irreplaceable voice and mind of the avant-garde school, the 'Muse of Darmstadt'. Berberian's performative intelligence turned her into the ideal vocalist of the avant-garde: it became almost fashionable for composers to entrust her with the creation of a work, as 'La Berberian' would secure an accurate and powerful delivery, and a successful synergy between her audience and the work. The components of such communicative acts were extra-musical, deriving from the assertive quality of Berberian's persuasive performative power and voice.

On the other hand, Cage's compositional agenda must have appealed to Berberian in unique ways. Cage maintained an open and speculative attitude towards his performers and moulded his music on their abilities, not on a pre-packaged ideal. In Cage's words:

> I had a conversation earlier that year with Karlheinz Stockhausen, and he asked, 'If you were writing a song would you write for the singer, or would you write music?' I said I would write for the singer. That's the difference between us. I would write the music. He was at the time thinking about writing a song for Cathy Berberian, and he wanted to make use of as many ways of vocal production as he could think of. He was interested in African clicking, and he was able to do that, so he put it in. He was also interested in whistling. It didn't occur to him that she couldn't whistle. She's absolutely incapable of whistling. So he gave her things to do that she was unable to do. That was why I left the theater piece unspecified. I didn't want anyone to do something he couldn't do.[33]

In addition to that, Cage and Berberian shared an intrinsic idea of the performative. Cage would refer to his experience as 'theatrical', a quality

---

[32] Vila, *Cathy Berberian Cant'atrice*, p. 42.   [33] Kostelanetz, *Conversing with Cage*, p. 115.

that made his work stand out from the others and that projected more broadly 'his lack of intentionality and planning; openness for what could occur; the impossibility of control; coincidence, transience, and perpetual transformation without any outside intervention'.[34] 4'33" incarnated this agenda perfectly: 'What could be more theatrical than the silent pieces – somebody comes on the stage and does absolutely nothing.'[35]

Berberian defined herself as a theatrical rather than a singing *persona* – a *cant'attrice* (a singing-actress) rather than a *cantante* – a belief that was apparent throughout her performing career as well as in her composition. *Stripsody* (premiered in 1966), which originated from her collaboration with the artists Eugenio Carmi and Roberto Zamarin, is a quintessential compendium of her playful spirit and is probably the most manifest synthesis of her vocal pioneering achievements, summed up in *Sequenza III* and *Aria*.

The *New Vocality* and transformations of modernist vocal performance

Cage and Berberian explored further their notions of the theatrical through their work on *Song Book* and their continual exchange in Cage's vocal repertoire. Prior to that, their work on *Aria* was perhaps crucial to Cage's developing notion of vocal performance, which carried on well into the 1980s and 1990s in his collaboration with Joan La Barbara.

With *Aria*, Berberian and Cage brought this theatrical and linguistic agenda to avant-garde vocal music, creating a space for embodied sounds in a grey area where up to that point, the voice was only used in such a manner by composers as a prolongation, or a juxtaposition, to artificial sound effects. By breaking down words from language, speech from a text, noises from different vocal emissions, Cage and Berberian re-created in vocal music the two utopias Artaud would define in his concept of *glossolalie*,[36] namely, a phonic utopia and its non-sense, a language in which each sound, syllable and idiom is scanned and explored and gives rise to *xenoglossie*, a language emerging from entangled sounds; and a somatic utopia, in which the flesh and blood of the vocal apparatus participates

---

[34] Erika Fischer-Lichte, *The Transformative Power of Performance: A New Aesthetics*, trans. Saskya Iris Jain (New York: Routledge, 2008), p. 124.
[35] Ibid.
[36] See Allen S. Weiss, 'La glossolalie et la glossographie dans les délires théologiques', trans. (French) Thomas Chantal, *Langages*, 23/91 (1988), *Les glossolalies*, 105–10; Andrew Kimbrough, *Dramatic Theories of Voice in the Twentieth Century* (Amherst: Cambria Press, 2011), pp. 112–15.

with all possible vocal noises and emissions through breath and the body to create not a simple imitation or transcription of sound but a new 'behaviour of the words'.[37]

However, the rediscovery of the voice and its palette of sound effects meant calling into play the unique performing skills and intellect of the body – in this case Berberian's – which stepped in authoritatively as a transformative agent of the composer's act, the performance platform and a range of vocabulary and possibilities that until that very moment had been entrusted only to the materiality of the sounding objects and their manipulation by the composer.

> I do not want to be misunderstood: the New Vocality is emphatically not based on the inventory of more or less unedited vocal effects which the composer may devise and the singer regurgitates, but rather on the singer's ability to use the voice in all aspects of the vocal process; a process which can be integrated as flexibly as the lines and expressions on a face.[38]

By focusing on the actual singer, capitalizing on her or his body and on the uniqueness of their performer intelligence, Berberian overturned the modernist notion of 'voice' with a new appraisal of 'singing', hence giving the singer her or his authority as a subject, relegating the singer's objectification as an apparatus of the composer's will, to that bygone gesture of modernism.

In fashioning the vocality of the avant-garde, though, the 'Muse of Darmstadt' evidenced its intrinsic contradiction: if the singer of the New Vocality was called to interact independently and in creative ways with the musical text, the voice was no longer only an ethereal medium detached from its body, but became the ultimate, yet not the only, emanation of the 'performer intelligence' of the singer. Berberian's impact on the compositional language of the avant-garde carried the 'performative scandal of the singing body',[39] which asserted itself over and over again through the live performances of a repertoire which had been instead conceived to deconstruct the performance act and deprive it of its carnality. *Aria* represented the first encounter of the 'private' and 'public' voice and thus enacted a liberating quality in affirming the bodily and subjective experience of the domestic self.[40]

---

[37] Michel Foucault, *The Order of Things: An Archaeology of the Human Sciences* (New York: Pantheon Books, 1971), pp. 47–8.
[38] Cathy Berberian, 'The New Vocality in Contemporary Music', p. 43.
[39] Duncan, 'The Operatic Scandal of the Singing Body'.
[40] Karantonis, 'Cathy Berberian and the Performative Art of Voice', p. 163.

The focus on the singing body represented a powerful shift compared to the compositional agenda of the avant-garde school and to the idiomatic language that they had associated with the voice up to that point. The anonymity typical of the *singing personae* stigmatized by Schoenberg's *Erwartung*, for instance, was conveyed in the early works of Berio, but also of Nono and Stockhausen. The powerful re-appropriation of the singer's authority in writing her or his own performance contradicted the notion of an avant-garde vocality, where the voice had to neglect the body in order to incarnate a naked ideal of purity, only attainable through electro-acoustic manipulation. The singer's voice was disembodied and reduced to a *medium*, a dehumanizing vehicle of vocal effects tending to expand the realm of artificial sounds, in total contrast with the sensually gratifying performance practices of nineteenth-century vocality. With her New Vocality, Berberian assigned creative freedom to the performer in the entirety of her or his capabilities. This attitude, just like the principles of the *recitar cantando*, restored avant-garde singing to the realm of the *affetti*, and of 'expressivity'. The communicative bridge instituted by the performer between the listener and the work was necessarily to take over the 'aesthetic of negativity', which rejected the reciprocal correspondence between emitter and recipient in an effort to shake the commodities of the subject's critical consciousness.[41]

This newly forged aesthetics resembled new notions of interiority embraced by 1980s modernist composers, a concept that 'encompassed the totality of the capacity of the feeling, desiring, thinking subject'.[42] The late twentieth-century reincarnation of this aesthetic included the figure of the avant-garde composer, among whom, obviously, John Cage needs to be mentioned. This new emphasis on the subject or, as Metzer defined it, recalling the Adornian idea of the Subject, this 'expressive persona', was to be embodied by the performer, able to effect the composer's work in original ways.[43]

Through *Aria* first and then her later formulations of the New Vocality, Berberian enacted that 'renewed emphasis on subjectivity' that projected itself in a newly found vocal expressivity, presiding over musical materials and favouring the unifying physicality of the performer over the deconstruction brought about by the text. In a few words, Berberian predicated the subjective over the objective, the power of the human over the dehumanization pursued by the avant-garde agenda of the Darmstadt school, in which, not by chance, neither Cage nor Berberian lingered.

---

[41] David Metzer, *Musical Modernism at the Turn of the Twenty-First Century* (Cambridge University Press, 2009), p. 15.
[42] Ibid. [43] Ibid.

In that new connection between the performer and the listener, enormously influential for the work's reception, the transformative power injected by Berberian created a new 'performative canon', in which the performer was called to assert her or his own identity beyond the *persona* represented on stage. The successful impersonation of the singer with her physical presence and vitality would turn the musical text into a living being, and the embodied persona could then begin to compose his or her part, thus living immanently through the song.[44]

Berberian's 'magic presence',[45] the transformative power of her performance, and her pioneering notion of the 'performative art of the voice' infused by her New Vocality, went beyond avant-garde vocality and started a different journey, beyond the ideal isolation proclaimed by an early modernist aesthetic. Berberian was able to create such impersonations successfully in all the vocal realms she crossed, reaching out to opera, chamber repertoires, avant-garde and even in her crossover covers of Beatles songs. Late modernist vocal repertoire endorsed the need for vocal gesture, the attention to the theatrical aura of the singing stage and the return to expression and communication with the audience. With that, musical composition and Western performing arts as a whole undertook the same journey, reinforcing for the new century the multilayered communicative interplay of the current scene.

---

[44] Edward T. Cone, 'Text and Texture: Song and Performance' in *The Composer's Voice* (Berkeley and Los Angeles, CA: University of California Press, 1974), p. 62, quoted in Karantonis, 'Cathy Berberian and the Performative Art of Voice', p. 156.

[45] For Eugenio Barba's theories of 'magic presence' and embodiment see Erika Fischer-Lichte, *The Transformative Power of Performance*, p. 97.

15 Radically idiomatic instrumental practice in works by Brian Ferneyhough

Anders Førisdal

Brian Ferneyhough and the radically idiomatic

The late twentieth century saw a vast proliferation of musicological discourses, one of the most interesting being the recognition of the voice of the performer. Speaking from within a musical practice, the voice of the performer can shed new light on well-known phenomena. Performance studies has been mostly directed towards historical practices rather than contemporary music, where the analytic tradition continues to prosper. Thus, despite the growing musicological interest in the music of Brian Ferneyhough, persuasive discussions of the function of instrumental practice in his work are few and far between. In this chapter I suggest that this shortcoming is the result of a possible bias towards the base matters of practice; thus one risks losing sight of the fact that Ferneyhough's work represents a transformation of the traditional function of instrumental practice in relation to composition. With Ferneyhough, the function of instrumental practice is not just a matter of translating dots into sounds, but rather an integral aspect of the compositional structure. It might very well be that this falls short of the traditional analytic framework; however, the privileged position of the performer-analyst offers a bifurcating perspective whose position from within the score, within the process of musical realization itself, might offer new insight.

Ferneyhough and instrumental practice

Ferneyhough's instrumental and vocal writing is often uncritically described in terms of defamiliarization,[1] resistance,[2] transcendental virtuosity[3] or even

---

[1] Ross Feller, 'Strategic Defamiliarization: The Process of Difficulty in Brian Ferneyhough's Music', *The Open Space Magazine*, 2 (2000), 197–202.

[2] Ross Feller, 'Resistant Strains of Postmodernism: The Music of Helmut Lachenmann and Brian Ferneyhough' in Judy Lochhead and Joseph Auner (eds.), *Postmodern Music, Postmodern Thought* (London and New York: Routledge, 2002), pp. 249–62.

[3] Fabien Lévy, 'Inintelligible, injouable, incompréhensible: La complexité musicales est-elle analytique, instrumentale, perceptive ou hétéronome?', *Itamar, revista de investigacion musical*, 1 (2008), 61–87.

unperformability[4] – in short, terms suggesting oppression and negativity. While these descriptions to a certain extent emanate from the composer's own words and might have been part of his own conceptualizations, they are not therefore necessarily valid as generalizable concepts. Such notions tend to hypostasize a rather uncritical concept of tradition and run the risk of falling into the ideological reification they often seek to address. They are also highly determined historically – after all, anything new by necessity represents a cognitive and practical challenge; otherwise it could not be called new in a strict sense and would rather have to be assessed against the background of a performer's individual history. In my view – founded both on traditional analysis and also on practical experience – this position both has methodological shortcomings and fails to grasp the transformed status of instrumental practice in these works. In the following I will sketch an alternative position with reference to the work of Jacques Derrida and Michel Foucault.

The radically idiomatic

The term *radically idiomatic* first appears in the texts and interviews of Richard Barrett in order to describe his own working methods. In his 1995 paper 'Standpoint and Sightlines (provisional) 1995', Barrett describes his attempt to let the 'generative ideas, the philosophy, of composition . . . take on a physical, *concrete* reality', which results in what he calls a '"radically idiomatic" approach to instrumental composition'.[5] This approach is further described as 'an attempt to engage as intimately as possible with the musical resources at the conjunction between performer and instrument' in order to 'dissolve the boundaries between instrumentalism and compositional materials'.[6] In a later paper, Barrett relates how the experience of improvised music has led the development of a '"radically idiomatic" conception of instrumentalism' in which 'the instrument/player combination itself, in all perspectives from ergonomic to historical, becomes the "material" from which the music is shaped'.[7] One will find evidence of the radically idiomatic approach in all of Barrett's work since *Ne songe plus à fuir* (1986) for solo cello. Barrett's concern with instrumental practice is certainly shared by his sometime teacher Brian

---

[4] Nicholas Darbon, 'Virtuosité et complexité: l'injouable selon Brian Ferneyhough', *Analyse musicale*, 52 (2005), 96–111.
[5] Richard Barret, 'Standpoint and Sightlines (provisional) 1995' in Nina Polaschegg, Uwe Hager and Tobias Richtsteig (eds.), *Diskurse zur gegenwärtigen Musikkultur* (Regensburg: ConBrio Verlagsgesellschaft, 1996), pp. 21–35, p. 26.
[6] Ibid., p. 27.
[7] Richard Barrett, 'The Possibility of Music', http://www.rogerreynolds.com/futureofmusic/barrett.html (accessed 24 February 2015).

Ferneyhough. For instance, in an interview from 1991, and in terms showing great affinities to those of Barrett, Ferneyhough states that he is 'very concerned that the things [he asks] an instrumentalist to do be so instrument-specific that they conspire to create a sort of "X-ray" of his instrument's inner essence', 'ensuring that one could not imagine any other instrument playing the same material in the same way'.[8] Similar statements are found scattered throughout his essays and interviews, although this fact is largely overlooked in the majority of analytic writing on individual works.

Practice as text and condition of discourse

With Ferneyhough, as with Barrett, this interest is pursued by including elements of the practice as material in the process of composition. In this way composition is pursued along two slopes: as the work structure embraces the conditions of its own realization, the inside of the work structure embraces its own outside so that the distinction between the inside and outside is blurred. This largely mirrors the 'double reading' associated with Jacques Derrida. The double reading takes the form of a scholarly reconstruction of the dominant interpretation of a text as well as a destabilization of this dominant interpretation by tracing an element of alterity or exteriority within the text itself.[9] Indeed one could say that in opening the work to the exteriority of practice – the simultaneous composition of the music as well as the specific practical conditions of the music – Ferneyhough similarly operates with 'two hands, two texts, two visions, two ways of listening',[10] structuring the practice and the work 'in a single gesture, but doubled'.[11] This moment of alterity marks an evasion of closure in the work. The alterity of the work is also related to Derrida's critique of presence. In an early essay, Derrida suggests that being present is being 'summarized (*résumé*) in some absolute simultaneity of instantaneity'.[12] The critique of presence is one of Derrida's central tenets, transferring Saussure's insistence on semiological difference – the recognition that any sign consists of a binary opposition of 'form' and a 'content', or a signifier and a signified – into the language of philosophy. With the

---

[8] Brian Ferneyhough, *Collected Writings*, ed. James Boros and Richard Toop, with foreword by Jonathan Harvey (Amsterdam: Harwood Academic Publishers, 1995), p. 375.
[9] Simon Critchley, *The Ethics of Deconstruction: Derrida and Levinas* (Edinburgh University Press, 1999), p. 26.
[10] Jacques Derrida, *Margins of Philosophy*, trans. Alan Bass (University of Chicago Press, 1982), p. 65.
[11] Jacques Derrida, *Dissemination*, trans. Barbara Johnson (University of Chicago Press, 1981), p. 64.
[12] Jacques Derrida, *Writing and Difference*, trans. Alan Bass (London: Routledge, 1978), p. 15.

recognition of the binary difference of the sign, a sign cannot be said to fully represent its referent; the referent can never be fully present and identical with itself. Now, the alterity of the radically idiomatic work suggests a similar critique of presence: a work embracing the structural nature of its own conditions stages the impossibility of identical interpretations, its inherent ambiguities disseminating rather than gathering meaning. This is of course at odds with the Hegelian idea of an instrument's 'inner essence' mentioned above.[13] For Derrida, the critique of presence is always a critique of metaphysics and the notion of the transcendental signifier. I will suggest reading the materially-founded instrumental practice found in Ferneyhough's work along the same line of this critique of presence. 'That which is written is never identical with itself',[14] Derrida writes; in this chapter I hope to show that this is the case with Ferneyhough's music.

Although the strict application of compositional procedures to single elements of instrumental practice has no clear precedent, it nevertheless finds its conditions in certain characteristics of earlier twentieth-century composition, all of which could be described as a transformation of the idea of composition as a writing. First, there is the emergence of sound and timbre as an important compositional determinant in composers such as Mahler, Debussy, Varèse and Webern, theorized by Schoenberg in the famous notion of *Klangfarbenmelodie*. Second, there is the recognition that musical elements could be ordered as a series, which thus allows for the serial treatment of any quantifiable entity and transforms composition into a specific form of writing (*écriture*). Third, there is the recognition of the importance of the act of performance itself, and the increasingly problematic nature of the performer's body and context from Mahler to Kagel and Lachenmann.

Often these tendencies have been interwoven, as in Messiaen's *Mode de valeurs et d'intensités*, where the structuring of articulation problematizes the relationship between received corporeal wisdom and a practical situation. While the modal structure of Messiaen's piano study results in a fixed relationship between pitch, register, articulation and other parameters, in Boulez's *Structures*, one of its many descendants, all the parameters are dissociated and timbre is decidedly decentred. Thus the performer has to reorganize his or her practice to accommodate the demands made on

---

[13] '[H]earing has to do with sound, with the vibration of a body; [here] there is merely a trembling of the object ... This ideal movement in which simple subjectivity, as it were *the soul of the body*, is expressed by its sound, is apprehended by the ear ...' Georg W. F. Hegel, *Aesthetics: Lectures on Fine Arts*, trans. T. M. Knox, 2 vols. (Oxford: Clarendon Press, 1975), vol. II, p. 621.

[14] Derrida, *Writing and Difference*, p. 29.

dynamic and timbral articulation across the whole span of the piano. With a composer like Kagel, performance as such is targeted more explicitly. Kagel's theatricalization of performance often results in a fragmentation of sound production as such, as in remarkable works like *Transición II* (1958), *Sonant (1960 . . .)* (1960) and *Improvisation ajoutée* (1962).

The double gesture of the radically idiomatic gathers these tendencies together, regulating the corporeality liberated by Kagel with the structural panopticon of parametric composition. This facilitates a decisive transformation of the function of instrumental practice within composition which now takes on a decidedly textual character. With the radically idiomatic, instrumental practice is robbed of any proximity to the 'natural', emerging rather as a cluster of multiple relationships between the instrument, the body and history, where the individual sound is a node in the network of materially concrete layers that 'are neither absolutely separate nor simply separable'.[15]

This notion of practice aligns with Michel Foucault's notion of a discursive practice as it emerges in his work from *The Archaeology of Knowledge* (1969) onwards. In Foucault's work, a discursive practice is a regulated activity that establishes certain structural conditions for the production of meaning.[16] In the present context, it suffices to note that describing instrumental practice as a discursive practice highlights the vital function practice has in the shaping of any form of music – indeed, one could argue that there is no such thing as a music which is not conditioned by a practice, something which suggests that the claims in this chapter have applications far beyond the realm of the works discussed here. However, the practice itself and the discursive relations it establishes do not form a part of the sounding music as such: '[the discursive relations] are, in a sense, at the limit of discourse: they determine the scaffold [*faisceau*] of relations that discourse must establish in order to speak . . . These relations characterize not the (*langue*) used by discourse, nor the circumstances in which it is deployed, but discourse itself as a practice.'[17] What I will look for in the analyses that follow – which is indeed what explicitly emerges with the notion of the radically idiomatic – is how the various elements of instrumental practice condition the musical surface. The discursive instrumental practice is that by which the work of music lets itself be heard, that by which the work of music comes into being as sound. The practice is not necessarily part of the music as sound, but the *condition* of the music as

---

[15] Derrida, *Dissemination*, p. 177.
[16] Michel Foucault, *The Archaeology of Knowledge*, trans. A. M. Sheridan Smith (New York: Pantheon Books, 1972), p. 117.
[17] Ibid., p. 46. Note that the English translation renders *faisceau* as *group*.

sounding expression. It is these conditions that are explicitly confronted with the radically idiomatic.

In the following I will make close readings of *Unity Capsule* and *Kurze Schatten II*, focusing on how the radically idiomatic approach is enacted in these works and showing how instrumental practice takes on a distinctly textual and discursive character. For lack of space, the analyses will necessarily only be partial, and I will leave issues of performance and interpretation aside in favour of the description of the emergence of the work as a structuring of practice – indeed, the composition of the work as a writing of the body.

Unity Capsule
There is the body, and a metal tube with holes and keys. Picking up the tube, the arms and hands position the shining object in relation to the body with a certain determined vigour, pull the loose end of the tube and wait, silently. Then, after fifteen seconds, a slight whisper is heard. Again there is silence. With the tube at the lips, another whisper as the tube is turned outwards, somehow dragging a quiet hiss out of the body which responds with activating the muscles of the lower belly in order to push the tongue down from the palate towards the teeth with a sudden flow of air from the lungs: [t]!, the muscles of the hand contracting simultaneously to produce a click on the keys of the tube.

Already in these first few bars of *Unity Capsule* (Example 15.1), one finds that the performance of the music is shaped as a result of the relationship between the body and the instrument taking part in a game of sound production – a discursive practice. The angle between

Example 15.1   Brian Ferneyhough, *Unity Capsule*, opening.

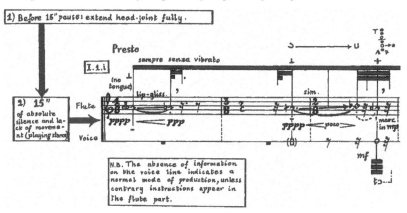

Example 15.2 Brian Ferneyhough, *Unity Capsule*, page 5, end of middle stave and opening of bottom stave.

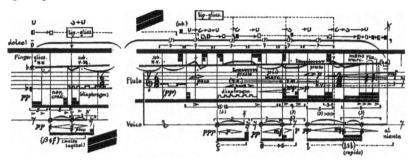

the flute and the mouth – both the angle between the mouthpiece as well as the distance to the instrument – the embouchure and breath of the player, various forms of vibrato and fingerings, as well as vocal sounds and various kinds of activity with the tongue, lips and cheeks are part of the elements that go into the subtle sculpting of the body involved in a performance of this work. It is clear that Ferneyhough is working from a constructivist principle, as one parameter is stacked on top of the other. These 'practical parameters' are no longer viewed as ornaments, but take on a decidedly structural function in the organization of the practice itself as well as the sounds that emerge from material conditions of the practice. The hierarchy between the parameters is in continual flux throughout the work, and often changes from sound to sound – indeed, single short events even constitute processual transitions in several parameters, as in Example 15.2.

The example shows section 1.4.v. In this little section, a glissando rises from a B-flat to an E. This is shown with a diamond note-head as the second partial of the E-flat square note-head, the 'o' above the diamond designating the harmonic. Above the 'o', there is a half-filled square that gives the level of embouchure tension (whereby open square = loose embouchure, half-filled square = medium embouchure and filled square = tight embouchure). The U above the embouchure square signifies the angle between the flute and the lips, graded according to five levels. The signs ⊃ and ⊂ mean that the flute should be turned inwards and outwards respectively, as far as possible 'whilst still producing recognisable pitch';[18] U means normal position, and the angled sign means a position between the normal and either extreme. One can observe how the practice takes on a textual character, single elements being identified with separate signs and

---

[18] Brian Ferneyhough (1975), *Unity Capsule*, notes for performance (London: Edition Peters).

inscribed in the notation. The score includes further instructions that will be clarified in the following.

The phrase is formed on the basis of the glissando of a given duration. The glissando, which is performed with the fingers, is confronted with another layer of glissandi performed by the lip, shown in the score as modifications to the basic line. The first lip glissando is below the basic glissando, the second above and below, then above, below, and finally above and below. However, there is further activity that affects the pitch content. For instance, there are two trills around the middle and second half of the 6/8 bar. Also, the turning of the flute as well as the change in embouchure tension subtly affects the pitch. Although the different levels are clearly articulated in the notation, in practice they rather produce what Derrida calls *dissemination*[19] – their structure is dispersed centrifugally rather than articulated, the single sound being the result of a dense and always local negotiation of practice.

Though uninterrupted, the glissando is subject to accentuations that are specified below the ledger line underneath the stave. In addition to the normal accents, a further layer of pulsation is found in the graded tremble of diaphragm impulses, which occurs twice in the example and is notated with a jagged line and marked '(diaphragm)'. These impulses also affect pitch. The sound is further sculpted by vibrato, marked n.v. or v.m. (non vibrato or molto vibrato, respectively), dynamics and, towards the end of the example, flutter tongue. The vibrato and diaphragm vibrato are in a sense conflictual, as vibrato in flute playing is often produced by diaphragm trembling.

In addition to the flute playing, the player performs certain vocal actions. These vocal sounds, which are notated on the line below the stave, are closely linked to the various shadings in the flute. The four vocal actions have a similar dynamic envelope. The first and last of these end with rapid tremulation, the former as a trill between ß and f, the latter on l. The first of these sounds, the ß, is produced by the same lip configuration used for normal flute playing – and normal embouchure should be synchronized with the start of the vocal action – which means that it is the f that stands out, further articulating another level of pulsation which is picked up by the diaphragm vibrato. The second vocal action is based on a single sound, and the third has a gradual transformation from a 'th' sound to an 's', thus gradually transforming from a dark to a bright sound not unlike the first vocal action.

---

[19] '[Dissemination] marks an irreducible and *generative* multiplicity.' Jacques Derrida, *Positions*, trans. Alan Bass (London and New York: Continuum, 2002), p. 45.

In my view, the vocal actions should not be seen as a complement to the sound of the flute proper. Rather, the two strands interact and interfere with each other in a way that could better be described as polymorphic rather than polyphonic. Indeed, the whole apparatus of the practice is polymorphic, as many of the levels of sound production operate in relation to the same flow of air or diaphragm inflexions. In the example, the various levels of articulation come together at certain critical junctures. This happens at the first lip glissando, where the basic sound is affected by the dip in pitch that is simultaneous with the vocal crescendo, the onset of diaphragm vibrato as well as normal vibrato and the turning of the flute away from the mouth. The flute is returned to normal position as the lip glissando is finished, and the normal vibrato stops. As the diaphragm settles, a new lip glissando develops, underscored by a small crescendo, along with rapid turning of the flute and change of embouchure tension. Again, from the normal sound a new vocal action and diaphragm vibrato sets in, seemingly to trigger yet another lip glissando, as well as the onset of a trill, the tightening of the embouchure and a turn of the flute. As the sound just about reaches normal, the third vocal sound sets in, this time reaching its maximum dynamic simultaneously with an increase in vibrato that commenced with the second vocal action and ends as the last one is fading in. Thus, the different practical elements inscribe themselves into each other reciprocally as a chain of signifiers, one level affecting the articulation of the other, making them neither absolutely separate nor simply separable.

The different articulations that I have described in detail form a single musical phrase. Now my question is, what is the material of such a phrase? Should the various transformations of sound and texture be seen merely as an addition, a colourful supplement to the allegedly basic finger glissando? Is it possible to sustain a position that views the different elements of the practice as something outside the music proper? I would say no. I suggest, instead, seeing the different elements of the practice as a play of meaning between the various parameters, a game where the differentiated interaction of the elements produces a structure of instrumental practice without a fixed centre. Excepting the vocal actions, the performer activities sculpted in this brief excerpt are all important and basic elements in flute playing. These are unhinged by Ferneyhough and given individual status in the compositional fabric, the intrinsic heterogeneity of the practice being unleashed with centrifugal force in the game of negotiation between the different practical parameters. This game negotiates the conditions of the musical surface, the relations of the discursive instrumental practice determining the scaffold from which the music as sound emanates. In

Unity Capsule, this practical game is spelled out visibly in the notation. In later pieces, like *Kurze Schatten II*, the double gesture of the radically idiomatic is not always upfront, but rather found below the surface.

Kurze Schatten II

Kurze Schatten II, Ferneyhough's only work for guitar solo, was written between 1983 and 1988 and was first performed by Magnus Andersson in 1990. The title refers to Walter Benjamin's *Kurze Schatten*, a collection of seven short texts. This format is reflected in the seven movements of the guitar piece, even though the music does not stand in an illustrative relation to the texts. The movements are arranged in three pairs of slow and fast movements, with a fantasy-like movement at the end. In the following, I will focus on three basic elements of classical guitar practice which are treated as musical material in the work: resonance, pitch, and left-hand fingering and left-hand position playing.

One of Benjamin's texts describes how the shadow of an object gradually shortens as the sun approaches the zenith, leaving the object fully exposed to the sunlight. One trajectory that runs through the whole of *Kurze Schatten II* is modelled on this process. At the beginning of the work, four of the six strings of the instrument are detuned. Strings 6, 5 and 1 return to standard tuning after movements two, four and six, respectively. The resonance of the instrument is altered in this process, from the eccentric towards the normal. However, the instrument does not quite reach its traditional identity: the second string never returns to its standard tuning, and the very last line of the seventh movement is written for this string only. The resonance of the instrument is found in the natural harmonics of the strings, which produce sympathetic reverberation while playing. So when the instrument is detuned the natural harmonics change, and the sympathetic resonance is transformed.

The importance of natural harmonics is clear from the first movement, where they take on a very specific structural function. The form of the first movement is quite straightforward in its presentation of a single process and the reversal of the same process from the middle of the movement. Two opposing layers of material take part in this process. The first is a two-part textural layer of natural harmonics, and the second layer juxtaposes six different types of gestural material – pizzicati, melodic lines, chords and so on. Simply put, in the first half of the movement, the gestural activity increases as the number of harmonics is gradually reduced. The second half of the movement, from the reintroduction of harmonics in bar 13 until the

Radically idiomatic instrumental practice 289

Example 15.3 *Kurze Schatten II*, mvt. 1, bars 1–6.

end, presents a reversal of this process. Example 15.3 shows the opening page of the score.

So, in principle, the process itself is very simple; what is more complex is the relationship between the two layers. The activity and the notation of the harmonic layer condition the activity of the other material, because as long as a string is occupied by a harmonic, it cannot be employed for the other layer of material. It should be noted that it is the notated duration that specifies what strings are occupied by harmonics – in many cases the actual sound of a harmonic has died out before the string in question is available for gestural activity. Because of the pitch layout of the guitar fingerboard and the quarter-tone scordatura, the occupation of strings by the harmonics influences the formation of the various gestures quite heavily – for instance, small intervals are often available only by way of long leaps across the fingerboard, and the number of possible chord voicings is highly reduced. Another result of the microtonal scordatura is that some pitches are available only on one string in a given context. Moreover, the contexts change as the harmonics change, resulting in a kaleidoscopic rearrangement of the pitches available and the possibilities for gestural activity.

Of course, a similar phenomenon occurs in any work for guitar where natural harmonics are supposed to be sustained across other types of material, such as Elliott Carter's *Changes* (1981). In this piece it is clear that harmonics are chosen for their pitch content and their use is a reference to the ringing changes to which the title of the piece alludes.[20] In the Carter, harmonics are not used to order or govern a structural process as they are in *Kurze Schatten II*.

A further important aspect is the relationship between the different layers of sound and the metric/rhythmic grid. The French composer Jean-Paul Chaigne has discussed the compositional procedures involved in this movement in detail.[21] I will briefly sum up the main points of the arithmetic procedure employed. The numerator 5 of the first metric designation 5/8 governs the number of parts in the whole movement; the numerators of the metres in the first part govern the number of bars in each part (5, 3, 4, 4 and 4 bars, respectively); the metres of the various parts are based on the metres from the first part. For the rhythms of the two harmonic parts, rhythmic subdivisions of the bars are calculated by simple procedures of addition and subdivision of values from the metres. Another calculation based on the same values is applied for how many of the subdivided rhythmic units should pass between each note. A similar procedure is used to generate rhythmic subdivisions of the bars that determine the entry points of the gestural material, the duration of the individual gestures as well as their order of appearance.

Though these seem like somewhat abstract procedures, it is important to note that with the radically idiomatic, the abstract turns concrete as the

---

[20] Elliott Carter (1983), *Changes* (New York: Boosey and Hawkes).
[21] Jean-Paul Chaigne, 'La complexité de la musique de Brian Ferneyhough: Étude philologique et esthétique', unpublished DMA dissertation, University of Nice – Sophia Antipolis (2008). See especially pp. 68–90.

instrumental practice reveals itself as a discursive practice. The basic procedure used to generate the number of parts of the movement, the metric structures as well as the density of activity directly affect the durations of the harmonics, and thus directly condition the practical possibilities for gestural activity on the surface – formal procedures actually condition the continually changing layout of the fingerboard and thus what pitches are available at a given moment. That is, the network of parameters forms a chain of signs, one signifier grafting itself onto the other.

Analyzing pitch structures in *Kurze Schatten II*, one is confronted with a very interesting theoretical, and indeed methodological, question: which set of pitches should be analyzed? The question concerning pitch in *Kurze Schatten II* is also rooted in the microtonal scordatura. Pitch structures in *Kurze Schatten II* are worked out and notated at fingered pitch, and not sounding pitch, the latter being the result of the filtering of the former through the scordatura. Given the established priority of pitch both in the theoretical and analytic tradition, the subtle dismantling of this superior musical parameter in *Kurze Schatten II* is of great interest. Although the non-identical relationship between notated and sounding pitch is a major issue in *Kurze Schatten II* as a whole, it is particularly pressed in the second movement. Before discussing pitch in some detail below, I will first explain the rhythmic level of this movement, which presents a bifurcating play of differences analogous to that of pitch.

The second movement has six sections, all of which consist of six bars. The musical flow of this movement is based on two opposing processes. While the notated tempo decreases with each new section, the notated density increases quite dramatically throughout the movement. The music transforms from a quasi-motivic texture with highly differentiated rhythms towards long chains of rather undifferentiated material at the end. Although these processes appear to be quite simple, for the reader of the score the effect is that the notation thus draws attention to its own status and function, the relationship between notation and perception being explicitly problematized as the notation represents a quite dramatic fall in pacing while the actual music is propelled forward with seemingly unhinged energy.

The level of pitch is also, at the outset, quite simple. A sequence of fifty pitches makes up the material for the first section. This material is repeated at the head of each section and is treated in a relatively free manner with ad hoc pitch repetitions and omissions (this is particularly the case with the first four pitches). The opening bars of the first and sixth sections provide examples of the varied disposition of the pitch material (see Example 15.4).

Example 15.4 *Kurze Schatten II*, mvt. 2, bars 1–4 (example 15.4a) and 31–32 (example 15.4b).

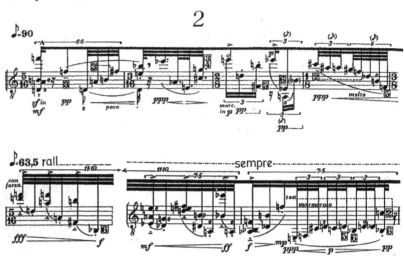

However, as the number of pitches required to fill each section increases along with the increase in rhythmic density, more pitches are added at the tail of the sequence, resulting in a series of 119 pitches in section six.

As in the first movement, the music is initially based on certain characteristic gestures – chords, linear passages, arpeggios and so on. The music seems to be worked out at notated pitch and with little regard for resulting pitch structures, surface continuity being rather achieved through motivic proximity. In the first movement, fingerings are specified for every note because of the continual reconfiguration of the fingerboard that conditions the different material types. In contrast, in the second movement there is a relative freedom of choice of fingering – *relative* freedom, because in practice there are often few decisions open to choice, the complex interplay of different materials being worked out with a specific fingering in mind even where this is not indicated in the score. The point is that the scordatura and the relative freedom of the performer ultimately leave pitch structures in the hands of the performer. The scordatura and fingering choices function as a filter for the end result, the notation of pitch signifying possibilities of fingering (i.e. a combination of string, fret number, left- and right-hand finger), which are translated into sounding pitch. Of course, this is part of the play of meaning in this movement, just as the level of notated tempo. This play of meaning is indeed a conditioned function of the notation – of the music as a form of *writing* – the bifurcation of a stable element where two independent levels that emerge 'together

Example 15.5 *Kurze Schatten II*, mvt. 2, bar 7.

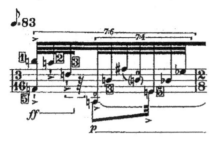

at once and separately'.[22] However, the play is staged in the notation on the level of pitch as it is on the level of tempo. The continual deferral of stable pitch structures is occasionally highlighted in the material as in bar 7, the opening bar of the second section (see Example 15.5).

In the example, the pitch B appears four times, the last time as a B-flat. However, only two of these sound as notated: the first B, on the first string, sounds a quarter-tone flat; the second sounds as written, the third, notated in parenthesis, which means it should be slurred on the second string, results in a B-flat like the last one, which needs to be played on the fourth string because the first finger has to fret the E-natural on the fifth string. Thus, rather than having three successive Bs and a B-flat, there is a B-quarter-flat, B, B-flat and B-flat. One could add that the A on the second string results in an A-flat, and that the low A open fifth string – indicated by the 'o' – results in a B-quarter-flat just like the B on the first string. Also, another interesting detail is that the sound of the E on the fifth string is higher than the F-sharp in the middle of the bar – the E results in an F-quarter-sharp, and the F-sharp results in an F-natural. It should be noted that in this particular example all fingerings are clearly implied in the notation. The play indicated here between the written material and the sounding result is present throughout the movement. However, due to one string returning to normal tuning between every other movement, the discrepancy between the notation and result is transformed throughout the work as a whole. Nevertheless, the explicit problematization of the relationship between notation and realization – one could also say, between its structure and phenomenology – is established within the work itself, and does not disappear from the process of interpretation even if, in comparison to an earlier work like *Unity Capsule*, it appears to have vanished from the immediate surface of the notation. The play of the signifier is not terminated even if it fades out of view – it is continuously

---

[22] Derrida, *Margins of Philosophy*, p. 65.

mediating the gap between the two slopes of the double gesture: the abstract and concrete levels of the notation.

If the dissemination of pitch structure in the first movement of *Kurze Schatten II* is worked out on the basis of a continual modification of the strings available, and in the second movement stages the interminable play of the signifier, in the fourth movement pitch material is based on the principle of position playing. Position playing is an important element in guitar technique and helps to orient the player around the fingerboard. Simply put, a position designates the fret where the left-hand index finger is and is marked in the score with roman numerals. Fingerboard position is a decisive trait of Ferneyhough's guitar-writing: he adheres to position playing very strictly, and the left hand is usually fixed in one position of the fingerboard at any one time with the fingers fixed in one fret each. This is in great contrast to what one finds in the guitar works of someone like Chris Dench, who has a much more flexible approach to left-hand activity.

A large matrix found among the sketch material held at the Paul Sacher Stiftung in Basel suggests how the left-hand activity for this hand was determined.[23] Now, if one places one finger in consecutive frets and on different strings, one gets a four-note handgrip,[24] or a six-note handgrip if the two open strings are played as well. In the fourth movement of *Kurze Schatten II*, these different elements are treated as separate parameters and combine to form the pitch material of the movement. To determine the handgrips that were to be employed, Ferneyhough worked out a system that designates the following parameters: left-hand position, string combination (always including open strings), finger pattern, the number of strings to be employed and which strings to be used. A large table of the required number of handgrips was worked out that specifies the patterns or values of the various parameters. Interestingly, a partial copy of a fully worked-out handwritten chart bears the heading 'Random string combinations',[25] suggesting that the parameters were not worked out according to specific rules meant to generate a structural coherence in the material. This is not to suggest that the music as such lacks coherence, but rather that what coherence is there is necessarily to be found at the surface of the music as sound, as it has been formed as practice on the instrument. In the sketches, the actual handgrips are also written out in succession in staff notation and this order is strictly adhered to throughout the movement. The generative procedure arguably does not result in a *structure* at all; it is

---

[23] Folder marked *Kurze Schatten II*, Paul Sacher Stiftung, Basel.
[24] I employ the term 'handgrip' rather than chord, as the combination of pitches has no structural function.
[25] Folder marked *Kurze Schatten II*, Paul Sacher Stiftung, Basel.

Radically idiomatic instrumental practice

Example 15.6 *Kurze Schatten II*, mvt. 4, bars 6–8.

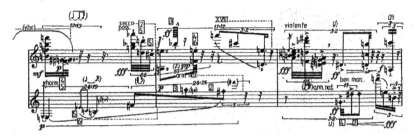

Example 15.7 *Kurze Schatten II*, mvt. 4, bars 26–27.

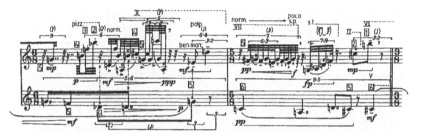

simply the dissemination of practical elements as a set of discursive relations that condition the aural surface.

One should notice that most practical parameters do not possess any aural correlate – the single elements of the practice are actually mute, sound only occurring when elements are brought together. A finger, string or fingerboard position has no sound in itself, thus relating clearly to the quote from Foucault above regarding the discursive relations being found at the limits of discourse: the elements of the practice are not themselves part of the music strictly speaking, but rather the conditions through which the music can emerge. Thus the relationship between the work and interpretation is deconstructed as mutually dependent. By extension the notation is analogously deconstructed, any clear distinction between the descriptive and the prescriptive being continually deferred.

The movement is a kind of scherzo in three parts. The first part, comprising nineteen bars in a steady 3/8 metre, is again based on different kinds of musical gestures as in movements one and two discussed above (see Example 15.6). The second part of the movement is based on the principle of melody and accompaniment (a rare texture in Ferneyhough's work), the soft, slow-moving melody being constructed on the basis of the succession of handgrips given, the remaining pitches of the handgrips being employed in rapid arpeggio figurations that often cover the melody (see Example 15.7).

Example 15.8 *Kurze Schatten II*, mvt. 4, bars 34–35.

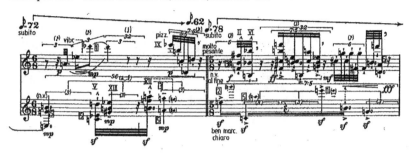

The last section sees the music regaining pace, and the two-part writing of section two becomes more complex. Full chords supplant the melody, and the function of the accompaniment is dismissed in favour of a more characteristic gestural material. This process is facilitated by the introduction of natural harmonics in the melodic part, which enables the left hand to change position even if a sound is sustained. However, it should be pointed out that this is only a possibility when two consecutive chords have an open string in common on which the harmonic can be played (see Example 15.8).

With regard to the examples from the fourth movement, it should be noted that strings 5, 2 and 1 are still at scordatura tuning.

There are many other generative processes that go into this movement which are beyond the scope of this chapter. Suffice it to mention that the density of position changes is much higher in the first than in the second section, suggesting the frequency of position changes has been worked out as a separate structural level. The changes and the chords that occur are largely counter-intuitive, especially as the player ventures into the upper regions of the fingerboard. Further, there is an interesting relationship between the pitch range of the material and the actual position; often one has to make a leap from a low to high position in order to play a descending line or vice versa, so that the surface materials are at odds with the result of the generative process, producing yet another bifurcation. In this way, a form of phrasing is implied that takes into account the inherent conflict between a legato melodic line and the formalist application of position playing, thus explicitly extending the compositional decisions into the domain of musical interpretation. This would mark the possibility of reading Ferneyhough's work along the lines of a critique of metaphysics. Any decisions with regard to form, musical material or local detail always seem to find its conditions in the materiality of the instrumental practice.

The radically idiomatic and the impossibility of closure

What should be clear from the examples from *Kurze Schatten II* as well as the discussion of the two brief excerpts from *Unity Capsule* is that the musical material and form of these works are inextricably linked to the practicalities of the instrumental forces for which they are written. The inherently conflicting generative methods employed suggest an affinity to the positive negation that Adorno located in the disruption of the orchestral body in Mahler, and which was such a powerful tool in his own thinking.[26] However, I suggest instead that, in the works considered here, the construction of the work must be seen as a double gesture that includes both the structuring of the aural musical surface while simultaneously constructing a work-specific instrumental practice that takes into account the corporeality of performance and the materiality of its instrumental forces.

A double writing, then, of music and the body, the inscription of the one into the other without the two ever becoming one, as the body of the other – the performer – is invited, indeed presupposed, to enact the emergence of the work through the process of interpretation and corporeal realization: the work structuring the body and the body structuring the work – a double writing marking a transformation of the relationship between practice and composition, a transformation facilitated from within musical writing. Returning to the notion of the radically idiomatic, it should be clear that what is found in Ferneyhough is not a mere defamiliarization or probing of the impossible. At work amid the conflicting lines of force of the compositional process, the works do so much more than push idiomatic writing towards idiomatic extremes in search of novel sounds and techniques. Rather, I would claim that these works spell out the deconstruction of the mutual dependence of work and body in their alterity, assessing this interdependence in the form of a reworking of their most basic common conditions.

'Deconstruction opens a reading by locating a moment of alterity within a text', writes Critchley,[27] and he quotes Derrida: 'Deconstruction is ... an opening towards the other.'[28] This is what I find in the musical texts of Ferneyhough and the radically idiomatic works of Barrett as well as Klaus K. Hübler and certain other composers: an alterity of work and body that evades closure with regard to its own identity. For the inclusion of the

---

[26] Theodor W. Adorno, *Mahler: A Musical Physiognomy*, trans. Edmund Jephcott (University of Chicago Press, 1992), p. 15.
[27] Critchley, *The Ethics of Deconstruction*, p. 28.
[28] Derrida quoted in Critchley, *The Ethics of Deconstruction*, p. 28.

outside is the opposite of closure: it is to explicitly open the work to the physical play of bodies. This alterity marks the impossibility of closure in a radically idiomatic instrumental practice, the recognition that musical notation always already presupposes the agency of a physical body and a practice by which it is conditioned and always already presupposes the undoing of its own structuration through the interminable play of signification.

16 The ethics of performance practice in complex music after 1945

Tanja Orning

Opus breve (1987)[1] for solo cello, by Klaus K. Hübler, is notated on three staves, decoupling the hands in a complex parametric polyphony of independently performed actions; the score pushes the boundaries of both the performer and the instrument to the extreme. The score is densely written, with multiple overlapping layers and cascades of nested irrational rhythms throughout. There is an explosive abundance of material, more than a human can grasp, much less execute in compliance with the score according to Western classical performance practice.

In this chapter, *Opus breve* provides a case study for discussing the development of performance practice in post-war complex contemporary music. I will argue that in the music of Hübler (and similar composers), there is a shift of focus from the score as musical text to the action embodied in performance, a shift that calls for a complementary shift in performance practice: a transformation of a linear and transparent model of performance practice, in which the idea of *Werktreue* is central, into a performance practice that embraces its own ambiguity and its critical and performative potential. Principally in the twentieth century, the *Werktreue* ideal came to reflect a positivistic approach to music, becoming an ideology of replication, of the possibility of a transparent rendering of what is notated. Accepting and embracing the ambiguity in a work's notation and performance, on the other hand, opens a creative space for the performer, a space where several areas are yet to be explored.

Hübler's music has been related to the 'New Complexity',[2] an aesthetic notational and performance direction emerging in the 1970s, associated

---

[1] Klaus K. Hübler, *Opus Breve Für Violoncello* (Wiesbaden: Breitkopf & Härtel). Composed in 1987 and published in 1988.
[2] The term was coined by Richard Toop in his article 'Four Facets of "the New Complexity"', *Contact*, 32 (1988), 4–50. Although the music that falls under this umbrella term is highly individualistic, and the composers come from different backgrounds and nationalities and have different intentions and styles, their music shares traits such as the use of micro intervals, highly complex rhythms, rapid changes and fluctuations, and – perhaps their strongest common characteristic – the employment of a notational intricacy that leads to dense and complex scores.

with, and represented in, works by Brian Ferneyhough, Klaus Hübler, James Dillon, Richard Barrett, Liza Lim and Michael Finnissy, among others. The term has been linked with the Darmstadt summer courses, as Ferneyhough coordinated the composition courses there between 1982 and 1996. The New Complexity can be seen partly as a reaction to the New Simplicity of the 1960s, but it is perhaps better understood as a continuation of avant-garde practices, pursuing the exploration of notational and performative potentials. Rather than rejecting history, these highly intricate and detailed notational practices sought to explore serialist parameters further, in specifying and separating performance actions down to the smallest detail. The scores are not theoretical constructs, but prescriptions for action – they have to be acted out and performed in order for the works to be constituted. Using concrete performance operations as compositional material, the work concept is challenged as the ontology of the work is now interwoven with the performance actions. This, then, is a performative transformation of the compositional material which foreshadows the emerging performative turn, offering an acute reflection on the mediation of music.

The extremely high demands this music makes upon its performers are an important part of this aesthetic direction, and the focus of my investigations. I argue in this chapter that the composer's and performer's aesthetics are not aligned and I will explore the unsolvable ethical dilemmas this disagreement causes for the performer. Elements in the performance practice discussed in this chapter can be understood as a continuation of qualities already latent within earlier modernist performance practice, but they also suggest a return to *pre*-modernist practices when musicians adopted a greater interpretational freedom.

Opus breve

The relatively small but original oeuvre of the German composer Klaus K. Hübler (b. 1956) has been overlooked to a certain extent, perhaps because of his sudden withdrawal from composition due to serious illness between 1989 and 1995.[3] Between 1981 and 1989, he explored an idiosyncratic polyphonic notational system, which facilitated the independent organization of performance actions. He used his decoupled notational approach for the first time in *'Feuerzauber' auch Augenmusik* (1981), for three flutes,

---

[3] The literature on Hübler is scarce. He was left out of the *New Grove II* (an article was added to the online edition in 2010) and does not have an entry in Wikipedia. He resumed composing in 1995 but has not pursued the radical instrumental aesthetics.

Example 16.1   Klaus K. Hübler, *Opus breve*, page 1.

harp and cello, going on to compose a series of solo works[4] in which he applied the decoupling of the physical actions, as well as *Cercar* (1983) for trombone,[5] *Grave e sfrenato* (1985) for oboe, *Opus breve* (1987) for solo cello and *Reißwerck* (1987) for solo guitar. The use of decoupled notation culminated in his third string quartet *Dialektische Fantasie* (1982–4), in which each individual instrument is notated on up to five staves. Although clearly drawing on the general advancement in notational and instrumental aesthetics,[6] he was a pioneer in systematically developing the decoupled notation technique.

Opus breve, as its title reflects, is a short work, consisting of only eleven measures and lasting approximately one and a half minutes in performance. Avery and Cox call *Opus breve* 'one of the most difficult [works] ever written for the cello', and note that it 'has received more than 200 performances in its first two decades'.[7]

The score is divided into three staves, which constitute separate musical, rhythmic and technical layers (see Example 16.1). The lowest stave represents the left hand's actions on the fingerboard. The four lines of the middle stave represent the four strings, and the rhythms notated indicate the movements between the strings. The top one-line stave indicates the to-and-fro rhythmic motion performed by the bow, sometimes coinciding with the change of string, which is then shown by a common stave drawn through the two staves, but more often prescribed independently of the

---

[4] Hübler did not use decoupled notation in *Sonetto LXXXIII del Michelangelo* (1986) for solo piano and *Finale und kurzes Glück* (1989) for solo trumpet, although the technical demands of both pieces are very high.

[5] In *Cercar*, Hübler separated the layers of breath impulse, slide, harmonics and mute.

[6] Several composers used multiple-stave notation, among them Brian Ferneyhough, Mauricio Kagel, Heinz Holliger and Aldo Clementi. Apart from specifying which string to play on, Aldo Clementi's four-stave score *Lento* (1994), for cello solo, is purely descriptive in its notation.

[7] James Avery and Franklin Cox, 'Hübler, Klaus K.' in Stanley Sadie and John Tyrrell (eds.), *The New Grove Dictionary of Music and Musicians*, 2nd edn. Version at Grove Music Online.

change and notated separately. The bow parameters are notated above the upper stave, describing point of contact as well as bowing techniques. Though not designated in a separate stave, these effectively function as a fourth layer. There are four dynamic parameters: the markings on staves 1–3 indicate the intensity of the percussive finger attack, the intensity of the bow pressure and the speed of the bow motion, and the fourth denotes the overall sonic result.

The idiosyncratic mixture of prescriptive[8] (tablature or action notation) and descriptive (result-oriented or traditional) notation facilitates the independent treatment of the performance actions. This parametric polyphony[9] or multi-parametric notational practice can be seen, on one level, as a continuation of the serialist conception of separating parameters, although it does not treat the performance parameters in serial structures. The parameters in question are unlike those of the serialists, as they are not traditional musical parameters – pitch, duration, dynamics and articulation – but technical ones: they indicate the separated playing techniques such as bow position, type of bowing, bow speed, bowing rhythms and left-hand articulations. The serialist attitude to parameter is now applied to the physical aspects of performance, a development that has occurred within a context of several kinds of innovation over the past forty years, including microtonal composition and work with recorded sound.[10] What is new with Hübler is that he breaks down every component in the instrumental practice and identifies and names separate parts of the instrumental practice that have not previously been considered on their own, but only heard together in a merged entity. He explores sonic details from the edges of instrumental practice, only reached by his hyper-detailed notation and combination of earlier uncoupled performance actions. Idiomatic boundaries are thus challenged, extended, isolated and renamed, something that will be discussed further in relation to an idea of *radically idiomatic instrumentalism*.

---

[8] Charles Seeger, 'Prescriptive and Descriptive Music-Writing', *The Musical Quarterly*, 44/2 (1958), 184–95; Mieko Kanno, 'Prescriptive Notation: Limits and Challenges', *Contemporary Music Review*, 26/2 (2007), 231–54.

[9] The term *parametric polyphony* was introduced by Brian Ferneyhough, describing his work *Unity Capsule* (in Brian Ferneyhough and James Boros, 'Shattering the Vessels of Received Wisdom', *Perspectives of New Music*, 28/2 (1990), 6–50, p. 24).

[10] Pierre Boulez and Karlheinz Stockhausen are examples of composers expanding the serial technique to multiple compositional parameters. Examples of early experiments with performance parameters as musical material are Messiaen's *Mode de valeur* (1950) prescribing twelve different types of attack and Stockhausen's wind quintet *Zeitmasse* (1956), which treats musical time as dependent on the abilities of the individual player, with indications like 'As fast as possible' and 'As slow as possible'.

Several new combinational techniques emerge from the continuous transitions between tone and noise in *Opus breve*. Different degrees of pressure applied with the left hand, in combination with different bow-speeds, produce a multitude of sound qualities, ranging from unpitched sounds to *flautando* whisperings. The left-hand techniques include tapping of the fingertips, harmonics and half-harmonics. Tapping, or 'hammer-on' as it is called, produces two pitches, one from either side of the stopping point. A half-harmonic occurs when the finger is pressed slightly harder than a harmonic, but does not reach the fingerboard. Both the harmonic and the fundamental will sound when the finger is placed on a natural harmonic, whereas a multiphonic will occur when placed between harmonics. In addition to these, Hübler prescribes several degrees of left-hand finger pressure on stopped notes. He makes extensive use of the wood of the bow, in *col legno* alone, as well as in transitions and combinations with *ordinario, sul pont* and *sul tasto*. Also novel is the use of the parameters that control the bow – velocity and pressure – as agents of dynamic nuance. The fast transitions back and forth between *sul pont, ordinario* and *sul tasto* create great timbral variations.

Viewed separately, the left-hand stave is written in descriptive notation, with pitches, rhythms and frequent trills and glissandos. The radical new aspect that arises from the decoupling is that the left hand becomes rhythmically autonomous. The fingers of the left hand play a rhythm that differs from both the bow's back-and-forth movements and the rhythm of the string transitions; together, they form a three-part rhythmic polyphony. Assigning different rhythmic functions to the separate performance actions is a prerequisite for the experience of the polyphonic strata in the sonic domain, as each rhythmic stratum filters the others when they all take place simultaneously. When the top one-line stave showing the rhythm of the bow's back-and-forth movements is filtered through the string transitions and the left-hand actions, the left hand's voice loses its fundamental pitch-creating function as we know it from traditional performance practice. The sound that comes out is scattered fragments of the left hand's voice. The widespread use of bracketed rhythms speed the music up and slow it down, as if shifting gears.

In a sense, Hübler has orchestrated the cello; he treats it almost like a keyboard instrument, with four-finger chords throughout the piece. Between the chords, one or more fingers of the left hand are almost always engaged in a glissando, producing a sound in constant flux. This juxtaposition of the vertical (chords) and horizontal (textural) layers roughly constitutes the musical material of *Opus breve*. The chords serve as markers – like structural columns, keeping the piece together and defining the sonic space in an almost architectural fashion. The visual representation bears likeness to traits in baroque scores, with fast black passages, trills and tremolandos leading to gestural chords, often with grace notes. This is not surprising when we know that Hübler studied musical rhetoric in renaissance and baroque music.[11]

While Hübler treats the cello as a chordal (keyboard) instrument, he undermines the very same function in the remaining material. By leaving the limitations of the well-tempered-keyboard way of thinking, Hübler explores, challenges and expands the sonic and microtonal world. By dissolving the diatonic paradigm, he allows a new world of sounds to break free, with subtle transitions between pitch and non-pitch, sound and noise, and sound and silence. This sound-world requires its own set of instrumental techniques and musical expression. It is not new, though: we know this world from Helmut Lachenmann, Brian Ferneyhough and numerous contemporary composers, as well as performers within freely improvised music.

Radically idiomatic instrumentalism

Polemical discussions about the nature and necessity of notation have always surrounded the music of the so-called New Complexity. A common criticism of this music has been that the scores are the epitome of theoretical constructs and intellectual fantasies, expressed in an excessive density of score writing that is not rooted in a musical performance, implying that the complex writing is intended only for the eye,[12] for the analysers and musicologists rather than for musicians. But, contrary to the impression given by the extremely intricate notation, Hübler's approach is entirely idiomatic in the sense that he uses the physical properties of the cello, the way it is played with all its mechanics and acoustic properties, as his starting point. His studies of the cello gave him the tools for a 'critical examination of the instrument',[13] while his main innovations are found in the separation of the different playing actions so that they can be combined

---

[11] Avery and Cox, 'Hübler, Klaus K'.

[12] The obvious discrepancy between Hübler's meticulous notation and the sound result has been associated with the term *Augenmusik* (Eye Music) – elaborate notation which portrays the music visually but when performed is unnoticed by listeners. Hübler plays with the term in naming his earlier work *'Feuerzauber' auch Augenmusik* (1981), and in his third string quartet there are long stretches of 'dumb' music, played almost inaudibly, but still meticulously notated in the score.

[13] Klaus K. Hübler, 'Expanding String Technique', trans. Frank Cox in Frank Cox, Wolfram Schurig and Claus-Steffen Mahnkopf (eds.), *Polyphony and Complexity: New Music and Aesthetics in the 21st Century* (Hofheim: Wolke Verlag, 2002), pp. 233–44, p. 233.

in countless new ways. Everything he has written in *Opus breve* is playable. It is beyond doubt very difficult, but nevertheless it is possible to execute.[14] Critical examination is also applied to the instrumental practice, which is challenged and stretched in all directions through the new perspective on the instrument. Hübler's aim is to superimpose dialectically his ideas upon the idiomatic materiality of the cello: 'there must be a permanent tension between the instrument and the intention'.[15] I would say, rather, that the dialectic tension takes place between the performer's intentions, ability and creativity in interpreting the scores and the composer's intentions and visions. This permanent tension, between his deep knowledge of the instrument's potential, coupled with his conceptual ideals concerning the disassembling of the physical gestures, has been named 'radically idiomatic instrumentalism'. According to composer/performer Richard Barrett, the term 'denotes music which radicalizes the concept of what it means for composition to be "idiomatic" to instruments'.[16]

Traditionally, the term 'idiomatic' is applied to music written within the natural physical limitations of specific instruments and the human body. Of course, the accepted boundaries of what constitutes idiomatic have been linked to certain criteria and have changed through history; they are also perceived differently in different communities. Nevertheless, idiomaticism is primarily associated with what is natural and comfortable to play. One of the radical aspects in radically idiomatic instrumentalism, then, is its challenging of the comfortable and familiar in relation to the instrument, leading the way into rare and unfamiliar techniques and sonic worlds. The fundamental meaning of 'radical' in this context is that it simply takes the way the instrument is played, from its very roots, and uses it as a starting point for composing. The physicality of playing, down to the smallest detail, becomes the material for composition. The works originate

---

[14] It is important to distinguish between compositions built upon an idiomatic reality and those that disregard what is practically possible. Ferneyhough is known to build dummies/models of instruments to be able to work out fingerings carefully. In addition, he has played several instruments himself: 'In younger years I managed tolerably almost everything that could blow; starting with the full spectrum of brass and, shortly thereafter, complementing this valuable experience with self-tutoring on most woodwinds. For a brief period in 1965, I was a professional trumpet player with the BBC in Birmingham; later, in London I was employed as a peripatetic woodwind teacher.' Ferneyhough in Christopher Fox, 'The Extended Clarinet: Four Contemporary Approaches' in Roger Heaton (ed.), *The Versatile Clarinet* (London: Routledge, 2006), pp. 15–30, pp. 16–17.

[15] Hübler, 'Expanding String Technique', p. 244.

[16] Richard Barrett, private email correspondence, 15 November 2011. The term was introduced by Barrett in 'Standpoint and Sightlines (provisional) 1995' in Nina Polaschegg, Uwe Hager and Tobias Richtsteig (eds.), *Diskurse zur gegenwärtigen Musikkultur* (Regensburg: ConBrio Verlagsgesellschaft, 1996), pp. 21–35, p. 26.

not from an abstract compositional idea but from the instrumental practice in all its chaotic, physical and inexhaustible glory. The composer Dominik Karski goes as far as saying, 'I do not consider an instrument to "become an instrument" until it is in the hands of a performer.'[17] The actions that arise between the instrument and performer, the manhandling of the object, become, then, a *new* instrument.[18]

Bringing the physical reality of playing into composition is, according to Richard Barrett, an attempt 'to engage as intimately as possible with the musical resources at the conjunction between performer and instrument, an engagement which attempts to dissolve the boundaries between instrumentalism and compositional materials'.[19] The performer's physical interface with the instrument as an explicit parameter can be seen as a continuation of Lachenmann's *musique concrète instrumentale*,[20] music that emphasizes the way sound is produced – the energetic aspect of sounds – rather than how it should be heard. Leaving the tonal system of consonance or dissonance and venturing into a '*mechanical modality* whose basis is the construction of the instrument and the "ergonomics" of fingerings, embouchure, breath, and so on'[21] introduces a new dimension of performer interactivity. Ferneyhough, the prime exponent of multi-layered notation, said of his own approach, 'I'm very concerned that the things I ask an instrumentalist to do be so instrument-specific that they conspire to create a sort of "X-ray" of his instrument's inner essence',[22] suggesting that something is hidden inside the instrument, an essence we cannot see with the naked eye, but which may be unleashed by interpretation. Avery and Cox say of Hübler's music:

> In each piece, the independent organization of performative actions is not treated in a typically serialist manner, such that any aspect organized by a series is a 'parameter' like any other and all elements organized are subsidiary to the total design, but rather is realized in light of what might be called the

---

[17] Dominik Karski quoted in 'The Music of Klaus K. Hübler' in Tim Rutherford-Johnson, 'The Rambler' (blog), http://johnsonsrambler.wordpress.com/tag/klaus-k-hubler/ (accessed 31 March 2015).

[18] This is not far from Lachenmann's statement that 'to compose is to build an instrument' (ein Instrument bauen). See his 'Über das Komponieren' in *Musik Als Existenzielle Erfahrung: Schriften 1966–1995*, 2nd edn (Wiesbaden: Breitkopf & Härtel, 2004), pp. 73–82, p. 77.

[19] Barrett, 'Standpoint and Sightlines', p. 27.

[20] The composer introduced the term (in German, *instrumentalen Musique concrète*) in his brief account of *Pression* first published in 1972: Lachenmann, *Musik als Existenzielle Erfahrung*, p. 381.

[21] Ibid.

[22] Brian Ferneyhough, *Collected Writings*, ed. James Boros and Richard Toop, with foreword by Jonathan Harvey (Amsterdam: Harwood Academic Publishers, 1995), p. 375.

piece's existential state, as an inextricable component of its expressive vision.[23]

An instrument's *inner essence* and a piece's *existential state* and *expressive vision* are expressions revealing a search for the unexploited, the inside, the depth of the instrumental practice and the work. A piece's existential state – its existence, or form of 'being in time and space' – can be defined in the form of notation or sound, which, in the case of Hübler's music, are interrelated to a high degree, as the physical playing parameters are part of the notation. The terms may also be associated with corporeality and concepts such as instinct, intuition and viscerality, which again are closely related to the subconscious, topics rarely discussed in relation to composed music, but which have been more relevant to discussions of improvised music.[24]

Modernist music performance practice

The common theory about performance practice of modernist music is that there is little room for interpretation, because the technical learning of the music demands all the resources. The ideals of *Werktreue* and *Neue Sachlickeit*, also, have given rise to an idealization of clean, unemotional, readings of modernist music. This is supported by Stravinsky's demand that the music should be executed rather than interpreted,[25] as well as Hindemith's recommendation, in *Kammermusik* no. 1 opus 24/1, that performers should never try to express their own feelings. For musicians educated in Western classical performance practices, with the ideal of *Werktreue* as a central element, approaching a complicated and seemingly 'unplayable' score can generate ethical questions. Since fidelity to the composer and the score are paramount, interpretation includes a moral and ethical aspect. But what does this fidelity consist of, and what duty of the performer is at stake?

The prevailing performance practice of modernist music is reflected in the direction Cox calls The 'High Modernist Model' of performance practice.[26] This model is a linear, noise free and transparent chain between

---

[23] Avery and Cox, 'Hübler, Klaus K'.
[24] For a further discussion of this, see Tanja Orning, 'The Polyphonic Performer: A Study of Performance Practice in Music for Solo Cello by Morton Feldman, Helmut Lachenmann, Klaus K. Hübler and Simon Steen-Andersen', unpublished PhD dissertation, Norwegian Academy of Music (2014).
[25] Igor Stravinsky, *Poetics of Music in the Form of Six Lessons* (Cambridge, MA: Harvard University Press, 1970), p. 18.
[26] See Frank Cox, 'Notes toward a Performance Practice for Complex Music' in Cox et al., *Polyphony and Complexity*, pp. 70–132.

conception, notation and realization, influenced by the objective style reinforced by the recording industry's ideal of perfection, and is familiar to practices taught worldwide in conservatories today. Cox calls this an 'ideal type' based on

> a direct-functional relationship between 1) notation, as indicating tasks demanding responsible technical mastery, 2) ... an adequate 'realization', in which all notes are correct, all the rhythms are accurately realized, all the dynamics, phrasing marks etc., are audibly projected ... and 3) ideal perception, which should be able to measure, based on the score, the correspondence of the former two aspects, and even more ideally perceive composed relationships from responsible realizations.[27]

Cox presents a 'soft' version of the model, in which 'the demands of responsible realization may occasionally be overridden by interpretational demands', but he maintains that 'in "hard" versions, the latter should always be subordinated to the former'.[28] In either version, the demands for transparency, correspondence and perception of composed relationships position this model within a *Werktreue* ideal. Cox repeatedly calls for *responsible* and *morally responsible* performance, the responsibility clearly being to realize the composer's intentions and his work. This hierarchical model gives the composer power to exert strict control over performances; however, it also carries with it the danger of producing unimaginative interpretations by restraining the creativity of the musicians.

The *Werktreue* ideal reflects a positivistic approach to music; it rests on the belief that there is something close to a truth when it comes to performing a work. This is naturally challenged when transferred to the practical realm of performance, where musicians have always been interpreting, inventing and modifying scores and have made their own contributions. In Lydia Goehr's words, 'To act and sing correctly under the composer's strict control involved a technique of self-denial, which was required if the mythic or aesthetic space of the work was to be transformed into an ideal, socialized space.'[29] This 'self-denial' reinforces the moral imperative and adds a psychological dimension to performance. The performers can feel inadequate in this paradigm, practising even more and stretching even further, to make the performance more 'true' to the text. Performers may lose their confidence – something so crucial in performing music. This loss of confidence was vividly described by the clarinetist Roger Heaton in 1987:

---

[27] Ibid., pp. 71–2.   [28] Ibid.
[29] Lydia Goehr, *The Quest for Voice: On Music, Politics, and the Limits of Philosophy* (Oxford University Press, 1998), p. 158.

> The absurdity of the excesses of the New Complexity lies not merely in the precise notation of 'expression', but in the subjugation and manipulation of the performer, who can only conclude that his efforts are ultimately of secondary importance. The player confronted by these impossible works, is defeated before even beginning, and ultimately discouraged and depressed by the approximations which occur, challenging his integrity.[30]

Within the discourse around performance, there is a sharp distinction between being genuine and not being genuine. The ideal of the diligent and honest musician, loyal to the work and the composer, is held up against that of the dilettante who fakes, cheats and takes shortcuts. This thinking is linked to the model of instrumentalists as craft workers, whose honour and pride reside in correctly executing their job as they have learned it, often from a master teacher. To 'fake it' is to produce faulty goods and is considered shameful. These attitudes are so strongly embedded in performance practice that challenges are met with powerful objections. Heaton writes as follows:

> Because the pieces are impossible, the performer has to fake and to improvise certain sections; players familiar with the style, and probably well practised through free improvisation, can get away with it. This leads to the possibility of the imaginative, but technically less competent, players performing these pieces, whereas a player with a sound traditional technique (the only one to have!) would not attempt something which has no regard for the instrument while still, by notation, setting out its terms of reference within the tradition from which that instrument comes.[31]

Heaton's comments go to the very core of how musicians often experience an absolute distinction between the 'playable' and the 'unplayable', and the perceived insult to the performer in using the traditional instruments and notation in this new way. Heaton's only alternative to playing the notes correctly, a position within the High Modernist Model of performance practice, is to fake or improvise. To be accused of faking is a serious insult for performers trained in Western classical music, with its ideals of authenticity, accuracy and fidelity to what is written. When 'faking' is understood as pretending, misleading or deceiving – producing faulty goods – it is understandable that the word has negative connotations, but the word can also mean imitating, simulating or substituting, skills highly operative in musical practice. Heaton equates being imaginative and improvising with being less technically competent, expressing an exclusive faith in the traditional view of performance practice where musicians do as

---

[30] Roger Heaton, 'The Performer's Point of View', *Contact*, 30 (1987), 30–3, p. 33.
[31] Ibid., p. 32.

they are told and where a score is a set of instructions to be followed without involving too much of the musician's creativity.

The common inclination towards perfection among performers of classical music can become an excuse for no further action. In a right/wrong paradigm, the imperative to 'get it right' is so self-explanatory that it relieves the performers of the responsibility of thinking for themselves. There is an interesting conflict, little discussed, between these (polarized) choices either to be active, make judgments and take personal responsibility or to be passive, correctly executing 'orders' from the composer, and thus be exempted from responsibility. There is, of course, a wide area between these poles, but the dominance of the latter model is clear to anyone who is classically trained. Orchestral institutions are largely dependent on performers who 'do as they are told', if admittedly on a very high level.

Many composers writing within the aesthetics of the New Complexity have clearly stated that a perfect rendition of the score is neither objective nor even necessarily desirable. Richard Barrett says, 'Notation to me is not a specification, but more of a proposal of a way of making music. The music doesn't make "demands," it makes proposals. The act of interpreting is one whereby such a "proposal" is transformed into music by the performer.'[32]

In interviews, Ferneyhough repeatedly denies that his music should follow the transparent and linear principles found in the High Modernist Model of performance practice: 'It is clear that no conceivable notation would ever be equal to the task of rendering every aspect of a work's physiognomy in a manner capable of reproduction; nor am I suggesting that this would even be desirable.'[33] When asked what he thought were the essential criteria for a good performance of his work, he answered,

> I would say the establishment of audible criteria of meaningful inexactitude. That is, from work to work, from one section of a work to another section, from one performer to another, from one performance situation to another, the level of meaningful inexactitude is one indication, one hint of the way in which a work 'means'.[34]

Ferneyhough's often-quoted 'meaningful inexactitude' goes to the heart of the matter: for him, music must create meaning, not *one* true meaning, but a multitude of meanings through multiple (personal) interpretations.

---

[32] Richard Barrett and Arne Deforce, 'The Resonant Box with Four Strings: Interview on the Musical Esthetics of Richard Barrett and the Genesis of His Cello Music', http://issuu.com/arnedeforce/docs/the_resonant_box_with_four_strings (accessed 31 March 2015).
[33] Brian Ferneyhough, 'Questionnaire Response' in Joël Bons (ed.), *Complexity in Music? An Inquiry into Its Nature, Motivation and Performability* (Rotterdam: Job Press, 1990), p. 19.
[34] Ferneyhough, *Collected Writings*, pp. 268–9.

Though *Werktreue* has primarily been a theoretical construct, we have seen that it exerts a powerful influence on performers and consequently on their practice. The challenge is that the notion of fidelity to the score is largely implicit in practice and rarely addressed – a culturally embedded truth that cannot be subjected to validity testing. An important premise for the fidelity/infidelity binary, which we have seen is so deeply rooted in performance practices, is the still-powerful work concept. What happens, then, when the work concept is challenged, when the work is no longer to be found complete and innate in the score, but is dependent upon performance to be fully constituted? How can a performer be loyal to a score with intricate notation that has multiple possible faithful readings?

The struggle idiom

A significant trait in compositions dating from after World War II is a resistance embedded in the score, a resistance that occurs in various degrees, but that can lead, at its most extreme, to a sense of struggle and even loss of control for the performer.[35] Several composers were experimenting with notational and instrumental expression, creating intricate scores that were pushing the capacity of the performers to the extreme. Ferneyhough's *Time and Motion Study II* (1973–6), for cello and electronics, was a groundbreaking work, with significant physical and mental struggle for the cellist who is wired with several microphones, including one throat microphone and two foot pedals. Two assistants are required, and the score is written on up to five staves (see Example 16.2). Ferneyhough refers to the ideas of Antonin Artaud, who proposed struggle as a prerequisite for freeing the spirit. The work investigates the filtering of memory through the human body, and through the cellist's performance, which is being looped and played back, building up to an inevitable breakdown composed into the work. According to Artaud's ideas, struggle and breakdown open up a new consciousness, transcending all that has gone before. His 'Theatre of Cruelty' aimed at breaking away from conventional text-based theatre to a physical theatre where all expressions were regarded as physical articulations in space. The body became the locus of action: 'The body is the body, alone it stands.'[36]

---

[35] Performance resistance is of course not new to musical modernism – it can be found in traditions of musical virtuosity in the nineteenth century and is already anticipated in works like Beethoven's *Hammerklavier* sonata.

[36] Antonin Artaud, 'The Body Is the Body', trans. Roger McKeon, *Semiotext(e)*, 2/3 (1977), 59–60, p. 59.

Example 16.2 *Time and Motion Study II* by Brian Ferneyhough.

Pianist Marc Couroux introduces the term 'critical virtuosity' to describe 'deliberately writing against conventional physical paradigms in order to trigger new relationships between body and matter'.[37] In writing about learning the piece *Evryali* (1973) by Xenakis, he claims that some passages are unplayable, which puts the performer in a very difficult position. At the same time, he criticizes the pianist Peter Hill for reducing and rewriting the score for pragmatic purposes, going as far as calling this an 'ethical violation'. When Couroux performs *Evryali*, he claims, 'the uneasiness remains, and so do the scars of having breached a seemingly unbreachable performative ethic'.[38]

Failure or breakdown is seen by most performers as something to avoid at all costs, even when deliberately composed into the score. They link the failure directly to individual moral responsibility, rather than looking at the work's aesthetics and navigating the practice into a more corresponding conception of interpretation. The realistic notion of what is playable is, as every performer knows, a movable factor, and ideally up to the diligence of the performer. Many performers speak of terms like *performance ethics* and *ethical violation*, reflecting the moral dimensions of performance, often combined with anxiety. An idealistic and utopian approach is called for, approaching seemingly unplayable or impossible tasks. According to Cox, 'one must work on each piece as though an authoritative realization/interpretation were possible, although it will in fact never be so', adding that 'the burden of proof here will lie on the performer, not the composer'.[39] Writing as a pianist, Michael Finnissy says, 'I have a tendency to always assume that it is my fault if things don't work.'[40]

These conflicting elements in performance can be described as the *struggle idiom*, which alludes to the performer's struggle with difficult and seemingly unplayable music. The struggle with the material becomes part of the aesthetic. Struggle and resistance have several functions: to expand perception, to prevent disobedience, to produce energy and vitality and to create multiple meanings.

Performing works on the threshold of performability opens up a new level of aesthetic experience. If the music contains challenges that bring the performer to the brink of breakdown, then the potential for breakdown is already present in the work, and must therefore be taken into

---

[37] Marc Couroux, '*Evryali* and the Exploding of the Interface: From Virtuosity to Anti-Virtuosity and Beyond', *Contemporary Music Review*, 21/2–3 (2002), 53–67, p. 54.
[38] Ibid.   [39] Cox, 'Notes toward a Performance Practice for Complex Music', pp. 105 and 125.
[40] Michael Finnissy, 'Biting the Hand That Feeds You', *Contemporary Music Review*, 21/1 (2002), 71–9, p. 72.

consideration. What happens to the performance, the performer and the work itself during the struggle, breakdown or collapse?

In connection with performing Ferneyhough's *Bone Alphabet*, Steven Schick wrote thus:

> If the interpretive skeleton, built up painstakingly during the learning process, is not sufficiently strong to support the weight of the complexities in the score, then the entire piece threatens to collapse into a simple and singularly unappealing mass.[41]

To argue that the musician's practice process is what prevents collapse makes the practitioner accountable if 'the complexities in the score' prove to be too much to handle in a performance situation. Taking responsibility for the performance is quite natural for performers, yet it is interesting to see the moral implication this statement entails. And what is this 'unappealing mass' that would appear after the 'interpretive skeleton' collapses? The struggle becomes a battle between performance ethics and the work's aesthetic. The built-in verge of collapse is fought with all means available since the performer cannot lose the battle, or she loses face. The psychological effect is strong: this music requires all the performer's resources in a battle of which the outcome remains uncertain.

Towards a new performance practice

As we have seen, if the complexity of the music is an intrinsic part of the composer's aesthetic, it is similarly an intrinsic part of the performance aesthetic. The complexity of performance creates the space for a new domain of aesthetic experience that calls for a new performance practice. The performance practice of complex music has three significant characteristics:

1. **A new emphasis of the role of the body.** The decoupling of the physically executed parameters in composition takes place in the instrumental and performative domain. The performance forefronts the instrumental practice, and thus the locus of performance, the body interacting with the instrument.
2. **Radically idiomatic instrumentalism – a move from *Werktreue* to work ambiguity.** A shift from a transparent and linear performance practice to a practice where the resistance, the struggle idiom and the breakdown of control are embedded in sound and action, embracing

---

[41] Steven Schick, 'Developing an Interpretative Context: Learning Brian Ferneyhough's *Bone Alphabet*', *Perspectives of New Music*, 32/1 (1994), 132–53, p. 133.

the expressions of internal contradictions. Central in this shift is the radical confrontation of the preconceived conception of instrument identity and technique. How the performer relates to this leads to the last point.

3. **The critical and self-reflective performer.** The work implicitly critiques conventional performance practice by challenging and confronting essential aspects of practice, causing the performer to question habits and ingrained patterns.

Recent literature offers a number of explorations of the implications of the new emphasis of the body's role in contemporary music, most notably from performers. In discussing the performance practice in Xenakis's *Mists*, the pianist Pavlos Antoniadis develops a model he calls 'corporeal navigation', which focuses 'on physicality and non-serial learning'.[42] He draws on cognitive science, acknowledges the hybridity and non-linearity in learning complex music and points to the importance of physical, gestural movements in learning. At the end of his article, 'Performance Practice for Complex Music', Cox introduces the concept of '"corporal thinking" transcending means/end-oriented training (for example of traditional virtuosity)'.[43] Corporeal navigation and thinking can be understood in the context of radically idiomatic instrumentalism, discussed above, where the idiomatic now encompasses all of the performer's performative equipment. Returning to Klaus Hübler, who acknowledges the central role of the body in his works:

> My compositions do not exceed the technical possibilities of the instruments ... but they break with the 'conditioned reflexes' of the performers. They require e.g., a new awareness of bodily processes at play, something Max Nyffeler called an 'analytical virtuosity', which of course is not an end in itself but a prerequisite for the realization of my ideas about sound. To settle this, it is sometimes a downright necessity to make demands that seem to exceed the human skills for conscious control of movement.[44]

'Analytical virtuosity' defines the performance practice through the perspective of the body, with a 'new awareness of bodily processes at play', not unrelated to Couroux's term 'critical virtuosity', discussed earlier.

---

[42] Pavlos Antoniadis, 'Physicality as a Performer-Specific Perspectival Point to I. Xenakis's Piano Work: Case Study *Mists*', paper presented at the the Xenakis International Symposium, Southbank Centre, London (2011). http://www.gold.ac.uk/media/07.3%20Pavlos%20Antoniadis.pdf (accessed 31 March 2015).
[43] Cox, 'Notes toward a Performance Practice for Complex Music', p. 128.
[44] Carola Dewenter, 'Neue Musik und Musikpädagogik: Ein Gespräch mit Klaus-Kart Hübler', *Zeitschrift für Musikpädagogik*, 11 (1986), 27–31, p. 29 (my translation).

However, there is an apparent contradiction at play between Hübler's statement that 'my compositions do not exceed the technical possibilities of the instruments', and the 'demands that seem to exceed the human skills for conscious control of movement'. What exceeds these conscious skills? Are we looking at subconscious skills, intuitive, latent, tacit or visceral skills? What is located in this space, between the technically controllable and what is situated beyond the conscious body movements? This is something central to this performance practice and confirms that it is a field still in the state of becoming.

Ambiguity

Many composers within the New Complexity movement use the word 'ambiguity' in a positive sense, as something creating a desired multi-dimensionality in music. In Liza Lim's words:

> My focus in instrumental exploration tends always to look at areas where I feel there there's a lot of ambiguity and flux in the quality of the sounds – inbetween states, like between 'solid'/'liquid', 'granulated'/'gaseous'.[45]

When uncertainty is used as part of the expressive content of the work, its function spills over to the instrumental practice. 'Ambiguity' is defined as 'the quality of being open to more than one interpretation; inexactness'.[46] When performers read ambiguity to mean 'inexactness' the result can be frustrating, simply because it is difficult to know exactly what the notation implies, what the composer wants and hence, what to do at the fundamental level (where to put the fingers, and so on). Approaching an ambiguous score, with the aim of certainty and clarity is thus futile. But if the performer can read ambiguity as 'the quality of being open to more than one interpretation', it becomes a positive attribute – an opportunity to interpret the work in a personal way.

As we have seen, Hübler claimed that his compositions broke with the 'conditioned reflexes' of the performers and required 'new awareness of bodily processes at play' outside the conscious domain. The sheer technical difficulty of the works forces the performers to examine their practice, as the tools they have learned are not sufficient in this context. This situation can be seen as an exaggeration of tendencies that have developed gradually

---

[45] Liza Lim quoted in 'The Music of Klaus K. Hübler' in Rutherford-Johnson, 'The Rambler' (blog).
[46] Oxford University Press, *Oxford Dictionaries* (website), 'Ambiguity', www.oxforddictionaries.com/definition/english/ambiguity?q=ambiguity (accessed 31 March 2015).

through the whole era of modernist music. Several years before Hübler, Adorno said the following:

> Adequate performance requires the formulation of the work as a problem, the recognition of the irreconcilable demands, arising from the relation of the content (*Gehalt*) of the work to its appearance, that confront the performer. In uncovering the tour de force of an artwork, the performance must find the point of indifference where the possibility of the impossible is hidden. Since the work is antinomic, a fully adequate performance is actually not possible, for every performance necessarily represses a contrary element. The highest criterion of performance is if, without repression, it makes itself the arena of those conflicts that have been emphatic in the tour the force.[47]

To view performance as an arena of conflict, in which the work confronts the performer and provokes a battle fought between the two, raises the temperature of the discussion; this is a long way from the well-trodden paths and familiar recipes taught in classical performance practice. In this light, *Opus breve* can be seen as a work that problematizes performance practice – the role and habits of the performer. The perceptual ambiguity of the piece works against the habitual patterns ingrained in the musician, questions every move and method and forces the performer to find new methods and approaches. For the performer of this music, it is a tremendous challenge to interrogate and examine one's own practice – to confront one's limits, work on the margins and accept the non-linearity of complexity that removes the idea of perfection from one's vocabulary. In doing so, the performer allows these scores to become an area of investigation into corporeal, analytical, perceptual and psychological aspects of performance, engaging the broad range of human capacities for expression.

In *Opus breve*, performance practice is not merely about what the performer does but also what constitutes the work. Hübler's sound-world is full of contradictions, ambiguities and flux in the quality of the sounds – it creates an in-between state with great potential for transformation. The extreme detail on every level leads to unlimited combinations of choice and represents a number of possible sounding outcomes. By conventional definitions, *Opus breve* may be considered an 'unfinished' piece, as it represents numerous possible performances and different interpretations. In this way, *Opus breve* highlights the way the ontology of the work is powerfully interwoven with the role of the performer. The work forces the performer to inhabit the physical and sonic space actively, in order to follow the requests of the score. This is a new direction in performance

---

[47] Theodor W. Adorno, *Aesthetic Theory*, ed. Gretel Adorno and Rolf Tiedemann, trans. Robert Hullot-Kentor, new edn (London: Continuum, 2004), p. 140.

practice, in which constitutive elements of the work are moved into the performative domain through instrumental practice. Each performer's physical and mental predispositions will thus be decisive factors in interpretation. Listening to the three available recordings of *Opus breve*,[48] in which it is difficult to recognize that the same piece is being played, further supports this argument. The question whether the piece can be realized – and what it means to 'realize' a work in this context – highlights the central role of performance practice, and the way any compositional aesthetic is dependent upon the performer's communal practice. It also leads to the need to revise the concept of realization to suit the practice in question.

The notational experiments of *Opus breve* and the other works mentioned here represent one important way in which contemporary music performance practice has been challenged and propelled. Performers' encounters with these works have triggered active and important discussions about the relationship between performer and composer and have opened up a space for the importance of questioning power hierarchies in music and confronting inherited beliefs about obedience, authority and creativity. A musical culture dominated by the figure of the 'great composer' is thus challenged. A culture in which the score, rather, can be seen as a starting point for interpretation, a springboard for any number of interpretations, each of which sheds light on the score, requires curious and exploratory performers with the will to experiment. The linear performance practice model with transparent layers between composer, work and performance now becomes opaque, muddled with noise and distortion in the chain of action. From the point of view of performers, this transitional time of experiment and uncertainty, ambiguity and openings, creates a new environment with unique opportunities for their own involvement. As Roland Barthes wrote, 'the Text is experienced only in an activity of production'.[49]

---

[48] The three available commercial recordings of *Opus breve*, performed by Frances Marie Uitti (Wergo), Friedrich Gauwerky (Albedo) and Franklin Cox (forthcoming on Centaur Records).

[49] Roland Barthes, 'From Work to Text' in *Image, Music, Text* (London: Fontana Press, 1977), pp. 155–64, p. 157.

Bibliography

Adlington, Robert, 'Into the Sensuous World: The Music of Rebecca Saunders', *The Musical Times*, 140/1868 (1999), 48–56.

Adorno, Theodor W., *Aesthetic Theory*, ed. Gretel Adorno and Rolf Tiedemann, trans. Robert Hullot-Kentor (London and New York: Continuum, 1997; new edn 2004).

Adorno, Theodor W., *Alban Berg: Der Meister des kleinsten Überganges* (Frankfurt am Main: Suhrkamp, 1995).

Adorno, Theodor W., *Essays on Music*, ed. Richard Leppert, trans. Susan H. Gillespie (Berkeley and Los Angeles, CA: University of California Press, 2002).

Adorno, Theodor W., *Introduction to the Sociology of Music*, trans. E. B. Ashton (New York: Seabury Press, 1976).

Adorno, Theodor W., *L'art et les arts*, trans. Jean Lauxerois (Paris: Desclée de Brouwer, 2002).

Adorno, Theodor W., *Mahler: A Musical Physiognomy*, trans. Edmund Jephcott (University of Chicago Press, 1992).

Adorno, Theodor W., *Musikalische Schriften*, ed. Rolf Tiedemann and Klaus Schultz (Frankfurt am Main: Suhrkamp, 2003).

Adorno, Theodor W., *Philosophy of New Music*, trans. and ed. Robert Hullot-Kentor (Minneapolis, MN: University of Minnesota Press, 2006).

Adorno, Theodor W., 'Rede zu Rudolf Kolisch's 60: Geburtstag', *Musiktheorie: Zeitschrift für Musikwissenschaft*, 24/3 (2009), 238–40.

Adorno, Theodor W., *Sound Figures*, trans. Richard Livingstone (Redwood City, CA: Stanford University Press, 1999).

Adorno, Theodor W., *Zu einer Theorie der musikalischen Reproduktion* (Frankfurt am Main: Suhrkamp, 2001); *Towards a Theory of Musical Reproduction*, ed. Henri Lonetz, trans. Weiland Honban (Cambridge: Polity Press, 2006).

Aguila, Jésus, *Le Domaine musical: Pierre Boulez et vingt ans de création contemporaine* (Paris: Fayard, 1992).

Aho, Kalevi, 'Bergman, Erik', *Komponisten der Gegenwart*, 32. Lfg. (Munich: Edition Text + Kritik, 2006).

Aho, Kalevi, Pekka Jalkanen, Erkki Salamenhaara and Keijo Virtamo, *Finnish Music*, trans. Timothy Binham and Philip Binham (Keuruu: Otava, 1996).

Albèra, Philippe, 'Avant-propos' in *György Kurtág: Entretien, Textes, Écrits sur son Œuvre* (Geneva: Contrechamps, 1995), pp. 7–10.

Alter, Robert, *The Five Books of Moses: A Translation with Commentary* (New York: W. W. Norton, 2004).

Amirkhanians, Charles, *Other Minds: Cathy Berberian on KPFA's Ode to Gravity Series* (MP3 audiofile), 1 min. 31 sec., 1 November 1972, 'RadiOM.Org/Interviews', available at: http://rediom.org/berberianotg.php (accessed 24 July 2010).

Anderson, Martin, 'Erik Bergman [Obituary]', *The Independent* (9 May 2006).

Appadurai, Arjun, *Modernity at Large: Cultural Dimensions of Globalization* (Minneapolis, MN: University of Minnesota Press, 1996).

Appiah, Anthony, *Cosmopolitanism: Ethics in a World of Strangers* (New York: W. W. Norton, 2006).

Artaud, Antonin, 'The Body Is the Body', trans. Roger McKeon, *Semiotext(e)*, 2/3 (1977), 59–60.

Ashby, Arved, *The Pleasure of Modernist Music: Listening, Meaning, Intention, Ideology* (University of Rochester Press, 2004).

Avery, James and Frank Cox, 'Hübler, Klaus K.' in Stanley Sadie and John Tyrrell (eds.), *The New Grove Dictionary of Music and Musicians*, 2nd edn (Version at Grove Music Online).

Babbitt, Milton, 'Who Cares If You Listen?', *High Fidelity* (February 1958).

Badiou, Alain, *Logics of Worlds: Being and Event (II)*, trans. Alberto Toscano (London: Continuum, 2009).

Balázs, Istvan, 'But, chemin, hésitation' in Philippe Albèra (ed.), *György Kurtág* (Geneva: Contrechamps, 1995), pp. 173–83.

Ballantine, Christopher, 'Modernism and Popular Music', *Journal of the Royal Musical Association*, 139/1 (2014), 200–4.

Bannister, Matthew, '"Loaded": Indie Guitar Rock, Canonism, White Masculinities', *Popular Music*, 25/1 (2006), 77–95.

Barrett, Richard, 'Standpoint and Sightlines (provisional) 1995' in Nina Polaschegg, Uwe Hager and Tobias Richtsteig (eds.), *Diskurse zur gegenwärtigen Musikkultur* (Regensburg: ConBrio Verlagsgesellschaft, 1996), pp. 21–35.

Barrett, Richard, and Arne Deforce, 'The Resonant Box with Four Strings: Interview on the Musical Esthetics of Richard Barrett and the Genesis of His Cello Music', http://www.arnedeforce.be/composerfiles_toelichtingen/barrettresbox.htm.

Barthes, Roland, 'From Work to Text' in *Image, Music, Text* (London: Fontana Press, 1977), pp. 155–64.

Bartók, Bela, *Essays*, ed. Benjamin Suchoff (London: Faber, 1993).

Bassetto, Luisa, 'Orient—Accident? *Pli selon pli*, ou l'"eurexcentrisme" selon Boulez' in Pierre Albèra (ed.), *Pli selon pli de Pierre Boulez: Entretiens et etudes* (Genève: Éditions Contrechamps, 2003), pp. 37–44.

Bauer, Amy, *Ligeti's Laments: Nostalgia, Exoticism and the Absolute* (Farnham: Ashgate, 2011).

Beck, Ulrich, *The Cosmopolitan Vision* (Cambridge: Polity Press, 2006).

Begbie, Jeremy, *Music, Modernity, and God: Essays in Listening* (Oxford University Press, 2014).

Bekker, Paul, 'Kunst und Krieg: Zwei Feldpostbriefe' in *Kritische Zeitbilder (Gesammelte Schriften, vol. 1)* (Berlin: Schuster & Loeffler, 1921), pp. 177–97.

Bekker, Paul, *Neue Musik* (Berlin: E. Reiss, 1920; reprinted Nendeln, Liechtenstein: Kraus Reprint, 1973).

Bellman, Jonathan (ed.), *The Exotic in Western Music* (Lebanon, NH: Northeastern University Press, 1998).
Benjamin, Walter, *The Origin of the German Tragic Drama*, trans. John Osborne (London: Verso, 2003).
Benjamin, Walter, 'Thesis on the Philosophy of History' in *Illuminations*, ed. with an introduction by Hannah Arendt, trans. Harry Zohn (New York: Schocken Books, 1969), pp. 253–67.
Benjamin, Walter, 'Über den Begriff der Geschichte' in Rolf Tiedemann and Hermann Schweppenhäuser, *Gesammelte Schriften*, 7 vols. (Frankfurt am Main: Suhrkamp, 1974), vol. I.
Berberian, Cathy, 'Cathy's Solo Talk Show' (1979), produced by Frans van Rossum and Frits Bloemink, audio material digitized by Joes Roelofs and edited by John Knap for CD (2010). Special transcript by Pamela Karantonis in Karantonis, Pamela, Francesca Placanica, Anna Sivuoja-Kauppala and Pieter Verstraete (eds.), *Cathy Berberian: Pioneer of Contemporary Vocality* (Farnham: Ashgate, 2014), pp. 33–44.
Berberian, Cathy, 'La nuova vocalità nell'opera contemporanea', *Discoteca*, 62 (1966), 34–5.
Berger, Karol, and Anthony Newcomb (eds.), *Music and the Aesthetics of Modernity: Essays* (Cambridge, MA: Harvard University Press, 2005).
Bernard, Jonathan W., 'Voice Leading as a Spatial Function in the Music of Ligeti', *Music Analysis*, 13/2–3 (1994), 227–53.
Bhabha, Homi, *The Location of Culture* (London: Routledge, 1994).
Bhabha, Homi, 'Unsatisfied: Notes on Vernacular Cosmopolitanism' in Laura Garcia-Morena and Peter C. Pfeiffer (eds.), *Text and Nation: Cross-Disciplinary Essays on Cultural and National Identities* (London: Camden House, 1996), pp. 191–207.
Bloom, Harold, *The Anxiety of Influence: A Theory of Poetry*, 2nd edn (Oxford University Press, 1997).
Bloom, Harold, *Poetics of Influence: New and Selected Criticism*, ed. with an introduction by John Hollander (New Haven, CT: Henry R. Schwab, 1988), pp. 213–34.
Bohlman, Philip V., 'Epilogue: Musics and Canons' in Katherine Bergeron and Philip V. Bohlman (eds.), *Disciplining Music: Musicology and Its Canons* (University of Chicago Press, 1992), pp. 197–210.
Bohrer, Karl Heinz, *Suddenness: On the Moment of Aesthetic Experience*, trans. Ruth Crowley (New York: Columbia University Press, 1994).
Bonds, Mark Evan, *Music as Thought: Listening to the Symphony in the Age of Beethoven* (Princeton University Press, 2006).
Bonds, Mark Evan, 'The Spatial Representation of Musical Form', *The Journal of Musicology*, 27/3 (2010), 265–307.
Born, Georgina, *Rationalizing Culture: IRCAM, Boulez, and the Institutionalization of the Musical Avant-Garde* (Berkeley, CA: University of California Press, 1995).
Born, Georgina, and David Hesmondhalgh (eds.), *Western Music and Its Others: Difference, Representation, and Appropriation in Music* (Berkeley, CA: University of California Press, 2000).
Botstein, Leon, 'Modernism', *The New Grove*, 2nd edn, 29 vols., ed. Stanley Sadie and John Tyrrell (London: Macmillan, 2001), vol. XVI.

Botstein, Leon, 'Out of Hungary: Bartók, Modernism, and the Cultural Politics of Twentieth-Century Music' in Peter Laki (ed.), *Bartók and His World* (Princeton University Press, 1995), pp. 3–63.

Boulez, Pierre, *Boulez on Music Today*, trans. Susan Bradshaw and Richard Rodney Bennett (London: Faber and Faber, 1971).

Boulez, Pierre, *Conversations with Célestin Deliège* (London: Eulenburg, 1976).

Boulez, Pierre, *Jalons (pour une décennie)* (Paris: Éditions Christian Bourgois, 1989).

Boulez, Pierre, *Leçons de musique (Points de repère III)*, collected and ed. Jean-Jacques Nattiez (Paris: Éditions Christian Bourgois, 2005).

Boulez, Pierre, 'L'informulé', *Révue d´esthetique: Adorno*, 8 (1985), 25–30.

Boulez, Pierre, *Orientations* (London: Faber and Faber, 1986).

Boulez, Pierre, *Penser la musique aujourd'hui* (Genève: Gonthier, 1963).

Boulez, Pierre, *Points de repère* (Paris: Éditions Christian Bourgois, 1985).

Boulez, Pierre, *Regards sur autrui (Points de repère II)*, collected and ed. Jean-Jacques Nattiez and Sophie Galaise (Paris: Éditions Christian Bourgois, 2005).

Boulez, Pierre, *Relevés d'apprenti* (Paris: Seuil, 1966).

Boulez, Pierre, *Stocktakings from an Apprenticeship*, collected and ed. Paule Thévenin, trans. Stephen Walsh (Oxford: Clarendon Press, 1991).

Boulez, Pierre, and Célestin Deliège, *Par volonté et par hasard* (Paris: Seuil, 1975).

Boulez, Pierre, Jean-Pierre Changeux and Philippe Manoury, *Les Neurones enchantés* (Paris: Odile Jacob, 2014).

Bowie, Andrew, *Music, Philosophy, and Modernity* (Cambridge University Press, 2007).

Boym, Svetlana, *The Future of Nostalgia* (New York: Basic Books, 2001).

Breckenridge, Carol A. (ed.), *Cosmopolitanism, Millennial Quartet* (Durham, NC: Duke University Press, 2002).

Brooker, Peter, and Andrew Thacker (eds.), *Geographies of Modernism: Literatures, Cultures, Spaces* (London and New York: Routledge, 2005).

Brunner, Raphaël, 'L'"Improvisation III sur Mallarmé" de Pierre Boulez: Éléments pour une mise en perspective', *Dissonanz/Dissonance*, 50 (1996), 4–14.

Bürger, Peter, *Theory of the Avant-Garde*, trans. Michael Shaw (Minneapolis, MN: University of Minnesota Press, 1984).

Burnham, Scott, *Beethoven Hero* (Princeton, NJ: Princeton University Press, 1995).

Burnham, Scott, *Sounding Values: Selected Essays* (Farnham: Ashgate, 2010).

Busch, Regina, 'Thematisch oder athematisch?', *Mitteilungen der internationalen Schönberg-Gesellschaft*, 3–4 (1989), 5–9.

Butor, Michel, 'Mallarmé selon Boulez', *Melos*, 28 (1961), 356–9.

Butt, John, *Bach's Dialogue with Modernity: Perspectives on the Passions* (Cambridge University Press, 2007).

Bye, Antony, 'Darkness at Noon: Anthony Bye Explores the Music of Simon Holt', *The Musical Times*, 134/1804 (1993), 313–16.

Campbell, Edward, *Boulez, Music and Philosophy* (Cambridge University Press, 2010).

Chaigne, Jean-Paul, '*La complexité de la musique de Brian Ferneyhough: Étude philologique et esthétique*', unpublished DMA dissertation, University of Nice – Sophia Antipolis (2008).

Cherlin, Michael, *Schoenberg's Musical Imagination* (Cambridge University Press, 2007).

Chernilo, Daniel, 'Cosmopolitanism and the Question of Universalism' in Gerard Delanty (ed.), *Routledge Handbook of Cosmopolitan Studies* (Abingdon: Routledge, 2012), pp. 47–59.

Cobussen, Marcel, *Thresholds: Rethinking Spirituality through Music* (Aldershot: Ashgate, 2010).

Cohen, Brigid, 'Limits of National History: Yoko Ono, Stefan Wolpe, and Dilemmas of Cosmopolitanism', *The Musical Quarterly*, 97/2 (2014), 181–237.

Cohen, Brigid, *Stefan Wolpe and the Avant-Garde Diaspora* (Cambridge University Press, 2012).

Cohn, Robert, *Towards the Poems of Mallarmé* (Berkeley, CA: University of California Press, 1980).

Cone, Edward T., *The Composer's Voice* (Berkeley and Los Angeles, CA: University of California Press, 1974).

Connor, Steven, 'The Decomposing Voice of Postmodern Music', *New Literary History*, 32/3 (2001), 467–83.

Connor, Steven, 'Edison's Teeth: Touching Hearing' in Veit Erlmann (ed.), *Hearing Cultures: Essays on Sound, Listening and Modernity* (Oxford: Berg, 2004), pp. 153–72.

Cook, Nicholas, and Anthony Pople (eds.), *The Cambridge History of Twentieth-Century Music* (Cambridge University Press, 2004).

Corrado, Omar, *Vanguardias al sur: la música de Juan Carlos Paz* (Buenos Aires: University Nacional de Quilmes Ed., 2012).

Coulembier, Klaas 'Multi-Temporality: Analysing Simultaneous Time Layers in Selected Compositions by Elliott Carter and Claus-Steffen Mahnkopf', unpublished PhD dissertation, University of Leuven (2013).

Couroux, Marc, '*Evryali* and the Exploding of the Interface: From Virtuosity to Anti-Virtuosity and Beyond', *Contemporary Music Review*, 21/2–3 (2002), 53–67.

Cox, Frank, 'Notes toward a Performance Practice for Complex Music' in Frank Cox, Wolfram Schurig and Claus-Steffen Mahnkopf (eds.), *Polyphony and Complexity: New Music and Aesthetics in the 21st Century* (Hofheim: Wolke Verlag, 2002) pp. 70–132.

Crang, Mike, *Cultural Geography* (London: Routledge, 1998).

Critchley, Simon, *The Ethics of Deconstruction: Derrida and Levinas* (Edinburgh University Press, 1999).

Csipák, Károly, 'Sehr schnelle Reflexe: Erinnerungen an das Kolisch-Quartett', *Musica* (1986), 518–24.

Dahlhaus, Carl, 'Adornos Begriff des musikalischen Materials' in *Schönberg und andere: Gesammelte Aufsätze zur Neuen Musik* (Mainz: Schott, 1978), pp. 336–9.

Dallmayr, Fred R., *Beyond Orientalism: Essays on Cross-Cultural Encounter* (Albany, NY: SUNY Press, 1996).

Danuser, Hermann, 'Zur Haut zurückkehren: zu Theodor W. Adornos Theorie der musikalischen Reproduktion', *Musik & Ästhetik*, 7/25 (2003), 5–22.

Darbon, Nicholas, 'Virtuosité et complexité: l'injouable selon Brian Ferneyhough', *Analyse musicale*, 52 (2005), 96–111.

Decroupet, Pascal, 'Comment Boulez pense sa musique au début des années soixante' in Pierre Albèra (ed.), *Pli selon pli de Pierre Boulez: Entretiens et etudes* (Genève: Éditions Contrechamps, 2003), pp. 49–58.

Delanty, Gerard, 'The Idea of Critical Cosmopolitanism' in Gerard Delanty (ed.), *Routledge Handbook of Cosmopolitan Studies* (Abingdon: Routledge, 2012), pp. 38–46.

Deleuze, Gilles, *The Fold: Leibniz and the Baroque*, trans. Tom Conley (London: Athlone, 1993).

Deleuze, Gilles, and Félix Guattari, *A Thousand Plateaus: Capitalism and Schizophrenia*, trans. Brian Massumi (London: Athlone, 1988).

Deleuze, Gilles, and Félix Guattari, *What is Philosophy?*, trans. Graham Burchell and Hugh Tomlinson (London: Verso, 1994).

de Man, Paul, *Blindness and Insight: Essays in the Rhetoric of Contemporary Criticism*, 2nd edn (Minneapolis, MN: Methuen, 1983).

Derrida, Jacques, *Dissemination*, trans. Barbara Johnson (The University of Chicago Press, 1981).

Derrida, Jacques, 'The Law of Genre', *Critical Inquiry*, 7 (1980), 55–81.

Derrida, Jacques, *Margins of Philosophy*, trans. Alan Bass (The University of Chicago Press, 1982).

Derrida, Jacques, *Positions*, trans. Alan Bass (London and New York: Continuum, 2002).

Derrida, Jacques, *Writing and Difference*, trans. Alan Bass (London: Routledge, 1978).

de Swaan, Carrie (dir.), *Music Is the Air I Breathe* (documentary) (Amsterdam: Swaan Produkties, 1995).

Dewenter, Carola, 'Neue Musik und Musikpädagogik: Ein Gespräch mit Klaus-Kart Hübler', *Zeitschrift für Musikpädagogik*, 11 (1986), 27–31.

Downes, Michael, *Jonathan Harvey: Song Offerings and White as Jasmine* (Farnham: Ashgate, 2009).

Doyle, Laura, and Laura A. Winkiel, *Geomodernisms: Race, Modernism, Modernity* (Bloomington, IN: Indiana University Press, 2005).

Duncan, Michelle, 'The Operatic Scandal of the Singing Body', *Cambridge Opera Journal*, 16/3 (2008), 283–306.

Duteurtre, Benoît, *Requiem pour une avant-garde* (Paris: Robert Laffont, 1995).

Dwyer, Benjamin, 'Transformational Ostinati in Györgi Ligeti's Sonatas for Solo Cello and Solo Viola' in Louise Duchesneau and Wolfgang Marx (eds.), *György Ligeti: Of Foreign Lands and Strange Sounds* (Woodbridge: Boydell and Brewer, 2011), pp. 19–52.

Edwards, Peter, *György Ligeti's Le Grand Macabre* (Farnham: Ashgate, 2016, forthcoming).

Edwards, Peter, 'Tradition and the Endless Now: A Study of György Ligeti's *Le Grand Macabre*', unpublished PhD dissertation, University of Oslo (2012).

Erauw, Willem, 'Canon Formation: Some More Reflections on Lydia Goehr's Imaginary Museum of Musical Works', *Acta Musicologica*, 70/2 (1998), 109–15.

Erdely, Stephen, 'Bartok and Folk Music' in Amanda Bayley (ed.), *The Cambridge Companion to Bartók* (Cambridge University Press, 2001), pp. 24–44.

Fanning, David, 'Expressionism' in Stanley Sadie and John Tyrrell (eds.), *The New Grove*, 2nd edn, 29 vols. (London: Macmillan, 2001), vol. IIX.

Feller, Ross, 'Resistant Strains of Postmodernism: The Music of Helmut Lachenmann and Brian Ferneyhough' in Judy Lochhead and Joseph Auner (eds.), *Postmodern Music, Postmodern Thought* (London and New York: Routledge, 2002), pp. 249–62.

Feller, Ross, 'Strategic Defamiliarization: The Process of Difficulty in Brian Ferneyhough's Music', *The Open Space Magazine*, 2 (2000), 197–202.

Ferneyhough, Brian, *Collected Writings*, ed. James Boros and Richard Toop, with foreword by Jonathan Harvey (Amsterdam: Harwood Academic Publishers, 1995).

Ferneyhough, Brian, 'Questionnaire Response' in Joël Bons (ed.), *Complexity in Music? An Inquiry into Its Nature, Motivation and Performability* (Rotterdam: Job Press, 1990).

Ferneyhough, Brian, and James Boros, 'Shattering the Vessels of Received Wisdom', *Perspectives of New Music*, 28/2 (1990), 6–50.

Finnissy, Michael, 'Biting the Hand That Feeds You', *Contemporary Music Review*, 21/1 (2002), 71–9.

Fischer-Lichte, Erika, *The Transformative Power of Performance: A New Aesthetics*, trans. Saskya Iris Jain (New York: Routledge, 2008).

Foege, Alec, *Confusion is Next: The Sonic Youth Story* (New York: St. Martin's Press, 1994).

Foucault, Michel, *The Archaeology of Knowledge*, trans. A. M. Sheridan Smith (New York: Pantheon Books, 1972).

Foucault, Michel, *The Order of Things: An Archaeology of the Human Sciences* (New York: Pantheon Books, 1971).

Foucault, Michel, and Pierre Boulez, 'Contemporary Music and the Public', *Perspectives of New Music*, 24/1 (1985), 6–12.

Fox, Christopher, 'The Extended Clarinet: Four Contemporary Approaches' in Roger Heaton (ed.), *The Versatile Clarinet* (London: Routledge, 2006), pp. 15–30.

Franklin, Peter, *Reclaiming Late-Romantic Music: Singing Devils and Distant Sounds* (Berkeley and Los Angeles, CA: University of California Press, 2014).

Freud, Sigmund, *Psychopathology of Everyday Life* (Seattle: Pacific Publishing Studio, 2010).

Gilroy, Paul, *The Black Atlantic: Modernity and Double-Consciousness* (Cambridge, MA: Harvard University Press, 1993).

Gloag, Kenneth, *Postmodernism in Music* (Cambridge University Press, 2012).
Goehr, Lydia, *The Imaginary Museum of Musical Works: An Essay in the Philosophy of Music* (Oxford: Clarendon Press, 1992; revised edn Oxford University Press, 2007).
Goehr, Lydia, *The Quest for Voice: On Music, Politics, and the Limits of Philosophy* (Oxford University Press, 1998).
Goldman, Jonathan, *The Musical Language of Pierre Boulez: Writings and Compositions* (Cambridge University Press, 2011).
Goldman, Jonathan, Jean-Jacques Nattiez and François Nicolas, *La Pensée de Pierre Boulez à Travers ses Écrits* (Paris: Delatour, 2010).
Gooley, Dana, 'Cosmopolitanism in the Age of Nationalism, 1848–1914', *Journal of the American Musicological Society*, 66/2 (2013), 523–49.
Grassl, Markus, and Reinhard Kapp (eds.), *Die Lehre von der musikalischen Aufführung in der Wiener Schule: Verhandlungen des Internationalen Colloquiums Wien 1995* (Vienna, Cologne and Weimar: Boehlau Verlag).
Greenberg, Clement, 'Modernist Painting' in John O'Brien (ed.), *Clement Greenberg: The Collected Essays and Criticism, Modernism with a Vengeance (1957–1969)*, 4 vols. (University of Chicago Press, 1993), vol. IV.
Greene, Jayson, 'Making Overtures: The Emergence of Indie Classical', *Pitchfork* (28 February 2012), http://pitchfork.com/features/articles/8778-indie-classical/ (accessed 24 March 2015).
Griffiths, Paul, *A Concise History of Western Music* (Cambridge University Press, 2006).
Guilbaut, Serge, *How New York Stole the Idea of Modern Art: Abstract Expressionism, Freedom, and the Cold War*, trans. Arthur Goldhammer (University of Chicago Press, 1985).
Guldbrandsen, Erling E., 'Casting New Light on Boulezian Serialism' in Edward Campbell and Peter O'Hagan (eds.), *Boulez Studies* (Cambridge University Press, 2016, forthcoming).
Guldbrandsen, Erling E., 'Modernist Composer and Mahler Conductor: Changing Conceptions of Performativity in Boulez', *Studia Musicologica Norvegica*, 32 (2006), 140–68.
Guldbrandsen, Erling E., 'New Light on Pierre Boulez and Postwar Modernism: On the Composition of "Improvisation I–III sur Mallarmé"' in Søren Møller Sørensen (ed.), *In the Plural: Institutions, Pluralism and Critical Self-Awareness in Contemporary Music* (University of Copenhagen, 1997), pp. 15–28.
Guldbrandsen, Erling E., 'Pierre Boulez in Interview, 1996 (I) Modernism, History and Tradition', *Tempo*, 65/255 (2011), 9–16.
Guldbrandsen, Erling E., 'Pierre Boulez in Interview, 1996 (II) Serialism Revisited', *Tempo*, 65/256 (2011), 18–24.
Guldbrandsen, Erling E., 'Pierre Boulez in Interview, 1996 (III) Mallarmé, Musical Form and Articulation', *Tempo*, 65/257 (2011), 11–21.
Guldbrandsen, Erling E., 'Pierre Boulez in Interview, 1996 (IV) Some Broader Topics', *Tempo*, 65/258 (2011), 37–43.

Guldbransen, Erling E., 'Tradisjon og tradisjonsbrudd: En studie i Pierre Boulez: Pli selon pli – portrait de Mallarmé', unpublished PhD dissertation, University of Oslo (1995).

Guldbrandsen, Erling E., *Tradisjon og tradisjonsbrudd: En studie i Pierre Boulez: Pli selon pli – portrait de Mallarmé* (Oslo: Scandinavian University Press, 1997).

Hakobian, Levon, *Music of the Soviet Age 1917–1987* (Stockholm: Melos Music Literature, 1998).

Hallam, Mandy, 'Conversation with James MacMillan', *Tempo*, 62/245 (2008), pp. 17–29.

Hannerz, Ulf, 'Cosmopolitans and Locals in World Culture', *Theory, Culture & Society*, 7/2 (1990), 237–51.

Harvey, Jonathan, 'The Mirror of Ambiguity' in Simon Emmerson (ed.), *The Language of Electronic Music* (London: Macmillan, 1986), pp. 177–90.

Heaton, Roger, 'The Performer's Point of View', *Contact*, 30 (1987), 30–3.

Hegel, Georg W. F., *Aesthetics: Lectures on Fine Arts*, trans. T. M. Knox, 2 vols. (Oxford: Clarendon Press, 1975).

Hegel, Georg W. F., *The Philosophy of Fine Art*, trans. F. P. B. Osmaston, 4 vols. (London: Bells and Sons, 1920), vol. III.

Heile, Björn, 'Weltmusik and the Globalization of New Music' in Björn Heile (ed.) *The Modernist Legacy: Essays on New Music* (Farnham: Ashgate, 2009), pp. 101–21.

Heininen, Paavo, 'Erik Bergman's Path to the New Music' in Jeremy Parsons (ed.), *Erik Bergman: A Seventieth Birthday Tribute* (Helsinki: Pan, 1981), pp.113–50.

Heiniö, Mikko, 'Bergman, Erik' in Hanns-Werner Heister and Walter-Wolfgang Sparrer (eds.), *Komponisten Der Gegenwart*, 10. Lfg. (Munich: Edition Text + Kritik, n.d.).

Hell, Julia, and Andreas Schölne (eds.), *Ruins of Modernity* (Durham, NC and London: Duke University Press, 2010).

Hewett, Ivan, *Music: Healing the Rift* (New York and London: Continuum 2003).

Hibbett, Ryan, 'What is Indie Rock?', *Popular Music and Society*, 28/1 (2005), 55–77.

Hobsbawm, Eric and Terence Ranger (eds.), *The Invention of Tradition* (Cambridge University Press, 1983).

Hoeckner, Berthold, *Programming the Absolute: Nineteenth-Century German Music and the Hermeneutics of the Moment* (Princeton University Press, 2002).

Hooper, Giles, *The Discourse of Musicology* (Aldershot: Ashgate, 2006).

Howell, Tim, *After Sibelius: Studies in Finnish Music* (Aldershot, UK and Burlington, VT: Ashgate, 2006).

Hübler, Klaus K., 'Expanding String Technique', trans. Frank Cox in Frank Cox, Wolfram Schurig and Claus-Steffen Mahnkopf (eds.), *Polyphony and Complexity: New Music and Aesthetics in the 21st Century*, pp. 233–44.

Hullot-Kentor, Robert, 'Right Listening and a New Type of Human Being' in *Things Beyond Resemblance: Collected Essays on Theodor W. Adorno* (New York: Columbia University Press, 2006), pp. 193–209.

Hutcheon, Linda, *A Theory of Parody: The Teachings of Twentieth-Century Art Forms* (New York: Methuen, 1985).
Huyssen, Andreas, *After the Great Divide: Modernism, Mass Culture, Postmodernism* (Bloomington, IN: Indiana University Press, 1987).
Huyssen, Andreas, 'Nostalgia for Ruins', *Grey Room*, 2 (2006), 6–21.
Iddon, Martin, *New Music at Darmstadt: Nono, Stockhausen, Cage, and Boulez* (Cambridge University Press, 2013).
Idel, Moshe, *Kabbalah and Eros* (New Haven, CT: Yale University Press, 2005).
Ivashkin, Alexander, *Alfred Schnittke* (London: Phaidon Books Ltd., 1996).
Jameson, Fredric, *Postmodernism, or, The Cultural Logic of Late Capitalism* (Durham, NC: Duke University Press, 1991).
Jameux, Dominique, *Pierre Boulez* (Paris: Fayard, 1984).
Jencks, Charles, *What is Post-Modernism?* (New York and London: St. Martin's Press, 1986; Chichester: Academy Editions, 1996).
Johnson, Julian, 'An Interview with Jonathan Harvey' in Peter O'Hagan (ed.), *Aspects of British Music of the 1990s* (Aldershot: Ashgate, 2003), pp. 119–30.
Johnson, Julian, *Mahler's Voices: Expression and Irony in the Songs and Symphonies* (Oxford University Press, 2009).
Johnson, Julian, *Out of Time: Music and the Making of Modernity* (Oxford University Press, 2015).
Johnson, Julian, *Webern and the Transformation of Nature* (Cambridge University Press, 1999).
Johnson, Julian, *Who Needs Classical Music?: Cultural Choice and Musical Value* (Oxford University Press, 2002).
Josephson, David, 'The German Musical Exile and the Course of American Musicology', *Current Musicology*, 79 and 80 (2005), 9–53.
Kanno, Mieko, 'Prescriptive Notation: Limits and Challenges', *Contemporary Music Review*, 26/2 (2007), 231–54.
Kant, Immanuel, *Perpetual Peace* (Minneapolis, MN: Filiquarian Publishing, LLC., 2007).
Karantonis, Pamela, 'Cathy Berberian and the Performative Art of Voice' in Pamela Karantonis, Francesca Placanica, Anna Sivuoja-Kauppala and Pieter Verstraete (eds.), *Cathy Berberian: Pioneer of Contemporary Vocality* (Farnham: Ashgate, 2014), pp. 151–68.
Karantonis, Pamela, Francesca Placanica, Anna Sivuoja-Kauppala and Pieter Verstraete (eds.), *Cathy Berberian: Pioneer of Contemporary Vocality* (Farnham: Ashgate, 2014).
Katz, Ruth, and Carl Dahlhaus (eds.), *Contemplating Music: Source Readings in the Aesthetics of Music* (Stuyvesant: Pendragon Press, 1992).
Kawabata, Mai, 'Virtuoso Codes of Violin Performance: Power, Military Heroism, and Gender (1789–1830)', *19th-Century Music*, 28/2 (2004), 89–107.
Kerman, Joseph, *The Beethoven Quartets* (New York: W. W. Norton, 1979).
Kerman, Joseph, *Contemplating Music: Challenges to Musicology* (Cambridge, MA: Harvard University Press, 1985).

Kerman, Joseph, *Musicology* (London: Fontana Press, 1985).

Kimbrough, Andrew, *Dramatic Theories of Voice in the Twentieth Century* (Amherst: Cambria Press, 2011).

Klotz, Heinrich, *Kunst im 20. Jahrhundert: Moderne-Postmoderne-Zweite Moderne* (Munich: C. H. Beck, 1994).

Kolisch, Rudolf, *Rudolf Kolisch: Zur Theorie der Aufführung* (Musik-Konzepte 29/30), ed. Heinz-Klaus Metzger and Rainer Riehn (Munich: edition text+kritik, 1983).

Kolisch, Rudolf, 'Tempo and Character in Beethoven's Music,' trans. Arthur Mendel, *The Musical Quarterly*, 29/2 (1943), 169–87 (part 1); 29/3 (1943), 291–311 (part 2).

Kolisch, Rudolf, and René Leibowitz, 'Aufführungsprobleme im Violinkonzert von Beethoven', *Musica*, 33/2 (1979), 148–55.

Kostelanetz, Richard, *Conversing with Cage* (New York: Routledge, 2003).

Kramer, Lawrence, *Why Classical Music Still Matters* (Berkeley and Los Angeles, CA: University of California Press, 2007).

Kurasawa, Fuyuki, 'A Cosmopolitanism from Below: Alternative Globalization and the Creation of a Solidarity without Bounds', *European Journal of Sociology/Archives Européennes de Sociologie*, 45/02 (2004), 233–55.

Lachenmann, Helmut, *Écrits et entretiens* (Genève: Contrechamps, 2009).

Lachenmann, Helmut, *Musik Als Existensielle Erfahrung: Schriften 1966–1995*, 2nd edn (Wiesbaden: Breitkopf & Härtel, 2004).

Leech-Wilkinson, Daniel, 'Musicology and Performance' in Zdravko Blazekovic (ed.), *Music's Intellectual History: Founders, Followers and Fads* (New York: RILM, 2009), pp. 791–804.

Leibowitz, René, 'Comment interprète-t-on Beethoven?', *Les Temps Modernes*, 175–6 (1960), 630–46.

Lester, Paul, 'Tank Boy', *The Guardian* (5 October 2001), http://www.guardian.co.uk/culture/2001/oct/05/artsfeatures3 (accessed 24 March 2015).

Levi, Erik, and Florian Scheding, *Music and Displacement: Diasporas, Mobilities, and Dislocations in Europe and Beyond* (Lanham, MD and Plymouth, UK: Scarecrow Press, 2010).

Levinas, Michaël, *Le compositeur trouvère: écrits et entretiens (1982–2002)*, collected and ed. Pierre A. Castanet and Danielle Cohen-Levinas (Paris: L'Harmattan, 2002).

Levitz, Tamara, 'Vogel, Wladimir' in Stanley Sadie and John Tyrrell (eds.), *The New Grove Dictionary of Music and Musicians*, 2nd edn. Version at Grove Music Online.

Lévy, Fabien, 'Inintelligible, injouable, incompréhensible: La complexité musicales est-elle analytique, instrumentale, perceptive ou hétéronome?', *Itamar, revista de investigacion musical*, 1 (2008), 61–87.

Lewin, David, *Studies in Music and Text* (Oxford University Press, 2006).

Ligeti, György, 'Form' in Ernst Thomas (ed.), *Darmstädter Beiträge zur Neuen Musik* (Mainz: Schott, 1966), pp. 23–35.

Locke, Ralph P., *Musical Exoticism: Images and Reflections* (Cambridge University Press, 2009).

Lutosławski, Witold, *Lutosławski on Music*, ed. and trans. Zbigniew Skowron (Lanham, MA: Rowman & Littlefield, 2007).

Lyotard, Jean-François, 'Musique et postmodernité', *Surfaces*, 6/203 (v.1.0 F – 27 November 1996), 4–16.

Lyotard, Jean-François, *The Postmodern Condition: A Report on Knowledge*, trans. Geoff Bennington and Brian Massumi (Manchester University Press, 1984; Minneapolis, MN: University of Minnesota Press, 1984; *La Condition Postmoderne: Rapport sur le Savoir*, Paris: Les Editions de Minuit, 1979).

Magaldi, Cristina, 'Cosmopolitanism and World Music in Rio de Janeiro at the Turn of the Twentieth Century', *The Musical Quarterly*, 92/3–4 (2009), 329–64.

Mahnkopf, Claus-Steffen, Frank Cox and Wolfram Schurig, Facets of the Second Modernity: New Music and Aesthetics in the 21st Century (Hofheim: Volke Verlag, 2008).

Makarius, Michel, *Ruins*, trans. David Radzinowicz (Paris: Fammarion, 2004).

Mallarmé, Stéphane, *Œuvres complètes* (Paris: Pléiade, 1989).

Mauser, Siegfried, 'Zum Begriff des musikalischen Charakters in Beethovens frühen Klaviersonaten' in Otto Kolleritsch (ed.), *Beethoven und die Zweite Wiener Schule* (Studien zur Wertungsforschung 25) (Wien: Universal, 1992), pp. 190–202.

McClary, Susan, *Conventional Wisdom: The Content of Musical Form* (Berkeley and Los Angeles, CA: University of California Press, 2000).

McClary, Susan, *Desire and Pleasure in Seventeenth-Century Music* (Berkeley and Los Angeles, CA: University of California Press, 2012).

McClary, Susan, *Georges Bizet: Carmen* (Cambridge: Cambridge University Press, 1992).

McClary, Susan, *Reading Music: Selected Essays* (Aldershot: Ashgate, 2007).

McClary, Susan, 'Soprano Masculinities' in Philip Purvis (ed.), *Masculinity in Opera*, (London: Routledge, 2013), pp. 51–79.

McClary, Susan, 'Terminal Prestige: The Case of Avant-Garde Music Composition', *Cultural Critique*, 12 (1989), 57–81.

McClary, Susan, 'The World According to Taruskin', *Music and Letters*, 87/3 (2006), 408–15.

McLeod, Kembrew, and Peter DiCola, *Creative License: The Law and Culture of Digital Sampling* (Durham, NC: Duke University Press, 2011).

Menger, Pierre-Michel, 'From the Domaine Musical to IRCAM: Pierre Boulez in conversation with Pierre-Michel Menger', trans. Jonathan W. Bernard, *Perspectives of New Music*, 28/1 (1990), 6–19.

Metzer, David, *Musical Modernism at the Turn of the Twenty-First Century* (Cambridge University Press, 2009).

Meyer, Thomas, 'Zum Tod von Hansjörg Pauli', *Dissonanz/Dissonance*, 98 (2007), 46–7.

Minor, Ryan, 'Beyond Heroism: Music, Ethics, and Everyday Cosmopolitanism', *Journal of the American Musicological Society*, 66/2 (2013), 529–34.

Moretti, Franco, *Atlas of the European Novel, 1800–1900* (London: Verso, 1998).
Morrison, Richard, 'Julian Anderson in Conversation with Richard Morrison', *The Times* 2 (30 April 2014), 8–9.
Mosch, Ulrich, '"Ihre Lieder Sind Stimmungsvoll Und Schön, Nur...": Erik Bergmans Studien Bei Heinz Tiessen Zwischen 1937 Und 1943', *Mitteilungen Der Paul Sacher Stiftung*, 24 (2011), 12–18, http://www.paul-sacher-stiftung.ch/de/forschung_publikationen/publikationen/mitteilungen/nr_24_april_2011.html.
Müller-Doohm, Stefan, *Adorno: A Biography* (Cambridge: Polity Press, 2009).
Nehemas, Alexander, *Only a Promise of Happiness: The Place of Beauty in a World of Art* (Princeton University Press, 2010).
Nelson, Maggie, *The Art of Cruelty: A Reckoning* (New York: W. W. Norton, 2012).
Newman, Michael Z., 'Indie Culture: In Pursuit of the Authentic Autonomous Alternative', *Cinema Journal*, 48/3 (2009), 16–34.
New York Times, 'Mark Oppenheimer, "Poetry's Cross-Dressing Kingmaker"', Sunday Magazine (14 September 2012).
Nietzsche, Friedrich W., *The Birth of Tragedy*, trans. Clifton Fadiman (New York: Dover Publications, 1995).
Nordwall, Ove, *György Ligeti: Eine Monographie* (Mainz: Schott, 1971).
Nyman, Michael, *Experimental Music: Cage and Beyond*, 2nd edn (Cambridge University Press, 1999).
O'Meara, Caroline, 'Clarity and Order in Sonic Youth's Early Noise Rock', *Journal of Popular Music Studies*, 25 (2013), 13–30.
Oesch, Hans, 'Exotisches Bei Erik Bergman' in Jeremy Parsons (ed.), *Erik Bergman: A Seventieth Birthday Tribute* (Helsinki: Pan, 1981), pp. 183–206.
Oramo, Ilkka, 'Bergmann [sic], Erik (Valdemar)' in Friedrich Blume (ed.), *Die Musik in Geschichte Und Gegenwart: Allgemeine Enzyklopädie der Musik*, revised 2nd edn, ed. Ludwig Finscher (Kassel, Stuttgart, etc.: Bärenreiter, Metzler, 1999), vol. 2, pp. 1271–7.
Orledge, Robert, 'Evocations of Exoticism', *The Cambridge Companion to Ravel* (Cambridge University Press, 2002), pp. 27–46.
Osmond-Smith, David, 'The Tenth Oscillator: The Work of Cathy Berberian 1958–1966', *Tempo*, 58/227 (2004), 2–13; reprinted in Pamela Karantonis, Francesca Placanica, Anna Sivuoja-Kauppala and Pieter Verstraete (eds.), *Cathy Berberian: Pioneer of Contemporary Vocality* (Farnham: Ashgate, 2014), pp. 19–31.
Paddison, Max, *Adorno's Aesthetics of Music* (Cambridge University Press, 1993).
Paddison, Max, 'Performance and the Silent Work', *Filigrane: Musique, esthétique, sciences, société*, http://revues.mshparisnord.org/filigrane/index.php?id=147 (accessed 27 May 2011).
Perloff, Marjorie, *21st-Century Modernism: The 'New' Poetics* (Oxford: Blackwell, 2002).
Piencikowski, Robert, 'Nature morte avec guitare' in Josef Häusler (ed.), *Festschrift Pierre Boulez* (Mainz: Schott, 1985), pp. 66–81.
Placanica, Francesca, 'Cathy Berberian: Performance as Composition', unpublished Master's thesis, Southern Methodist University (Dallas, 2007).

Potter, Keith, Kyle Gann and Pwyll ap Siôn (eds.), *The Ashgate Research Companion to Minimalist and Postminimalist Music* (Farnham: Ashgate, 2013).

Pousseur, Henri, *Musiques croisées* (Paris: L'Harmattan, 1997).

Proust, Françoise, *L'Histoire à Contretemps: Le Temps Historique Chez Walter Benjamin (Passages)* (Paris: Éditions du Cerf, 1994).

Rancière, Jacques, *The Politics of Aesthetics: The Distribution of the Sensible*, trans. Gabriel Rockhill (London: Continuum, 2004).

Rehding, Alexander, *Music and Monumentality: Commemoration and Wonderment in Nineteenth-Century Germany* (Oxford University Press, 2009).

Revuluri, Sindhumathi, 'Review: Musical Exoticism: Images and Reflections', *Journal of the American Musicological Society*, 64/1 (2011), 253–61.

Reynolds, Simon, 'Review: Public Enemy, Fear of a Black Planet,' *Melody Maker* (April 1990).

Richard, Jean-Pierre, *L'univers imaginaire de Mallarmé* (Paris: Seuil, 1961).

Riegl, Alois, 'The Modern Cult of Monuments: Its Character and Its Origin' (1928), trans. Kurt W. Forster and Diane Ghirardo, *Oppositions*, 25 (1982), 21–51.

Rihm, Wolfgang, *Ausgesprochen: Schriften und Gespräche*, ed. Ulrihc Mosch, 2 vols (Mainz: Schott, 2002).

Rose, Tricia, *Black Noise: Rap Music and Black Culture in Contemporary America* (Hanover and London: Wesleyan University Press, 1994).

Rosen, Charles, 'Music and the Cold War,' *New York Review of Books* (7 April 2011).

Rosen, Charles, 'The Piano Music' in William Glock (ed.), *Pierre Boulez: A Symposium* (London: Eulenburg, 1986), pp. 85–97.

Rosen, Charles, *The Romantic Generation* (Cambridge, MA: Harvard University Press, 1995).

Ross, Alex, 'American Sublime', *The New Yorker* (19 June 2006).

Ross, Alex, *Listen to This* (New York: Farrar, Straus and Giroux, 2010).

Said, Edward, *Orientalism* (London: Penguin Books, 2003).

Saunders, James (ed.), *The Ashgate Research Companion to Experimental Music* (Farnham: Ashgate, 2009).

Savenko, Svetlana, 'Valentin Silvestrov's Lyrical Universe' in Valeria Tsenova (ed.), *Underground Music from the Former USSR* (Amsterdam: Harwood Academic Publishers, 1998), pp. 66–83.

Scaldaferri, Nicola, *Musica nel laboratorio elettroacustico* (Lucca: Libreria Musicale Italiana, 1994).

Schäfer, Thomas, 'Zwischen Schönberg und Stockhausen: Rudolf Kolisch bei den Internationalen Ferienkursen' in Rudolf Stephan, Lothar Knessl, Otto Tomek, Claus Trapp and Christopher Fox (eds.), *Von Kranichstein zur Gegenwart* (Stuttgart: DACO, 1996), pp. 104–11.

Scherer, Jacques, *Le 'Livre' de Mallarmé* (Paris: Gallimard, 1957).

Schick, Steven, 'Developing an Interpretative Context: Learning Brian Ferneyhough's Bone Alphabet', *Perspectives of New Music*, 32/1 (1994), 132–53.

Schiff, David, 'Unreconstructed Modernist', *The Atlantic Monthly* (September 1995), 104–8.

Schlegel, Friedrich, *Philosophical Fragments*, trans. Peter Firchow (Minneapolis, MN: University of Minnesota Press, 1991).

Schmalfeldt, Janet, *In the Process of Becoming: Analytic and Philosophical Perspectives on Form in Early Nineteenth-Century Music* (Oxford University Press, 2011).

Schmelz, Peter J., *Such Freedom, If Only Musical: Unofficial Soviet Music during the Thaw* (Oxford University Press, 2009).

Schmelz, Peter J., 'Valentin Silvestrov and the Echoes of Music History', *The Journal of Musicology*, 31/2 (2014), 231–71.

Schmelz, Peter J., 'What Was "Shostakovich", and What Came Next?', *The Journal of Musicology*, 24/3 (2007), 297–338.

Schoenberg, Arnold, 'Aphorismen', *Die Musik*, 9/21 (1909/10), 159–63.

Scholem, Gershom G., *Major Trends in Jewish Mysticism* (New York: Schocken Books, 1961).

Scholem, Gershom G. *On the Mystical Shape of the Godhead*, trans. Joachim Neugroschel (New York: Schocken Books, 1991).

Schönle, Andreas, *Architecture of Oblivion: Ruins and Historical Consciousness in Modern Russia* (DeKalb: Northern Illinois University Press, 2011).

Schwarz, David, Anahid Kassabian and Lawrence Siegel (eds.), *Keeping Score: Music, Disciplinarity, Culture* (Charlottesville, VA: University Press of Virginia, 1997).

Scruton, Roger, *Death-Devoted Heart: Sex and the Sacred in Wagner's Tristan und Isolde* (Oxford University Press, 2004).

Seabrook, Mike, '"Dark Fire": Simon Holt and His Music', *Tempo*, 201 (1997), 21–7.

Seeger, Charles, 'Prescriptive and Descriptive Music-Writing', *The Musical Quarterly*, 44/2 (1958), 184–95.

Seherr-Thoss, Peter von, *György Ligetis Oper Le Grand Macabre: Erste Fassung: Entstehung und Deutung: von der Imagination bis zur Realisation einer musikdramatischen Idee* (Eisenach: Wagner, 1998).

Shaw, Jennifer, 'New Performance Sources and Old Modernist Productions: *Die Jakobsleiter* in the Age of Mechanical Reproduction', *The Journal of Musicology*, 19/3 (2002), 434–60.

Shenk, David, *Data Smog: Surviving the Information Glut* (New York: Harper Collins, 1997).

Simmel, Georg, 'The Ruin' (1911) in Kurt H Wolff (ed.), *Georg Simmel, 1858–1918: A Collection of Essays, With Translations and a Bibliography*, trans. David Kettler (Columbus: The Ohio State University Press, 1959), pp. 259–66.

Small, Christopher, *Music of the Common Tongue: Survival and Celebration in African-American Music*, 2nd edn (Middletown, CT: Wesleyan University Press, 1998).

Small, Christopher, *Music, Society, Education*, 2nd edn (Middletown, CT: Wesleyan University Press, 1996).

Small, Christopher, *Musicking: The Meanings of Performing and Listening* (Middletown, CT: Wesleyan University Press, 1998).

Small, Christopher, *Schoenberg* (London: John Calder, 1978).

Steinitz, Richard, *György Ligeti: Music of the Imagination* (London: Faber, 2003).

Stokes, Martin, 'On Musical Cosmopolitanism', *The Macalester International Roundtable* (2007), http://digitalcommons.macalester.edu/intlrdtable/3.

Stoler, Ann Laura, 'Imperial Debris: Reflections on Ruins and Ruination', *Cultural Anthropology*, 23/2 (2008), 191–219.

Straus, Joseph, 'The Myth of Serial "Tyranny" in the 1950s and 1960s', *The Musical Quarterly*, 83/3 (1999), 301–43.

Stravinsky, Igor, *Poetics of Music in the Form of Six Lessons* (Cambridge, MA: Harvard University Press, 1970).

Sturken, Marita, 'Monuments – Historical Overview' in Michael Kelly (ed.), *Encyclopedia of Aesthetics in Oxford Art Online* (accessed 4 September 2012).

Suarès, Carlo, *The Song of Songs: The Canonical Song of Solomon Deciphered According to the Original Code of the Qabala* (Boston, MA: Shambala, 1972).

Taruskin, Richard, 'Afterword: *Nicht Blutbefleckt?*', *The Journal of Musicology*, 26/2 (2009), 274–84.

Taruskin, Richard, *The Oxford History of Western Music*, 6 vols. (Oxford University Press, 2005; 5. vols., 2010).

Tommasini, Anthony, 'Drifting Back to the Real World', *New York Times* (8 June 2014).

Toop, Richard, 'Against a Theory of Musical (New) Complexity' in Max Paddison and Irène Deliège (eds.), *Contemporary Music: Theoretical and Philosophical Perspectives*, (Farnham: Ashgate, 2010), pp. 89–97.

Toop, Richard, 'Four Facets of "the New Complexity"', *Contact*, 32 (1988), 4–50.

Torvinen, Juha, 'The Tone of the North', *Finnish Music Quarterly* (September 2010), http://www.fmq.fi/2010/09/the-tone-of-the-north/.

Trigg, Dylan, *The Aesthetics of Decay: Nothingness, Nostalgia, and the Absence of Reason* (New York: Peter Lang Publishing, 2006).

Várnai, Péter, Josef Häusler, Claude Samuel and György Ligeti, *György Ligeti in Conversation with Péter Várnai, Josef Häusler, Claude Samuel and Himself* (London: Eulenburg Books, 1983).

Vila, Marie-Christine, *Cathy Berberian Cant'atrice* (Paris: Fayard, 2003).

Wagner, Richard, *Richard Wagner: Briefe* (Stuttgart: Reclam, 1995).

Wald, Elijah, *How the Beatles Destroyed Rock and Roll: An Alternative History of American Popular Music* (Oxford University Press, 2009).

Wason, Robert, 'Webern's "Variations for Piano", Op. 27: Musical Structure and the Performance Score', *Intégral*, 1 (1987), 57–103.

Watkins, Holly, 'Schoenberg's Interior Designs', *Journal of the American Musicological Society*, 61/1 (2008), 123–206.

Weber, William, *The Rise of Musical Classics: A Study in Canon, Ritual and Ideology* (Oxford University Press, 1992).

Weiss, Allen S., 'La glossolalie et la glossographie dans les délires théologiques', trans. (French) Thomas Chantal, *Langages*, 23/91 (1988), *Les glossolalies*, 105–10.

Wells, Dominic P., 'In the Footsteps of Bach: Passion Settings of David Lang and James MacMillan', *Tempo*, 67/264 (2013), 40–51.

Wells, Dominic P., 'James MacMillan: Retrospective Modernist', unpublished PhD dissertation, University of Durham (2012).
Werbner, Pnina, 'Anthropology and the New Ethical Cosmopolitanism' in Gerard Delanty (ed.) *Routledge Handbook of Cosmopolitan Studies* (Abingdon: Routledge, 2012), pp. 153–65.
Werbner, Pnina, 'Global Pathways. Working Class Cosmopolitans and the Creation of Transnational Ethnic Worlds', *Social Anthropology*, 7/1 (1999), 17–35.
White, Hayden, 'Anomalies of Genre: The Utility of Theory and History for the Study of Literary Genres', *New Literary History*, 34 (2003), 597–615.
White, John D., and Jean Christensen, *New Music of the Nordic Countries* (Hillsdale, NY: Pendragon Press, 2002).
Whittall, Arnold, 'Boulez at 80: The Path from the New Music', *Tempo*, 59/233 (2005), 3–15.
Whittall, Arnold, *Musical Composition in the Twentieth Century*, revised edn (Oxford University Press, 1999).
Whittall, Arnold, 'Schoenberg and the "True Tradition": Theme and Form in the String Trio', *Musical Times*, 115/1579 (1974), 739–43.
Whittall, Arnold, '"Unbounded visions": Boulez, Mallarmé and Modern Classicism,' *Twentieth-Century Music*, 1/1 (2004), 65–80.
Wilson, Samuel, 'An Aesthetics of Past-Present Relations in the Experience of Late 20th- and Early 21st-Century Art Music', unpublished PhD dissertation, Royal Holloway, University of London (2013).
Wilson, Samuel, 'After Beethoven, After Hegel: Legacies of Selfhood in Schnittke's String Quartet No. 4', *International Review of the Aesthetics and Sociology of Music*, 45/2 (2014), 311–34.
Wilson, Samuel, 'Building an Instrument, Building an Instrumentalist: Helmut Lachenmann's Serynade', *Contemporary Music Review*, 32/5 (2013), 425–36.
Wolff, Christoph, 'Schoenberg, Kolisch, and the Continuity of Viennese Quartet Culture' in Reinhold Brinkmann and Christoph Wolff (eds.), *Music of My Future: The Schoenberg Quartets and Trio* (Cambridge, MA: Harvard University Press, 2000), pp. 13–24.
Zenck, Martin, 'Auswirkungen einer "musique informelle" auf die neue Musik: Zu Theodor W. Adornos Formvorstellung', *International Review of the Aesthetics and Sociology of Music*, 10/2 (1979), 137–65.
Zimmermann, Bernd Alois, 'Intervalle et temps' in Philippe Albéra (ed.), *Bernd Alois Zimmermann* (Contrechamps 5), (Lausanne: Édition L'Age d'Homme, 1985), pp. 32–35.
Zoppelli, Luca, 'Processo compositivo, "furor poeticus" e Werkcharakter nell'opera romantica italiana: Osservazioni su un "continuity draft" di Donizetti' in *Il Saggiatore Musicale*, 12/2 (2005), 301–38.

Index of names

Adams, John, 4, 21n, 22, 33, 35, 56
Adès, Thomas, 35
Adlington, Robert, 60, 60n
Adorno, Gretel, 147n, 159n, 248n, 317n
Adorno, Theodor W., 9, 10, 12, 14–15, 26, 78, 82, 99–100, 110, 115, 145–9, 153, 156–60, 162–3, 165–6, 193n, 216, 216n, 236, 236n, 246–63, 277
  Aesthetic Theory 147n, 154, 159, 317; 'Beethoven im Geist der Moderne', 257; *Alban Berg* 230, 230n; *Essays on Music* 26n; *Introduction to the Sociology of Music* 26n, 'Kolisch und die neue Interpretation' 262; *L'art et les arts* 145n; *Mahler* 148n, 149n, 156n, 203, 211, 218, 297; *Philosophy of New Music* 47–9, 77, 99n, 156, 188, 246; 'Rede zu Rudolf Kolisch's 60. Geburtstag' 249; *Sound Figures* 178n; *Towards a Theory of Musical Reproduction* 246–51
Aguila, Jésus, 230n
Aho, Kalevi, 82n, 84, 84n, 87n
Alarm Will Sound, 107–8
Albéniz, Isaac 46
Albéra, Philippe, 150n, 151n, 152, 152n, 225n, 235n
Alter, Robert, 126n
American Contemporary Music Ensemble, 108, 108n
Amirkhanians, Charles, 266n
Anderson, Julian, 73
Andersson, Magnus, 288
Angius, Marco, 34n
Antoniadis, Pavlos, 315, 315n
Aphex Twin, 10, 113, 116
  'Cock/Ver10' 104, 107
Appiah, Anthony, 80, 80n
Applebaum, Stanley, 130
Arendt, Hannah, 119n
Armstrong, Louis, 103n
Aron, Simha, 37
Artaud, Antonín, 29, 175, 178, 187, 275, 311, 311n

Ashby, Arved, 1, 1n, 172, 172n
Ashton, E.B., 26n
Auner, Joseph, 279n
Avery, James, 301, 301n, 304n, 306

Babbitt, Milton, 22, 25–7, 115, 121, 142, 172
Bach, Carl Philipp Emanuel, 30
Bach, Johann Sebastian, 3, 5n, 39, 51, 188, 192, 205–6
  St. Matthew Passion [*Matthäus-Passion*] 129
Badiou, Alain, 13, 173, 183, 185–9, 185n
Baez, Joan, 273
Baker, Chet, 176
Balázs, István, 151, 151n
Ballantine, Christopher, 98n
Balter, Marcos, 97
Bang On A Can, 107
Bannister, Matthew, 114n
Barba, Antonio, 278n
Barrett, Natasha, 158
Barrett, Richard, 69, 280–1, 280n, 297, 300, 305–6, 305n, 306n, 310, 310n
  Ne songe plus à fuir 280
Barthes, Roland, 238, 318, 318n
Bartók, Bela, 4, 9, 37–43, 37n, 44n, 46–9, 48n, 50n, 56, 78, 82, 121, 172, 179, 186
  Sonata for Solo Violin 9, 39–42
Bass, Alan, 281n, 286n
Bassetto, Luisa, 225n, 238, 238n
Baudelaire, Charles, 180
Bauer, Amy, 38, 38n, 191n, 193n, 197–8, 197n
Bayley, Amanda, 41n
BBC Symphony Orchestra, 227n, 230, 253–4
Beardslee, Bethany, 27
The Beatles, 98, 278
Beck, Ulrich, 81n
Beckett, Samuel, 49, 59, 63, 151, 165, 165n
Beethoven, Ludwig van, 2, 12, 28, 50–2, 52n, 154, 169, 188, 194, 202n, 207, 247n, 248
  Hammerklavier sonata 311n; *Ninth Symphony* 23; *Sixth Symphony* 164–6;

Index of names

Sonata op. 31, no. 2 159; Sonata op. 81a 197; Violin Concerto 249, 255–62
Begbie, Jeremy, 5n
Bekker, Paul, 82, 82n
Bellman, Jonathan, 77n
Benjamin, George, 8, 22, 30, 34n, 189, 201, 201n
   Written on Skin 33–5
Benjamin, Walter, 12, 119–20, 119n, 145–6, 145n, 151, 157, 200, 200n, 218, 218n, 288
Bennett, Richard Rodney, 224n
Bennici, Aldo, 43
Bennington, Geoff, 3n
Berberian, Cathy, 16, 43, 45, 264–78
Berg, Alban, 4, 172, 178–9, 186, 231, 230n, 246, 247n, 248
   Lulu 28, 141; *Lyric Suite* 230; *Wozzeck* 23, 141
Berger, Karol, 5n
Bergeron, Katherine, 207n
Bergman, Eric, 10, 74–96
   Adagio for baritone, flute, male choir and vibraphone 84; *Arctica* 93; *Aubade* for orchestra 84–6; *Bardo Thödol* 91–2; *Borealis* 93; *Circulo* 84; *Colori ed Improvvisazioni* 87–8; *Det Sjungande Trädet* 89, 93; *Espressivo* for piano 83, 91; *Kalevala* 93; *Lament and Incantation* 93–4; *Lapponia* 93, 95; *Lemmikäinen* 93; *Loleila* 93; *Rubaiyat* 90–1, 95; *Simbolo* 86; *Three Fantasies* for clarinet and piano 83; *Le voyage* 91, 95
Bergson, Henri, 146, 194
Berio, Cristina, 268–9, 271
Berio, Luciano, 4, 11, 14, 43n, 142, 157, 163–6, 164n, 169, 172, 223, 264, 267–8, 267n, 271, 277
   Circles 273; *Coro* 44n; *Epifanie* 273; *Folk Songs* 273; *Naturale* 48; *Recital I (for Cathy)* 273; *Sequenza I* 182; *Sequenza III* 273; *Sequenza VIII* 182; *Sinfonia* 12, 32, 164–66, 171; *Thema (Omaggio a Joyce)* 273n; *Visage* 273; *Voci* 9, 43–6
Berlin, Irving, 31
Berlioz, Hector, 30, 184
Bernard, Jonathan W., 180n, 191n
Beyer, Robert, 267n
Bhabha, Homi, 74, 74n, 78–9, 78n, 79n, 81, 81n, 95, 95n
Binham, Philip, 82n

Binham, Timothy, 82n
Birtwistle, Harrison, 67
Bizet, Georges, 31, 31n
Blanchot, Maurice, 163
Blake, William, 28
Blazekovic, Zdravko, 245n
Bloemink, Frits, 268n
Bloom, Harold, 12, 119–20, 119n, 120n
Blume, Friedrich, 84n
Boethius, 26
Bohlman, Philip V., 207, 207n
Bohrer, Karl-Heinz, 12, 160–1, 160n, 161n, 166–9, 167n, 168n
Bonds, Mark Evan, 202n, 207n, 214–5, 214n, 215n
Bons, Joël, 310n
Boop, Betty, 273
Born, Georgina, 89n, 174–5, 174n, 175n, 187
Boros, James, 70n, 281n, 302n, 306n
Botstein, Leon, 47, 48n, 53n
Boulez, Pierre, 1, 4, 4n, 5n, 9, 11, 13, 16, 26–7, 27n, 30, 35, 50, 55–6, 70, 85n, 89, 89n, 114, 142, 172–89, 221–44, 245n, 263, 302n
   Anthèmes 2 174; *... explosante-fixe ...* 174, 181; *Dérive I* 173; *Dialogue de l'ombre double* 174, 224; *Improvisation III sur Mallarmé* 15, 173, 223–44; *Le Marteau sans maître* 22, 175–6, 178, 224; *Mémoriale* 173; *Pli selon pli* 173, 179, 225–44; *Poésie pour pouvoir* 174; *Polyphonie X* 174, 178; *Répons* 50, 173, 186, 224, 230; *Rituel in memoriam Maderna* 139, 181, 224; *Second Piano Sonata* 49, 174, 224; *Sonatine* for flute and piano 174; *Structures I* 174, 178, 235, 282; *Third Sonata* for piano 179, 237
Bourdieu, Pierre, 114
Bowie, Andrew, 5n
Boym, Svetlana, 208, 208n, 218n, 220, 220n
Bradshaw, Susan, 224n
Brahms, Johannes, 3, 121, 178, 188, 197
Braun, Ethan, 35
Braxton, Anthony, 103n
Brecht, Bertolt, 266
Breckenridge, Carol A., 80n
Brinkmann, Reinhold, 255n
Britten, Benjamin, 4, 51, 55, 70
   Death in Venice 72; *A Midsummer Night's Dream* 34
Brown, James, 103

Index of names

Bruckner, Anton, 203, 208, 218
Brunner, Raphaël, 225n, 238, 238n
Bryn-Julson, Phyllis, 227n
Burchell, Graham, 184n
Burden, Chris, 29
Bürger, Peter, 157, 169
Burke, Edmund, 28, 166n, 167
Burnham, Scott, 202n, 207n
Burns, Robert, 119
Busch, Regina, 255, 255n
Bussotti, Sylvano, 264, 271, 273
Butor, Michel, 240n
Butt, John, 5n
Bye, Anthony, 63n

Cage, John, 4, 22, 46, 55, 55n, 85n, 87, 101n, 174, 176, 184–5, 188
   Aria 16, 264–78
Callas, Maria, 273
Campbell, Edward, 13, 172–89, 173n, 174n, 175n, 181n, 224n, 238n
Cardew, Cornelius, 101n
Carmi, Eugenio, 275
Carter, Elliott, 56, 104, 121, 142, 189n
   Changes 290, 290n
Castanet, Pierre A., 187n
Cerha, Friedrich, 51
Cézanne, Paul, 179, 184–5, 188
Chaigne, Jean-Paul, 290, 290n
Chamber Orchestra of Europe, 261n
Changeux, Jean-Pierre, 176n
Chantal, Thomas, 275n
Char, René, 243
Cherlin, Michael, 11–12, 27, 27n, 119–44
Chernilo, Daniel, 81, 81n
Clarke, James, 60, 69
Clarke, Kenneth, 78
Clementi, Aldo, 301n
Clifford, James, 80
Cobussen, Marcel, 30, 30n
Cohen, Brigid, 75n, 79, 79n
Cohen-Levinas, Danielle, 187n
Cohn, Robert Greer, 240n
Coleman, Ornette, 103n
Coltrane, John, 26
Cone, Edward T., 278n
Conley, Tom, 183n
Connor, Steven, 45, 45n
Cook, Christopher, 170n
Cook, Nicholas, 76n

Cooper, Martin, 254n
Copland, Aaron, 28
Corrado, Omar, 87n
Coulembier, Klaas, 189n
Couroux, Marc, 313, 313n, 315
Cox, Franklin, 3n, 105n, 301, 301n, 304n, 306–8, 307n, 313, 313n, 315, 315n, 318n
Crang, Mike, 75–6, 75n
Crimp, Martin, 34n
Critchley, Simon, 281n, 297, 297n
Crossing Brooklyn Ferry, 109
Crowley, Ruth, 160n
Crumb, George, 32
   Ancient Voices of Children 32
Csipák, Károly, 254n

Dahlhaus, Carl, 99n, 151, 199n
Dallapiccola, Luigi, 84
Dallmayr, Fred R., 81, 81n
Danuser, Hermann, 248n
Darbon, Nicholas, 280n
Davis, Miles, 103n
Deacon, Dan, 109
Debussy, Claude, 46, 50, 82, 121, 172, 177, 179, 184–6, 188, 191, 230–1, 282
   Jeux 213; *Pelléas et Mélisande* 141; *Prélude à l'après-midi d'un faune* 141
Decroupet, Pascal, 235n
Deerhof, 97
de Falla, Manuel, 46
Deforce, Arne, 310n
Delanty, Gerard, 74n, 80n, 81n
Deleuze, Gilles, 13, 173, 188–9, 238
   The Fold: Leibniz and the Baroque, 183; *A Thousand Plateaus: Capitalism and Schizophrenia* (with Guattari) 183–5, 189; *What Is Philosophy?* (with Guattari) 184–9
Deliège, Célestin, 177, 177n, 237n, 242
Deliège, Irène, 55n
de Man, Paul, 4, 4n, 11
Dench, Chris, 294
Derrida, Jacques, 16, 280–2, 297, 297n
   La dissémination 238, 281n, 283n, 286; 'The Law of Genre' 110; *Margins of Philosophy* 281n, 293n; *Positions* 286n; *Writing and Difference* 281n, 282n
Dessner, Bryce, 109, 115n
Dewenter, Carola, 315n
Dickinson, Emily, 68

Index of names

DiCola, Peter, 102
Dietrich, Marlene, 270, 272–3
Dillon, James, 4, 11–12, 60–1, 119–144, 158, 300
    Book of Elements 121–3; *Come live with me* 119–44; *Dillug-Kefitsah* 122–3; *Nine Rivers* 121: *Philomela* 122
Le Domaine Musical, 180n
Donizetti, Gaetano, 195n
Dósa, Lidi, 41
Downes, Michael, 71n
Duchamp, Marcel, 168
Duchesneau, Louise, 37n
Duncan, Michelle, 266n, 276n
Duteurtre, Benoît, 172, 172n
Dwyer, Benjamin, 37–8
Dylan, Bob, 26

Ecstatic Music Festival, 97–8, 109, 116
Edwards, Peter, 13, 27n, 190–200
Eimert, Herbert, 267n
Einstein, Albert, 25
Eisler, Hanns, 10, 51
Ellington, Duke, 88, 103n
Emmerson, Simon, 71n
Emsley, Richard, 9, 56–60, 73
    for piano 1 56; *for piano 2* 56; *for piano 15* 57–60; *Still/s* 59
Ensemble Dal Niente, 97
Ensemble InterContemporain, 227n, 230
Erauw, Willem, 206n
Erdely, Stephen, 41n, 42, 42n
Erlmann, Veit, 45n
Ethel Quartet, 108, 108n
Evans, Bill, 37n

Fadiman, Clifton, 161n
Fanning, David, 53n
Feldman, Morton, 7, 22, 35, 50n, 62, 307n
    Rothko Chapel 49; *The Viola in My Life* 49
Feller, Ross, 279n
Ferneyhough, Brian, 4, 55, 60, 63, 70, 70n, 187, 279–98, 300, 301n, 302n, 304, 306, 306n, 310n, 314n
    Bone Alphabet 314; *Kurze Schatten II* 16, 279–98; *Time and Motion Study II* 311–12; *Unity Capsule* 16, 279–98
Finnissy, Michael, 55, 60, 300, 313, 313n
Fischer-Lichte, Erika, 275n, 278n
Fitzgerald, Ella, 194

Foege, Alec, 100n
Førisdal, Anders, 16, 279–98
Forkel, Johann Nicolas, 205, 205n
Forster, E.M., 106
Forster, Kurt W., 206n
Foucault, Michel, 5, 16, 182, 238n, 280, 295
    The Archaeology of Knowledge 283, 283n; 'Contemporary Music and the Public' 182, 183n; *The Order of Things* 276, 276n
Fox, Christopher, 251n, 305n
Freud, Sigmund, 149, 199n
    Psychopathology of Everyday Life 199
Furtwängler, Wilhelm, 23, 159

Galaise, Sophie, 180n, 224n
Gann, Kyle, 56
Garcia-Morena, Laura, 81n
Garden, Mary, 273
Gauwerky, Friedrich, 318n
Gershwin, George, 31
Gesualdo, Carlo, 34
Ghirardo, Diane, 206n
Gilbert, Anthony, 63
Gillespie, Susan H., 26n
Gilroy, Paul, 103n
Ginastera, Alberto, 87
Glass, Philip, 21n, 32, 56, 104n
    Akhnaten 34
Gloag, Kenneth, 106n
Globokar, Vinko, 165
Glock, William, 235n
Goebbels, Joseph, 23
Goehr, Lydia, 205n, 206n, 226n, 308, 308n
Goethe, Johann Wolfgang von, 28
Goldhammer, Arthur, 25n
Goldie, 104
Goldman, Jonathan, 5n, 173, 173n, 231, 231n, 238n, 243n
Gonson, Claudia, 113
Gooley, Dana, 75n
Goya, Francisco, 28
Grassl, Markus, 247n
Greenberg, Clement, 99–100, 99n, 110, 115
Greene, Jayson, 109n
Greenstein, Judd, 108–9, 108n
Griffiths, Paul, 53n
Grisey, Gérard, 38n
    Les Éspaces acoustiques 50
Guattari, Félix, 13, 173, 183n, 184n, 185n, 188–9

A Thousand Plateaus: Capitalism and Schizophrenia (with Deleuze) 183–5, 189; *What Is Philosophy?* (with Deleuze) 184–9
Gubaidulina, Sofia, 4, 183n
Guilbaut, Serge, 25n
Guldbrandsen, Erling E., 1, 4n, 15, 27, 27n, 173, 173n, 177n, 201n, 221–44

Hagen, Lars Petter, 158
Hager, Uwe, 280n, 305n
Hakobian, Levon, 203n
Hallam, Mandy, 65–6
Handler, David, 109
Hannerz, Ulf, 81, 81n
Hannigan, Barbara, 34n
Harnoncourt, Nikolaus, 261
Harvey, Jonathan, 9, 30, 70–73, 281n, 306n
    80 Breaths 73; *Advaya* 71; *Bhakti* 70; *Birdconcerto with pianosong* 71; *Body Mandala* 72; *Cello Concerto* 71; *Madonna of Winter and Spring* 70; *Messages* 72; *Mortuous plango, vivos voco* 70; *Passion and Resurrection* 70; *Speakings* 72; *Sprechgesang* 72; *The Summer Cloud's Awakening* 73; *Thebans* 73; *Tombeau de Messiaen* 71; *… towards a Pure Land* 72; *Wagner Dream* 71–2; *Weltethos* 72
Häusler, Joseph, 192n, 232n
Heaton, Roger, 305n, 308–9, 309n
Hegel, Georg Wilhelm Friedrich, 2, 47–8, 50–1, 189, 202n
    Aesthetics: Lectures on Fine Arts 282, 282n; *The Philosophy of Fine Art* 215, 215n
Heifetz, Jascha, 257
Heile, Björn, 10, 74–96, 89n
Heininen, Paavo, 86, 86n
Heiniö, Mikko, 84, 84n
Heister, Hanns-Werner, 84n
Hell, Richard, 101n
Hendrix, Jimi, 101
Henze, Hans Werner, 4
Heraclitus, 199
Herbert, Matthew, 158
Hesmondhalgh, David, 89n
Hestholm, Marion, 12–13, 155–71
Hewett, Ian, 64, 64n, 65
Hibbett, Ryan, 114n
Hill, Peter, 313
Hindemith, Paul, 51, 83, 165

Kammermusik op. 24/1 307; *Murder, Hope of Women* 28
Hitler, Adolf, 83
Hobsbawm, Eric, 76n
Hoeckner, Berthold, 158, 158n, 159n, 160n
Hölderlin, Friedrich, 51, 153–4, 171
Holliger, Heinz, 60, 301n
Holocaust, 26
Holt, Simon, 9, 63–70, 73
    A Book of Shadows 69; *Black Lanterns* 67–8; *Boots of Lead* 69; *Ellsworth 2* 69; *… era Madrugada* 67; *Morpheus Wakes* 70; *Troubled Light* 69; *Witness to a Snow Miracle* 69
Honban, Weiland, 246n
Hooper, Giles, 206, 207n
Howell, Tim, 82n, 87, 87n
Hübler, Klaus K., 16, 297, 299–318, 307n
    Cercar 301; *Dialektische Fantasie* 301; *'Feuerzauber' auch Augenmusik* 300–1; *Grave e sfrenato* 301; *Opus breve* 299–318; *Reißwerck* 301
Hullot-Kentor, Robert, 47, 47n, 77n, 99n, 147n, 156n, 159n, 255, 255n, 263n, 317n
Husserl, Edmund, 146
Hutcheon, Linda, 157, 157n
Huyssen, Andreas, 14, 31, 31n, 201, 201n, 209, 209n

Iddon, Martin, 85n
Idel, Mosche, 119, 123, 132, 132n
International Summer Courses for New Music in Darmstadt [Internationale Ferienkurse für Neue Musik Darmstadt], 10, 15, 23, 24, 33, 46, 85, 85n, 89, 174–5, 188, 245–6, 248, 248n, 249n, 251, 251n, 252n, 256, 267n, 268, 271, 273–4, 276–7, 300
IRCAM (Institut de Recherche et de Coordination Acoustique-Musique), 23, 24, 33, 70, 174, 174n, 180n, 230
ISCM (International Society for Contemporary Music), 82n
Ivashkin, Alexander, 208n
Ives, Charles, 4, 54, 104, 163, 194

Jackson, Jesse, 103
Jain, Saskya Iris, 275n
Jalkanen, Pekka, 82n
James, Richard David, 104
James, William, 133

Index of names

Jameson, Fredric, 176, 177n
Jameux, Dominique, 225n
Janáček, Leos, 46-7, 78, 82
    Intimate Letters 49; *Kát'a Kabanová* 49
The J.B., 103
Jencks, Charles, 106n, 177, 177n
Jephcott, Edmund, 148n, 156n, 203n, 297n
Jeune, Claude le, 34
Joachim, Josef, 260
Jochum, Eugen, 258n
Johnson, Barbara, 281n
Johnson, Julian, 1, 5n, 9, 36-52, 70n, 201n, 202n, 209n, 210n, 211, 212n
Joplin, Scott, 194
Josephson, David, 25n
Joyce, James, 157, 178-9, 236, 238
    Finnegans Wake 226; *Ulysses* 63
Jung, Carl Gustav, 63

Kafka, Franz, 170-1, 170n
Kagel, Mauricio, 4, 7, 79, 282-3, 301n
    Improvisation ajoutée 283; *Sonant (1960 ...)* 283; *Transición* 283
Kanno, Mieko, 302n
Kant, Immanuel, 15, 28, 79, 79n, 160-1, 243
Kapp, Reinhard, 247n
Karantonis, Pamela, 264n, 265n, 266, 269n, 273n, 276n, 278n
Karski, Dominik, 306, 306n
Kashkashian, Kim, 43n
Kassabian, Anahid, 21n
Katz, Ruth, 199n
Kawabata, Mai, 259n
Kay, Jean, 59
Kelly, Ellsworth, 69
Kelly, Michael, 206n
Kerman, Joseph, 25n, 52, 52n, 224n, 236
Kettler, David, 201n
Khayyam, Omar, 90
Killmayer, Wilhelm, 51
Kimbrough, Andrew, 275n
Klee, Paul, 181, 184-5, 188
Kleist, Heinrich von, 168
Klotz, Heinrich, 105n
Knap, John, 268n
Knessl, Lothar, 251n
Knox, T. M., 282n
Kolisch, Rudolf, 14, 15, 246-63
Kolisch Quartet [Kolisch Quartett], 247, 247n, 262

Kolleritsch, Otto, 258n
Korgues, Milizia, 273
Kostelanetz, Richard, 269n, 274n
Kramer, Lawrence, 26
Kraus, Karl, 250
Kreidler, Johannes, 158
Kreisler, Fritz, 260
Kremer, Gidon, 261
Krenek, Ernst, 252n
Kristeva, Julia, 81
Kubrick, Stanley, 191
Kurasawa, Fuyuki, 80n
Kurtág, György, 4, 11-12, 14, 51, 151n, 152n, 154, 163
    Kafka Fragments 151-2, 170-1

La Barbara, Joan, 275
Lachenmann, Helmut, 4, 60, 64, 99, 114, 158, 187, 187n, 279n, 282, 304, 307n
    musique concrète instrumentale 17, 306
Laki, Peter, 48n
Lang, David, 66n
Latham, Alison, 53n
Le Poisson Rouge, 109, 109n, 111
Leech-Wilkinson, Daniel, 245n
Leibowitz, René, 51, 186, 256-62, 257n, 260n
Leppert, Richard, 26
Lester, Paul, 104n
Levi, Erik, 75n
Lévi-Strauss, Claude, 45
Lévinas, Emmanuel, 281n
Levinas, Michaël, 187, 187n
Levitz, Tamara, 84n
Lévy, Fabien, 279n
Lewin, David, 27, 27n
Leydi, Roberto, 267n
Lietti, Alfredo, 267n
Ligeti, Gabor, 37n
Ligeti, György, 4, 11, 13-14, 22, 27, 35-40, 36n, 37n, 39n, 43, 45-6, 48-9, 50n, 51, 142, 172, 190-200, 223
    Atmosphères 101, 191-200; *Aventures* 193-200; *Cello Concerto* 197; *Double Concerto* 197; *Hamburg Concerto* 197; *Le Grand Macabre* 27n, 194-200; *Lontano* 197; *Nouvelles Aventures* 193-200; *Sonata for Solo Viola*, 9, 36-40; *Trio* for violin, horn and piano 182, 198; *Violin Concerto* 196-200; *Volumina* 191-200
Lim, Liza, 300, 316, 316n

Index of names

Lindberg, Magnus, 87
Liszt, Franz, iv, 37, 54, 191
Livingstone, Richard, 178n
Lochhead, Judy, 279n
Locke, Ralph P., 77n
Lonetz, Henri, 246n
Longinus, 167
Loos, Adolf, 215n
Lorca, Federico García, 67
Louis XIV, 23
Luening, Otto, 25
Lukomska, Halina, 227n
Lutosławski, Witold, 87, 87n
Lyotard, Jean-François, 3, 17, 29, 176
  'Musique et postmodernité' 176n; *The Postmodern Condition: A Report on Knowledge* 3n, 29n, 157n

Machaut, Guillaume de, 194
Mackey, Steve, 22
MacMillan, James, 9, 63–70, 73
  The Confessions of Isobel Gowdie 64–5, 67; *Miserere* 66; *St John Passion* 65–7; *The Sacrifice* 65
Maderna, Bruno, 181, 264, 268
Magaldi, Cristina, 80n
Mahler, Gustav, 12, 14–15, 46, 48, 54, 82, 148–9, 148n, 149n, 152, 156n, 163, 165, 194, 203, 203n, 208, 209n, 211n, 218, 218n, 243n, 282, 297, 297n
  Fifth Symphony 204, 210; *Ninth Symphony* 156, 204; *Sixth Symphony* 211
Mahnkopf, Claus-Steffen, 3, 3n, 105n, 189, 189n, 304n
Makarius, Michel, 204, 205n
Malipiero, Gian Francesco, 84
Mallarmé, Stéphane, 15, 178–80, 223, 225, 228, 236–40, 236n, 242
  'A la nue accablante tu' 227, 240; *Le 'Livre' de Mallarmé* 237; *Œuvres Complètes* 237n, 240n
Manet, Édouard, 179
Mann, Thomas, 72
Manoury, Philippe, 176
Marlowe, Christopher, 119
Marx, Wolfgang, 37n
Massumi, Brian, 3n
Mattheson, Johann, 214, 215n
Mattes, Arnulf, 15, 245–63
Mauser, Siegfried, 258n

Mawer, Deborah, iv
Maxwell Davies, Peter, xv
Mazzoli, Missy, 108
MC Chuck D, 102
McClary, Susan, 8–9, 8n, 21–35, 26n, 28n, 172n, 202n
McKeon, Roger, 311n
McLeod, Kembrew, 102n
Mehta, Bejun, 34n
Mendel, Arthur, 256n
Menger, Pierre-Michel, 180, 180n
Menuhin, Yehudi, 42
Merikanto, Aarre, 82
Messiaen, Olivier, 4, 7, 22, 35, 71, 125, 185–6, 223, 228
  Mode de valeurs et d'intensités 282, 302n; *Saint François d'Assis* 30, 33
Metzer, David, 10, 97–116, 98n, 99n, 106n, 155, 155n, 163n, 170, 170n, 190n, 277, 277n
Metzger, Heinz-Klaus, 248n
Meyer, Thomas, 257n
Meyer-Eppler, 267n
Michaux, Henri, 243n
Miedl, Christian, 34n
Minor, Ryan, 75, 75n
Mitchell, Katie, 34n
Monk, Thelonius, 37n
Monroe, Marilyn, 270, 273
Monteverdi, Claudio, 16, 266
  L'Orfeo 194–5
Moore, Thurston, 100
Moretti, Franco, 78n
Morrison, Richard, 73n
Mosch, Ulrich, 74n, 83, 189n
Mozart, Wolfgang Amadeus, 31, 194, 216–7, 247n, 260, 263
Muhammad, Khalid Abdul, 103
Muhly, Nico, 108, 108n, 112, 115n
Müller-Doohm, Stefan, 248n
MusicNOW, 109
Mussorgsky, Modest, 177, 179

Nancarrow, Conlon, 104, 107
Nattiez, Jean-Jacques, 5n, 175n, 180n, 224n, 243n
Nehamas, Alexander, 29, 29n
Nelson, Maggie, 29
Neugroschel, Joachim, 128n
Neuwirth, Olga, 99
The New York Philharmonic, 230

Index of names

Newcomb, Anthony, 5n
Newman, Michael Z., 112n, 113, 113n, 114n
Nicolas, François, 5n, 243n
Nietzsche, Friedrich, 2, 161, 161n, 166–8, 168n, 171, 184
Nono, Luigi, 4, 11, 14, 31, 85n, 142, 163, 172, 257, 263, 268, 273, 277
   Fragmente – Stille, An Diotima 12, 153–4, 170–1; *Il Canto sospeso* 85–6; *Prometheus* 153
Nordwall, Ove, 191n
Novalis, 162, 162n
Nyffeler, Max, 315
Nyman, Michael, 55n

O'Brien, John, 99n
Ockeghem, Johannes, 154
Oesch, Hans, 90–1, 90n, 93n
O'Hagan, Peter, 70n, 173n, 224n
Olive, Jean-Paul, 12, 145–54
O'Meara, Caroline, 100n
Ono, Yoko, 75n, 79
Oppenheimer, Mark, 113n
Oramo, Ilkka, 84, 84n
Orledge, Robert, 252n
Orning, Tanja, 16, 299–318
Osborne, John, 201n
Osmaston, F.P.B., 215n
Osmond-Smith, David, 264, 264n, 268, 268n, 273n
Ottieri, Silvana, 269n

Pace, Ian, 50, 59n
Paddison, Max, 55n, 99n, 178n, 216n, 247n
Pallett, Owen 108
Parker, Charlie, 103n
Parsons, Jeremy, 86n, 90n
Pärt, Arvo, 4, 56, 65
Partch, Harry, 49, 197, 197n
Paul, Jean, 159
Paul Sacher Foundation [Paul Sacher Stiftung], 74n, 83n, 84, 194n, 232, 256n, 260n, 294, 294n
Pauli, Hans-Jörg, 256–7, 257n
Paz, Juan Carlos, 87, 87n
Penderecki, Krzysztof, 101
   Threnody for the Victims of Hiroshima 101
Perloff, Marjorie, 105n
Pfeiffer, Peter C., 81n
Piazzolla, Astor, 87

Picasso, Pablo, 157
Piencikowski, Robert, 232n
Pintscher, Matthias, 189
Placanica, Francesca, 16, 264–78
Plato, 23, 160, 160n, 167, 183
Poggioli, Renato, 157
Polaschegg, Nina, 280n, 305n
Pople, Anthony, 76n
Porter, Cole, 31
Potter, Keith, 56n
Potter, Rosie, 122
Pound, Ezra, 150
Pousseur, Henri, 172–3, 173n
Prieberg, Fred K., 83n
Pro Arte Quartett, 262
Prokofiev, Sergei, 157
Proust, Françoise, 145–6, 145n, 146n, 152, 152n
Proust, Marcel, 41, 230
Public Enemy, 10, 103n, 113, 116
   'Bring the Noise' 103; *Fear of a Black Planet* 102; *It Takes a Nation of Millions to Hold Us Back* 101–2; 'Night of the Living Baseheads' 102
Purvis, Philip, 34n
Pushkin, Alexander, 269
Pythagoras, 25

Rachmaninoff, Serge, 28
Radio Orchestra Beromünster, 256
Radzinowicz, David, 205n
The Ramones, 100
Rancière, Jacques, 13, 188–9, 188n
Ranger, Terence, 76n
Rautavaara, Einojuhani, 87
Ravel, Maurice, 252n
   Miroirs 50; *Rapsodie Espagnole* 196; *Trois Poèmes de Mallarmé* 268; *Tzigane* 252
RCA Orchestra, 257
Rehding, Alexander, 205n, 206, 206n
Reich, Steve, 4, 30, 32, 56, 101n
Reger, Max, 51, 191–2, 256
Revuluri, Sindhumathi, 77n
Reynolds, Simon, 102, 102n
Richard, Jean-Pierre, 240n
Richtsteig, Tobias, 280n, 305n
Riegl, Alois, 206, 206n
Riehn, Rainer, 248n
Riemann, Hugo, 250n
Rihm, Wolfgang, 4, 51, 158, 189, 189n

Index of names

Rimbaud, Arthur, 2, 29
Rimsky-Korsakov, 121, 196
Robertson, Robby, 22
Rockhill, Gabriel, 188n
Roelofs, Joes, 268n
Rognoni, Luigi, 267n
The Rolling Stones, 143
Rose, Tricia, 102, 102n
Rosen, Charles, 24n, 162, 162n, 204–5, 204n, 235, 235n
Ross, Alex, 49, 50n, 102, 102n
Rossini, Giacomo, 194
Rossum, Frans van, 268n
Rothko, Mark, 59–60
Rougier, Louis, 175
Rudel, Jaufré, 33
Rufer, Josef, 247n
Rushdie, Salman, 157
Russolo, Luigi, 4
Rutherford-Johnson, Tim, 306n, 316n

Saariaho, Kaija, 4, 8, 22, 30, 46, 51, 99, 223
    Adriana Mater 33; *L'Amour de loin* 33–5; *Émilie* 33; *La Passion de Simone* 33
Sadie, Stanley, 53n, 84n, 301n
Sadler, Eric, 102
Sahran, Francois, 158
Said, Edward, 77n
Salamenhaara, Erkki, 82n
Salonen, Esa-Pekka, 33, 87
Samuel, Claude, 192
Sandow, Greg, 26, 26n, 108n, 109n
Sartre, Jean-Paul, 257
Satie, Eric, 10, 55
Saunders, James, 55n, 60n
Saunders, Rebecca, 9, 69, 73
    Crimson 60–3; *Shadow (2013). Study for piano* 63; *Solitude* for solo cello 63; *Violin Concerto* 63
Saussure, Ferdinand de, 281
Savenko, Svetlana, 203, 203n, 209, 209n, 212, 212n, 215, 215n
Scaldaferri, Nicola, 267n
Scelsi, Giacinto, 4
Schaeffer, Pierre, 46, 102, 174, 267n
Schaeffner, André, 238n
Schäfer, Christine, 227n
Schäfer, Thomas, 251n
Scheding, Florian, 75n

Schenk, David, 192n
Schenker, Heinrich, 159
Scherer, Jacques, 237, 237n
Schick, Steven, 314, 314n
Schiff, David, 175, 176n
Schiller, Friedrich, 160–1
Schlegel, Friedrich, 155, 155n, 161, 161n, 170
Schmalfeldt, Janet, 207n
Schmelz, Peter J., 218n, 219, 219n
Schnebel, Dieter, 158
Schneiderhan, Wolfgang, 258–60, 258n
Schnittke, Alfred, 4, 202n, 208n
    Symphony No. 3 208
Schoenberg, Arnold, 1, 3–4, 9–10, 12, 14, 27n, 32, 32n, 35, 46, 49, 54–6, 60, 82, 99n, 115, 121, 124, 132–3, 146, 163n, 172, 174, 177–8, 180, 185–6, 188–9, 215n, 231–2, 236, 245–63, 266, 282
    Die Jakobsleiter 245n; *Erwartung* 23, 277; *Gurrelieder* 141; *Moses und Aron* 30, 163; *Pelleas und Melisande* 141; *Phantasy* for violin with piano accompaniment 249, 251–5, 262; *Pierrot Lunaire* 177; *Verklärte Nacht* 132, 141
Schoenberg, Nuria, 268
Scholem, Gershom, 122, 123, 123n, 126n, 128n
Schopenhauer, Arthur, 166n
Schubert, Franz, 163, 203, 218, 247n, 248
Schulkowsky, Robyn, 43n
Schultz, Klaus, 257n, 262n
Schumann, Robert, 13, 162n, 197, 203
Schurig, Wolfram, 3n, 105n, 304n
Schwarz, David, 21n
Schweppenhäuser, Hermann, 200n
Schwitters, Kurt, 168, 194
Sciarrino, Salvatore, 8, 22, 34n, 158, 223
    Luci mie traditrici 34–5
Scorsese, Martin, 22
Scruton, Roger, 66, 66n
Seabrook, Mike, 63–4, 63n, 66
Sooger, Charles, 302n
Seherr-Toss, Peter von, 194n
Sellars, Peter, 33
Sessions, Roger, 26
Shaw, Jennifer, 245n
Shaw, Michael, 157n
Shreidan Smith, A. M., 283n

Sherman, Cindy, 157
Shostakovich, Dmitri, 55, 208
Shreffler, Anne C., 249n
Sibelius, Jean, 31, 46–7, 82, 87n
Siegel, Lawrence, 21n
Silverthorne, Paul, 51
Silvestrov, Valentin, 4, 11–14, 201–220
  Symphony No. 5 201–220
Simmel, Georg, 201–2, 201n, 202n, 209, 209n, 211, 211n, 219, 219n
Siôn, Pwyll ap, 56n
Sivuoja-Kauppala, Anna, 264n
Skowron, Zbigniew, 87n
Sly and the Family Stone, 103
Small, Christopher, 31, 31n
Smirnov, Dmitri, 51
Smith, Patti, 101n
Soderbergh, Steven, 113
Sonic Youth, 10, 106, 113, 116
  Goodbye Twentieth Century 101n; 'Silver Rocket' 100–1
Society for Private Musical Performance [Gesellschaft für musikalische Privataufführungen], 115
Sparrer, Walter-Wolfgang, 84n
Stadlen, Peter, 245n
Steen-Andersen, Simon, 307n
Steinitz, Richard, 36, 36n
Stenzl, Jürg, 45
Stephan, Rudolf, 251n
Steuermann, Eduard, 248, 252n
Stevens, Sufjan, 109, 115n
Still, Clyfford, 69
Stock, Else, 252n
Stockhausen, Karlheinz, 1, 4, 7, 9–10, 30, 70, 85, 85n, 107, 121, 142, 172, 185, 188, 223, 263, 267n, 273–4, 277
  Gesang der Jünglinge 22, 45; *Gruppen* 86; *Hymnen* 44n; *Zeitmasse* 302n
Stokes, Martin, 80n
Stoler, Ann Laura, 215, 215n
Straus, Joseph N., 21n
Strauss, Richard, 28, 34, 51, 83
Stravinsky, Igor, 4, 28, 82, 121, 129, 131n, 146, 156, 172, 184, 186, 188–9, 230–1, 307, 307n
  Abraham and Isaac 30, 125, 132; *The Firebird* 196; *The Flood* 132; *Les Noces* 12, 125, 130, 138, 181; *Oedipus Rex* 12, 132;

Pribaoutki 268; *Renard* 30; *The Rite of Spring* 28, 177, 228; *Symphonies of Wind Instruments* 39, 181; *Symphony of Psalms* 30
Stuckenschmidt, Hans Heinz, 247n
Sturken, Marita, 206, 206n
Suarès, Carlo, 123, 123n, 126, 128, 129n
Suchoff, Benjamin, 42n
Sun Ra, 103n
Swaan, Carrie de, 270n
Swarthout, Gladys, 273

Tarandek, Nina, 34n
Taruskin, Richard, 1, 1n, 24n, 32, 32n, 76, 76n, 78, 78n, 172, 172n, 196n
Tavener, John, 30, 56, 65
Thévenin, Paule, 89n, 175n, 223n
Thomas, Ernst, 199n
Thomson, Virgil, 30
Tiedemann, Rolf, 147n, 159n, 200n, 257n, 262n, 317n
Tiessen, Fritz, 83
Tomek, Otto, 251n
Tomlinson, Hugh, 184n
Tommasini, Anthony, 34, 34n
Toop, Richard, 55n, 70n, 281n, 299n, 306n
Toscanini, Arturo, 257
Toscano, Alberto, 185n
Torvinen, Juha, 74n, 93, 93n
Trapp, Claus, 251n
Trapp, Max, 83
Trautwein, Friedrich, 267n
Trigg, Dylan, 202n
Tsenova, Valeria, 203n
Tyrrell, John, 53n, 84n, 301n

Uitti, Frances Marie, 318n
Ullmann, Viktor, 51
Ussachevsky, Vladimir, 25

Varèse, Edgar, 4, 69, 99, 101, 106–7, 125, 172, 184–6, 188, 267n, 282
Varga, Tibor, 252–5, 252n, 254n
Várnai, Péter, 192n, 194n
Vaughan, Sarah, 273
Velvet Underground, 98
Verdi, Giuseppe, 154
Veress, Sándor, 37

Verlaine, Paul, 179
Verstraete, Pieter, 264n
Vienna Philharmonic Orchestra [Wiener Philharmoniker], 258n
Vienna Radio Symphony Orchestra, 43n
Vila, Marie-Christine, 268n, 274n
Virtamo, Keijo, 82n
Vogel, Wladimir, 84, 84n

Wagner, Richard, 9, 15, 54, 66, 66n, 71–2, 121, 178, 188, 194, 230–1, 230n
  Das Rheingold 209–10; *Tristan und Isolde* 209
Wagner Festival in Bayreuth [Bayreuther Festspiele], 230
Wald, Elijah, 31n
Walsh, Stephen, 89n, 175n, 223n
Walshe, Jennifer, 158
Wason, Robert, 245n
Watkins, Holly, 215n
Weber, William, 25n
Webern, Anton von, 4, 10, 49, 54, 56, 60, 172, 178, 186, 188, 212n, 226, 226n, 230–2, 245, 247n, 263, 282
  Variations for Piano 245n
Weill, Kurt, 10, 266
Weiss, Allen S., 275n
Wells, Dominic P., 66n
Werbner, Pnina, 80n, 81n
Wesendonck, Mathilde, 230n

White, Hayden, 110, 110n
Whittall, Arnold, 5, 5n, 9–10, 13, 53–73, 180n, 187, 225n, 255n
Widmann, Jörg, 189
Wiener, Oswald, 168
Wiener Streichquartett, 262
Willman, Alan, 252n
Wilson, Samuel, 12–14, 201–220
Wolff, Christian, 101n
Wolff, Christoph, 255n
Wolff, Kurt H., 201n
Wolpe, Stefan, 51, 75n, 79, 79n
Wright, Roger, 122

Xenakis, Iannis, 4, 7, 109, 121, 125, 142, 172, 223, 315n
  Evryali 313; *Mists* 315

Zamarin, Roberto, 275
Zemlinsky, Alexander, 124
Zenck, Martin, 193n
Zender, Hans, 158
Zimmermann, Bernd Alois, 4, 11–12, 150–52, 150n, 154
Zimmermann, Tabea, 36–7
Zohn, Harry, 119n
Zoppelli, Luca, 195n
Zorn, John, 22
Zuccheri, Marion, 267n

Index of subjects

abstraction 8, 24, 38, 48–50, 178, 199, 232–3, 239
aesthetic experience 8, 17, 72, 159, 160n, 166–7, 205, 313, 314
aesthetics 3n, 5n, 10, 49, 145, 166, 188n, 201n, 202n, 203, 206n, 230, 266, 277, 282n, 300n, 313
   avant-garde 267
   elitist 6
   history of 9
   modernist 72, 161
   montage 156
   nationalist 93
   philosophical 190
   romantic 162
   of Adorno 10, 99n, 160, 178n, 216n
   of compositional writing 7, 15
   of Darmstadt 10
   of music 193n, 199n
   of new music 15, 105n
   of performance 15–16, 247, 265, 275, 300, 301
   of ruins 201, 202n, 208–9
   of the Schoenberg School 14, 247
   of the twentieth century 155
aleatory, aleatoric, aleatoricism 6, 10, 74, 87
analysis 5, 7, 17, 29n, 33, 38, 49, 85–6, 115n, 155, 158, 160, 165, 165n, 169, 190, 191n, 195n, 197n, 207, 209, 223–4, 224n, 236, 244, 255n, 258, 260, 280
autonomy 156–7, 161, 178, 181, 207
atonal, atonality, 1, 3, 45, 54–5, 59, 151, 175
avant-garde 4, 7, 8n, 9–10, 21–2, 21n, 26, 38, 47–8, 50, 54–6, 69–70, 75, 78, 85–7, 89, 91, 95, 145, 148, 157–8, 157n, 158, 168–70, 172, 172n, 174n, 176, 178, 180, 265–7, 274–8, 300

body 6–7, 14, 16–17, 50, 60, 68, 72, 129, 138, 186, 265, 266n, 267, 276–7, 276n, 282–5, 282n, 297–98

capitalist, capitalism 153, 177n, 183n
   anti-capitalist 274
colonialism 77–9, 89
   neo-colonialist 89
   postcolonialism 77

compositional
   aesthetics 9, 15, 318
   agenda 274, 277
   career 89
   choices 225
   control 223, 225
   creation 13
   decisions 296
   development 13, 190
   ideas 44, 306
   fabric 287
   freedom 186
   language 276
   manifestos 245
   material 44, 280, 300, 306
   parameters 302n
   poetics 16
   practices 225, 265
   problem 253
   procedures 230, 282, 290
   process 224, 238, 297
   self-reflection 6
   states 191n
   studies 184
   structure 279
   style 231
   subject 236
   system 190
   technique 7, 86, 223–4, 230
   tendencies 10
   thinking 55, 224
   thought 14
   tradition 253
   unity 12
   unpredictability 243
   voice 125, 172
   writing 7, 11, 14, 18, 225, 237, 239
construction 6, 55, 77, 149, 152, 199, 205, 211–12, 242, 297, 306
culture 2, 5, 7–8, 10, 16, 21n, 24, 29–31, 31n, 45n, 59, 66, 72–3, 74–96, 97–116, 124, 149, 154, 157n, 172n, 174n, 175, 175n, 177, 202, 204–5, 208–14, 246, 248, 252–4, 255n, 262, 318

deconstruction 16, 156–7, 162, 181, 240, 276–7, 281n, 295, 297, 297n

dissonance, dissonant 1, 28, 38, 54, 64, 114, 192, 210, 216, 218, 225n, 257n, 306
dodecaphony, dodecaphonic 3, 5, 10, 74, 83–4, 86, 89, 91, 179, 186, 188

elitism, elitist 6, 113, 177
ethical, ethics 16, 24, 26, 75, 75n, 79, 80, 80n, 81n, 154, 250, 281n, 297n, 299–318
ethos 38, 55–6, 59, 72–3, 121
experience 34, 42, 48, 56–7, 59, 68, 70–1, 80, 83, 85, 89, 113, 132, 145–6, 152, 155, 159, 160n, 163, 170, 175, 203, 212, 220, 237, 263, 267n, 274, 280, 303, 305n, 318
  aesthetic 8, 17, 72, 157, 159, 160n, 166–7, 205, 267, 313, 314
  composer's 199, 225, 229
  conductor's 15, 87–8, 225, 228–30
  cultural 81, 93, 96
  existential 167, 171
  human 145, 150, 211, 214
  listener's 6–8, 11, 15, 104, 157, 223
  momentary 157
  musical 2, 93, 97, 201n, 207, 218, 244
  performer's 16, 51, 265, 265, 309
  subjective 276
expression 1–2, 11, 14, 22, 52, 53, 71, 82, 90, 122, 132, 142, 146–7, 149–50, 159, 160, 177, 182, 191, 193–8, 200, 202, 205, 209n, 210, 217, 246, 249–51, 255, 261–2, 267, 272, 276, 278, 284, 304, 307, 309, 311, 315, 317
expressionism 1, 9–10, 25n, 53–73

feminist 6
formalism, formalist 5–7, 168, 224, 233, 244, 296
fragment 1, 10–13, 44–5, 50, 63, 99, 106, 133, 145–54, 155–71, 190, 196, 198, 200, 204–5, 210, 216–19, 246, 283, 303

gesture 6, 33–4, 36, 40–41, 43, 48, 64, 193, 212, 214, 228, 235, 239, 242n, 246, 251–3, 255, 258, 263, 272, 276, 278, 281, 283, 288, 290, 292, 294–5, 297, 305
globalization 77, 79–80, 79n, 80n, 89n

hearing, rehearing 8, 17, 45n, 103, 153
hegemonic, hegemony 21, 172n, 207, 223
hermeneutic, hermeneutics 81, 155, 158n, 160, 160n
history 2, 4–7, 17, 42, 70, 75–6, 151, 206
  and aesthetics 5n, 9
  and memory 14, 200, 205

and modernity 2, 4–5, 4n, 5n, 13, 15–16, 32, 35, 39, 46–50, 79n, 103n, 145–54, 172–89, 201, 210
and montage 146–8, 154
and present 220
and ruin 201–220
as progress 5, 48, 74, 176
canonic 74
literary 4, 4n, 11, 45n, 110, 110n
musical 2–5, 10–11, 17, 22, 29, 47, 49, 53, 102, 168, 176, 180, 191–2, 199, 203, 205, 218, 245n, 265, 205
national 75n, 79, 79n
of colonialism 79
of concert programming 25n
of musical language 150
of musical modernism 5, 17, 78, 96, 98–9, 102, 114–15, 162, 177, 208
of performance 226–32, 263, 280, 283, 300
of popular music 31n
of twentieth-century music 9, 46, 74, 186, 208
of Western music 1, 22, 25, 32, 76–7, 76n, 77n, 78n, 172n, 203
historiography, historiographical 5–7, 11, 15, 46, 82, 223–4, 226, 243–4

ideology, ideological 1n, 9, 21, 24, 25n, 47, 50, 64–5, 71, 75, 78, 149, 172n, 202, 207, 245–6, 263, 280, 299
intelligibility, intelligible 8, 22, 162, 279n

jazz 22, 26, 31, 37, 37n, 103n, 151, 175, 177, 270, 272

listener 1, 6, 23, 26–31, 33–4, 37, 57, 59–60, 104–5, 107, 109, 111, 116, 157–60, 163–5, 168–9, 171, 175, 190, 193–9, 203, 242, 249, 252–3, 255, 257, 259, 263, 277–8, 304n
listening 1, 1n, 5n, 7–8, 13–14, 18, 31, 31n, 45n, 49, 93, 116, 153, 172n, 183, 199, 202n, 240, 254, 255n, 263n, 281
  analytical 157
  atomistic 159
  body 17
  casual 26n
  categories of musical 242n
  easy 1
  experience 7, 11, 15, 223, 236
  habits 26
  modes of 191, 263
  musical 247
  'new way of' 178
  phenomenology of 12

Index of subjects

practices of 76
re-listening 263
strategies of 190
structural 159
subject 215

meaning 1n, 6, 8, 21, 23, 31n, 36, 80, 126, 145, 147, 149, 152, 156–7, 157n, 161–6, 165n, 168, 172n, 202–3, 282, 305, 310
  crisis of 162
  cultural 27
  emergent 200
  historical 47
  loss of 156
  multiple 126, 310, 313
  musical 171, 243
  new 123
  nexus of 250
  nonreferential 171
  original 39
  play of 287, 292
  plurality of 6
  poetic 242
  production of 283
  referential 157, 162, 164
  rhetorical 258
  semantic 240
  structural 258
  symbolic 129
  withdrawal of 171
meaningful 32, 159, 310
  meaningful inexactitude 310
meaningless, meaninglessness 66, 157, 162, 181, 202
montage 12, 145–54, 156–8, 164, 166, 168–9
musical form 1, 3, 11, 28n, 174, 179–81, 196, 199, 202n, 214n, 215, 215n, 226, 228, 230–1, 232–6, 237n, 239–41
musical material 1, 11–12, 15–16, 37, 47, 50, 64, 90, 95, 98–9, 125–6, 149, 170, 191n, 192, 216–18, 232, 266, 277, 288, 296–7, 302n, 303
modernity 2, 3n, 4–5, 4n, 5n, 12–13, 15–16, 31–2, 35, 39–41, 45n, 46, 50, 79n, 103n, 105n, 145–54, 172–3, 177, 180, 182–5, 188–9, 201–2, 205, 208, 210

particularity, 9, 36–52, 249
perception, perceive 6, 22, 26, 52, 59, 87, 89, 106, 123, 150, 153, 159, 162, 165, 171, 190–1, 193, 199, 212, 230, 242, 291, 305, 308–9, 313
  aesthetic perception 167, 169
  perceptual 169, 317

perceptible, perceivable, 11, 90, 149, 154, 184, 219
  perceptibility 173, 175
  imperceptible 93
performer, performance 1, 5–8, 14–18, 25–6, 29, 33n, 34, 34n, 45–6, 101n, 114–15, 153, 170, 174, 182, 192, 205, 207, 216–17, 226–7, 230, 236, 239–40, 245–63, 264–78, 279–98, 299–318
performative
  actions 306
  acts 7
  aesthetics 16
  art of the voice 266n, 273n, 276n, 278
  'canon' 278
  dimensions 244
  domain 314, 318
  ethic 313
  intelligence 274
  potential 299–300
  power 274
  procedure 237
  scandal 276
  self-reflection 6
  transformations 14–5, 226–32, 239, 300
  turn 14, 300
  vocality 266
philosophy 17, 24, 155, 160, 174n, 175n, 176n, 181n, 185, 238, 238n, 280–1, 281n, 293n, 308n
  after Nietzsche 184
  and modernity 5n
  of history 2–4, 6–7, 11, 17, 119, 119n, 151, 160, 175n
  of fine art 215, 215n
  of music 205n
  of new music 47n, 77, 77n, 99n, 146, 156, 156n, 188, 188n, 246
  what is 184, 184n
pleasure 1n, 6, 28, 31–2, 38, 64, 119, 129, 157, 167, 172, 172n, 202n, 253, 272
poetics 7, 9, 15–16, 105n, 120n, 151, 177–8, 225–6, 236–9, 243, 269, 307n
politics, political 1, 7, 9, 23, 49, 65, 82–3, 102–3, 153–4, 188n, 207, 308n
  cultural politics 48n
  geopolitics 77
  identity politics 81
popular music 6–7, 10, 25–6, 31–2, 77, 97–116, 140, 142, 144, 148
postmodern, postmodernism 1–3, 8, 21, 27, 29, 29n, 31n, 32, 34–5, 45n, 81, 105–6, 105n, 106n, 126, 156–7, 157n, 162, 169, 176–7, 176n, 177n, 180, 182–3, 182n, 188–9, 206, 208, 261, 279n

progress, progressive 1, 5–6, 15, 24, 29, 31, 38, 40, 47–8, 50, 65, 74–6, 78, 147, 174, 176, 180, 199, 202, 208, 223, 226, 238, 245–6, 253, 263

radically idiomatic, 16, 279–98, 302, 304–5, 314–5
rational, rationalist, rationalization 9, 15, 38–9, 40, 50, 147, 169, 174n, 175, 175n, 202, 223–5, 236, 240, 246, 249–50, 261–2
reception 6–8, 35, 90, 165, 190, 192, 205, 245, 245n, 248n, 264, 278
   reception history 165, 205
reduction 152, 204, 210, 213–14, 233–4
religion, religious 30, 65–6, 73, 82, 90–1, 254n
ruin 12–14, 146, 149, 161, 201–220

sensual, sensuality 8–9, 12, 33, 57, 64, 123, 133, 223, 277
serial, serialist 13, 15, 21, 21n, 32, 49, 84–6, 151, 156, 172–4, 185–7, 189, 223–6, 231–2, 236–7, 237n, 239, 244, 244n, 245, 282, 300, 302, 302n, 306
   post-serial 172, 189
serialism 4, 10, 21, 27n, 31, 46, 74, 84–6, 148, 156, 172–3, 173n, 187, 195, 223–4, 224n, 237–8, 237n, 243–4, 244n
sound 6, 22, 29n, 31–5, 36, 41, 49–50, 57, 60–1, 63, 70, 74, 86, 93, 95, 99–110, 113, 121–3, 153–4, 159, 162, 170, 184, 186–8, 192–3, 197, 203, 210, 216, 236, 239, 249, 252–5, 260, 263, 265–6, 275–7, 279, 282–6, 282n, 290–7, 302–3, 306–7, 314–16
   acoustic properties of 38
   'breath sound' 209, 218
   electronic 33, 45, 45n, 104, 110, 187
   emancipation of 176
   'found sounds' 102–3
   'grain of sound' 122
   musical 9, 48, 283
   particularity of 37
   soundscape 2, 12, 45, 126, 269
   soundtrack 17, 23
   sound art 109
   sound experience 71
   sound mass 99, 101
   sound object 60, 191
   sound shapes 191
   sound studies 8
   sound production 17, 283–4, 287, 306
   sound recording, recorded sound 23–5, 32, 43, 46, 49, 71
   sound world 69, 101, 104, 261, 304, 317
   transformation of 99, 187, 287

vocal 138, 285–7
structure 6, 48, 64, 84, 114, 121, 159, 161–2, 171, 198, 207, 214, 218, 242, 250–1, 260, 262, 281, 286–7, 293–4
   compositional 279
   depth of 56, 59
   expressive 211
   formal 38, 199, 240, 242
   metric 291
   micro- 147
   mise-en-abyme- 240
   modal 90, 282
   motivic-thematic 255
   musical 86, 214–15, 219, 241, 245n, 250
   phrase 104
   pitch 291–4
   rhythmic 177
   serial 15, 85–6, 226, 231, 232–6, 302
   subcutaneous 262
   symphonic 203
style 1–2, 76, 82–3, 100, 102, 104, 106, 112, 114, 133, 163, 168, 177–8, 180, 198, 200, 251, 270–2, 299n, 308–9
   banal 152
   canonic 191
   classical 148
   compositional 231
   dance 104
   global 6
   'guitarist' 238
   historical 6
   indie 116
   international 86
   'late' 51
   modernist 114
   musical 1–2, 83, 96, 263
   national 76
   performance 245n, 249, 252, 254, 263
   personal 113, 198
   popular 98–9, 106, 114–15
   rock 100, 107, 113
   'post-' 203n
   'style history' 168
   vocal 265, 269–72
   writing 230
sublime, the 8–9, 19–35, 50n, 73, 166–7, 166n, 209–10

taste 25, 28, 31, 36, 114–15, 124, 129, 204, 225, 230, 260–1
transformation 1–17, 25, 37, 38n, 46, 52, 98–9, 120–1, 173, 202n, 207, 212n, 223, 225, 259, 262, 275, 286–7, 297, 300, 317
   aesthetic 236
   generative 226, 232–6

Index of subjects

historiographical 226, 243–4
in scholarly work 190
of appearance 155–71
of consciousness 123
of instrumental practice 17, 279, 283, 299
of musical geography 74–96
of poetics 226, 236–9
of the ruin 205
of sound 99, 187, 287
of texture 287
of vocal performance 265, 275–8
performative 14, 226–32, 239
spiritual 133

universal, universalist 8, 10, 75–6, 78–9, 81, 81n, 89–90, 267

voice 12, 14, 16, 22, 34, 40–1, 43–6, 45n, 66, 87, 89, 102, 121, 122n, 124–7, 129, 136–8, 149, 164, 166n, 170, 191n, 197n, 209n, 210, 210n, 228, 233, 235–8, 235n, 264–78, 303, 308n
author's 236
composer's 165n, 237, 278n
corporeality of 46
human 37, 45, 48, 87
instrumental 133
Jewish-Bohemian 46
melodic 41
musical 9, 37, 73
multiple 151
particularity of 9, 38, 44, 48
performer's 279
Sicilian folk 45
specificity of 37, 44

world music 6, 10, 80n

Lightning Source UK Ltd.
Milton Keynes UK
UKHW05n2201140918
328935UK00008B/56/P